Robert Surtees and Early Victorian Society

Robert Surtees and Early Victorian Society

NORMAN GASH

CLARENDON PRESS · OXFORD

Oxford University Press, Walton Street, Oxford OX2 6DP
Oxford New York
Athens Auckland Bangkok Bombay
Calcutta Cape Town Dar es Salaam Delhi
Florence Hong Kong Istanbul Karachi
Kuala Lumpur Madras Madrid Melbourne
Mexico City Nairobi Paris Singapore
Taipei Tokyo Toronto
and associated companies in
Berlin Ibadan

Oxford is a trade mark of Oxford University Press

Published in the United States
by Oxford University Press Inc., New York

British Library Cataloguing in Publication Data
Data available

Library of Congress Cataloging-in-Publication Data
Gash, Norman.
Robert Surtees and early Victorian society / Robert Gash.
p. cm.
Includes bibliographical references and index.
1. Surtees, Robert Smith, 1805–1864—Criticism and interpretation.
2. Literature and society—England—History—19th century.
3. England—Social life and customs—19th century. 4. Social
history in literature. I. Title.
PR5499.S4Z68 1993 823'.8—dc20 93–13963
ISBN 0 19 820429 9

Printed in Great Britain
on acid-free paper by
Ipswich Book Co. Ltd. Suffolk

PREFACE

This is not a treatise on the history of fox-hunting nor an exercise in literary criticism. I have no qualifications for the first and only amateur status for the second. My purpose is simply to use historical evidence to create a background for the Surtees novels and his novels to enlarge the historical evidence.

It is often said that Surtees' writings furnish much material for social historians. Yet the only other book about them by a professional historian, as far as I know, is Anthony Steel's *Jorrocks's England*, published in 1932. Steel was a Fellow of Christ's College, Cambridge, and University Lecturer in History from 1930 to 1949. His meticulous and comprehensive analysis of the social detail in Surtees' novels is one which, within its self-imposed limits, could hardly be bettered. Yet the limits are there. For the most part Steel restricted himself to the information contained in the novels; he did not think it his business to take into account other historical evidence. He failed to provide source-references; and apparently did not believe that there was serious historical value in what he had done.

This study, by contrast, was designed as a contribution both to Surteesian literature and to Victorian social history. The advantage of using a single novelist in this way is that it gives structure and unity to what is by its nature a shapeless subject. The disadvantage is that one has to accept the limitations present in the novelist himself. Surtees paid little attention to much that was historically important in his day and was to become even more important later. A book based on his interests and observations, however broadly interpreted, is bound to be one-sided. Nevertheless, it is useful to look at a familiar historical landscape from an unusual angle and explore parts of the scene usually left unvisited. This implies selection but not necessarily distortion. Though the traditional preoccupations of social historians have been in topics he neglected or ignored, Surtees' world was one which half his contemporaries would have recognized.

It is now over thirty years since I bought a worn but almost complete set of Surtees' novels, many of them first editions, which had been discarded by Douglas & Foulis's Circulating Library in Castle St., Edinburgh. I formed a hope then of one day writing something about them; and I am indebted to the Oxford University Press now for the opportunity to publish this book. It only remains for me to thank all those who encouraged me to write it, answered my queries, or found material which otherwise I would have missed. I would like in particular to mention Michael Brock, Charles Esdaile, Charles Sisson, Arnold Taylor, and above all my two daughters.

Langport, Somerset   NORMAN GASH

CONTENTS

INTRODUCTION

In the literary landscape of the early nineteenth century, Robert Smith Surtees, creator of Jorrocks and some of the best fox-hunting scenes in the English language, is an isolated figure. That such a man was a novelist at all is an oddity. Squire of Hamsterley Hall in County Durham, landowner, magistrate, member of a family which could trace its ancestry back to the eleventh century, he was typical of the gentry who ruled the countryside but a rare animal among the middle-class intelligentsia who formed the literati of his time. It is significant that while he took little trouble to conceal his authorship, he never allowed his name to be affixed to any of his novels. When one magazine editor disobeyed his express injunction to that effect, Surtees at once broke off the connection and (supreme sacrifice for a writer) abandoned the story in midstream. Even more untypical of the literary establishment of the age than the author himself are his novels. They were neither improving, nor compassionate, nor propagandist. Surtees was a satirist but the aim of his satire was not the amendment of manners but the entertainment of his readers. Most men, he once privately noted, take pleasure in satire as long as it is not directed against themselves.

The genuine country gentry to whom he belonged escaped his censure. His province was the middle-class society of the countryside and small provincial town with an occasional foray into the seedier parts of the metropolis. His stock-in-trade are families with independent means rather than inherited wealth, though it is true that with some of them the independence is more apparent than the means. They included retired tradespeople, parvenus, adventurers, social climbers, farmers, doctors, lawyers, bank managers; scheming mammas seeking eligible husbands for their daughters; impecunious bachelors seeking brides with a sufficiency for two; the young virgin ladies themselves, either sharp-witted and calculating or vain and simpering; and eccentric middle-aged men pursuing their hobbies and recreations with bland indifference to what others thought of them. Maintaining and maintained by this hearty philistine society are a great concourse of servants—butlers, house-keepers, valets, maids, cooks, grooms, and gardeners —the indispensable under-structure of the Victorian middle classes. No other nineteenth-century novelist, perhaps, devoted more space than Surtees to the char-acters and activities of servants. Thackeray in his *Yellowplush Papers* used them to provide a particular view of the middle classes. Dickens introduced them as indi-vidual personalities to provide colour, humour, and sentimental interest. Surtees did that too; his James Pigg, though not so well known, is at least the equal of Sam Weller; and his 'Dirtiest of the Dirties' is not far short of the Marchioness in the *Old Curiosity Shop*. But he does more; he describes the world below stairs, its organiza-tion, its attitudes, its manners, and its morals, both in small households and in large, more completely than anything Dickens ever attempted.

Yet though Surtees' world is thoroughly explored, it remains a small world. The few members of the higher aristocracy that make their appearance are libellous cari-catures—senile wenchers or pompous fools. The occa-sional rural labourer who shambles out of the hedgerow is an inarticulate clodhopper. No sympathy is wasted on the poor, deserving or otherwise. What is most re-markable, perhaps, in Surtees' novels are the principal characters. The roles of what with most other novelists would be hero and heroine are taken by self-assured, semi-respectable rogues living on the gullibility of society and a few physical accomplishments of their own in the hunting and shooting line; in the other sex by dashing young ladies from the theatrical profession who combine a firm seat in the saddle with a more flexible attitude out of it. His inimitable character Jorrocks, to whom he devoted three of his eight novels, was a self-made City of London grocer with a Cockney accent and a misplaced passion for fox-hunting.

Not surprisingly, the Victorian public was slow to appreciate Surtees. It was the kind of person he wrote about, and the way he wrote about them, that perplexed them. They thought his characters, if not positively coarse, undoubtedly low; his plots perverse if not actually immoral. An old friend, who being a QC might be thought not unacquainted with the shadier aspects of life, once asked Surtees despairingly whether he could not introduce 'a good character, man or woman; honest, truthful, domestic, trying to do what duty requires to God and Man, and happy accordingly'. One is reminded of Harriet Martineau's tart comment, even after the appearance of *Pendennis* and *Henry Esmond*, that Thackeray has apparently never known a good sensible woman such as 'abound among the matronage of England'. From the evidence of his novels the limitations of Surtees' range of social acquaintances might appear to be still more severe than that of his friend Thackeray. Even among his male characters he never produced a Major Dobbin; and when he once came within measurable distance of doing so, in Jovey Jessop of *Plain or Ringlets*, the delineation is half-hearted, the role distinctly minor. As for good sensible women, one may search Surtees' novels in vain for such paragons. His one female who unites virtuousness with a degree of spirit is Belinda Jorrocks and she is only permitted a brief walking-on part in *Handley Cross*.

Such reputation as Surtees acquired outside sporting circles was therefore of a dubious nature and clung to him long after his death in 1864. A publisher's advertisement which appeared early in this century introduced him as 'a well known country gentleman, who was passionately devoted to the healthy sport of fox-hunting, and gifted with a keen spirit of manly humour of a Rabelaisian tinge'.[1] The description does not argue much acquaintance with either Surtees or Rabelais; but it helps to explain why in his own lifetime he was never regarded as a serious novelist. Though he was included in the *Dictionary of National Biography* (1885–1900), Andrew

Lang apparently saw no reason to mention him in his *History of English Literature* (1912). It was just as well, perhaps, that he did not depend on his pen for a living. Only one of his novels was a real success when it appeared and some were decided failures.

Yet his reputation grew steadily after his death and today his place among English novelists needs no advertisement whether of a Rabelaisian tinge or otherwise. Even in his own century there were one or two appreciative fellow-craftsmen. One was Thackeray, who not only, like Surtees, lacked the optimism of the time but, seeking a broader canvas, chafed against the restrictive conventions under which he had to write. Thackeray's admiring remark about the character of Lord Scamperdale in *Mr Sponge*—'perfectly odious and admirable'— was a juxtaposition of adjectives that would not have come naturally to most of the literary public. Another but later Victorian writer who clearly enjoyed Surtees was Kipling. *Stalky & Co.* (1899) is full of joyous Surtees quotations. The very first episode in the book finds Stalky reading *Handley Cross* and the chapter entitled 'The Last Term' is so stuffed with unexplained allusions to, and quotations from, that immortal work that it must mystify the uninitiated. Presumably those for whom *Stalky & Co.* was designed were deemed to be among the elect. Like Kipling, Surtees' posthumous reputation is unaffected by fashion. His readership may be limited but its members constitute a freemasonry of their own. His novels are regularly reprinted and old copies rarely remain on the shelves of second-hand bookshops for long.

Nobody of course would pretend that Surtees offers either a comprehensive or unbiased picture of Victorian society. It is because his bias ran counter to the main literary tendencies of his age that he deserves attention. That he was a satirist and not a sentimentalist, an observer and not a reformer, does not in itself make him a more reliable historical witness; but the contrast with more widely read and more highly praised novelists of his time can at least illuminate a few complexities in a society which has had too many simplified generalizations applied to it. Surtees was an unusual figure among early Victorian novelists; he was not an unrepresentative figure in the ordinary England of his time. If he was not one of those writers who helped to form what might be called the 'moral tone' of the period, he at least belonged to that larger part of the population which that moral tone was meant to influence; and he was not very malleable material. 'I never push myself an inch forward,' he once remarked, 'but I damned well see that I'm never pushed an inch back.' He was conservative by instinct though not against all change. He was a humane man who nevertheless disliked the cant of humanitarianism; a proud man who retained a certain hardness towards himself and others; an honest man who could not bear humbug; a good man who had only limited faith in the goodness of mankind.

Yet because he distanced himself from his novels, in a manner impossible for Dickens or Thackeray, those qualities remain in the background. Unlike many professional writers, he had a complete life outside his books; his feelings were less engaged; his literary ambitions more modest. He could afford to be objective and prosaic. There was no place in his fiction for Bulwer Lytton's grand topics of crime and passion; Surtees did not deal in the sublime. In his novels, as for most people most of the time, life goes at a jogtrot. He took his characters from the mass of ordinary, indifferently honest, moderately selfish human beings which at all time make up the great part of the race. There are no villains and no saints; no tragedies, no romanticism, no idealism, and precious little innocence. In his most disreputable characters there is always something to admire, even if it is no more than physical courage and strength of will. In his most respectable characters there is always something shoddy or ludicrous, even if for the most part they are well-intentioned and harmless. What they all have in common (perhaps these are the basic Victorian virtues) are robustness, vitality, and self-confidence. They are energetic individuals, busy on their own affairs, tolerant of the idiosyncrasies of others, but more intent on doing what they want in their own little circle. They are not given to introspection; they rarely feel remorse. Optimism and a thick skin carry them through life; and life in the Surtees novels has no particular distributive justice. In the succession of events which is his substitute for a plot, virtue is rarely rewarded; fools are made to pay for their folly; the respectable often meet with undeserved disappointment; and the unscrupulous do uncommonly well for themselves. As moral tales the Surtees novels are not to be recommended; for teaching ingenuous youth something about life they have their points.

For the historian Surtees has other useful qualities. He does not go outside the field of his own observation. Like Jane Austen, he is strictly a contemporary observer; that, and a skill in constructing conversation to display character, are perhaps the only things they have in common. Being a man, he had a wider field. The beat of the great world which is so muffled in Miss Austen's novels is more audible with Surtees. From casual allusions to public personages and political events, to the weather at home and happenings abroad, the reader can tell almost to the year when the action of the book is supposed to take place; and usually it is only a year or two before the date of publication. Surtees is the minor chronicler of the age of Sir Robert Peel and Lord John Russell, of the repeal of the Corn Laws, of the coming of the railways, of the Great Exhibition, the Crimean War, of the bloomer and the crinoline. It is not that he makes much of these matters; they are simply there. He has no need to explain them to his readers; allusion is enough. As each novel replaces the preceding one, the backcloth imperceptibly changes, like a landscape slowly moving past the window of a crawling stage-coach. Few novelists have so consistently sited their books in such a firm historical setting without allowing the purely historical events to affect the essentially private and domestic narrative.

Two other characteristics add to Surtees' virtues as a social witness. He is a writer obsessed with the details of everyday life—the clothes people wore, the dishes they ate, the wines they drank, the furniture in their houses,

the carriages which took them about their businesses
and pleasures. The minuteness and particularity of his
descriptions of these mundane matters prompts one to
reflect that even though Surtees was not a Grub Street
penny-a-liner, for whom every additional word brought
a commensurate reward, at least he was under no necessity to exercise literary self-discipline. All his novels
originally appeared in serial form, usually in monthly
parts, and this normal Victorian method of publication
fostered a leisurely and discursive style. Apart from
Hawbuck Grange, the weakest of the novels, and
Jorrocks's Jaunts and Jollities, which is not really a novel
at all but a collection of sketches, all Surtees' books are
long ones, perhaps too long from a literary point of view;
and their prolixity is assisted by Surtees' indifference to
plot. With most of his novels, in fact, there seems no
compelling reason why they should ever end; and when
the practical requirements of publishers eventually bring
them to a halt, Surtees bundles his characters away like
a Punch and Judy man packing his puppets into a box
before moving on to the next fairground. What may be
useless lumber in the eye of a literary critic, however,
can yield useful pickings to a historian. In few other
novelists of the period is he likely to find such a quantity
of information about the small details of Victorian life:
details which in most writers go unrecorded because
they are too ordinary and obvious to be part of serious
literature.

There is another trait in Surtees as a novelist which
makes him interesting to the historian, though it does
nothing for his reputation as a literary craftsman. He has
a trick of drawing his reader to one side and delivering
his views on something of which he has apparently just
been reminded, whether it is the inadequacies of farmers, the effect of London clubs on the habits of young
men, the pitfalls of buying horses at an auction, or the
absurdities of female costume. Surtees had no illusions
about his novels; he never thought they served any purpose other than to entertain and even that with a limited
public. Yet he enjoyed his scribbling; he would hardly

have continued to produce his books otherwise, since he had no need for money and no expectation of literary fame. He was always a reserved and reticent man; and though his novels were only part of his life they gave him an opportunity to express his thoughts more freely perhaps than anywhere else. It is in his soliloquies and incidental comments that one comes closest to the man; and through him to a better knowledge of his society.

Surtees died in 1864 when his last novel was about to appear. His continuous recollection of the world, therefore, if we may judge from common experience, started about the time of Waterloo when he was 10; his adult perception from the reign of George IV. To cover this half-century the term 'early-Victorian' has been given here a slightly generous latitude, starting in 1815 and lasting until the second Reform Act of 1867, a date which conveniently marks the half-way point of Victoria's reign. There is logic as well as convenience in this extended use. Victoria's accession in 1837 marked no significant change; it aroused no expectations; it affected nothing of importance except the personal relations between monarch and ministers. Much of what we regard as typically Victorian was already in existence in the two or even three preceding decades. The men and women who were prominent in English society in the first thirty years of her reign were for the most part born in the reign of George III: Dickens and Thackeray before the end of the Napoleonic Wars, the three Brontë sisters between 1816 and 1820, George Eliot in 1819, John Stuart Mill in 1806, Carlyle as early as 1795. Mrs Somerville, the scientific bluestocking who lived into the age of Bismarck and the Franco-German War, was born in 1780; George Stephenson, the engineer, in 1781; Paxton, the creator of the Crystal Palace, in 1801; Playfair the chemist in 1818. Nearly all the senior officers in the Crimean War, including Admiral Dundas, Admiral Napier, and the army commander Lord Raglan, were born before the end of the eighteenth century; as were all Victoria's prime ministers until 1868. The use of dates to mark off convenient historical periods obscures the element of human continuity; people do not change their habits and outlooks overnight. Surtees, dying at the comparatively early age of 59, was not markedly older or younger than his better-known literary contemporaries. With many of them he shared a common social background and a common historical experience.

G. M. Young, in his classic *Portrait of an Age*, used the fictional device of 'a boy born in 1810' to illuminate the transformation of English society between the first Reform Act in 1832 and the death of Palmerston in 1865. Surtees, five years older than G. M. Young's boy, was a real person who may serve something of the same purpose, in the modest sense of offering sidelights on that society if not a complete portrait. It was Young also who observed that he was continually being told that the Victorians did this or thought that whereas his difficulty was to find anything on which they agreed, any assumption which was not at some time fiercely challenged. Equally, any historian who tries to penetrate 'Victorian society' finds himself faced instead by individuals. Among them Surtees has some claim to be heard, the more so since he is an example of what Young called 'the large ironic English mind' on which the fashionable moral and intellectual forces of the age were seeking to impose themselves.

PART ONE
Surtees' England

1

THE MAN AND HIS BOOKS

I

That such an unlikely figure as Surtees ever became a novelist is largely ascribable to the fact that he was born a younger son and remained in that inauspicious state for the first twenty-six years of his life. He came of an old but not particularly wealthy family of small landowners in County Durham, another branch of which had produced his namesake and cousin, the well-known antiquarian and local historian. His name and local connections provided him therefore with a more spacious background than his actual prospects seemed likely to perpetuate. Like many a thrifty squire's son he was educated locally, first at a small private school in the neighbourhood, and then for one year at Durham Grammar School. At the age of 14 his formal schooling came to an end. He thus escaped one of the worst misfortunes that could have befallen a future novelist—six or seven years unrelenting subjection to the mechanical grind of Latin and Greek which passed for education in the great public schools and the two ancient universities of England at that time. Whatever else can be said of Surtees' style, it is free from the ponderousness and rotundity which characterize the prose of most formally educated mid-Victorians.

He escaped the drudgery of the classics, however, only to fall into the even deadlier drudgery of the law. In 1822 he was articled to a solicitor in Newcastle upon Tyne in whose office he had possibly been working previously as a clerk. Law was one of the traditional careers for younger sons, though it was less fashionable to be a solicitor than a barrister. The unglamorous branch of the profession offered, on the other hand, a more certain livelihood than the overcrowded ranks of the Bar. In the spring of 1825 a crucial stage in his life opened when he was further articled to a solicitor in London and made his first long journey away from home. Distance is as much a matter of time as of space. Surtees took two days and a night to go from Newcastle to the capital. 'The fare was £6 inside,' he later recalled, 'and it was considered very fine travelling.' In London he soon wearied of the life of a law student, if indeed he had not already taken a dislike to it in Newcastle. His sketch of Charley Stobbs in *Handley Cross* (ch. xxiv) is clearly based on his own experiences, and from that account it was a stultifying existence. Young Mr Stobbs was attached, we are told, to the chambers of the great Mr Twister, 'one of those legal nuisances called conveyancers'.

Having plenty to do himself, he took as many pupils as ever he could get, to help each other to do nothing. Each of these paid him a hundred guineas a year, in return for which they had the run of a dingey, carpetless room, the use of some repulsive-looking desks, and liberty to copy twenty volumes of manuscript precedents, that the great Mr Twister had copied himself when a pupil with great Mr Somebody else.

It is not surprising that in his novels lawyers do not emerge as engaging characters. Surtees did not easily forget and rarely forgave.

Nevertheless, there is not a great deal of exaggeration in his description of the legal education of his day. Even those who, unlike Surtees and Thackeray, endured their apprenticeship and remained in the profession, in later life expressed much the same sentiments. That eminent Victorian lawyer Roundell Palmer, an Oxford graduate who proposed to practise at the Chancery Bar, went through the customary course of one year's pupillage in a conveyancer's chambers and another with an Equity draughtsman. He found the contrast with university life a painful one. 'To descend', he wrote feelingly fifty years later, 'from the flowers of history, poetry, and philosophy, to those dry bones of technical systems, and especially to the dull copying clerk's work and mechanical processes of conveyancing, was dispiriting enough.' It also explained to his doubtless partisan mind why there were so many more Cambridge men than Oxford men high in the profession.

Not being a product of either university, Surtees had to find his consolations elsewhere. At least in London there were endless diversions to excite his provincial curiosity. The great capital, with its million and a half population, half as big again as the next nine largest towns in England put together, the centre of power and wealth, the home of every imaginable trade and profession, the place where the highest and lowest in society lived side by side, was an inexhaustible field for observation and entertainment. Youthful students away from home are not as a rule conspicuous for social decorum and virtuous domesticity. There are indications in the novels that Surtees knew a good deal about the London underworld; at all events it is clear that his education was not limited to the equivalent of Mr Twister's chambers. He was duly called to the Court of Chancery in 1828 but, more important, in the following year he began writing for the *Sporting Magazine*. Then in 1831 he joined Ackermann in founding the *New Sporting Magazine* and became its editor. Apart from his professional journeys into the provinces as hunting correspondent, his literary earnings enabled him to indulge in a little private travel—to Margate and other seaside resorts beloved of the Cockney tourist and across the Channel to Boulogne and Paris. In 1835 he signified his abandonment of the law as a career by removing his name from the Law List.

His future had taken on a new colour, however, long before that step was taken. In 1831 his elder brother died unmarried and Robert was now heir to the family estate. In due course, on the death of his father seven years later, he became squire of Hamsterley Hall and in 1841 consolidated his social position in the county by his marriage to Elizabeth Jane Fenwick, daughter and co-heiress of a neighbouring magistrate. In the next few years he assumed all the outward trappings of an active,

public-spirited, provincial landowner. He was appointed
JP and deputy-lieutenant for County Durham; major in
the Durham militia; president of the local agricultural
association; and Poor Law Guardian. In 1837 he stood
as Conservative candidate for Gateshead against an
unpopular Liberal sitting member but withdrew before
polling-day to give a second Liberal candidate a clear
run. The next year he became vice-president of the local
Conservative Association, that new class of party organization springing up all over England. He remained influential in local politics for another decade, though he
declined to stand again himself. A parliamentary career
demanded more money and more commitment than
perhaps his purse or his sceptical temperament provided.
Moreover, it would have interfered with his sport; and
sport was one of his enduring passions. Throughout his
life he continued to hunt. He even for a few years (1838–
40) kept a pack of hounds; though this, if less ruinous
than electioneering, was expensive enough.

Outwardly, then, Surtees became a conventional provincial squire of modest means and purely local activities. There were hundreds of men like him in the English
countryside, leaders in their little rural world but hardly
known outside it. But for Surtees there was the other,
largely hidden, compartment of his life, his novel-writing.
The urge to write had been with him from an early age.
Even in the 1820s, before his first magazine article had
been published, he had started and then destroyed the
draft of a 'semi-sporting novel'. His first book developed
out of his journalistic contributions to the *Old* and *New
Sporting Magazines*. As early as 1831 he was writing about
Jorrocks, the sporting grocer of Great Coram Street,
whose various adventures enabled him to expand his
repertory beyond the range of a mere hunting correspondent. The separate articles were collected and published in 1838 as *Jorrocks's Jaunts and Jollities*. Falling in
love with his own creation, he produced a riper and more
rounded version as the central character of what more
nearly resembled a real novel. It appeared in monthly
parts in the *New Sporting Magazine* in 1838–9 and
eventually in book form under the title of *Handley Cross*

in 1842. Though it did not arouse much interest, it must have pleased its creator, since another Jorrocks novel, in no way inferior to *Handley Cross*, followed under the title of *Hillingdon Hall*, serialized in 1843–4.

By now the habit of writing was too strong to shake off. As he soliloquized in *Hawbuck Grange* a few years later, writing 'is something like snuffing or smoking— men get into the way of it, and can't well leave it off. Like smoking it serves to beguile an idle hour. Individually speaking, writing makes us tolerably independent, both of the world and the weather.' For the rest of his life he was never long without something on the stocks. Yet in parting with Jorrocks he lost for a time a certain inspiration. His next two books were the weakest in the whole corpus of Surtees literature. The first, in 1846, was the misleadingly named *Analysis of the Hunting Field*, a compilation of papers published in *Bell's Life* the previous winter. It sketches a gallery of hunting characters from the master of hounds to the humble earth-stopper, together with a few well-known types encountered among the followers in the field. In form the *Analysis* seems to have been modelled on the traditional manual of hunting since it contains, along with much practical information and advice, a great deal of anecdotal entertainment. It is not commonly classed with Surtees' novels since it has neither plot nor continuity of characters. It is also Surtees at his blandest, as though he has one eye on his editor and the other on his readers, and is anxious to offend neither. Masters of Hounds are the most honoured of mankind; fox-hunters are the salt of the earth; farmers are public-spirited and hospitable even when they do not hunt themselves; hunt servants are loyal and devoted. Even the peerage, in the person of Lord Evergreen, who has the additional distinction of being a Cabinet Minister, earns some deferential remarks. It is almost as if he was taking a few leaves from Nimrod's book. That famous, older, sporting journalist, in private life C. J. Apperley (1779–1843), had been the first of the gentleman hunting-correspondents of the *Sporting Magazine*. In this capacity he had moved in a more exalted and fashionable set of men than Surtees ever did, and his articles, though knowledgeable, had a characteristic flavour of snobbery and effusiveness which Surtees was tempted to caricature rather than to copy. It is only in the *Analysis*, in fact, that he runs any risk of being likened to his better-known predecessor on the magazine.

Fortunately, enough genuine Surteesian bitters is added to the honey to make it palatable. There are a few characteristically mordant epigrams—'More people are flattered into virtue than are bullied out of vice.' 'Many people prefer finding fault to praising. They think it shows acuteness on their part.' 'The man must lead a wretched life who troubles himself with thinking what "the world thinks of him".' 'A man is not a match for a woman till he's married.' In the procession of blameless characters a few reprehensible types are introduced to add interest and a touch of satire—Elijah Bullwaist, the gross, clumsy blacksmith and incompetent horse-doctor; Captain Shabbyhounds, adventurer, steeplechaser, gambler, and horse-dealer; Colonel Codshead, militia officer and local major, who preferred talking about his hunting to actually riding across country. More revealing still, as the book progresses, is the author's increasing tendency to allow his analysis of characters to stray into embryonic plots and episodes. The story of Captain Shabbyhounds, for example, with his spectral groom Job Tod, and their dealings with the Hon. Julius Milksop; or Miss Henrietta Cottonwool's matrimonial capture of that dashing hunter, Sir Rasper Smashgate, are episodes that could have found a place in any of Surtees' novels.

In his next book, *Hawbuck Grange*, published in 1847, he returned to a more fictional form, but it was not a good book. It is the shortest of the novels, has no plot, and its hero Tom Scott is remarkably colourless. If, as has been surmised, *Hawbuck Grange* is largely autobiographical in the sense that it draws on Surtees' own experiences as a hunting correspondent, the flatness in the leading character is understandable; it is a form of self-suppression, almost amounting to anonymity, typical of the man. What the book did do was enable Surtees to give his own sharp and independent opinions on hunting in general, fashionable or otherwise, and its accompaniments, human and material. It is a novel only one remove from sporting journalism, just as the *Analysis* is sporting journalism constantly edging towards the form of a novel.

The uncertainties and shapelessness of this middle period gave way towards the end of the decade to the certitude and maturity of his last five books; and with them came at last a degree of public recognition. The Jorrocks books had not caught on; *Hawbuck Grange* was a decided failure. *Mr Sponge's Sporting Tour* (1848–51) was his first real success. He might have achieved a second in *Young Tom Hall* (1851–3) had he not dropped it as a result of his quarrel with his editor Harrison Ainsworth over the breach of his anonymity. After that setback he experimented with the wider canvas of *Ask Mamma* in 1857–8 and *Plain or Ringlets* in 1859–60, two society novels which suffer from a lack of strong leading characters though there is a cast of entertaining minor roles and both books are full of matter for the social historian. Finally, in 1864 he returned to the sporting world with *Mr Facey Romford's Hounds*, which he regarded as a good sequel to *Mr Sponge* and some later critics have deemed to be technically the best of all his novels. It was while waiting for its publication in book form that he turned from fiction to the preparation of his projected sporting and social recollections. He had hardly got beyond the compilation of a few scattered notes when a heart-attack in a Brighton hotel carried him off on the night of 16 March 1864.

Undeniably, then, Surtees had, as he put it, a 'taste for scribbling'. The deprecatory tone is characteristic. He never put on airs about his writing; he simply enjoyed doing it. To get into print was reward enough; to be paid for it was delightful. Few English authors have so consistently followed the English habit of understatement about their own achievements. 'The work merely professes to be a tale,' he observes in the preface to *Handley Cross*, 'and does not aspire to the dignity of a novel.' In *Ask Mamma* he warns his readers that 'the following story

does not involve the complication of a plot. It is a mere
continuous narrative of an almost everyday exaggeration, interspersed with sporting scenes and excellent illustrations by Leech.' Later in the same book he asserts
that 'we have only aimed at nothing but the natural
throughout'. In *Hawbuck Grange* (ch. xv) he inserts a brief,
perhaps not entirely fictional, conversation with a candid
friend on the subject of his 'queer books' in which he
expresses his own surprise that publishers print them
and the public read them, even paying good money for
the privilege. With this attitude towards his creations he
never sought personal literary prestige and clung to his
cloak of anonymity long after it had become transparent.
For a man in his position this is understandable, particularly at the outset of his writing career. A journalist at
the start of Victoria's reign was hardly a gentleman, and
though gentlemen (especially politicians) indulged in
journalism, they usually concealed their names and affected to despise its regular practitioners. Moreover, the
members of the various hunts he attended in his capacity
as sporting correspondent would have looked at him
rather oddly had they guessed his real purpose among
them. Anonymity protected his social status and left him
free to air his own sometimes unorthodox views. As he
observed in the *Analysis*, once fashionable London
periodicals took to printing occasional articles on contemporary fox-hunting, 'people have become rather
suspicious of strangers in the hunting field . . . Authorship somehow is not a popular trade in the country.
Nimrod was the only author on horseback who could
fairly face a hunting field in *propria personae* [*sic*].'

He carried this professional secretiveness into his
novel-writing. 'I find,' he confessed when negotiating the
publication of *Tom Hall* in 1851, 'I can write much better
and with far more pleasure to myself, when I am free to
deny an article if I like.' Yet there was more perhaps to
his passion for anonymity than this. In the sporting rural
society to which he belonged books were valued for utility
rather than literary merit. In *Hawbuck Grange* (ch. xi)
Surtees disinterestedly advises the fox-hunter deprived

of his sport by frost to stay at home and read the *Post Office Directory* or the *Annual Register* or 'any work that is not encumbered with a plot'. This maxim is carried to extremes by his character Soapey Sponge, whose habitual reading-matter was *Mogg's Omnibus and Cab Time Table*. It was to this unpromising class that for the first twenty years of his career Surtees was looking to provide his readership. He had no illusions about their literary shortcomings. 'The sporting world is altogether different from the general world of literature,' he observed wryly in 1852 when reflecting on the unexpected success of *Mr Sponge*, 'a book serving many sportsmen a long time; some indeed get on capitally without any.' This consideration must have been a powerful inducement to write a racy colloquial prose with almost a deliberate indifference to either fine writing or fine sentiments. Pitching his novels at this level, it is hardly surprising that he tried to prevent his daughters from reading them. As one of them reported, 'Papa said there was nothing worse for young people than reading bad literature.' By bad, no doubt, he meant low literature as contrasted with the conventional moral tone of respectable literature. In much the same vein, when he came to publish *Mr Sponge's Sporting Tour* in book form with a dedication to Lord Elcho, he added a brief preface defending his choice of 'such a characterless character as Mr Sponge' as the hero of the story, on the unconvincing grounds that it would serve to put the rising generation on their guard against specious, promiscuous acquaintances. Such a relapse into the primness of orthodox respectability was rare. It did not stop him making an even more promiscuous rogue, Facey Romford, the hero of his very last novel.

At bottom there seems, in fact, to have been a discordancy between his consciousness that novel-writing was not a proper occupation for a man of his class and the personal pleasure he got out of writing them. The kind of book that in these circumstances he came to write had at least this advantage. He was spared the need to observe the conventions and subscribe to the aspirations of a moral and reforming age. While other novelists pursued virtuousness, he wrote about the cakes and ale of actual life, not forgetting even the cheese and onions.

II

Like many novelists, especially those who rely on observation rather than imagination, Surtees often took real persons and actual landscapes as models for his books; even though, like most novelists, he modified them to suit his needs. Just as he used his journalistic tours in the English counties and in France to provide material for *Jorrocks's Jaunts and Jollities*, so he used some of his early acquaintances as bases for his characters. Two were well-known figures in Georgian Brighton—Captain Eld, the effusive MC, and the eccentric foreign baron Gablenz. He did not apparently spare even highly placed neighbours. The duke of Donkeyton in *Hillingdon Hall* is said to have been modelled on a contemporary duke of Northumberland and, less probably, Lord Scamperdale in *Mr Sponge* on the earl of Wemyss. Even Jorrocks may have had a real-life original, though research has failed to identify him. The north-country, however, presented him with a prototype of James Pigg in a local man, Josh Kirk. Pomponius Ego, on the other hand, was a deliberate and malicious, not to say unmistakable, portrait of C. J. Apperley, the celebrated Nimrod of sporting journalism as Surtees, when challenged by his indignant victim, contemptuously acknowledged. It was an admission that almost certainly would have led to a duel, except that within a few weeks Apperley, then in debtor's exile at Calais, died of peritonitis in May 1843.

It is clear also that Surtees drew extensively on his own neighbourhood for the settings of his novels. Take, for example, the scene in *Hillingdon Hall* (ch. xxiv) when Jorrocks encounters a herd of 'Scotch kyloes' driven by his former huntsman James Pigg. It was a sight with which Surtees must have been familiar since his boyhood, though when he came to write the novel he had to record

regretfully that the incident took place on 'one of these
now rarely met with passages, a green lane . . . one of
those continuous lines of by-roads frequented chiefly
by cattle drovers'. A contemporary work, *Spas of England*, published by Dr Granville in 1841, fixes the location. Describing the Roman road which ran close to
Hamsterley Hall (he calls it Watling Street though it
appears on modern maps as Dere Street), he observes
that though it was now obstructed in parts, 'the Scotch
drovers, tenacious of their traditional rights, still insist
on tracking it, throughout its whole extent, with their
cattle'. A captious critic might point to a certain incon-
gruousness in making Jorrocks, a Cockney grocer, pitch
on County Durham for his retirement home; but for
Surtees the convenience of placing his fictitious localities
in a setting he knew so well outweighed any such trivial
objections.

Even Featherbedshire, Lord Ladythorne's country in
Ask Mamma, has a north-country feel to it, if we may
judge from the remark of a casual bystander in chapter
xxxii: 'what, you're gannen to him—are ye.' We meet the
same dialect in *Mr Romford* when a rustic, explaining just
where his cur had turned Romford's fox, says, 'Just by
yon bit bush beyond the stone heap.' These are not accents found anywhere south of the Trent. The same
topographical preference helps to explain what is otherwise a mystifying episode in chapter xlv of *Handley Cross*
when the lost and benighted Jorrocks is given hospitality
for the night in a smuggler's cave presided over by a
young lady in tight blue bodice and red flannel petticoat
whose delicate white legs attract the admiring eyes of
the impressionable sportsman. The modern reader, to
whom smuggling at this period conjures up visions of
brandy and lace and the coasts of Kent and Sussex,
may be mildly puzzled at the introduction of an inland
smuggler called Whisky Jim who follows his romantic
calling in a district of hills, heather, and dense forests.
Any native of Durham or Northumberland at the time
would have recognized its authenticity. In the early part
of the century there was a flourishing contraband trade

in whisky across the Border to avoid the excise duty of
2s. 6d. a gallon. In an effort to stop this illegal traffic an
act was passed in 1820 prohibiting the carriage of whisky
by land from Scotland to England. This draconian statute seems if anything to have stimulated smuggling, as
the numerous prosecutions for illicit trading in Scottish
spirits in Northumberland and Durham in the 1820s
testify. Public sympathy was naturally with the law-
breakers, and the smugglers were credited with all kinds
of ingenious tricks and bold exploits. Remarkably, it was
not until Gladstone equalized the duty on spirits in the
two countries in his 1853 budget that Border smuggling
came to an end. It is probable, as a local historian, Mr
Thomson, suggests, that the railways (those agents of
progress and civilization) had a hand in bringing this
about.[1] Until then the Caledonian and North British
railway companies had been constrained to warn their
passengers that the transport of spirits from Scotland to
England was illegal and any quantity, however small,
was liable to seizure. In an age of fast travel, delays
between Gretna and Carlisle to allow excise officials
to search for contraband liquor seemed singularly
anachronistic.

There are other reasons for giving *Handley Cross*, as
well as *Hillingdon Hall*, a north-country location. The
invitation to Jorrocks to become MFH at Handley Cross
was part of a local campaign to turn the town into a spa
and tourist resort. That in itself was a contemporary
theme. The late 1830s and 1840s saw the first great wave
of railway building when property speculators and enterprising builders flourished and grandiose schemes
of local development were floated by civic communities
with an eye on private profit. The presence of a natural
spring, a favourable chemical analysis of the water, and
the recommendations of a couple of local doctors, was
enough to encourage dozens of insignificant towns to
aspire to the dignity of a spa. With a larger, wealthier,
and more leisured middle class, tourism in Surtees' day
was a booming industry. In the great urban expansion of

the first half of the nineteenth century, the fastest growing group of towns was not London and the industrial
aggregations of the North and Midlands but watering
places and holiday resorts.

It was because the development ironically described
by Surtees in chapter ii of *Handley Cross* was so typical
of the time that several places have been suggested as
originals. E. D. Cuming's claim for Shotley Bridge in
County Durham is, however, convincing on several
grounds. It was only a few miles from his home; and
while he was actually writing *Handley Cross* the town was
being actively promoted as a spa. Two rival practitioners
there, according to a Surtees family tradition, were the
originals of Doctors Mello and Swizzle in the novel. In
his work on English spas, which appeared at this time,
Dr Granville devoted a whole chapter to Shotley Bridge,
not forgetting to blow a few complimentary puffs in
Surtees' direction. In his notes for a description of County
Durham which Surtees compiled towards the end of his
life, he drily mentions Granville's attempts to inflate
Shotley Bridge into a fashionable spa. By that time it had
long been clear that the flattering forecast in his book
that 'Shotley Bridge will emulate the celebrity of Harro
gate, Cheltenham and Leamington' had gone the way of
similar prophecies for equally forgotten places in his
enthusiastic survey.

Sardonically as Surtees viewed Shotley Bridge and the
sycophantic Dr Augustus Bozzi Granville, the episode
does at least show his knack of weaving into his novels
whatever was catching the attention of the public at the
time. His books are scattered with topical allusions, some
to subjects which still find a place in the history books,
others of only ephemeral interest. The rage for phre-
nology in 1843, for example, is reflected in *Hillingdon Hall*
where it enables Jorrocks to indulge in his own brand
of amatory investigation. In *Tom Hall* (1851–3) there is
mention of the Great Exhibition, the new Prince President of France, and the gold discoveries in California
and Australia; all of which made headlines at the

time when he was writing. In *Mr Sponge* (ch. xv) Mr Jawleyford is shown tastefully composed to meet Soapey Sponge with a copy of Disraeli's *Life of Lord George Bentinck* in his hand. In the serial version a couple of years earlier, it had been a volume of Macaulay's *History*; but Disraeli's book recently published in December 1851, was of much more immediate interest, particularly to protectionist politicians and landowners. Topicality could hardly go further than this.[2]

The same journalistic zest for contemporaneity appears in other novels. In *Ask Mamma* (1857–8) there are references to the Crimean War (1854–6) and Indian Mutiny (1857) and even to the approaching marriage of the Princess Royal which did not take place until January 1858. It is noticeable, incidentally, that on the subject of the Crimean War there is nothing in the novels to indicate that Surtees shared either the jingoism or the sentimentality of the British public. The heroic pathos of Tennyson's 'Charge of the Light Brigade' (1854) was not for him. His allusions to that blundering act of courageous folly are brief and mocking. He observes in *Plain or Ringlets* (ch. xcvii) that 'talk of the courage of facing an enemy, or Cardiganising a cannon—what are such exploits compared with the courage of a man who deliberately risks his all in a concern over which he has no more control than he would over a runaway steam engine?' In *Mr Romford* he is even more disrespectful. He is describing the arrival at the county ball of his disreputable party of adventurers—Facey himself, Mrs Somerville, Miss Howard, and Sir Roger Furguson—none of whom were what they purported to be and all but Facey under assumed names. 'On, on, our gallant party went, just as Lord Cardigan went against the cannon', he writes, as they enter the dance room under the scrutiny of a battery of diamonded dowagers. He has only a solitary reference to the Indian Mutiny, that spectacular and bloody episode which evoked a hysterical cry for vengeance from the Victorian public; and, such as it is, it does not suggest that he had much sympathy with the popular fury. When he makes that seedy rogue Cuddy

Flintoff in *Ask Mamma* (ch. xxxviii) while away a vacant hour in studying *Bell's Life in London* (a popular and sensational weekly newspaper) and 'considering whether Nana Sahib, the Indian fiend, should be roasted alive or carried round the world in a cage', only the dullest reader could be unconscious of the irony.

The novel with the firmest chronological setting of all is *Plain or Ringlets*, the action of which takes place in 1858, the 'year of the comet'. This was Donati's comet and it brought with it the hottest summer in living memory—a 'real continental summer', wrote Surtees appreciatively—when people left town early and took to the open air and the seaside. In the letters of the time the comet vies for attention with the heat. One of the table-anecdotes of the Revd W. H. Brookfield, who besides being the much-overshadowed husband of a celebrated society hostess was also a school inspector, concerned a little girl whom he had set to write an essay on the comet. 'Comets are very useful,' wrote the artless child. 'They have long tails and are something to talk about. We should get on very badly without comets.' As the year advanced, however, the comet was eclipsed by the weather as a talking-point. June was scorching, the second hottest for nearly ninety years. On one day, the 16th, the temperature rose even at the seaside to 88 °F and in some places inland to 95 °F. And that was not the end. Though July saw a return to normal, August was good, and September had average temperatures exceeded only four times since 1779, the last of those occasions being in 1818.

Mr Jorrocks opined once that an English summer generally totalled 'three 'ot days and a thunderstorm', a view which most of his countrymen then and since are frequently tempted to echo. It was fitting, therefore, that 1858 should be meteorologically commemorated in Surtees' novel. It was made, moreover, on good aesthetic principles, not merely a casual feature but the prime reason why the assorted cast of *Plain or Ringlets* found themselves, along with several thousand other visitors, at his fictitious seaside resort of Roseberry Rocks—'the

ladies are all beautiful and elegantly attired', writes
Surtees with mild satire, 'and the men look as if LSD
were for once banished from their thoughts—a combination of circumstances extremely favourable to
authorship'.

III

Surtees had his prejudices and did not mind displaying
them. There was no need for concealment, since they
were shared by a large number of his readers. He did
not, for example, care for Irishmen, if we may judge from
his sketch of Mr Dennis O'Brien in *Handley Cross* and
Johnny O'Dicey the gambler in *Plain or Ringlets*. His
attitude towards European nationalities shows the same
mixture of amusement, condescension, and mild contempt that one finds in the contemporary pages of *Punch*.
Yet foreigners are also cunning and avaricious. Jorrocks,
in one of the more farcical episodes of *Jaunts and Jollities*, is bamboozled and fleeced by the self-styled Countess Benvolio. In *Plain or Ringlets* there is her male
counterpart Prince Pirouetteza, the son of an Italian
dancing-master. His easy impudence and delightful
dancing flutter the ladies, but to the men he reveals the
true depths of his depravity by shooting a fox at a ducal
battue. Another variant on this theme is Jean Rougier
(alias Jack Rogers) in *Ask Mamma*. This true-born English rogue, who for professional reasons passes himself
off as French, exploits simultaneously the snobbish
preference of employers for a foreign valet and the in-
eradicable conviction of Englishmen that a Frenchman
can always be confidently backed to lose in a matter of
horsemanship.

The attitude of the Victorian public towards France
was remarkably illogical. It was natural enough that,
separated from their neighbour not only by the Channel
and profound differences of temperament but by centuries of national rivalry, they should nourish certain

prejudices. What is striking is John Bull's habit of treating individual Frenchmen as slightly comic characters and the French nation collectively as a permanent threat to British security. The latter conviction had at least some history behind it. Most people at the accession of Victoria could remember Waterloo. It is true that twenty years later France was to be Britain's ally in the Crimean War; but the British commander-in-chief's absent-minded tendency during that campaign to refer to the enemy as 'the French' innocently reflected an inborn attitude which even after the Franco-German war of 1870 was slow to disappear. Even Englishmen who knew France and could enjoy what it had to offer were not free from the common prejudice. Thackeray, for example, who spent much time in Paris, persistently wrote of the French in what Pope-Hennessy has called 'tones of adolescent ridicule'. Yet it was also Thackeray who about the year 1840 was declaring more seriously that there was only one thing for his countrymen to remember in France—'that they hate us'. He was not peculiar in this. When the great duke of Wellington to the end of his life believed in the inevitability of a French war of revenge on Britain, civilians could be excused for sharing his conviction of the permanently aggressive intentions of their nearest Continental neighbour. The strained relations with France over the Tahiti affair in 1844, and the fear of Napoleon III which led to the Volunteer movement of 1859, were proofs of a profound and widespread English distrust. The 'new Boney', as Mrs Blunt, the colonel's lady, called him in Young Tom Hall, struck a sensitive nerve in the Victorian psychology. We forget how long a shadow was cast over the nineteenth century by that other 'Great War' which ended in 1815, imposed a strain on the British state equal proportionately to that of the 1914–18 war, and lasted five times as long.

Surtees' greatest prejudices, however, were against the army and the Jews. Of the two, his anti-Semitism, though less frequently expressed, was the more violent. Unpleasant as it now appears, it was less exceptional then; and there were contemporary circumstances which

explain even if they do not excuse his feelings. His dislike is mainly directed against rich Jews. An exception is
the episode in *Handley Cross* when Benjamin is tricked
into buying, at what he thinks is a bargain price of 10s,
a second-hand pair of top-boots which turn out to be
made of varnished brown paper. The shop-owner who
sold them is a certain Levy Aaron of Holywell Street,
London. Yet the incident is related without rancour and
the laugh is directed against the conceited little Benjamin
for being such a greenhorn. Surtees' real animus is reserved for the urban plutocrats; not the proletarian Jews
of the London slums. It has something of the resentment
of the English country squire against the alien parvenu
from the big city. What has also to be remembered is
that at the time he was writing the campaign for placing
English Jews on a footing of complete civil equality with
native English was winning success after success. Contemporary events gave a sharper sting to his comments,
for his was the losing side.

It was an issue of principle rather than of politics. There
were not many Jews in Britain in Surtees' time—about
30,000 at the start of Victoria's reign, about two-thirds
of them in London, and about twice that number when
he died in 1864. The great increase, mainly as result of
persecution in Russia, came at the end of the century.
Until then British Jews were a small minority group, the
poorer members of which were clearly distinguished from
native English by their speech, their names, their occupations, and their localities. This distinctiveness, almost
as obvious to non-Jews as a different colour of skin, made
them a popular object of contempt and ridicule. Prejudice
feeds on instantly recognizable physical differences. We
have forgotten how strong the outward and visible marks
of Hebraism once were in English society. Surtees,
searching on one occasion for suitable similes to emphasize the peculiarities of old-fashioned blacksmiths, wrote
that they were 'as much a distinct class or breed of men
as coachmen, sailors or Jews'. Yet there were, particularly
in the City of London, Jews of acknowledged respectability and high social standing, including some of considerable wealth and culture, such as the Rothschilds,

the Montefiores, the Goldsmids, and the Salomons. Some of the upper-class Jews had even penetrated to the titled aristocracy. The first Jew to become a baronet was Sir Isaac Goldsmid, financier and philanthropist, in 1841. A Montefiore was given a baronetcy by Peel in 1846; a Rothschild by Russell immediately afterwards. This rise in social status inevitably strengthened the case for complete civil equality. Between 1829 and 1845 most of the barriers which prevented Jews from entering professional life and local government were removed. The right to sit in parliament took longest to achieve, mainly because of the opposition of the House of Lords. The great campaign which started with Lionel de Rothschild's election for the City of London in 1847 (the first of five such elections before he was finally allowed to take his seat) was protracted and acrimonious. Eleven years, five bills, and several lawsuits later, the deadlock between Lords and Commons was broken by an act which allowed each House to frame its own oath of admittance. It was not until after Surtees' death that the Lords were deprived of their veto and not until 1885 that the first Jewish peer was admitted in the person of Nathaniel de Rothschild.

The Jewish question was, therefore, a controversial topic which repeatedly came before the public in the years when Surtees was writing. The tenacious anti-Jewish feeling in the country (better expressed by the Lords than the liberal-minded majority in the House of Commons) was both racial and religious. Jews were not only not Christians but, in the opinion of many, not really British. It was a supporter of the relief bill of 1841, the Bishop of St David's, who admitted that the Jews would always remain to some extent foreigners and aliens. In the 1847 debates the evangelical and humanitarian Ashley, better known as Lord Shaftesbury, cited Dr Arnold's argument that Jews were 'voluntary strangers' in Britain and had no claim on citizenship. The age-old prejudice was particularly strong in the class to which Surtees himself belonged. In the same 1847 debates one of the leading Tory backbenchers, George Bankes, expressed his horror at the possibility of seeing a Jewish prime minister in the House of Commons. Fortunately for his peace of mind, he died a dozen years before that fearful contingency took place.

Surtees' savage depiction of Sir Moses Mainchance in *Ask Mamma* shows how deeply he was imbued with these feelings. It is true that Sir Moses has the atoning grace of being a fox-hunter ('a passion for hunting is variously distributed', observes Surtees almost apologetically), but apart from that he is spared nothing. He is an avaricious swindler who cheats his neighbours, furnishes his house on the cheap, has bad servants because he is too mean to pay good wages, and cannot even manage his estate efficiently. Even more odious are the Hebraic vignettes in *Plain or Ringlets*—the 'party of cigar-smoking Israelites' lolling in a barouche at the races 'with their great arms over the side, like half-drunken sailors on a spree', and the troop of Misses Jewisons 'turning up their oiley hook noses at everything'. These verbal descriptions are accompanied by sketches by Leech which are as vicious as the text. The illustrations are important because the collaboration between Leech and Surtees was a close one, and the author would not have sanctioned any of which he did not approve. Surtees' anti-Semitism, though only a small part of the novels as a whole, is unforgettable (and, some might think, unforgivable) because it is pure malevolence, unredeemed by either wit or humour. What is also striking is that nobody, neither publisher nor public, apparently protested against it. Anti-Semitism has to be accepted as one of those hard and uncomfortable features of Victorian life difficult to reconcile with the proclaimed liberalism and morality of the age.

It was an issue which affected the artistic as well as the political world. Dickens had to defend his creation of Fagin in *Oliver Twist* by pointing out that in London such figures usually were Jews. Charles Kingsley and Monckton Milnes were sympathetic to the Jewish cause; others less so. Haydon, after lecturing on Fuseli to a Jewish audience, observed disdainfully that 'there is an air of suspicious spite on all Jewish expressions'. Leech, who illustrated so many of Surtees' novels, clearly shared his anti-Semitic prejudices. A cartoon he contributed to

Punch in 1845 entitled 'The Cheap Tailor and his Workmen' depicts a fat hook-nosed Jew puffing at a cigar while he surveys a workroom of cross-legged female skeletons stitching away on the benches. Thackeray disliked Jews despite being on friendly terms with some of them, including Lady Rothschild. Carlyle's anti-Semitism is notorious. Standing outside Rothschild's great house at Hyde Park Corner one day, he observed that, if he had to choose, he preferred King John's methods of dealing with Jews to a society which allowed them to flaunt such opulence.

Almost everywhere in Victorian society one comes up against this deep prejudice—among public schoolboys and the impoverished Irish community in Wapping, in lawcourts and in street ballads. One need not doubt Bishop Thirlwall's remark in the House of Lords in 1848 that Jews in Britain 'have not yet ceased to be the objects of a very general hereditary, unreasoning prejudice, aversion and contempt'. Surtees' Sir Moses Mainchance, like Disraeli, was a Christianized Jew. In Surtees this is reason for additional scorn. The family history he invents for Sir Moses makes him descend from a tribe of street pedlars who accumulate money by sharp practices and calculated marriages, discarding their name of Levy along with their religion on the way up the social ladder, until they attain the coveted distinction of a sheriffdom in the City of London, a knighthood, and finally a baronetcy. Having reached this pinnacle of worldly ambition, Sir Moses abandons commerce and sets up as a landed gentleman. It would not be difficult to find parallels for this in real life. Surtees is recording a feature of contemporary society as well as his distaste for it.

His portrayal of the military profession, though more humorously expressed, is almost as contemptuous as his anti-Semitism. Just as he concentrates on wealthy Jews and largely ignores their poorer co-religionists, so he ridicules army officers rather than the other ranks. The centre-piece of his military sketches is Colonel Blunt and his regiment in *Tom Hall*: an amusing but appallingly libellous picture of a regular army garrison in which the officers are devoid of both decency and discipline and are sometimes not even in full command of the Queen's English. Even greater ridicule is poured on the part-time volunteers, the county militia and the yeomanry, as their cavalry units were generally known. Lord Lavender's hussars are satirically described in ch. v of the same novel as the pick of the yeomanry cavalry of England, officered by noblemen and swells of the first water. The rapid transport provided by the new railways enables these exquisites to descend on their commanding officer's country seat at a moment's notice to eat, drink, and play at soldiers in his park. Lord Lavender himself has the soul of a tailor in the body of a nobleman. The magnificence of the uniforms he prescribes for his corps is such that only the very wealthy can afford to accept a commission in it. As for the officers of those two floral units, the Royal Lavender Dragoons and the Hyacinth Hussars, who achieve the remarkable feat of being heavy cavalry in the morning and hussars at night, they are demolished in a single phrase—'hairy heavies'.

Why Surtees picked on this particular target for his literary arrows is not clear. Either he disliked army officers very much or he found them an easy subject for satire. His grotesqueries can hardly be accepted as a veracious account of the state of the British army at the time; but they probably convey something of the prejudices of the sporting gentry for whom he was writing. It was a very English prejudice. In no other leading European country, it is probable, would a novelist of Surtees' social class have lampooned the military profession in this unsparing fashion. It is impossible to imagine it happening in France, for instance, or Prussia. In England it was different. The English had the singularity of being a martial nation without being a militaristic one. They were convinced that one Englishman was worth two or even three Frenchmen in the field. Yet they did not venerate the army as an institution. No particular prestige attached to the holding of a commission. So innate was this characteristic that they were hardly conscious of it either as a prejudice or a paradox. It took a foreigner to see the oddity. 'Nothing is perhaps more striking to a Berliner', observed a German professor in 1835, 'than the almost total absence of uniforms and orders [i.e. medals] in England.' He cited it as an example of profound national differences that 'the Englishman thinks a universal liability to military service tyrannical'. Visiting the Custom House in London he noted the surprising absence, compared to the Continent, of soldiers and sentinels. 'Generally speaking,' he explained to his German correspondent, 'soldiers are hated, and their interference still more so.'[3]

This civilian outlook, made possible by insular security, had long historical roots in English society. But there were also contemporary circumstances to keep it alive. To the gentry in the Commons the armed forces were the main item of parliamentary expenditure: tolerable perhaps in time of war, but always unpopular in time of peace. To the middle classes the professional army offered the spectacle of an officer caste drawn from the aristocracy, and a rank and file from the lowest of society. England was not like other European countries where universal conscription made a bond between bourgeois families and the profession of arms. This social alienation was increased by the peculiar nature of the army's domestic role. Before the creation of an efficient local police in counties and boroughs (which outside London did not happen until the middle of the century), the function of the army at home was to act as the executive arm of the Home Office for the enforcement of law and order in time of social unrest. In carrying out that task it was liable to be denounced both as a tool of party and as a danger to constitutional liberties. Even after the Napoleonic Wars it was customary for opposition speakers to denounce the whole concept of a professional standing army and argue that the only proper constitutional force was the militia. The prejudice against the army was therefore to be found among country gentry as well as radical politicians, as the 1828–30 Tory press attacks on Wellington as a would-be military dictator demonstrated.

The militia, being a part-time volunteer force, locally

raised and officered, generally escaped the political unpopularity of the regular army. If they notoriously posed
no threat to a foreign invader, they also constituted no
threat to constitutional liberty. Though harmless, however, they were also regarded by many as useless. Surtees
himself held a commission in the Durham militia for a
short time; but he boasted that he never once wore a
sword during that time and took the first decent opportunity to resign. Military command of that amateurish
nature was more a social perquisite than a serious responsibility. An even greater north-country sportsman,
George Osbaldeston, recalled in later life that he was
commissioned as a colonel in the Yorkshire militia during the latter years of the Napoleonic War 'not on account
of any military knowledge I possessed, but merely
because, owing to my large estates in that part of the
country, I had influence in the neighbourhood'. His
majors and captains, he observed parenthetically, were
as inexperienced as himself.[4] Between public indifference and government parsimony, however, the militia at
the start of Victoria's reign was a moribund organization.
In the 1830s it was no longer enrolled for service and in
the 1840s almost ceased to exist, only a small headquarters
cadre being maintained. It is not surprising that Surtees
was unable to take his militia commission seriously. It
was not until 1852 that the force began to be reorganized
and training recommenced. In *Hawbuck Grange* (ch. xiii)
the yeomanry come in for some cutting comments on
the occasion when Tom Scott encounters a troop of them
clattering along 'in all the pomp and terror of cart-horse
cavalry . . . as if they were going to quell a rebellion or
extinguish a fire at the least'. 'Who,' enquires Tom unkindly of one of their officers known to him personally,
'who looks after the shop when you are out soldiering?'

Behind his scorn was perhaps the jealousy of the
squirearchy against the great peers and landowners who
often treated the militia and yeomanry as their peculiar
social perquisite. The general prejudice against the profession of arms to which Surtees gave expression probably had an effect even on regular officers. An intelligent

Guards officer whom Sir Thomas Acland met in 1866 singled out lack of professional knowledge as the chief weakness of army officers and was inclined to ascribe it to 'the fact that military men are not held in such honour as abroad, so that a man tries to sink his military character, and only to be an agreeable gentleman'.[5] Certainly Guards officers, exposed to all the social distractions of the capital, were conspicuous for this tendency. If we can trust the anecdotal evidence of Grantley F. Berkeley, who held a commission in the Coldstream Guards in the immediate post-Waterloo years, neglect of regimental duties in order to enjoy the amenities of social life was endemic in his regiment.

It was to this casual attitude among army officers that Lytton Bulwer in 1833 attributed not only the lack of any proper system of recruitment and of serious study of military science but also 'the low moral standard of our army, and the consequent difficulty of abolishing corporal punishment'. Sympathy with the army could hardly be expected from one who was both a literary man and a radical politician. Nevertheless, if Gronow (another ex-Guards officer) is to be believed, even more trenchant criticism came from within the military establishment itself. Shortly before his death at Waterloo, General Picton declared that with fifty thousand British troops commanded by French officers he could march from one end of Europe to the other. When an affronted member of his staff protested that this was the first time he had heard that French officers were superior to others, his peppery superior exclaimed, 'What, never heard they were superior to ours? Why, damn it, where is our military education? Where our military schools and colleges? . . . Nine French officers out of ten can command an army, whilst our fellows, though as brave as lions, are totally and utterly ignorant of their profession. Damn it, sir, they know nothing. We are saved by our non-commissioned officers, who are the best in the world.' Picton was a rough-tongued, hot-tempered Welshman, who was not much concerned with nice discrimination when expressing his convictions. There were always honourable exceptions: officers who attended foreign academies, read military history, and learnt foreign languages. Nevertheless, exceptions prove the rule. Gronow, though angry at the time, when he came to record the conversation forty years later admitted that Picton was right.[6]

At bottom the problem with the army was that its officer corps was a social rather than a professional organization. It was a charge that retained its force for most of the century. In a reforming age the army proved remarkably resistant to reform. Compared with the best Continental armies, the British military system remained both old-fashioned and inefficient. The practice of purchasing commissions, together with the inability of junior officers to live on their pay, ensured that the infantry and cavalry continued to be the preserve of the wealthier classes and the traditional refuge for the 'fool of the family'. Those with little family or financial backing had to look to the less fashionable artillery and engineer corps for a career. The system, in short, discouraged professionalism. Even the post-Crimea reforms, though they improved some aspects of the army, did not change its fundamental nature. Virtually for the whole of the nineteenth century, despite advances in organization, training, and equipment, the army remained a service which would have been familiar to Picton—long-service privates enlisted for escape, drink, or adventure, led by gallant upper-class amateurs, and held together by professional non-commissioned and warrant officers.

IV

With or without his prejudices, Surtees remains a paradox: the conventional landowner who was an unconventional novelist; the man who shared the likes and dislikes of his class and yet flouted the literary orthodoxies of his age. An illustration of this is the contrast between his hunting novels and C. J. Apperley's *Life of a Sportsman*.

This is a biographical novel and its subject matter is much the same as that which fills the pages of Surtees' sporting stories. Yet in style and character it is utterly different. Where Surtees is racy and vigorous, Apperley is tame and vapid. As a novel it is flat and lifeless; not surprisingly it is rarely read today, or even mentioned. It describes a world which Apperley had not so much lost as only briefly tasted. He was too anxious to be considered a gentleman and a fine writer to be either. Men like Osbaldeston, Assheton Smith, George Bentinck, Surtees himself, took their social position for granted; and though some of them accepted that they had a duty imposed on them by God and man, they did not talk about it. It is hard to imagine any of them writing a book in which, to quote Apperley's preface, 'the bright side of human nature is displayed, and the cultivation of cheerfulness and good humour earnestly recommended'; still less one in which 'there may be something to amuse if not to instruct the female mind'. Somehow Apperley creates the impression of being the gentleman's gentleman of the sporting world, a polished imitation but not quite the genuine article.

Surtees disliked Nimrod and it is not difficult to see why. He thought him pretentious (the nickname of Pomponius Ego he gave him in *Handley Cross* was meant to wound); he had no patience with the extravagant, hell-for-leather style of the Meltonian exquisites; and he grudged Nimrod's literary fame. This is illuminating, but it does not quite resolve the paradox of Surtees himself. Nor do we get much enlightenment from the records of his physical appearance. His portraits and a surviving photograph have the same enigmatic quality as his career. The photograph shows a typical hardbitten squire. The spare athletic frame, the thin face with prominent nose and cheekbones, the determined cleft chin, the sinewy hands, seem the outward and visible marks of the sporting country gentleman of the period. The portraits are more suggestive, as not uncommonly happens. In them the painters seem to have caught—or inserted —something which is not present in the unnaturally

rigid pose which the technique of photography at the
time inflicted on those who submitted to its rigours. In
the earlier paintings there is a thoughtful, introspective
look; in the later, done in old age, there is a touch of
melancholy.

Mere physiognomy, however, can be deceptive. There
are better clues to Surtees the man than the few records
of his physical characteristics which have survived. Not
many squires, one may hazard, were introspective;
Surtees clearly was. He ruminated on the world and his
conclusions were not particularly cheerful. 'Man is an
amusing animal.' he wrote unamusedly in one of his
notebooks. 'The vision of a mole would enable him to
discover the vices of his fellows, while that of a vulture
would scarcely detect a folly of his own.' Or take this
single mordant sentence. 'They reconciled us; we embraced; and from that time have been mortal foes.' Another of his jottings observed that when an elder brother
is in possession of all the family wealth, he would be
well advised not to go on a shooting party with his
younger brother. All this sounds savagely cynical; but it
may be doubted whether Surtees was really a cynic. The
man who takes the trouble to write down such caustic
sentences in his commonplace book is more likely to be
a man of sensibility who would like the world to be better
than it is but knows that this is impossible. Surtees' sardonic utterances are a form of emotional relief. He is not
trying to justify himself for taking a habitually low view
of human nature; he is indulging in a kind of mental
purge. It is not, after all, to be supposed that Anthony
Surtees was ever in danger when he went out shooting
with his younger brother. In the event he died prosai-
cally in Malta of smallpox contracted several thousand
miles away from the fields and coverts of Hamsterley.

What is fundamental to Surtees is not cynicism but
pessimism. It was this that led him to disbelieve in the
hopeful morality of his time. He could not bear what
often seemed to him to be merely affectation or hypocrisy. Out of this came a particular dislike of dealers in
cheap moral currency. 'Beware', he wrote in *Plain or*

Ringlets, 'of those who profess to be better than their neighbours.' At a time when philanthropy and humanitarianism were fashionable virtues, even if more preached perhaps than practised, he was stubborn enough to question these received truths of society. In one of Jorrocks' *Hillingdon Hall* 'lectors' he makes the great man observe that 'I knows in these 'umanity, anti-'anging times, punishment is quite out o' fashion, and everything must be done by the noble spirit of emulation'. How far these reflect Surtees' own sentiments is shown later in the same novel when he remarks in his capacity as author that 'Mr Green was an indiscriminate humanity-monger, a man who made as much to do about committing a hardened vagabond as others would with a reclaimable first offender, and always tried how little justice he could do and how great a show of feeling he could make. Many men do the same. It is a cheap way of gaining credit for kind-heartedness.' It was the cheapness, falsity, and sentimentality in much that passed for humanitarianism (then as in any other age where it becomes a modish attitude) that Surtees despised. He preferred an honest rogue to a sanctimonious hypocrite. On the whole he did not expect much of life. He was a melancholy as well as a pessimistic man; but he was determined to see people as they were, not as they claimed to be.

2
TOWN AND COUNTRY

I

In his novels Surtees ignores industrial Britain. He has
no interest in the cotton operatives of Manchester, the
out-workers of Birmingham, the handloom workers of
Spitalfields; none in Chartism, or the distress and rioting
of 1842. The nearest he comes to the problems of the
Industrial Revolution is in *Hillingdon Hall*, where much
of the plot revolves round the intervention of an Anti-
Corn Law candidate in a local parliamentary election.
Yet it would be wrong to conclude that this omission
makes him less representative of his age than, for instance, Charles Dickens or Mrs Gaskell. In his lifetime
England remained a largely rural and agricultural country—provided, that is to say, the criterion is not statistics
of manufacture and commerce but how people lived
and what they saw around them in their daily lives. The
England Surtees portrayed was more familiar to the
majority of his countrymen than the London of *Oliver
Twist* or the Manchester of *North and South*.

One of the commonplaces of demographic history is
that by the date of the 1851 census the urban population
of England and Wales reached equality with the rural
population for the first time in English history. Yet that
statistical event turns out to be less dramatic than it appears. The nature of urban life, that which sets it apart
from the countryside, depends to a large extent on the
size of the town. In early Victorian Britain the 'average
size' of towns was distorted by the exceptionally large
population of London. With its 2.3 million inhabitants in
1851 it was more than six times greater than the second
largest city, Liverpool. In such circumstances the concept

of an 'average town' is more of an abstraction than ever. What, in any case, was a 'town'? For the purpose of dividing the population into 'town' and 'country' the Census Commissioners of 1851 took as their definition of a town all cities, county towns, and places large enough to have regular markets. In England and Wales these totalled no less than 580. Only seven of them (Liverpool, Manchester, Birmingham, Leeds, Bristol, Sheffield, and Bradford) had populations larger than 100,000. If this group, together with London, are deducted from the national total, we are left with only five million 'town' population belonging to the remaining 572 towns. This gives an average of only 9,000. Even this figure is misleading. In reality the majority of towns were smaller than this. When, for example, the Census Commissioners came to consider the 196 boroughs or incorporated towns of England and Wales, they observed that the size of borough most commonly met with was between 2,000 and 7,000. They meant by this that towns within this range formed the largest and therefore most characteristic group, numbering eighty-seven out of a total of 196. If this was true of the boroughs, the majority of the 580 towns which the Commissioners distinguished from 'country' were even smaller. Few of them could be described as 'urban' or even industrial. W. F. Spackman, a contemporary statistician, reckoned that there were only seven counties, together with the West Riding of Yorkshire, in which the majority of the population was dependent on industry or manufacturing. In the forty-four other counties of England and Wales what were called 'towns' were for the most part little townships embedded in the countryside and part of its economy. Of Scotland and Ireland this was even truer.

The conclusion is inescapable that during Surtees' lifetime the majority of the British people lived either in the countryside or in towns of less than 20,000 inhabitants; and that the majority of British towns had populations of less than 10,000. It is therefore not unreasonable to conclude that the novels of Surtees, which are set predominantly in the country and small towns, are perhaps more characteristic of early-Victorian England than those of most of his better-known contemporaries. London, of course, was unique. The 1851 Census Commissioners were moved almost to lyricism when they contemplated its 2,362,236 inhabitants spread over 78,029 acres on either side of the Thames—'comprising the commerce of a great seaport, the manufacture of many towns,—the emporium of the empire—the palace of the sovereign—the seat of government, of the legislature, of the central courts, of the heads of commerce, of the learned professions, of literature, and of science'. It was also, though the Commissioners were too serious-minded to notice it, the centre of fashionable society whose houses and servants dominated the quarter between Park Lane, Oxford Street, Piccadilly, and Regent Street, and whose magnificent equipages, rolling through Hyde Park on every fine Sunday during the season, provided one of the great free spectacles of the metropolis.

Even in Surtees' provincial novels London is always a distant presence, the place from which people come and to which they return, the supplier of all known wants, the purveyor of horses, carriages, choice food, smart clothes, lively young ladies from the stage, and trained servants. Two of his leading characters, Mr Jorrocks and Soapey Sponge, are Londoners, though not Facey Romford. Surtees himself, unusually for a squire, had lived for a dozen years in London, and his sketches of London scenes have the sharpness of personal observation. Take the description of the entry into the capital, in the dusk of a December day, of the coach carrying Mr Pringle senior and his future wife in *Ask Mamma* (ch. iii):

the first distant curve of glow-worm-like lamps in the distance, and presently the great white invitations to 'TRY WARREN'S' or 'DAY AND MARTIN'S BLACKING' began to loom through the darkness of the dead walls of the outskirts of London. They were fast approaching the metropolis. The gaunt elms and leafless poplars presently became fewer, while castellated and sentry-box-looking summerhouses stood dark in the little paled-off gardens. At last the villas, and semi-detached villas, collapsed into one continuous gas-lit shop-dotted street. The shops soon became better and more frequent—more ribbons and flowers, and fewer periwinkle stalls. They now got upon the stones.

A similar journey, but by omnibus in the reverse direction and by daylight, figures in *Mr Sponge* when Soapey makes a journey into the country to look at horses (ch. ii).

The gradual emergence from the brick and mortar of London being marked as well by the telling out of passengers as by the increasing distances between the houses. First, it is all close huddle with both. Austere iron railings guard the subterranean kitchen areas, and austere looks indicate a desire on the part of the passengers to guard their own pockets; gradually little gardens usurp the places of the cramped areas . . . Presently a glimpse of green country or of distant hills may be caught between the wider spaces of the houses, and frequent setting-down increases the space between passengers, gradually conservatories appear and conversation strikes up; then comes the exclusiveness of villas, some detached and others running out at last into real pure green fields, studded with trees and picturesque pot-houses, before one of which latter a sudden wheel round and a jerk announces the journey done.

Even when the motor replaced the horse, journeys out of town by little country buses had some of these features.

This is straight visual reporting. A more original judgement is by Mr Jorrocks (*Handley Cross*, ch. lix) in the course of one of his famous 'lectors'. 'If a man has plenty of blunt, it's all werry well. London is an undeniable place for gettin' rid of it in. Frinds abound for rich men . . . To London let the rich man go. Whatever is gay, or grand, or expensive, will be his.' After running through a long list of alleged pleasures—riding in the Park attended by a smart groom, dinners at Greenwich, ballet and opera, billiards and gambling saloons—the sporting moralist concludes that London is the rich man's paradise, the poor man's purgatory; and that those who think it socially obligatory to make an annual pilgrimage to the metropolis are usually glad to come home again from that 'crowded, 'eartless, busy, bustlin', jadin' city'.

Huge and overgrown as this modern Babylon seemed

to contemporaries, it was still not difficult to reach the open country. The Post Office Directory map for 1846 shows large empty spaces round West Ham, Hackney Wick, and Kentish Town. Belsize Park was still a real park, standing in rural isolation between the Hampstead and Finchley Roads. South of the park was open ground all the way to Primrose Hill. In the 1840s all this area was regarded by Londoners as countryside. 'We who live in smoky, foggy, pent-up London,' Surtees wrote in the *Analysis*, 'to whom Primrose Hill or the tree-clad heights of Hampstead are a luxury.' There were already long ribbons of houses each side of Edgware Road, one of the great highways into London from the north-west; but the Great Western Railway ran to its terminus at Paddington along a tongue of open land; and even though its iron line bisected Westbourne Park, that too still appeared on the map as a spacious enclosure of grass and trees with a large private house in its own grounds. Kensington and Bayswater were sufficiently detached from the main mass of the metropolis to appear almost as separate villages, though further south Chelsea had pushed its houses along the north bank of the Thames to Battersea Bridge. Over the river and west of the Oval there was much unoccupied space; the area enclosed by the great loop of the Thames between Bermondsey and Deptford was still largely open, though traversed now by the two lines of the railway to Greenwich and Croydon.

Croydon itself remained the principal market town for east Surrey though near enough to town to attract Cockney sportsmen like Jorrocks. It was there, according to Surtees, that during the 1820s and 1830s at the Saturday meets of the Surrey Hounds 'groups of grinning cits may be seen pouring in from the London side, some on the top of Cloud's coaches, some in taxed carts, but the greater number mounted on good serviceable-looking nags, of the invaluable species, calculated for sport or business'. There had been another pack which met at Croydon, the Surrey Stag Hounds to which Surtees devoted a chapter in *Jaunts and Jollities*. By the time he came to publish the book in 1838, however, it had ceased to exist, no doubt for the same reasons that brought about the termination of Grantley Berkeley's staghounds in the Vale of Harrow. Stags, being carted, were a convenient way of ensuring sport on the outskirts of the metropolis from which foxes had departed, but the nature of the district brought its own peculiar problems. Berkeley's pack, which flourished between 1823 and 1829, included among its regular followers many middle-class tradespeople among whom Jorrocks would have felt at home—Gunter the famous pastry-cook, Mr Norton the coal merchant, Mr Canley the auctioneer—as well as Guards officers off duty. Being so close to London it attracted a horde of miscellaneous sportsmen completely unknown to the master. The great cavalcade of riders, amounting sometimes to some two hundred, made fearful havoc with hedges and fences. Compensation for damage was a heavy item in Berkeley's accounts and there were frequent scuffles with angry farmers, labourers, and private residents. Another problem was the tendency of Thames barges and town louts with bulldogs and lurchers to join in the chase. The terrain itself offered a variety of hazards, being covered with market-gardens, greenhouses, and private residences. Unlike 'Old Tunbridge', the veteran of the Surrey Stag Hounds who knew his part to perfection, Berkeley's stags, which came from the Berkeley Castle herd and were changed each season, had a certain wildness and wilfulness unusual in carted animals. On one occasion the stag took a line through Hounslow, Twickenham, and Teddington, finally taking refuge in the Thames. Among the riders that day was the famous wit, Alvanley. Returning later to White's Club he was asked what sport he had had. 'Oh,' he replied, 'the melon and asparagus-beds were devilish heavy—up to our hocks in glass all day; and all Berkeley wanted was a landing-net to get his deer out of the water.'[1]

The famous episode of Pigg in the melon-frame in *Handley Cross* clearly had its counterpart in real life; but sport of this eccentric nature, though it would have delighted Surtees' sense of the ridiculous, could not continue indefinitely. Yet while London's remorseless outward expansion was driving field sports further and further away, the sights and sounds (and smells) of the capital remained surprisingly rural. Universal dependence on the horse for transport, the demand for such delicacies as fresh eggs and milk, ensured the survival of pockets of rural economy even in the heart of the City. Take, for instance, the description in *Plain or Ringlets* (ch. lviii) of the mews in Rochester Square where Mr Bunting went in search for that rarity in London, an equine bargain. 'It was a long narrow alley running the whole length of the Square, interspersed with dunghills, dairies, coal-sheds, and cabbage-shops, with here and there a marine-store-dealer.' Rochester Square (if we assume that Surtees was referring to the actual place of that name) was in St Pancras, but even the fine houses of Mayfair had their mews and no doubt their dungheaps running behind their fashionable fronts. Further east the roads leading to Smithfield saw the daily passage of hundreds of sheep and pigs to add to the noise and filth of London. In the year after Victoria's accession nearly $1\frac{1}{2}$ million sheep trotted through the streets on their way to Smithfield. Corn was sold at Mark Lane; vegetables and fruit at Covent Garden; hay and straw at five great markets in Whitechapel, Smithfield, Southwark, Haymarket, and Paddington.

What chiefly brought the odours of the farmyard into central London, however, were the thousands of horses used in the capital. Each weekday the main thoroughfares of London were choked with a slow procession of vehicles—wagons, carts, chaises, coaches, cabs, omnibuses, and drays—passing in two almost continuous streams. The lines of traffic were so solid that it was often a matter of difficulty for a pedestrian to cross from one crowded pavement to the other. There were also the hazards of what lay underfoot. Everyone agreed that London was the dirtiest of all English cities. The central streets were covered with a thick layer of filth, the principal ingredients of which were horse manure, stone-dust from the constant grinding of iron tyres on the paving stones, and soot descending from the forest of London chimneys. The resultant compound resembled a black paste which clung glutinously to everything it touched and emitted a characteristic odour reminiscent of a cattle-market. Though contractors were employed to clean the streets, the work was hard and ill-paid; it could only be done at night; and the filth carried away had little commercial value. London produced in fact such a vast amount of excrement, both animal and human, that the surrounding agricultural districts were unable to absorb it. As a result the streets seemed to remain permanently foul. To get across busy streets, especially in wet weather, was a hazardous business except at the regular paths—'isthmuses of comparative dry land', as one observer called them—kept clean by the unremitting work of the crossing-sweepers. This was a recognized profession in London, even though it depended for its remuneration on the charity of grateful foot-passengers. So far from being the last resort of the weak and destitute, like Dickens' Jo in *Bleak House*, the crossings in the more important streets of central London were the jealously guarded monopoly of professional sweepers and were bought and sold on a commercial basis. In the quieter areas and in the outer suburbs, where the pitches were less lucrative, they were occupied by a more marginal and shifting race of sweepers. In Chelsea, for instance, Carlyle noted that the severity of economic depressions could be gauged by the increase both in the number of crossing-sweepers—men, women, and children—and in the importunity of their requests for money.[2]

Away from the main roads there were other smells to assail the nostrils of the Londoner; those emanating from stables, cow-byres, cess-pits, night-soil heaps, earth-closets, defective sewers, and in warm weather from the fetid exhalations rising from the Thames, that *cloaca maxima* of the metropolis. No doubt the native Londoner was inured to his odiferous environment, or at any rate resigned to its necessity. As a caustic article in *Chambers's Edinburgh Journal* in July 1841 heartlessly observed, 'when it so happens that 1,800,000 persons choose to huddle themselves into a space about five miles in mean diameter . . . such a place naturally inclines to be (pardon salutarily plain language) one vast dung-hill'. The final ingredient was supplied by the reek of humanity itself: the mass of ordinary Londoners, to whom soap and hot water were luxuries and baths unknown. The Victorian synonym for the masses—'the great unwashed'—had a literal significance for contemporaries.

London was not only smelly and dirty; it was also noisy. In the central streets during the day there was the interminable rumble of wheels and shouting of drivers. Minor accidents gave rise to sudden crescendos of sound. There is a lively description of one such in *Mr Sponge* (ch. ii) as Soapey waits for a bus at Piccadilly Circus. His chosen vehicle had got itself wedged among some Bayswater buses and three more drivers had cut across their path.

What a row! How the ruffians whip, and stamp, and storm, and all but pick each other's horses' teeth with their poles, how the cads gesticulate, and the passengers imprecate! how the bonnets are out of the windows, and the row increases. Six coachmen cutting and storming, six cads sawing the air, sixteen ladies in flowers screaming, six-and-twenty sturdy passengers swearing they will 'fine them all'.

There is little sign here of the legendary patience and phlegm of the British public.

Even away from the traffic there was little refuge from noise. In the side-streets, perhaps because only there could they be heard, were the itinerant vendors calling their wares—milkmaids, muffin-men, sellers of catsmeat, ballad-mongers dolefully chanting their songs, pedlars and cheapjacks proclaiming the virtues of their stock-in-trade—while rising above the clamour were the occasional notes of a barrel-organ. Even the passing of daylight did not bring peace. When Mr Bunting leaves Rochester Square, dusk is falling, the oil and gas lamps are beginning to be lit, and 'the me-a-u of the milkmaid, and call of the crumpet-man began to awaken the areas'. Dawn brought another sound. In *Jaunts and Jollities* Mr Jorrocks rises for his trip to Margate as the dawn is being greeted by all the cocks of Coram Street and its neighbourhood 'in every gradation of noise from the free street-scouring chanticleer before the door, to the faint response of the cooped and prisoned victims of the neighbouring poulterer's'. Those who are familiar with the life of Thomas Carlyle will remember how he suffered in the 1850s from the noisiness of Chelsea, particularly 'the crowings, shriekings, and half-maddening noises of a stock of fowls which my poor neighbour has set up for his profit and amusement'. In the end the only way he found to escape from the combined assault of street-cries and farmyard cackles was by building a soundproof room under the roof of his house in Cheyne Row, while Mrs Carlyle's diplomacy and a judicious £5 note disposed of the fowls.

Carlyle was a naturally irritable man; but other writers complained of being tortured in the same way. According to the journalist Cyrus Redding, alluding to the 1840s, outside the cloistered quadrangles of the Inns of Court there was little peace to be had in London except at the very top of the house. 'Even there, barrel organs, yelling brats, costermongers with cries not less musical than the howls of the savage, grinding carriage wheels, screaming fruit sellers, and vagabonds with blackened faces, semi-musical, playing childish antics, outdo, in the modern Babylon, all that the ancient could have produced to torment the student.'[3] Surtees himself is among the ranks of the complaining literary men. In the *Analysis* (ch. iv) he has a good-humoured reference to 'that confounded organ-grinder, who has just struck up under our window, for the third time this morning . . . Thank God, he's gone at last, though he has sorely put us out.'

Organ-grinders were generally of Italian origin, but the Cockneys themselves contributed to the general din of street-life. Sharp-witted, precociously impudent, and verbally dextrous, the shop-boys, casual urchins, costermongers, and newsboys, together with other idle inhabitants, were quick with ribald comment on any untoward happening or unusual figure passing by. What they lacked in material possessions they made up by their

independence, vitality, and crushing lack of respect for
their social superiors. Listen to the volley of remarks from
the newspaper vendors waiting outside the office of the
Morning Chronicle when Jorrocks rides past in hunting
costume bound for Croydon and the meet of the Surrey
hounds.

A hunter! a hunter! crikey, a hunter! My eye, there's a
gamecock for you! Vot a beauty! Vere do you turn out today?
Vere's the stag? Don't tumble off, old boy! 'Ave you got ever
a rope in your pocket? Take 'Bell's Life in London' vot contains all the sporting news of the country! Vot a vip the
gemman's got! Vot a precious basternadering he could give
us!—my eye, vot a swell! vot a shocking bad hat!—vot shocking bad breeches!

There was little opportunity on the London streets to be
condescending to the poor.

Indeed, whether working-class or middle-class, the
outstanding trait of the true Cockney, according to
Douglas Jerrold, playwright, journalist, and wit, was a
conviction of his immense superiority in worldly wisdom to the benighted inhabitants of the English countryside or peculiar foreigners from abroad. It was when
Cockneys were away from their natural environment,
Jerrold argued, that this good conceit of themselves was
most fully revealed: as witness his archetypal Cockney in
Paris who commemorated his visit to the gardens of the
Tuileries by writing on the right leg of a statue of Diana
the immortal message *'John Wiggins, Muffin-maker, Wild
Street, Drury Lane, was here on 20 July 1839'.*[4]

Given the never-ending growth of London's population, the noise, and the dirt, it is not surprising that, as
Victoria's reign wore on, the habit of slipping away for
the weekend increased among those who had the time
and money. Saturday, Surtees observed in *Ask Mamma*
(ch. xlix), which in the country was a good day for trans-
acting business, in London was 'the lazy day of the week',
when people with umbrellas and carpet-bags departed
on pleasure jaunts, either by steamer down river to
Margate or by the new means of transportation, the train,

into the country. Annual holidays were also becoming a regular feature of ordinary life. There was already, of course, the traditional migration of polite society away from the capital once the season (closely linked to the parliamentary session) was over. Now increasingly when August came round Londoners of all kinds fell into the habit of flying 'in every direction' as Carlyle put it as early as 1834, 'to sea coasts and mineral wells' to relieve the trials of their urban existence.

Despite being a countryman at heart, Surtees clearly relished the independence and sharp tongue of the Cockney. He would hardly otherwise have made a Londoner his greatest and most lovingly drawn character or devoted three books to him. Equally, though he decried the specious attractions of the metropolis and adored country pursuits, Jorrocks was always a townsman. In the novels, however, we see little of him in his native habitat. Half the humour arises from the fact that he is a townsman abroad, transported from Coram Street and the City to display his comic qualities in the world of small towns and countryside which Surtees knew so well.

II

The inland and seaside holiday resorts to which Londoners were fleeing in increasing numbers during the summer months formed a class of their own between the metropolis on the one hand and the more nondescript country towns on the other. While to the Londoner the resorts provided life in a cleaner atmosphere and more leisurely style, to the provincial they gave a taste of a more sophisticated and fashionable existence than could be offered by his own quiet and monotonous surroundings. With growing popularity the old social barriers at such places were breaking down. Brighton, for example, in the Regency period had been beyond the aspirations of most people, being both exclusive and expensive. Nevertheless, the fashions of Brighton and Bath helped

to shape the newer resorts. The conditions for a successful spa were listed by the industrious Dr Granville in
1841. They included baths, a master of ceremonies, a
band, a public promenade, good quality hotels, and
picturesque walks. Most towns aiming at the status of a
spa tried to follow this formula. When Mrs Brookfield
visited Tunbridge Wells in 1842 she found that the élite
of the visitors were expected to promenade at set times
in the morning and afternoon in the Pantiles where a
band played twice a day. At Broadstairs in the 1820s, still
a little village though one which 'affected select gentility', the social centre was the Assembly Room which was
open for cards and conversaziones each evening and two
or three times a week for dancing.[5]

In the early decades of the century the amenities of the
smaller spas sometimes left a little to be desired. When
old General Dyott dutifully experimented with baths and
mineral potations at Buxton in 1827 he found his hotel
charges reasonable enough at 10s. a week for board and
lodging, but there were few other attractions beyond a
coffee-room where he had access to all the London
newspapers for the price of a 6s. season ticket. At the
Buxton races in June he found mainly a socially inferior
'pedestrian population' and at the ball in the evening his
son noticed only nine ladies. For men who were not in
pursuit of either a medicinal cure or a wife, the availabil-
ity of some outdoor sport was a decided attraction in the
sometimes limited repertoire of amusements offered by
the smaller resorts. When the inhabitants of Handley
Cross decided to take over the pack of hounds left
leaderless by the death of Michael Hardey, it was with
the conscious object of adding to their existing assets of
a mineral spring, a pump room, an MC, a lover's walk,
and a waterfall. Though this was an ingenious device for
bringing Mr Jorrocks on the scene, it was a piece of civic
enterprise which at the time would have seemed perfectly natural. According to Granville, hunting had
contributed as much as water-drinking to the rise of
Leamington as a spa, there being no less than five hunts
within twenty-five miles of the town. At Cheltenham

the local races and the Cheltenham staghounds were prominent among the attractions of that famous watering-place, even though the staghounds had to be maintained out of the pockets of the townspeople and the visitors.

The rise of ordinary seaside resorts claiming no special medicinal virtues besides fresh air and salt water was a sign of increasing wealth and leisure among classes a little lower in social scale than Mrs Brookfield or General Dyott. Under this widening demand, even the towns which had enjoyed the favour of royalty in the preceding generation soon lost their exclusiveness. Victoria and Albert abandoned Brighton and the Royal Pavilion because they wanted more privacy. Their new rural retreat was Osborne on the Isle of Wight, obtained for the royal couple in 1845. Brighton, which up to 1837 had served almost as a second royal seat, soon became irredeemably middle-class, the favourite resort of London clerks and shopkeepers. This social decline was mourned by the elderly and snobbish, but Surtees, who knew Brighton well in its Regency days, would have been unimpressed by laments for vanished exclusiveness. He preferred the Brighton of the 1850s to the fashionable and expensive place of his youth.

His fictitious Roseberry Rocks in *Plain or Ringlets*, as is half suggested in the opening chapter, was probably a blend of many seaside resorts known to him. 'Other places may boast their specialties; Scarborough her pay bridge and newly built Dovecote, Hastings her castle, St Leonard's her silence, Weymouth her sands, Dover her castle, Margate her merriment, and Broadstairs her lugubrious solemnity, but the individual attractions of each particular place will be found concentrated at the Rocks.' Distance from London preserved a certain distinction of character. Nearer the capital life was more plebeian. Margate was a prime resort for Cockneys even before the railway age because of cheap access by steamer down the Thames. From the account of Jorrocks' trip in *Jaunts and Jollities* we learn that husbands detained in London often took season tickets so that they could go down each weekend to visit their families. But it was not the only place to profit from the taste for seaside holidays among London's teeming population. At the time of the Reform Act, Herne Bay was emerging as a keen rival. A large hotel and pier had been built by a private company; three squares, several wide streets, and a church were under construction. With its good bathing and quiet neighbourhood it enjoyed the additional advantage of being closer to London for day trips, being fourteen miles nearer the capital than Margate. The new pier allowed steam packets to disembark goods and passengers at all states of the tide and a mile-long promenade along the shore catered for both riders and pedestrians. The new pier was inaugurated on 4 June 1832 with the arrival of the steam-packet *Venus* bedecked with flags and flowers, with a military band on board, having fired gun salutes off every town it passed on its passage down the river. That was the day when the famous reform bill received its third reading, but even in 1832 the English people had their minds on many other things besides politics.

III

The mushroom growth of spas and seaside resorts helped to loosen still further the old framework of provincial society. The role of the county town, not only as the seat of administration and focus of trade but as a social centre, had long been declining as roads improved and coach-makers devised more comfortable vehicles. The time had been when local gentry and their families had taken refuge in their county town during the winter, away from the wet and mud of the countryside, the cold and draughts of their isolated houses. Living sometimes in modest hotels, sometimes in their own town houses, they created a kind of provincial town season in imitation of the great season in the metropolis. But this custom, thought the Revd T. Mozley, writing of Derby in the latter years of the Napoleonic Wars, was already extinct even then. Such gentry families who still lived in the town were there by accident, not as part of a migratory social pattern. The county towns were now dominated by tradespeople, manufacturers, clergy, lawyers, and doctors, who made their own society, patronized concerts, formed literary and philosophical societies, started subscription libraries, promoted schools, hospitals, and asylums, took shares in local gas companies and waterworks, without feeling the need for assistance, financial or otherwise, from outside.

A typical non-industrial county town like Reading, for example, with a population in 1841 of 18,000, possessed at the start of Victoria's reign two new Anglican churches in addition to its historic three pre-Reformation parish churches, a Roman Catholic church, eight dissenting chapels, a county hospital and medical dispensary, a literary institution, a philosophical institution, a horticultural society, three philanthropic institutions, a temperance society, a masonic hall, a life and pension insurance society for the poorer classes, a savings bank, and no less than seven private charitable associations ranging from the 'Infants Friend Society' and the 'Maternal Society' to the 'Society for supplying at cost price fuel and clothes to the Poor during the winter'. Though they might draw much of their wealth from the surrounding countryside, such towns had a social and intellectual life of their own, they did not take their tone from the county gentry and aristocracy.[6]

Perhaps for that reason towns of that size and character do not figure much in Surtees' novels. The nearest approach to them is perhaps Fleecyborough in *Tom Hall*, and it is not described in very flattering terms, 'with its railway station, its spiral churches, its tall-chimnied opposition gasometers, its barn-like opposition tanneries, and towering town hall', not to mention its 'half-acre allotments and little sentry-box summer-housed gardens of the outskirts', its bad pavements, and of course its military barracks which housed Colonel Blunt's Heavysteed Dragoons.

In Surtees' jaundiced view, such county towns lacked

the elegance and style of the metropolis without retaining the honesty and earthiness of the country.
'Fleecyborough . . . though more of an agricultural than
a manufacturing town, was large enough to have many
of the attributes of a manufacturing one: fairs, assizes,
races and so on; also a theatre and assembly rooms,
where town and country met in scornful defiance.' What
Surtees disliked most about such places was their pretentiousness. Young Tom himself, son and heir of the
town's wealthiest banker, was sufficiently exempt from
financial cares to set up as 'gent'—but 'the worst feature
of Fleecyborough for a gent was that there was no gents
to keep him company' during the day, at least not until
the lawyers' clerks and shop-assistants were free to
blossom out likewise as gents when they had come home
from work in the evening and changed into more or-
namental attire. Even then they were liable to be cut out
by Colonel Blunt's officers, 'the military being to a country
town pretty much what the nobility are to London town'.
Given Surtees' opinion of the army, this was hardly
complimentary to the young local 'gents'.

  He was more sympathetic to the small rural towns left
on one side by the march of progress—in other words,
the railways. Take his description of the towns of the
Heavyside Hunt country, Minshull Vernon and Dirlingford, in *Mr Romford* (ch. viii).

There were no factories, no tall chimnies, no coal pits, no
potteries, no nothing. The grass grew in the streets of what
were called the principal towns, where the rattle of a chaise
would draw all heads to the windows. The people seemed
happy and contented, more inclined to enjoy what they had
than disposed to risk its possession in the pursuit of more.

Minshull Vernon was on a single-line branch railway, its
small station too unimportant for any advertiser except
a Temperance Hotel and a soda-water manufacturer.
There were no cabs, buses, or vehicles of any kind to
meet the traveller, only a small boy to carry luggage. In
Mr Sponge (ch. xxviii) there is the little agricultural town
of Barleyboll.

It differed nothing from the ordinary run of small towns. It had a pond at one end, an inn in the middle, a church at one side, a fashionable milliner from London, a merchant tailor from the same place, and a hardware shop or two, where they also sold treacle, Dartford gunpowder, pocket-handkerchiefs, sheep nets, patent medicines, cheese, blacking, marbles, mole-traps, men's hats, and other miscellaneous articles.

One wonders how the milliner and the tailor made a living in such a place.

Pitched half-way in the scale of values between Fleecyborough and Minshull Vernon is Mayfield, one of the type of small country towns that, according to Surtees, seemed so flat and insipid to anyone returning from a visit to London, or, in the case of Miss McDermott, from Roseberry Rocks.

So it was with the star-fish-shaped town of Mayfield stretching its finger-like streets out upon the rich green meadows around. One such is a type of the whole. A square stone-towered church on one side of a market-place, a brick town-hall upon arches in the middle, with a perpetually 'going' but never gone mugger [vagrant] behind, large stone or flaming red brick houses with green doors and bright brass knockers alternating with inns and smaller houses around, and the aforesaid finger-like streets stretching out in all directions, generally tapering towards turnpike gates in the distance. And yet these outlandish places generally contain an amazing amount of comfortable self complacency the residents think-ing there are no such people as themselves, that they give the tone to the rest of the world.

Travel invites comparisons, and though these are pro-verbially odious, it is not in human nature to refrain from making them. After the delicious visits to Madame Bergamotte's beautiful bonnet-shop at Roseberry Rocks, it vexed Miss McDermott, as it would most women, to have to return to her local *modiste* Mrs Muslins with her millinery display-counter competing with the books and muffins on the other side of the shop.

Shops, for men perhaps as well as women, were an infallible indication of a town's status. The poorer the town, the more heterogeneous its establishments, each by an apparently iron law of economics seeking to supplement its principal trade by encroaching on that of its neighbours until all character was gradually lost. At Minshull Vernon all the shops did double duty 'with no apparent pre-eminence among them. Jugs and basins commingled with ladies' hoops, flour and fruit stood side by side, marbles and mustard were in the same bowl. Besom-makers and beer shops seemed to predominate.' A similar confusion of wares was found in the shops at Sellborough in *Hillingdon Hall* (ch. xix), formerly a parliamentary borough but cruelly deprived of both its MPs by the Reform Act of 1832. It had lost in consequence much of its trade and social importance; and since we may assume from its appearance in Schedule A of that famous Act that it was a small as well as a corrupt borough, it had no social or economic reserves on which to fall back once its parliamentary status was withdrawn.

It was a drowsy-looking place—a wide, scrambling sort of town, forming something like a square, with little off-shoot streets, starting off in all directions. There were two churches and two parsonage-houses, enclosed with high walls, among trees, and the usual sort of store-shops—grocers selling ribbons and British wines, booksellers dealing in candles and confectionery, and milliners in soap and crockery ware. Trade there was none, save on a market day, and that was purely agricultural produce, varied, perhaps, by an itinerant hawker and pedlar pitching his cart and selling his edgeless knives and pointless needles.

It was not only a dearth of specialist shops from which the young ladies suffered. There was an even more desperate dearth of eligible young men and of the social entertainments where they might be found. A race meeting and a New Year's Eve ball were all that there was to look forward to from one year's end to the next. 'This is generally the case in towns without trade; the young men leave them as soon as they are fledged in search of more bustling places, from whence', Surtees added heartlessly, 'they are seldom suffered to return—*single.*' As might be expected in such unpromising circumstances, the deprived young ladies of Sellborough were 'terribly moped'.

On village life Surtees is almost completely silent. This may seem odd in a writer whose roots were in the countryside. It may even seem an opportunity missed, in view of the fact that two of his contemporaries, Mrs Gaskell and Miss Mitford, had demonstrated in *Cranford* and *Our Village* respectively how successfully scenes of village life could be turned into entertaining literature. Yet the charm of those two classics has perhaps made posterity take too indulgent if not a positively romantic view of the English rural scene in the early nineteenth century. Cranford is usually said to be partly founded on Mrs Gaskell's childhood recollections of Knutsford; but that Cheshire township can hardly be considered a typical village of the period. Even in 1821, when the author was only 11, it had a population of some 3,000, which made it larger than many towns. Three Mile Cross near Reading, the home of Miss Mitford, was a more genuine village, as is reflected in the narrower scope of her book.

Even so, villages outside the industrial districts were often more socially cramped and economically depressed than might be inferred from fictional sources. In many the labourers and their families provided the majority of the inhabitants, with a shopkeeper, a beerhouse-keeper, and one or two skilled artisans to leaven the lump. In southern and eastern England the agricultural slump which followed Waterloo had brought pauperism and unemployment. Long before the rise of the Chartists, the agricultural proletariat had demonstrated their social discontent in the worst outbreaks of rural violence that England had known for nearly two centuries—the riots in East Anglia in 1816 and in the southern counties in 1830. The judicial aftermath of these two episodes—five executions in 1816, three in 1831, and hundreds of men transported to Australia—was hardly the stuff from which either sentimental or satiric novels of rural life could be constructed.

Even in the north of England, where labour was more in demand, wages higher, and diet marginally better, life for the rural poor was often hard and isolated. The only people in better social circumstances with whom they habitually came in contact were the farmers and the parish clergyman. Farmers were not conspicuous for their sympathy with labourers. Also, they did not as a rule write their memoirs. Clergy often did, and their accounts are rarely reminiscent of Miss Mitford's sketches, however charitable and conscientious they were in their pastoral work. Indeed, the harder they tried to do their Christian duty, the more likely they were to testify to the difficult social problems which they daily encountered. Take the testimony of the Revd Thomas Mozley, sometime Fellow of Oriel College, Oxford, brother-in-law of Henry Newman, parish priest, author, and journalist. In 1832, at the age of 26, he left the comforts of college life to take up the rural living of Moreton Pinckney in Northamptonshire. He found himself, as he later recorded, 'as much thrown on my own resources, and obliged to do myself whatever had to be done, as if I had been cast on an island of the Pacific, among rude and generally inoffensive savages'. The more aggressive and independent of the inhabitants did much as they pleased, in defiance of the local gentry and farmers. The parish poor-law administration, by a haphazard process of concession and neglect, had been reduced to a mere mechanism for pacifying the village population. In general, 'there existed no adequate means for the maintenance of order, health, or decency in the place'.

When in 1836 Mozley was promoted to the rectorship of Cholderton on Salisbury Plain, his social and intellectual solitude was almost as great. It was, he remarked ruefully, 'a place where Sydney Smith would have perished of isolation in a week'. He had no friends or neighbours of his own class within five miles; he saw nobody except his own parishioners; he spent his time talking with them, visiting their houses, listening to their troubles, and relieving, as far as he could from his own resources, their wants.[7]

This cannot be dismissed as the biased reminiscences of a frustrated academic. Mozley, a Tractarian and member of the Oxford Movement, was a singularly conscientious parish priest; and there are many other clerical witnesses to the rough and primitive habits found in rural districts at the beginning of the Victorian period. When Charles Kingsley went to his wild, neglected, poaching parish of Eversley in Hampshire, only thirty miles from London, he found (in his wife's words) that 'he had to redeem it from barbarism'. The Revd J. C. Atkinson, who spent forty years in a semi-pagan parish on the Cleveland Moors in Yorkshire in the middle of the century, and the Revd A. Barnard, a Congregational minister in East Anglia in the 1840s, offer similar evidence on the rudimentary state of morals and manners, little affected by either civilization or Christianity, to be found among the labouring population of the countryside. There should be no surprise in this. It is a commonplace that the agricultural labourers, particularly in the south of England and East Anglia, were the worst paid of all the larger occupational groups at this time. The human consequences of overcrowding and under-employment were inevitable. It would be mere sentimentality to assume that because the rural classes were ill-used by society they were in some way ennobled by their sufferings. In real life degrading conditions tend to degrade. In fiction, however, the instinct to make the victims of society attractive human beings often evades the uncomfortable truth. Even Thomas Hardy, for all his tragic view of life, uses the rustic characters in his Wessex novels as a kind of comic chorus to the main action of the story. Only occasionally, as with the gang of Trantridge women in *Tess of the D'Urbervilles*, or in short stories like 'The Fiddler of the Reels', do we touch on the harsher realities of country life. For a more realistic account of the Dorset peasant in the middle of the nineteenth century one has to turn to the correspondence of that outspoken aristocratic reformer the Revd Sidney Godolphin Osborne, who wrote in 1846 that the Dorset labourers 'are socially so degraded, that they have been for years, and are for the most part still, content to go through life on terms implying a want of all sense of the value of customs and feelings without the existence of which man becomes a mere reproducer of his race, working to live, but content to buy life at its very cheapest price'. On another occasion he wrote even more succinctly that in such circumstances 'human life is simply pig-life, glazed and stair-cased'.⁸

Not being a reformer, and not given to either moralism or romanticism, Surtees simply ignored the rural poor. Perhaps his kindest comment comes in *Plain or Ringlets* (ch. lxii) when he compares rural with mining villages. He wrote of his fictional Burton St Leger that

there cannot perhaps be a greater contrast to the now thatched, now blue-roofed, now stone-slated miscellany of houses and cottages constituting a real straggling country village than the long monotonous repetitions of dwellings containing a window, a numbered door, and a peep-hole, peculiar to a mining one. The former always look healthy and nice, while the latter too often present a combination of mud, tawdry squalor, and unbecoming finery.

But this is an architectural rather than a human description. The country labourers themselves rarely enter into his novels; and when they do make a momentary appearance, to hold a horse or answer (or more often, to be unable to answer) a request for direction, they are treated with a certain contempt. 'A yokel can't declare his ignorance', he observes testily in *Hawbuck Grange* (ch. xi), 'without exposing his stupidity.' For the rest, the one episode which hints at those aspects of rural life usually left decently veiled in conventional literature is Farmer Heavytail's Harvest Home ball in chapter xxv of *Hillingdon Hall*, where the labourers had 'all dressed up, men as women, women as men, and so on'. As he describes it, it is not so much a gathering of transvestites as a kind of pagan saturnalia. Outside in the darkness couples make love; inside most of the company are dressed up in animal masks—rams, goats, asses, cocks, and ducks. Among the frolics of this rude company Jorrocks had a bunch of nettles stuffed up his kilt and the young marquis of Bray, who had misguidedly agreed to go attired as a young lady, is pinched and pulled about by the males unaware of his sex, and has to make a hurried escape to avoid the 'tender advances of a liquorish young husbandman'.

This is a far cry from *Our Village*; but there is no doubt that, for example, Harriet Martineau would have sided with Surtees rather than Miss Mitford in this vignette of rural pastimes. 'Sensual vice abounds in rural districts,' she wrote in 1846 from her observation post in the Lake District. 'Here it is flagrant beyond anything I ever could have looked for . . . While every justice of the peace is filled with disgust and every clergyman with (almost) despair . . . here is dear, good, old, Wordsworth for ever talking of rural innocence.' A further reason why Surtees said so little about village life is perhaps that there was so little of it in his neighbourhood. When in 1832 Cobbett ventured up into what might be called the Surtees country—Northumberland and Durham—what struck his southern eye was the predominance of cattle-husbandry over arable farming, the absence of villages, churches, and roadside cottages, the sparseness of the population, and the fact that for the most part agricultural labourers lived in the farmhouse or buildings attached to it. Though his statistics were not entirely accurate, a modern calculation of regional variations in the size of parish populations in 1811 confirms his general picture. One group of counties in the south of England—Dorset, Hampshire, and Wiltshire—had three times the number of parishes that existed in Cumberland, Northumberland, Durham, and Westmorland though comprising only three quarters of their combined acreage.[9]

With Surtees' north-country background, it was natural that he should make less of village life than a novelist brought up in the south of England. In the years when he was a hunting correspondent he must have seen a good deal of southern and midland territory; but he never acquired the kind of intimate knowledge that comes from living as one of a village community. In his rural landscapes villages are few and the poor largely absent.

3
SQUIRES AND PEERS

I

One of the interesting minor debates in Victorian public life was over the definition of a gentleman: a debate which, if it did not reach a definite conclusion, at least revealed the confused standards of a rapidly changing society. Historically the term indicated a describable, if not definable, social status. It was the closest post-medieval England came to a caste. In their memoirs men could write without selfconsciousness that 'I was born a gentleman'; on their tombstones 'Gent.' would appear after their name as a sufficient description of their rank. In this time-honoured sense, 'gentlemen' and the collective word 'gentry' were an extension of the hereditary aristocracy: men of good blood but not necessarily with a title. The gentry class was not a close caste; it was always losing impoverished members and gaining afflu-ent recruits. The duke of Wellington was fond of a saying attributed to Charles II that he could make a hundred noblemen but not a single gentleman. 'Foreigners', he told Raikes, 'hardly know our definition of the term. They are always enquiring "si tel ou tel est un gentilhomme"; they do not understand what is meant by a real English gentleman.'[1]

For de Tocqueville in 1837 this was one of the illu-minating differences between English and French society. '"Gentlemen" in England is applied to every well-educated man whatever his birth, while in France gentilhomme applies only to a noble by birth.' In appar-ently making education his sole criterion de Tocqueville was going further than most Englishmen would have been ready to go at that date; but it would be difficult to dispute his other remark that while one could see clearly where the aristocracy in England began, it was impossible to say where it ended.[2] That it was impossible, however, did not deter people from trying. Hence the Victorian debate on what constituted a gentleman. To be one was in some sense to be a member, however remote, of the aristocracy; and the aristocracy was a class which, though attacked by a few, was envied by many and respected by most middle-class Victorians.

The external trappings of gentility were acquirable by the purchase of an estate and, for the fortunate, the conferment of a title—a knighthood, or, better still, a baronetcy since it would be passed to one's descendants. Estates and titles were passports to the gentry class. What of those who called themselves gentlemen without being obviously gentry? A characteristic of the gentry was that they were financially independent; their possession of property dispensed with the need for a career or a profession. An extension of this principle of economic independence was the popular notion of a gentleman as one who did not have to work for his living. Consider this exchange before a parliamentary committee in 1857.

Mr Edward Proom, sworn.
What are you?—A gentleman.
No occupation?—No.
Have you ever been in any business?—Yes, an omnibus proprietor.
Were you an elector of the borough of Lambeth?—I was.
You are a gentleman of some property, and own a considerable number of houses there?—I do.
How many tenants have you?—Forty five.[3]

The QC conducting the interrogation does not seem to have been indulging in any irony. Yet the concept of 'gentleman' that included a former omnibus proprietor was clearly more influenced by considerations of his financial independence than anything else. When to this is added the growing lower-class genteelism of referring to any unknown person as 'the gentleman' instead of 'the man', mid-Victorian vagueness could hardly reach further.

Instant recognition of who was or was not a gentleman proved difficult, according to Surtees, even for such
experienced practitioners in social differences as waiters
and hotel-keepers. When the top-booted, green-coated
Tom Scott in *Hawbuck Grange* turns up unannounced in
the dusk of a winter's day at the Goldtrap Arms, the
landlord, though as a former butler he considers himself
a judge of a gentleman, is puzzled to know whether he
is dealing with a fox-hunter or his groom. Only when he
learns that Tom actually owns the mare he is riding does
he touch his hat and give his guest a bow. Yet to a society in which public opinion was becoming more serious and moral, the word 'gentleman' suggested to many
something more than mere wealth or even title. The
original meaning of 'gentle', implying noble birth, was
forgotten; in its place came the modern sense of 'cour-
teous', 'kind', 'considerate'. This ethical concept had the
advantage of being a qualification in which only personal
merit counted and to which therefore all could aspire.
Yet the historic social attributes could not be brushed
aside so easily. Between being a gentleman by birth, one
by property, and one by nature were gaps not easily
bridged. Victorians had to make do with muddled compromises between all three notions. If it was difficult to
accept that a man could achieve the status by material
prosperity, it was even harder to accept that a rogue
could be a gentleman because of his family.

In the literary intelligentsia were some who pronounced
decisively in favour of moral qualities as the essence of
gentlemanliness. As early as 1833 in *Lady Vere de Vere*
the youthful Tennyson had delivered his much-quoted
assertion that kind hearts were worth more than coronets
and simple faith than Norman blood. By the time Mrs
Craik published *John Halifax, Gentleman* in 1857 the
calculated defiance of the title did not bring the same
shock as, for instance, Thomas Hardy's subtitle of 'A Pure
Woman' to his novel *Tess of the D'Urbervilles* thirty-four
years later. In proclaiming that honesty and integrity were
more important than riches or family, she was merely
enunciating a familiar liberal view. In 1860 Charles
Kingsley was writing to his son that his grandfather

(Kingsley's father, the Rector of Chelsea) 'was a *gentleman*, and never did in his life, or even thought, a mean or false thing', and urging him to bear in mind that honesty and modesty, the two marks of a gentleman, were the only principles on which to bring up his own family. It is only a short step from this to Dr Arnold's idea of a 'Christian gentleman' as the ideal aim of education. Indeed, Kingsley had earlier given his opinion that 'all gentlemen owe that name to church influence over themselves or their parents'.[4]

How far this idealized definition of what constituted a gentleman was establishing a foothold can be illustrated by that great organ of middle-class opinion *The Times*. In 1851 Sir Charles Napier, full of years and glory, retired from his post of Commander-in-Chief in India. Before laying down his office he published a General Order condemning luxury and extravagance among army officers and asserting bluntly that to drink un-paid-for champagne and ride un-paid-for horses was to be a cheat and not a gentleman. *The Times*, in the course of a long, approving article, denounced in turn the 'slip-shod code of ethics' prevalent in military circles and drew an unkind distinction between being an officer and being a gentleman.[5]

This was what may be styled the liberal progressive view. It was not universally held, least of all by those who normally passed as gentlemen. They could have pointed out that there was a difference between legal debts and debts of honour. Racing and gambling debts fell into the second category since they were unrecoverable in a court of law, usually were unwritten, and depended on mutual trust. Gentlemen did not lie to each other. Credit from tradesmen, on the other hand, was a matter of business calculation; no honour was involved. It was a limited conception of 'honour' but so powerful as almost in itself to constitute the test of a gentleman. There is an anecdote of the imperious Lord George Bentinck who, observing a man who owed him a racing debt doing himself rather well in Crockford's dining-room, took his bill from the waiter as he passed, glanced at it, and then called out, 'Before Sir St Vincent

Cotton ordered so expensive a dinner, he ought to have
paid his debts.' On the other hand, Bentinck himself
deliberately delayed payment on a lost wager with George
Osbaldeston because he believed that he had been the
victim of a racing ruse. He paid up when challenged, but
used such offensive language that a duel resulted.

The view that gentlemen of the traditional type entertained of their 'honour' was not the same as middle-class
moralists thought it should be. Certainly it had little to
do with business integrity. Jorrocks with his unfailing
realism put the matter clearly in *Handley Cross* (ch. xvi).

Folk talk about the different grades o' society but arter all's
said and done there are but two sorts of folks i' the world,
Peerage folks, and Post Hoffice Directory folks. Peerage folks
wot think it's all right and proper to do their tailors, and Post
Hoffice Directory folks wot think it's the greatest sin under the
sun not to pay twenty shillens i' the pund.

Napier and *The Times* notwithstanding, there is little
evidence that there was any sudden decline in the traditional aristocratic habit of allowing debts to tailors and
wine merchants to drag on indefinitely while regarding
debts on cards and horses as matters requiring immediate settlement.

It was left to the sceptical Thackeray to point out that
while there might be no connection in principle between
wealth and good behaviour, yet, as an observable social
fact, good family, good education, good upbringing, and
easy habits of life did in the course of a few generations
tend to produce what were generally accepted as
'gentlemen'. Outside the ranks of novelists, leader-writers,
clergymen, and headmasters, there probably remained
a not altogether foolish notion that to be a gentleman
implied a certain social status even if other qualities had
to be added to make the definition complete. Surtees
himself admitted the confusion and to some extent shared
it. So few agreed on the definition of a gentleman, he
wrote in *Ask Mamma* (ch. i), that the only infallible rule
he knew was that the man who was always talking about
being a gentleman never was.

On what did constitute a gentleman he was as am-
biguous as most of his contemporaries. In *Handley Cross*
(ch. xxiv) Charley Stobbs is described as the son 'of a
rich Yorkshire yeoman—of a man who, clinging to the
style of his ancestors, called himself gentleman instead
of esquire—Gentlemen they had been styled for many
generations, and son had succeeded sire without wishing for a change.' In *Hawbuck Grange* Tom Scott is called
a gentleman farmer (though we hear little about his
farming occupations) and in his behaviour is certainly
more gentlemanly than Soapey Sponge or Facey Romford. Yet in the preface Scott is made to disclaim the title
of esquire and prefers the plainness of Mr Thomas Scott,
Farmer. At various points in the *Analysis of the Hunting
Field* Surtees talks more about the subject. He refers to
'the idle acceptation of the term, meaning a man with
nothing to do'. When he comes to consider the business
of buying and selling horses, he expresses a doubt
whether anybody who pursued that trade for any length
of time could retain the title of gentleman. His reasons
are curious. Horse-selling, he argues, if it was to avoid
ruinous sacrifice, involved concealing, or at least slurring
over, an animal's defects. To practise that degree of
deception regularly was impossible without the assistance of a groom; but what gentleman would wish to
place himself to that extent in the power of a servant?
'Lying is never allowed among gentlemen—above all,
lying for self interest.' In plainer language horse-dealing
required a gentleman to behave in a not very gentlemanly
manner and, worse still, risk having his behaviour betrayed to others. As a trade, therefore, it was better
avoided. It was not a highly moral argument but a very
persuasive one.

At the start of the same book, however, he expresses
more conventional views. In chapter iii he has a passage
on the duties of a Master of Foxhounds which, if one
may use such an adjective about Surtees, is slightly naïve.

The fact is, a man won't do for a Master of Hounds unless he
is a gentleman. Wealth, birth, keenness, all combined, won't

do unless he has that indescribable quality which may be
defined as a sincere desire to please, with a nervous dread of
saying or doing anything that may hurt the feelings of another.

This definition might have appealed to Kingsley or Dr
Arnold, but one may wonder how many MFHs at that
time were noted for this quality in the hunting-field.
To keep in order a mob of riders who might include
fashionable Meltonian thrusters, wild, hard-riding
Irishmen, nervous beginners, and downright incompetents, demanded not so much a sincere desire to please
as a penetrating voice and a command of suitably deterrent language. Not only were sportsmen accustomed to
it but examples of the choicer pieces of invective were
treasured by those fortunate enough to overhear them.
'You think because I'm a lord, and can't swear or use
coarse language, that you may do what you like', shouted
Lord Scamperdale to Soapey Sponge when he threatened
to override the hounds. But not many frequenters of
the hunting-field would have entertained that delusion.
The colourful vocabulary of Lord Scamperdale and Mr
Jorrocks in the novels was matched, in abusiveness at
any rate if not in wit, by many contemporary MFHs such
as the Earl Fitzhardinge, Lord Southampton, Lord Ducie,
Grantley Berkeley, and Assheton Smith. Of Assheton
Smith, generally recognized as the greatest fox-hunter
of the day, it was said by his friend Charles Newdegate,
the MP for Warwickshire in the 1840s, that he 'was in
the field sometimes very rough-tempered and cared
not whom he offended. He thus made many personal
enemies.' Yet nobody would have regarded him as other
than a gentleman. One must charitably conclude that
this passage in the *Analysis* was a momentary and un-
characteristic lapse into journalistic sentimentality. An
MFH afflicted by a nervous dread of hurting people's
feelings would not have lasted very long, then or at any
other time.

What does emerge from the novels is Surtees' dislike
of pretensions to the status of a gentleman by those who

were not. There are plenty of these hybrid characters in
his books. He describes Soapey Sponge, for example,
as 'a good pushing, free-and-easy sort of man, wishing
to be a gentleman without knowing how'. The opening
words of *Tom Hall*—'Our Tom shall be a gent'—sets the
tone for all that follows. The satire, of course, is part of
his general attack on all social climbers. In *Handley Cross*
Marmaduke Muleygrubs is a jumped-up staymaker from
London who, having inherited a fortune from a 'great
drysalting uncle in Bermondsey', bought Cockolorum
Hall, turned it into an architectural semblance of a castle,
and furnished it in baronial style complete with portraits
of fictitious ancestors. In *Mr Sponge* the Puffingtons—he
a wealthy starchmaker from Stepney, she the daughter
of a Worcester china manufacturer—resolved (like the
Halls) to make their only son a gentleman. For that laudable purpose they sent him to Eton and Christ Church,
where he met titled young bucks to whom he would
refer simply by their surnames in 'the easy style that
marks the perfect gentleman'; and in case we miss the
sarcasm there is an asterisk against the word and a note,
'Query "snob?"'—Printer's Devil'. In *Mr Romford* 'Squire
Watkins' is a former painter and glazier who went out to
Australia, made a fortune in the gold-fields, came back,
bought an old country house, placed armorial crests on
his front gates, and engaged a staff of servants on the
novel principle of taking only those who had once been
in the employment of a peer of the realm.

The list could be extended. Mr Large of Pippin Priory
later in the same book is a rich manufacturer of teapot
handles, carrying on the trade in both London and
Birmingham, whose ambition is to mix in high society
and marry his son off to a nobleman's daughter. In *Tom
Hall* Sir Thomas Thimbleton, son of an army tailor, was
a 'Dublin Castle knight' who called his villa and twenty
acres of land Thimbleton Park and was apt when making
speeches on formal occasions to refer to the rank and
station which privileged him to do so. Surtees is never
tired of mocking these uneasy aspirants to gentility whose
money is so undeniably from trade and whose manners

so conspicuously middle-class. What saves him from the accusation of mere class-prejudice are two considerations. In the first place he is attacking not humble social origins in themselves but the pretentiousness that sought to hide those origins. Second, the affectionate creator of Jorrocks, who never attempted to disguise what he was, can hardly be convicted of snobbery.

For Surtees probably, as for most of his countrymen, the term 'gentleman' was a blend of meanings. It embraced both status and manners in indefinite, and perhaps indefinable, proportions. He too had a Victorian sense that being a gentleman involved a certain code of behaviour which went beyond the conventional requirements of gentlemanly 'honour'. His ideal is that of a man of independence, preferably of good family, perhaps a landowner, but with education and integrity, from whom a measure of consideration for others could be expected. There is a thumbnail sketch of such a paragon in *Hillingdon Hall* (ch. xxix) where he describes the chairman of the St Boswell Agricultural Society show to which Jorrocks took his prize bull. He is a local squire of large estate, through whose disinterested efforts the society was founded, who 'combined the polished manners of the modern school with the sterling characteristics of the old-fashioned English gentleman. He was at home everywhere, from the palace of the sovereign to the cottage of the labourer. Liberal, high-minded, and gentlemanly, he was looked up to and respected by all.'

II

What coloured Surtees' attitude was clearly pride in his own order: the country gentlemen of England. Though the *Analysis of the Hunting Field* suffers from a certain blandness, there is no mistaking the sincerity of the passage at the beginning of chapter xvi in which he eulogizes the resident country gentry. It was the absence of such a class in other countries, he writes, which had made him realize their importance in his own. In no other state did a class of men, who ranked as no more than commoners, possess so much power. It was because of them that the ancient title of Esquire, despite its appropriation by lesser ranks in society (he quotes the latter-day dictum of a judge that everybody who was not a gentleman was entitled to be called esquire), still retained an honourable place in English society, particularly in the familiar abbreviation of 'Squire'. This was the true 'esquire', he argues, the landowner, the country resident, the JP, above all, the sportsman. 'This is the sort of being that the title "Esquire" suggests to the minds of Englishmen, and this is the sort of "Squire" that the country people look up to as the highest authority within the scope of their imaginations.' A well-educated, right-thinking gentleman was an ornament to local society and a pillar of local administration.

Historically there was a great deal in his contention. The English squirearchy had not only contributed to the social stability of the eighteenth century but through their political moderation and practical experience had made the parliament of England, alone among the great states of Europe, an effective and sensible restraint on royal executive government. This in the fullness of time enabled the country in the nineteenth century to cross the difficult gap, between personal monarchical rule and a more democratic representative system, without the political upheavals which marked the evolution of the great Continental states. In the early Victorian period many, perhaps most, educated and prosperous Englishmen, even though they did not belong to the landed gentry themselves, regarded their presence as a national benefit and their mode of life supremely enviable. At its best it seemed to combine power and responsibility, public duty and private independence, prestige and pleasure, in admirable proportions, rivalling if not surpassing that of the titled aristocracy itself.

It was not only outsiders who felt this. Milnes senior, for example, the father of the more famous Richard Monckton Milnes, refused a peerage from Palmerston

and left it on record that 'with no disrespect to the House
of Lords, I consider there is no position higher than that
of an English country gentleman'. As far as Surtees was
concerned, this pride in his own order was accompanied
by a markedly critical attitude towards the higher ranks
of the aristocracy. In his novels their representatives
invariably come in for satirical treatment. Lord Lionel
Lazytongs in *Hawbuck Grange* is vain, self-important,
selfish, a monopolizer of domestic conversation in a circle
of obsequious guests. The duke of Donkeyton in *Hillingdon Hall* is a pompous fool. Lord Scamperdale in *Mr
Sponge* is coarse and mean, living for the most part as
though he were a groom or small farmer. He breakfasts
on cowheel, batter-pudding, and gin; and after a hard
day's run sits down to his regular Monday dinner of
bubble and squeak. Kept on a miserable allowance by
his long-lived father, the seventh earl, he had contracted
such stingy habits that had it not been for his love of
hunting he would have been a regular miser. The duke
of Tergiversation in *Plain or Ringlets* is extravagant with
pounds but mean with pence, disputing over a halfpenny
at a toll-gate but spending hundreds on flowers for an
evening party. It is a rare concession when Surtees speaks
in *Hillingdon Hall* (ch. xxxiv) of 'that easy affability and
kindness of manner almost invariably the attribute of the
high-born'. Even that compliment is paid to the duchess
of Donkeyton rather than to her spouse.

It is not an engaging gallery of noble portraits, and his
generalizations on the peerage are no kinder. 'Dukes are
people who generally have their own way, let them be
ever so unreasonable', he observes in *Hawbuck Grange*
(ch. xiii). Rank and power, he suggests, breed ignorance
and selfishness. Peers who count for little in London,
where they are overshadowed by the Court and the many
other members of their order, in their own districts rule
as despots. Many of them lead 'luxurious, inert lives'.
Though naturally clannish, exclusive, and tenacious of
their pedigree, they are nevertheless always seduced by
wealth. 'They can get over any little deficiency of birth if
there is a sufficiency of cash.' Their own conceit and the

snobbish adulation of others create isolation and delusion. Real truth, he says, seldom penetrates castle walls. The elderly duke of Donkeyton, for example—thickheaded and self-sufficient—'wrapped himself in the mantle of his order, and procured as much ignorance of the world by exclusiveness as his son possessed from inexperience'. When he chose on occasions to unbend and do the affable, he offended as many by his blunders as he pleased by his laboured condescension. Yet, for all that, 'his Grace believed himself extremely popular, and a perfect pattern of what an English nobleman ought to be'.

As a satire on the foibles of individuals this is amusing enough; as an indictment of a whole class it is so severe as to prompt the reflection that perhaps the peerage should be added to army officers and wealthy Jews among Surtees' inveterate prejudices. If so, some explanation seems called for. Historians have tended to emphasize the solidarity of county society; and there is much to support that view. The picture is a familiar one and is reflected in Surtees' own novels. With the Lord-Lieutenant at the apex, flanked by a few great titled landowners, the social pyramid slopes down through the squirearchy, the yeomen, and tenant farmers to the landless labourers at the foot, with parsons, lawyers, doctors, merchants, innkeepers, and bankers filling the interstices of the structure with their own form of social cement. The conventions of rural hospitality, in which propinquity was necessarily more important than personal preference, resulted in a network of friendly relations. Everyone had their place in what Surtees called the 'sliding scale of condescension' in which each could bestow gratification by deigning to visit those socially lower and be gratified by invitations to visit those socially higher than himself. Neighbourliness, snobbery, and self-interest were the bonds of country society.

Yet there were some cracks and fissures in the apparent solidity of this county structure. Town versus country was one; industry against agriculture another. A third was religion, especially the deep cleavage between Anglicans and Dissenters. Party politics was a fourth. Even before the Reform Act of 1832 the faction fights of Tory and Whig, Blues and Yellows, were a feature of local politics even if they were no more than a cover for traditional personal and family rivalries. After 1834 the growth of party electoral organization hardened the political divisions. There was also another kind of jealousy with a long history behind it: the resentment of the small landowners against the great. A century earlier Squire Western, in Fielding's *Tom Jones*, when rejecting his sister's aspirations to marry her niece off advantageously, growled that 'most o' zuch great estates be in the hands of lords and I hate the very name of themmun'. That great lords in the reign of George II tended to be Whigs and the generality of country squires Tory was only an additional irritant. In the provincial politics of the eighteenth century and later there was the well-known phenomenon of the 'independent interest' at election time in opposition to the great territorial magnates suspected of treating the representation of the county as their private perquisite. It was a tradition by no means exhausted at the start of Victoria's reign. That acute student of Victorian society W. L. Burn, for example, doubted the remark in F. M. L. Thompson's *English Landed Society in the 19th Century* that 'the squire who could not abide the aristo-crat . . . had in any case never been more than a rarity'. Burn instanced Surtees, Trollope, and (in real life) Lady Knightley's *Journal* in support of his scepticism. Other witnesses could be cited. In the middle of the century the Revd Thomas Mozley noted the existence of a type, if not a class, of 'middle class gentry' who, without either a threat to their social position or an ambition to rise still higher, 'have generally been *frondeurs*, content to grumble at their little difficulties and their want of open-ings'. He made the further comment that this species of lesser landowner was continually strengthened by alliances with urban tradesmen, manufacturers, bankers, and brewers.[6]

It is probably a mistake to regard landowners as a homogeneous class. Between the great aristocracy and the lesser gentry there were significant social and

economic differences. The outstanding territorial peers—
the dukes of Sutherland, Northumberland, Devonshire,
and Buccleuch, other peers like Fitzwilliam, Derby, and
Lansdowne, with between 100,000 and 200,000 acres
(some even more) and rent-rolls of upwards of £100,000
per annum—could run their estates on almost feudal lines.
At his biannual audit days in the 1830s the Earl of
Leicester used to entertain over a hundred tenants when
they came to Holkham to pay their rents. At Wentworth
Woodhouse the Earl Fitzwilliam still preserved the
spacious custom of 'open days' when all his neighbours
who wished could come to dine, by simply booking a
seat in advance with the housekeeper, and when the
guests processed into the dining-hall headed by the
resident chaplain in full canonicals. These large estates,
with their agricultural rents often reinforced by invest-
ments, urban leases, harbour dues, mines, and mineral
rights, made their owners almost invulnerable to the rise
and fall of agricultural prices. Only personal folly and
extravagance could cause their fiefdoms to collapse, as
that of the duke of Buckingham did so sensationally
in 1848. Their wealth, their social prestige, their wider
interests, and more frequent participation in national
politics, placed them in a different world to that in which
squires like Surtees lived.

That class was less wealthy and less numerous than is
often assumed. The parliamentary *Return of Owners of
Land 1873*, and various subsequent statistical analyses
based on it, threw fresh light on the number and revenues
of Victorian landowners. G. C. Brodrick in his analysis
divided them into several different classes. The peers
and great landowners (over 1600 in all) owning 3,000
acres or more possessed over 40 per cent of the land in
England and Wales. The 'squire class', on the other hand,
generously defined as landowners with 1,000 to 2,999
acres, possessed only just over 14 per cent. More than 41
per cent was in the hands of what were described as
yeomen, small proprietors and cottagers. As a class the
'squires' numbered about 2,500, only a thousand more
than the peers and other great landowners. With their

small estates, usually concentrated in one county, and their incomes dependent largely or almost exclusively on farm rents, the squirearchy was closely identified with the fortunes of the agricultural industry.

Since there had been no major changes in the social and economic structure of the landed classes in the fifty years preceding these surveys, their conclusions were broadly applicable to Surtees' generation also. All definitions of social class in purely economic terms are imperfect; and no doubt many wealthy commoners with estates of more than 3,000 acres would have regarded themselves as no more than country squires, as also some with less than 1,000 acres. Surtees himself barely met Brodrick's qualification. He is credited with farming some 250 acres himself and managing 700 acres of woodland. In the 1873 *Return* the estate of A. Surtees of Hamsterley, his son and heir, is given as only 687 acres bringing in less than £1,000 per annum. Nevertheless, as a pointer to the position of the squirearchy in relation to the great landowning aristocracy above them and the working farmers and small proprietors below them, Brodrick's estimates are of value. What is particularly striking about them is the modest number and modest wealth of this bottom tier of the landed aristocracy.

Yet it was this class that formed the backbone of county administration. Unlike the great nobility, who tended to be migratory or at least peripatetic in their seasonal habits, the squires prided themselves on being 'the resident gentry', always present, always available, whether as magistrates, Poor Law Guardians, or Grand Jurymen. Studies of local politics in this period make it clear that such men liked to manage affairs in their own way. They valued their independence and integrity, and they were less committed to party allegiances than the great peers. In most English counties they continued to have a preponderant influence over the parliamentary representation until the Second Reform Act of 1867, even though few of them nursed ambitions to become MPs themselves. Loath as they usually were to become embroiled in open opposition to the territorial magnates of their county, there was always room for private resentment and jealousy against great landowners who flaunted their wealth too obviously or exerted their power too insensitively.

III

In constructing his portrait gallery of titled libertines and boobies Surtees was amusing himself and hoping to amuse his readers. Satire depends on selection and emphasis. It would not be difficult to discover in real life very different representatives of the class he lampooned so cheerfully in his novels. The fifth earl Stanhope was President of the Society of Arts, a considerable historian in his own right, and principal creator of the Historical Manuscripts Commission. The third duke of Northumberland certainly supported his ducal dignity with great pomp; but for all that he was an able, disinterested administrator who had earned Peel's praise when Lord-Lieutenant of Ireland in 1829–30. The seventh duke of Buccleuch, who succeeded to the title in 1858, was a first-class Cambridge mathematician who became chancellor of three universities. The evangelical seventh earl of Shaftesbury devoted his public life to campaigns on behalf of women and children in factories and mines, chimneysweeps, education for the poor, and other social reforms. The wealthy Lord Egremont, besides being a famous stock-breeder, racing owner, and patron of the arts, was fond of dispensing charity to the poor of his neighbourhood. In 1834 Greville was present when he entertained 6,000 to a feast of beef and plum-pudding in his park and admitted 10,000 to see a firework display in the evening. The third earl of Radnor was a religious radical reformer, friend of Cobbett, and parliamentary advocate of the rights of the unenfranchised masses.

These examples are selective; but they caution against generalization. The peerage, like any other sizeable body of human beings (there were more than 350 of them on

the eve of Victoria's accession), showed almost every
variety of character and mode of life. The one thing most
of them had in common besides their titles was wealth;
and wealth, as pulpit moralists were once accustomed
to argue, brought its peculiar temptations. Wealth bred
power and power independence. It was easy for them to
do whatever they wanted; and the habits of their class
predisposed them to concede that right to others. They
were therefore more likely to be broad-minded and
tolerant of each other's eccentricities than the middle
classes. Constantly surrounded by servants, they lived
semi-public lives, always under observation: a fact which
led to a certain indifference to gossip and criticism. 'The
aristocracy are charged', wrote Thomas Mozley, 'with
being above public opinion; but the truth is they cannot
help it, they must brave it out.' They had less need for
hypocrisy, or even what Mozley called 'superfluous decency'. In this respect they had something in common
with the status-less poor as compared to the respectable
classes which formed the middle layers of society. The
middle classes had positions to preserve and reputations
to protect; they could not afford to flout society. The very
wealthy, like the very poor, did not have to concern
themselves too much with either status or respectability.
It was a sociological truth enunciated in a characteristically passionate form by the painter Robert Haydon.
'Higher and Lower Classes equally unrestrained in their
appetites—the modes of gratification only different,' he
noted in 1818. 'Middle Class—the heart, core and strength
of the country.'[7] The pious Lord Radnor was touching on
the same theme when he told de Tocqueville in 1833 that
the state of morals of the upper classes was as bad as
that of the lower classes, which he thought was very
bad, especially in the country districts.

One minor temptation of wealth and power which did
not escape Surtees' critical eye was sycophancy. As with
kings and dictators, flatterers and toadies gravitated to
the side of great men, providing them with ingratiating
company, fortifying their self-esteem, and keeping uncomfortable truths at a distance. The novels provide an

assortment of them. Lord Scamperdale was too mean to maintain a whole set of such men, but in Jack Spraggon he had a boon companion of considerably inferior social rank. Mr Jawleyford was no doubt justified in dismissing him as 'just a hanger-on of his lordship's; the creature has nothing—nothing whatever: he lives on my lord— eats his venison, drinks his claret, rides his horses, bullies those his lordship doesn't like to tackle with, and makes himself generally useful'. Jack Spraggon perhaps earned his keep. Lord Lionel Lazytongs, on the other hand, had a shallower circle of admirers to listen to his interminable monologues. They were led by Captain Windeyhash, 'a sort of general hanger-on of the house', one of whose functions was to act as 'trotter out, leading his lordship on to his stories, and helping him out with the lame ones'. Lord Lavender's weakness took a more esoteric, military turn: the recruitment into the Hyacinth Hussars of sprigs of the nobility who periodically came down from London to eat and drink at his expense.

The human toady is an immortal species and Surtees would not have needed to look round the society of his own time very long to find models for his portraits. There was the third marquess of Hertford, of whom Greville wrote that after he had acceded to the title and become the possessor of an enormous property, 'he was puffed up with vulgar pride, very unlike the real scion of a noble race; he loved nothing but dull pomp and ceremony, and could only endure people who paid him court and homage'. Better men than Hertford succumbed to this weakness. When Haydon visited Lord Egremont at Petworth in 1826 he met there two old military cronies, a Colonel Meade and a Count Bruhl (the son of Egremont's step-father), who for 'five years have drunk his wine, eat his game, rode his horses' and were decidedly put out by the appearance of a rival in the shape of a Mr King who had the undeniable advantage of having married Charlotte, one of Egremont's natural daughters.

The most striking feature of Surtees' depiction of the aristocracy, however, is his remarkably uninhibited references to their sexual habits. Lord Ladythorne in *Ask*

Mamma is a collector of fine women (with a preference
for larger ladies) and was accustomed to attend meets in
his carriage with the reigning favourite at his side. 'No
pretty women either in town or country ever wanted a
friend if he was aware of it.' We learn the names of some
of his conquests: Mrs Pringle, Miss Blissland, Miss Peach,
Mrs Spangles (an actress), and Miss Hybrid (Imperial
Jane), whose brother is set up in one of his lordship's
farms and who later is married off to one of his lordship's
tenants. Imperial Jane had been succeeded by Mrs Moffat,
who reigned as 'housekeeper' at Tantivy Castle but to
whom Lord Ladythorne was already looking around for
a successor. In *Plain or Ringlets* Lord Marchhare, son and
heir of the duke of Tergiversation, also pursued his
amours among girls 'belonging more to the aristocracy
of usefulness than the aristocracy of birth'. His current
liaison is with Miss Wrigglesworth, the milliner, 'a lady
of great personal attractions, though somewhat his senior,
an advantage that she knew how to turn to account', who
had supplanted Clara Brown, a baker's daughter.

In *Tom Hall* Lord Heartycheer has a roving and indiscriminate eye for pretty women ranging from Mrs
Ringdove of Cupid Grove to the buxom chambermaid at
the Crown Inn. At Heartycheer Castle there had been as
great a succession of favourites as of sportsmen turning
out with the hounds. Though over 70 he still kept wedded
ladies dangling with assurances of marriage once
Providence had pleased to make them widows, while at
the same time keeping himself informed of all the comely
unattached ladies in the neighbourhood through the
medium of his huntsman Dicky Thorndyke, whose duty
was to pursue more than one kind of game at his master's behest. In chapter xxv we are told explicitly of his
'long career of unbridled libertinism'. This prepares us
for the scheme in chapter xlv where he shows Angelena
and her mother the delights of his art gallery, including
'a voluptuous Etty that generally brought spectators
up short' and a copy of Power's *Greek Slave*, the nude
female statue which, on its revolving pedestal against a
background of red plush, so titillated the Victorian public at the Great Exhibition of 1851. This is followed, not

without a certain strain on the credulity of the reader, by the lascivious peer's plot to administer drugged wine to Angelena's mother and her ingenuous escort Ensign Jug, so that he can lead Angelena off to the hunt unencumbered by third parties.

Though some of Surtees' public may have been offended, they could hardly have been startled, by the raciness of these portrayals of upper-class life. Most men would have heard of similar characters in real life. The Berkeley peerage case, for example, was as well known in the early part of the century as the Tichborne case sixty years later. The fifth earl of Berkeley had four illegitimate children by Mary Cole, an innkeeper's daughter known under the alias of Miss Tudor, whom he eventually married. The couple then made an attempt to legitimize their elder children by forging a page in the parish register. The eldest son William inherited the estate but the House of Lords dismissed his claim to the title brought after his father's death in 1810. This was only part of the Berkeley saga. William Fitzhardinge, who through his electoral influence with the Whigs after 1830 became successively Lord Segrave and Earl Fitzhardinge, lived a life that was far more scandalous than his father's. In the 1830s he was keeping a string of mistresses at Berkeley Castle—first Miss Foote, described by his younger brother Grantley Berkeley as graceful and ladylike, followed by Mrs Bunn, who seems to have possessed the homely but nutritious qualities her name suggests. A third lady was later installed as first favourite—a Mrs Barker, wife of a singer and ex-mistress of Lord Coventry, with Mrs Bunn retained in second place. All this, while deplorable, was commonplace enough; but he then shocked respectable opinion at Cheltenham by establishing both ladies in separate residences in the town. Female society was offended by the way in which Mrs Barker flaunted her finery and talked of the Fitzhardinge hunt as 'our hounds'; the gentlemen by the appearance in the hunting field of the complaisant husband Mr Barker mounted on a Berkeley horse and attended by a groom in the crimson Berkeley livery.

From his connection with Cheltenham Surtees must

have been familiar with the details of the Berkeley scandals; and the parallels with Lord Ladythorne are close enough to suggest that he may have taken Lord Fitzhardinge as a model. There were plenty of other scandals in high places, however, to provide food for gossips and novelists as well as provoking the censure of the respectable. The fourth duke of Marlborough in the 1830s lived in seclusion with his mistress, allowing Blenheim Palace to fall into dilapidation; Lord Hertford's life in his latter years was a European scandal which put him outside the pale even of aristocratic tolerance. With others like the first marquess of Cholmondely, the third marquess of Waterford, the seventh earl of Stair, and the second baron Alvanley, they all served as public examples of sin in high places. Yet public opinion, even radical opinion, does not seem to have allowed the excesses of a few individuals to have coloured its attitude towards the aristocracy as a whole. It is true that the pompous, proud, or wicked lord was a stock character in early-Victorian fiction, from the novels of Dickens and Thackeray to the Gothic romances serialized in penny illustrated newspapers. By the middle of the century it had become a literary cliché. Popular literary conventions, however, are not a safe guide to the actual convictions of the readers. In fiction, as in life, rank and wealth added a certain fascination to vice; and disapproving curiosity about the private life of some of its members was not incompatible with respect for the aristocracy as a whole.

Working on the side of the aristocracy were some powerful instincts in English society. One was the plain fact that the social attributes which distinguished them were regarded as both desirable and attainable by the classes immediately below them. Even in the days of their greatest political unpopularity attacks on wealth and title were remarkably few. Property was respected at all levels of Victorian society, as also was rank. Both were legitimate objects of ambition; both procurable by those virtues of industriousness, perseverance, sobriety, and prudence that were given so high a place in both utilitarian and evangelical scales of value. The *Extraordinary*

Black Book of 1832, the most popular of the several works which set out the cause for radical reform in Church and State, dismissed any notion of criticizing the peers for their wealth.

It is nothing to us, nor is it much to the public, that the marquess of Stafford has £360,000 per annum; the duke of Northumberland £300,000; the duke of Buccleuch £250,000; and that there are other dukes and marquesses with nearly as much . . . It is neither the mansions nor parks of the peerage that excite popular cupidity.

The reasons for this lack of enviousness were clear to contemporaries.

In the first place was the absence of rigid barriers which might have prevented the fulfilment of social ambition. One of the great strengths of the English aristocracy, in de Tocqueville's opinion, was the national belief that anyone could hope to become rich, and anyone who was rich could enter the ranks of the titled and privileged. It was this general persuasion rather than its admittedly circumscribed reality that mattered. What is important in a lottery is not that there are relatively few prizes but that the chances of winning are open to all. A popular work on English society in 1840 laid it down almost as a truism that

In this country, which is happily devoid of every trace of caste, whatever astounding differences may exist among contemporaries, there is no degree of wealth, rank, or dignity that the successful merchant or great trader need deem beyond his own reach, or at any rate, need despair of seeing reflect lustre on himself from its possession by his son.[8]

Complementing this optimistic outlook went the standard view of the middle classes that it was not only a right but a duty for a man to try to better himself in whatever career he had chosen; to improve his position in society rather than be satisfied with his existing state. Nor was it an attitude peculiar to the business world, though the edge of competition was stronger there than elsewhere. The gospel of hard work, ambition, and dedication was almost universal. 'No-one enters life,' wrote the Revd Thomas Mozley in his *Reminiscences*, 'no-one goes to college, no-one is thrown into a neighbourhood or a new employment, without receiving on all sides the advice to rise, because there is no mean between that and falling; to attach himself to the best society, and beware of all that is lower.' Even among the clergy, he believed, the hope of advancing up the social ladder was an important element in the speculation involved in going to a university and taking holy orders.[9]

The less attractive aspects of this urge for upward mobility were an easy target for novelists like Surtees. What escaped much attention was the equally important current setting in the opposite direction. Possibly an even greater influence in integrating the upper and middle classes was insensibly exercised by that neglected class, the younger sons and daughters of the aristocracy. Daughters of peers could, and often did, marry heirs to titles; but they could not all do so, since there were always more daughters than titles to go round. They also had additional competition, both from the occasional actress or opera singer who could bring beauty to the altar and from the more numerous daughters of wealthy commoners who could bring their father's money-bags. Here are a few examples taken at random from Burke's 1853 *Peerage*. The fourth viscount Bolingbroke, who died in 1851, had four daughters of whom two married commoners, a third a cavalry officer, and the fourth was unmarried. The ninth duke of St Albans, who died in 1849, had six daughters to dispose of; one married an earl, one a baronet, and two commoners, the remaining two being unmarried. The second baron Wodehouse, who died in 1846, also had four daughters, one of whom married an MP, another a parson, the third a barrister, and the last a simple esquire. In all the total number of daughters of peers married to commoners runs to over 900.

The equivalent for younger sons was to enter one of the professions deemed suitable for a gentleman, normally the Church, the Bar, the Army, the Navy, and that relative newcomer to the list, the Indian Civil Service. There were sometimes unexpected additions to this select list. Lord Radnor told de Tocqueville that of his three younger brothers one was in the Church, another in the Navy, and the third was a banker in London. Usually, however, it was a repetitive pattern. The earl of Albemarle, for example, who succeeded his elder brother in the title in 1851, had three younger brothers: two in the Church, and the third in the Navy. The first marquess of Normanby also had three brothers: one a colonel in the Scots Guards, another a barrister and recorder of Scarborough, and a third in holy orders as rector of a Suffolk parish. Just as in genealogy the concentration on a single line of descent from father to son ignores the greater part of the total ancestry, so the preoccupation with the transmission of titles conceals the fact that in each generation of the aristocracy the majority were destined to a process of reabsorption by the community at large. It was a gentle process but inexorable and never-ending. Though in the first generation a courtesy title or a share in the patrimony might prolong, and in the next the possession of a titled grandfather might encourage, a certain aristocratic distinctiveness, in the end most of these families would merge imperceptibly with the middle classes proper.

It is not surprising, therefore, that another foreign observer, von Raumer, thought that while English society was in many ways democratic, in other respects it was still penetrated by the aristocracy and founded on it. His opinion is more notable since it was voiced in 1835 when there was still a groundswell of feeling against the House of Lords dating from the reform bill excitements of 1831–2 and prolonged by the hostility of the peers to some of the post-reform legislation of the Whig government. But though the agitation against the upper house lasted from 1831 to 1835, the complaints were not against the profligacy and irresponsibility of members of the aristocracy, but against their excessive power over the parliamentary process and against the preservation of their economic monopoly through primogeniture and entail. With the repeal of the Corn Laws in 1846 the last of the serious grievances disappeared. The electoral

power of the peers had been trimmed by the Reform Act
of 1832 and from 1837 onward the House of Lords showed
remarkable powers of political acclimatization. They ac-
quiesced in Peel's income tax of 1842 which hit their
pockets; they co-operated in the social reforms of the
1840s; they accepted free trade and the repeal of the
Corn Laws with less complaint than the protectionist
squires in the Commons. With public confidence in the
upper house restored, it proved increasingly difficult to
agitate successfully against it. The Cobdenite campaign
in the 1850s and 1860s to abolish primogeniture as a
principle of land inheritance failed to attract any more
support from the liberal middle classes than radical efforts in the 1830s to abolish the House of Lords outright.
Even proposals in the 1840s to introduce into county
administration the same representative structure given
to the boroughs in 1835 fell on stony soil. Among the
working classes of the industrial districts the peers were
probably more popular than those middle-class heroes
Cobden and Bright. When the Ten Hours factory bill
finally passed in 1847, the Lancashire Short Time Committee issued a formal resolution thanking 'the Duke of
Richmond, the bishops of Oxford, London and St David's,
and all the peers who spoke and voted in favour of the
Ten Hours' Bill'. By the time Surtees died in 1864 the
social and political position of the aristocracy was as
assured as it had ever been in his lifetime. Once the
charges of privilege and monopoly had been disarmed
by the concessions of the 1832–48 era of reform, the
peerage resumed its traditional place in English society.
The aristocracy was not exempt from criticism; but it
was levelled against individuals, not the whole order.

It would be an exaggeration to say that individual
members of the aristocracy in the early Victorian period
were judged by more severe standards than lesser men;
but they were more exposed to judgement and those
judgements tended to be more censorious. It was, after
all, an old Christian maxim that from those who had
much, much was required. Peers who blatantly sinned
against the morality of their age were felt, not only by

the public at large, but often by their own class, to be failing in what could legitimately be expected of them. The aristocracy were supposed at least to behave like gentlemen. Even in the sphere of sexual morals, where they were most open to censure, the criticism was not often of what they did but how they did it. There could not have been many men, even in the respectable middle classes, who thought that all aristocrats were models of domestic decorum. What offended public opinion was a failure to exercise that decent degree of concealment which at least indicated respect for other people's sensibilities.

Lord Fitzhardinge's real offence at Cheltenham was to have thrust his amours under the very noses of its inhabitants; and one of Greville's main charges against Lord Hertford was that 'he never seems to have thought it necessary to throw the slightest veil over the habits he pursued'. In October 1842, when he learnt casually about the effect of the Hertford scandal on public opinion in Germany, he was driven to reflect that nobody could be surprised if people on the Continent, from what they saw of Englishmen abroad and what they read in their newspapers, came to the conclusion that the English aristocracy was 'to the last degree profligate and unprincipled', however unfair and unwarranted that opinion was. Any dubious or discreditable behaviour by a member of the aristocracy which came before the public was 'to be deplored for the mischief they do, and the false notions they create'. Posterity has been inclined to call this attitude hypocrisy. Most Victorians thought otherwise. In their view it was undesirable for anybody, but especially someone in a position of social eminence, to be seen publicly to be undermining standards of social morality even if as a private individual he could not live up to them.

No serious challenge, however, can be made to Greville's argument that it would be wrong to lump together the many aristocratic scandals of his day to form a general picture of that class. Had such an indictment been justified, all their wealth and titles would hardly have protected them against growing public hostility. It was because those scandals were the exception rather than the rule that the aristocracy continued to be a respected and integral element in English society. Most of them, whether from inclination, duty, or habit, seem to have made some attempt to meet their social responsibilities. The duke of Rutland, for instance, whom Greville thought 'as selfish a man as any of his class' though neither foolish nor bad, served as Poor Law Guardian of a large local Union and not only attended its meetings when he was in residence at Belvoir during the winter months but visited the homes of those receiving outdoor relief and chatted with them about their problems. Constitutionally the House of Lords, though cautious and prudent, played an active role in legislation. Peers formed a large, and not merely decorative, presence in the higher reaches of government. From the Reform Act of 1832 to Gladstone's ministry of 1868, at least half the seats in every cabinet were filled by peers or sons of peers. Lord-Lieutenants of counties were almost invariably chosen from noblemen with large estates in the area. In civil life the aristocracy were patrons of innumerable local and national societies and institutions, charitable, literary, and scientific. They gave the lead in agricultural reform. The signatories to the public announcement which led to the formation of the Royal Agricultural Society in 1838 were headed by the duke of Richmond and eight other peers. They were patrons of the arts and often possessed more than an amateurish knowledge of the subject. In the hunting field and at the racecourse they were members of a large sporting public which embraced all classes.

For all this they were rewarded by the real, if sometimes quizzical and half-humorous, respect of their countrymen. Snobbery, of course, in the sense of respect for rank and admiration of wealth, played its part, to the irritation of critics from Dickens and Thackeray to Cobden and Bright. 'We are a servile, aristocracy-loving, lord-ridden people, who regard the land with as much reverence as we still do the peerage and baronetage', wrote

Cobden contemptuously in 1849. What he did not ask was the more interesting question why this was so. As it was, his protests only served to underline the impossibility of dislodging the aristocracy from their position of social ascendancy. Carlyle was a more acute social observer when he wrote in 1867 that 'our Aristocracy are not hated or disliked by any class of the People—but on the contrary are looked up to—with a certain vulgarly human admiration, a spontaneous recognition of their good qualities and good fortune, which is by no means wholly envious or wholly servile—by all classes, lower and lowest class included'.[10] Early Victorian society, though liberal and progressive, was not egalitarian; full of class distinctions, it was not riven by class jealousies. Surtees probably believed as much as anyone in the virtues of an ordered, hierarchical society. His satire on the nobility differed from similar manifestations in Victorian fiction in that it came from within, rather than from outside, the aristocracy. It was an expression of internal rivalry: a veiled vendetta carried on by a man who, as a country gentleman of ancient family, considered himself the social equal of any peer of the realm.

4
COUNTY SOCIETY

I

On one feature of aristocratic country life—the great house-parties which figure so prominently in Victorian diaries and correspondence—Surtees has little to say. Possibly he never took part in any. There is Jorrocks' accidental incursion into the company at Onger Castle; but the occasion was the young earl's twenty-first birthday and the party consisted of 'people in the neighbourhood, sprinkled with a few idle Honourables, who lend themselves out to garnish country-houses in the dull season'—and on whom the author is plainly indisposed to linger. Otherwise all we have is a derisive fling at that secondary form of aristocratic hospitality which was exercised in the interests of electoral power. Since, after the recognizable parody of the duke of Donkeyton in *Hillingdon Hall*, Surtees and his family had been struck off the duke of Northumberland's guest list, this was perhaps paying off a personal score. In *Plain or Ringlets* the duke of Tergiversation has a fixed scale of appropriate entertainment, depending on whether the guests are loyal adherents, probable supporters, or possible defectors—dinners for the first category, lunches for the second, and fêtes for the third. 'A person may be brought to the neutral ground of a *fête*', observes Surtees, 'who might shy at the apparent downright committal of a dinner.' This system of graduated hospitality was capable of further refinement, for the duke on another occasion invites Captain Cambo and Mr Cheadle for a day's shooting followed by dinner in the hope of getting them to cast both their votes for his party instead of splitting them.

This was politics rather than neighbourliness. The

county MPs might dispense hospitality in calculated doses, but most county entertainment was carried on without political motives. The object was simply to foster friendly relationships among residents, provide a diversion from the routine of domestic life, and show social status. It was done mainly on the give and take, or what Surtees called the debtor and creditor, principle. Paying off accumulated social obligations was more common than efforts to bring together congenial personalities or strengthen special friendships; the choice in the countryside was too restricted for those more elevated criteria— except, of course, when marriageable daughters came into the calculation. As a result such parties tended to be too ambitious for the means available. Surtees remarks that eighteen was considered 'the most serviceable-sized party in the country'. Even for the capacious mahogany dining-tables of the period this number would often be too large for comfort and necessitate hiring a temporary footman to assist the hard-pressed domestic staff: an expedient which, while adding to the expense, did not necessarily increase the comfort of the occasion.

There were problems for the guests as well as their hosts. One of the great social advantages of London over the provinces was that evening entertainment could be carried on, even in the winter, almost continuously since the streets were lighted at night. In the country it was necessary to wait for the period around the full moon when better illumination might be expected for journeying along country lanes than was provided by flickering carriage-lamps. That meant that dates had to be fixed well in advance to avoid clashing with other events in this congested period. For people in evening finery a vehicle was indispensable even for short distances. This brought added difficulties. Not all family carriages were watertight, especially the dual purpose, all-the-year-round, hooded variety. 'It is not nice to drive eight or ten miles in the dark', wrote Surtees, no doubt from experience, 'with the keen wind whistling through its pet aperture into one's ear, or for a lady to feel the drop, drop, drop of the neatsfoot-oiled water from the head upon her rich pink silk or beautiful moire antique.'

Hired cabs from the local inn, for those too poor to have a vehicle of their own, were rarely better, and the driver, horse, and harness often in worse condition. Then on arrival there was the question of stabling for the horse and accommodation for the driver. 'Providing proper stable accommodation for the visitors' horses', Surtees writes feelingly, 'is another of the difficulties peculiar to country gaiety.' To cope with an influx of a dozen or more horses and vehicles would tax the resources of most country villas of the period. Not many owners would relish having their animals stand out in the open for several hours on a winter's night. Not many hosts would relish the sight of deep ruts on the lawn and horse-manure on the gravel the following morning. Parking problems are not peculiar to the age of the internal combustion engine.

Not surprisingly, the problem for the country hostess was not which people to choose as her guests but how to persuade enough of them to come; with the subordinate problem of preventing those promoted from her reserve list, for what Surtees called 'stopping gaps', from finding out that they had only been invited to make up numbers. In rural society, where gossip was a way of life for servants, if not their employers, and (said Surtees) 'people seem to have nothing whatever to do but to note their neighbours' movements', this was always a risk; and if the secret got out it was a moot point whether the belated invitation created more resentment than gratification. These, however, are permanent vexations of social life; and for the more physical hazards Victorians were hardened by long experience to the discomforts of travelling round the countryside after dark and in wet weather.

II

In addition to sport and the superintendence of their estates, there was one other important occupation for the resident gentry: participation in local administration.

To take any prominent part in this it was necessary to be a magistrate; and that office was in consequence a mark of status for those who possessed it and an object of ambition for those who did not. Appointments to the magistracy, though legally made by the Lord Chancellor, in practice were on the recommendation of the Lord-Lieutenant of the county. When Henry Brougham was Lord Chancellor in the early 1830s, he would have liked to have broken this monopoly; and when Lord John Russell was Home Secretary at the start of Victoria's reign he explored the possibility of recruiting new types of men for the magistracy. Little came of these reforming efforts. Only in manufacturing districts like south Lancashire, where there was in any case a dearth of country gentlemen ready to become guardians of law and order in those notoriously indisciplined areas, did manufacturers come on the bench in any quantity. The Lord-Lieutenants themselves were appointed by the prime minister, usually from great peers (exceptionally from wealthy commoners) who were political supporters and had substantial property in the county in question. The Whig Lord-Lieutenants appointed after 1830, however, were no more inclined than their Tory counterparts to surrender their traditional powers.

In their turn Lord-Lieutenants usually consulted the existing bench of magistrates on new appointments and would rarely recommend a candidate in the teeth of local opposition. The statutory property-qualification for a magistrate (normally the possession of real estate of the yearly value of £100) would have allowed the selection of comparatively obscure individuals; but social pressures in the rural counties virtually confined the bench to the gentry. It seems clear that while the legal qualifications of some magistrates were dubious, mere ownership of the requisite amount of landed property was not in itself an overriding consideration. The essential requirement was gentlemanly status and social acceptability. The Quarter Sessions in some respects resembled a select county club in which the older members jealously scrutinized the credentials of new candidates. Sporadic campaigns to introduce a paid magistracy appointed by government failed to shake this entrenched social system. The combination of aristocratic influence and judicial independence proved an insuperable obstacle for reformers. Even when the industrial disturbances of 1842 brought to light some equivocal conduct on the part of a few borough magistrates, the government, though sorely tried, in the end refrained from any exemplary dismissals. An alternative proposal from the Home Secretary, to appoint professional barristers to stiffen the amateur justices of Quarter Sessions, was equally disliked by the cabinet. It would have been invidious to have distinguished between county and borough magistrates and politically impossible to alter the system as a whole. With some notorious defects, that system had the considerable merit, in a society which proclaimed cheap government as a virtue, of being unpaid and, on the whole, tolerably effective.

Equally important, it was the administrative embodiment of what was still the most influential class in English society. Even more than the House of Commons, J. S. Mill said in 1861, the Quarter Sessions was the most aristocratic institution left in England. The slow development of centralized Victorian bureaucracy made little impact on county administration during Surtees' lifetime. The new Poor Law of 1834 certainly removed much work from petty sessions. Simultaneously, however, magistrates were made ex-officio members of the new boards of Poor Law Guardians and continued to administer poor relief as they thought fit, without too much regard for the regulations and injunctions emanating from the central board in London. The only other great innovation of the period in local government was the police; and this too remained firmly under local control. A Constabulary Act of 1839 authorized (but did not oblige) magistrates in Quarter Sessions to establish police forces, under the direction of a chief constable to be approved by the Home Office, and levy a county rate to defray the costs of administration. Another Act in 1842 provided for the appointment by parish vestries of one or more local constables to be paid from the parish rate, and for superintendents in each division of the county to supervise them, whose salary was to be met from the county rate. The effect of this legislation, though salutary in the long run, was not immediately or universally apparent, while its shortcomings were only too obvious. Not until 1856 did a general act require every county to set up a police force (up to 1852 only twenty-two had done so completely, seven others partially) and give powers of inspection and limited financial control to the Home Office. When Surtees died in 1864, there were still only some 16,000 police outside London to enforce law and order.

Until the institution of county councils in 1888, the counties remained therefore largely under local control. In 1839, in his charge to the Grand Jury at Leicester Summer Assizes, the presiding judge Lord Abinger described the constitution of the country as 'a number of small republics'. In each parish, he pointed out, the inhabitants, through their local vestry, repaired their roads, provided for their poor, maintained their parson, appointed their parish officers, and in general superintended their own local interests without interference from the government. At Quarter Sessions each division of the county met four times a year in grand and petty juries 'presided over by the gentlemen who act as justices of the peace'. In the county at large 'twice in the year are assembled the principal gentlemen of the county, to meet the judges, and to render the most important assistance in the administration of justice'. The language was a trifle old-fashioned (judges are among the most conservative of creatures) but it was familiar and it was unlikely to have been received with anything except complacency by the magistrates who formed his audience.[1]

That was the accepted theory of local government enshrined in the constitutional textbooks as well as in judicial utterances. Surtees, who knew the system from the inside, took a more irreverent view. He has a good deal to say about the magistracy and the administration of justice; and what he says is satirical in the extreme. Much of it, of course, is exaggerated, though whether it is all exaggeration may be doubted. Certainly it is hardly credible that in real life someone like Jorrocks would ever have been appointed a county magistrate, however strong his support for the brand of politics favoured by his Lord-Lieutenant. Even Surtees has to think up some special explanation in *Hillingdon Hall* for this unlikely event. The duke of Donkeyton's son has been smitten with the charms of Eliza Trotter, a protegée of Mrs Jorrocks. Having visited the Jorrocks house in further-ance of his suit, he reports favourably on them to his father, who happens to be the Lord-Lieutenant. As a result the duke and duchess 'made no doubt they were most worthy respectable people, with considerable influence'. Within a few days Jorrocks receives the ducal proposal to put his name on the commission of the peace for the county. This borders on the farcical; but once Surtees decided to get Jorrocks on the bench, as part of the comic plot of the novel, it was as good an explanation as any. Calf-love and parental fondness are not rational emotions.

Another untypical JP, though playing only a minor role, is the wealthy Marmaduke Muleygrubs in *Handley Cross* who, we are told, 'having been a rampant Radical in the City, was rewarded by a JP-ship in the country' on his retirement by, presumably, a Whig government and a Whig Lord-Lieutenant. That at least was a possibility; and Surtees is equally realistic elsewhere. Major Guinea-fowle (the gentleman of commercial antecedents and illiterate speech in *Tom Hall*) ratted to the Whig side in a county election after promising his vote to the Tories. He was, however, only rewarded with a commission in the militia instead of being made, as he had hoped, a JP—'the justices of his petty-sessional division vowing they would all resign if he was'. This is much closer to real life.

Unlikely as the appointment of Jorrocks as magistrate must appear, the fiction at least enabled Surtees to take his readers behind the scenes at both Quarter Sessions and meetings of Poor Law Guardians. The portrait he draws of his fellow magistrates is not flattering.

With the exception of those who take their seats as a matter of course, and who elevate the office, rather than the office elevating them, the envy, jealousy, and detraction that take place on the appearance of a newcomer is truly ridiculous. Each questionable occupant man feels himself personally injured—*lowered*.

The coarse-grained Captain Bluster provoked an uproar when as a solitary Whig he had been forced on a Tory bench at Sellborough. Some magistrates resigned, and the Lord-Lieutenant had been obliged to intimate that, unless they pulled together, he would have to create more magistrates. Jorrocks' appointment renewed the mutters of 'insult to the bench', 'disgrace to the county', and the Lord-Lieutenant's insanity. Only the ineffable Bluster welcomed him to the bench on his first appearance and congratulated him on 'becoming one of them'.

The trial scene which follows, in which the prolixity of the rustic witnesses and the prevarication of the defendants are matched by the collective ignorance and individual prejudices of the magistrates, is Dickensian in its humour. Half a dozen years before *Hillingdon Hall*, the sessions court at Croydon had come in for similar treatment in *Jaunts and Jollities*. The chairman Mr Tomkins, described as a 'perfect prototype of a county magistrate', is a slow, solemn-faced man of great natural stupidity. When Jorrocks' counsel rises to address the court, half the JPs pull out a newspaper and the rest compose themselves for a nap. Afterwards they spend more time discussing private matters than the evidence presented to them; the apparently minor matter of the actual verdicts is decided largely by personal motives. The law, on this showing, is not only an ass but an unpredictable ass.

In *Handley Cross* (ch. lxiv) we are introduced to the mysteries of grand and petty juries. The proceedings at Walsington are seasoned by the cynical *sotto-voce* reflections of the presiding judge Baron Funnyfile, as he praises the experience and conscientiousness of the resident magistracy in a charge to the Grand Jury which reads like an abbreviated parody of Lord Abinger's rotund oratory at Leicester. The course of justice is hardly less turbid than in the lower courts. The grand jury, whose function it is to decide whether there is a prima facie case to be answered, is portrayed as being as casual and arbitrary as the magistrates at Croydon. The special jury to decide the great horse-sale case of *Doleful* v. *Jorrocks* is drawn from men 'who have little to do in court, and less at home, and yet think themselves desperately oppressed by being called on at all'. The common jurors are 'tradesmen, mechanics, farmers and so on, drawn from their homes at a great inconvenience, for four-pence, a verdict, and no thanks'. Baron Botherem, who sits in Jorrocks' court, thinks that special jury cases are peculiarly the affair of rich men and has no compunction in leaving them to the end. The Jorrocks action comes on as the last but one on the last day of the assizes. The previous case did not finish until eight o'clock in the evening, but as both judges are anxious to get away the next day to dine with the Lord-Lieutenant, the court continues even at that late hour. The jury consisted of five sporting gentlemen in top-boots, five in trousers, and two in 'drabs and continuations (described on the panel as merchants)'. The trial is memorable for the appearance of James Pigg in the witness box, a scene comparable to Sam Weller's evidence in *Bardell* v. *Pickwick*. Returning from the suffocating heat of the courtroom to their dank, candle-lit retiring-room, the jury have their deliberations unbearably prolonged by the resistance of one of the merchants who is under an obligation to Captain Doleful. The sporting gentlemen, who had probably all done in their time what Jorrocks was alleged to have done on this occasion, are naturally on his side; but it is not until half-past four in the morning that cold and hunger finally wear down the opposition and sleepy officials are woken to deliver the verdict in an almost deserted court.

Most people, as Surtees observes, in the course of their lives come into contact with the law as either witnesses, jurymen, or parties to a case. All suffer from its delays, many from its expense, and some from its verdicts. It is a universal target for satire. What strikes one about Surtees' description of the operation of the law at county level is not just the dominant role of the gentry but the amateurish quality of the justice they administered. The sporting squires he so much admired themselves contribute to the general air of casualness by their incessant conversation about hunting when they should be bending their minds to judicial matters. Even the meeting of Poor Law Guardians, briefly touched on in *Hawbuck Grange* (ch. xi), suffered from this distraction. Muff and his crony Tinhead use the opportunity of the meeting to twit Tom Scott on his failure to turn out in a brief interval of good weather during the generally bad winter of 1846–7. The routine reading by the clerk to the Board of the petty expenditure on poor relief in the period since their last meeting is drowned by the pointed remarks of Scott's two persecutors about the splendid runs he had missed. Reality might not have been quite so deplorable as Surtees' satire suggests; but, human nature being an imperfect thing, it is equally unlikely that all magistrates invariably maintained the strictest standards in what was after all a voluntary, unpaid, and sometimes tedious duty. Hard-riding, hard drinking men were not likely to suffer from undue sensitivity in such matters; and it would be unrealistic to expect it. Even when it exaggerates, satire usually reflects a certain truth.

Whether Mr Jorrocks' more personal and eccentric use of his magisterial authority is anything more than burlesque is open to question. In *Hillingdon Hall* he orders a boy caught stealing gooseberries and another caught stealing peas to be summarily chastised by his redoubtable maid Betsy. Since the penalty prescribed by law was somewhat more severe and many householders rather than prosecute would have inflicted similar punishment as the best way of disposing of the offence, Jorrocks can at least be defended on grounds of common sense, even if in the process he takes a broad view of his judicial powers. He was running little risk by so doing. By law a magistrate was open to civil action for injuries sustained as a result of his illegal actions, as well as to criminal

proceedings for corrupt or malicious use of his authority. But law and custom also guarded magistrates against
any personal consequences for bona fide errors of
judgement. Their actions in the course of their duty were
treated with 'great lenity and indulgence' in the higher
courts, according to one contemporary legal textbook,
and it would have taken more than the complaints of a
whimpering boy or his indignant parents to hamper the
discretion of a magistrate in dealing with the petty crime
of a parish. Only when Benjamin takes his master's place
and, with the connivance of the parish constable, fines a
drunken mechanic on the tramp 5s. (which the two split
between them) does Surtees stray into the realm of farce.

Jorrocks, however, is not the only magistrate in the
novels to display certain idiosyncrasies. In *Handley Cross*
Mr Muleygrubs JP has an economical habit of putting
beggars and vagrants to work in his grounds under threat
of enforcing the Vagrant Act against them. Though he
goes through the form of offering to pay them for their
work, in practice the men make themselves scarce at
the first opportunity without waiting for their wages.
'That's one of the few pulls we magistrates have', he
remarks complacently to Jorrocks. 'I keep my avenue in
repair and my walks weeded by the vagrants.' Another
of Muleygrubs' ingenious practices as a magistrate is to
employ the constables in his division on similar duties
about his estate. This was, he explains to Jorrocks, 'by
far the best way of disposing of the force . . . for you see,
in a thinly populated district, where each man has a
considerable range, you never know where to lay hands
on a policeman whereas, about here, they know that they
have only to send to his worship's to get one directly'—
a remark which directs Jorrocks' thoughts to the possibility of employing them as earth-stoppers for his hunt.

Surtees seems to have had a low opinion of the new
county police. Since Durham was one of the counties
which adopted the 1839 Act, he had the opportunity of
seeing them in action in his own neighbourhood. His
impression was clearly less than favourable since in 1854,
when he gave to the world his expanded version of

Handley Cross, he produced his classic portrait of those two rogues Superintendents Shark and Chizeler. Shark gets his job on the strength of a recommendation from the chief constable of another county who wants to get rid of him. Once appointed he sets up a private system of extortion and corruption, and looks on his official salary as merely a kind of retaining fee. He runs up fictitious expense accounts, persuades private individuals to undertake unnecessary prosecutions, and gets commissions from an unscrupulous attorney on the business he steers his way. In short, he and his crony in the adjoining district, Chizeler, are sharp, active scoundrels who make the most of a position of authority which lacks any effective supervision from above.

This is a very different picture from that presented by the more conventional police histories. The establishment of a national police force was undoubtedly one of the great Victorian achievements; but posterity is apt to overlook the undeniable flaws in the early county police organization. Part of this was due to the muddled and contradictory nature of the early legislation. The Act of 1839 pointed the way to the ultimate establishment of a professional police in every county on the model of Peel's Metropolitan force. That of 1842, in a concession to critics of the earlier Act, attempted to preserve the traditional system of unpaid parish constables by superimposing a thin layer of full-time paid police—superintendents and county constables—appointed by the magistrates in Quarter Sessions. The magistracy, however, was not an effective body for controlling professional police and the men they appointed were uneven in quality. The constables were mostly ex-soldiers or ordinary labourers. Their hours were long; their work sometimes dangerous; their pay inadequate. The superintendents, designed to provide a stiffening of authority, themselves went largely unsuperintended. It is not unlikely that some indulged in the same forms of malpractices to eke out their salary as those which characterized Superintendents Shark and Chizeler. For all its aspirations towards order and efficiency, Victorian society could not produce overnight

enough men of intelligence and probity to administer all
the reforms introduced by the legislature.[2]

Only after 1856 did a thorough and sustained improvement take place in the county police forces under
the combined impetus of the chief constables, many of
whom were former officers of the Army and Navy, and
the Home Office inspectors of constabulary. Surtees'
novels reflect not only the innate prejudices of the
country squires, but also the real defects of the piecemeal
legislation of the earlier years. Yet even before 1856 the
work of the county police, with all their defects, seems
to have resulted in a reduction in crime. Surtees himself
pays them a grudging compliment. In *Ask Mamma*, which
came out in 1858, there is a rascally publican Geordey
Gallon, who had made a practice of suborning 'the short-
lived superintendents' of his county. In the end, however,
the existence of 'that troublesome obnoxious corps, the
Hit-im-and-Hold-im-shire Rural Police' is a factor in his
calculations when he decides to give up his surreptitious
trade as receiver of stolen goods and turn respectable.

III

Chief constables and chief superintendents were new-
comers to county society. There were other middle-class
professional people with a longer history. In *Ask Mamma*
(ch. xi) Surtees describes the arrival at Tantivy Castle
for the opening meet of the season of what he calls
'the gentlemen of the second class' connected with the
estate—the auditor, the land agent, the architect, the
doctor, the builder, and others. Such men constituted a
class who, while depending on the wealthy for their livelihood, for social purposes acted as a kind of cushion
between the aristocracy and the gentry above, and the
farmers, publicans, and shopkeepers below who had
no claim to be gentlemen even of a third order. Though
these second-class gentlemen embraced a variety of
occupations, their strongest representatives were the

three ancient professions of the law, medicine, and the Church.

In provincial society the lawyers perhaps ranked lowest of the three. The revealing test is eligibility for the magistracy. Clergy were frequently put on the bench; physicians sometimes; attorneys hardly ever. The contrast is made all the more striking by the fact that a retired London barrister, perhaps a QC, would probably find little difficulty in getting himself put on the bench. The conventional excuse was that a solicitor's professional responsibilities might conflict with his judicial duties; but it is not easy to believe that this was the only reason, or even the chief one. The root of the objection to having lawyers as magistrates lay in the nature of their profession. With no law school or law degree (other than honorary ones) at Oxford and Cambridge, the intending lawyer had to qualify through a practical apprenticeship, usually for a period of five years. Not only was he a paid professional, a kind of superior tradesman, but his trade was not considered a particularly gentlemanly one. While sons of the landowning gentry class are to be found qualifying as solicitors, in social terms they were taking a slightly downward step in doing so. When In 1859 Lady Charlotte Guest's legal adviser conceived an attachment to her daughter, she initially discouraged the match, despite her personal liking for the young man, since she doubted, even if Maria was willing, whether 'her brothers and her sisters and her other friends would have been pleased with the union, on account of his profession, that of a solicitor'.

Nevertheless, solicitors, even if matrimonially ineligible, were indispensable to the aristocracy. A wealthy man might go through life without ever needing the services of a barrister; but everyone with property needed a lawyer, not so much to defend his interests in court as to keep him out of them. Drawing up wills, marriage settlements, and conveyances was only part of their work. Even more important was the experienced advice they could give on innumerable delicate matters and the private negotiations they could undertake to smooth away difficulties. The lawyer was the confidential man of business. Sometimes the close relationship established in this way might lead on to the general management of property. Sometimes a trusted lawyer would look after the electoral interests of a client or a political party in his neighbourhood. Given the state of electoral politics which existed for most of Victoria's reign, this often involved interviews with those whom it was better for their client not to meet and transactions which it was better that he should not know. In short, all who had money to safeguard, property to look after, daughters to protect, interests to promote, were in need of a good lawyer. If the strength of the barristers was in London, that of solicitors was without doubt in the provinces.

Surtees has captured several of the species in his novels. Indeed, it would have been difficult to have dealt with country society without introducing them. Two examples, however, may be sufficient. In *Hillingdon Hall* there is the faint-hearted, deferential, trimming Mr Smoothington, solicitor to the duke of Donkeyton. He is the man who buys off Bill Bowker, the electoral candidate opposing the marquis of Bray, for the sum of £1,000 paid out of his own private account. For this he is recompensed by the grateful duke with a cheque for £1,500: a rate of profit which enables one to understand his devotion to the duke's service. In *Plain or Ringlets* comes the contrasting figure of Mr Bullivant, solicitor to Mrs McDermott. Socially clumsy, he is 'a rough man but an honest one' and a good deal shrewder than Mr Smoothington. He puts the not unresourceful Mr Bunting through a searching cross-examination, carefully probes his notional claim to propertied wealth, and quietly steers Rosa McDermott away from his fortune-hunting embrace. There were clearly social differences among solicitors as in most professions. Mr Smoothington probably considers himself a gentleman. Does not the duke condescend to shake hands with him at the start of their interview and (rare mark of affability—or uneasiness) also at the end? Mr Bullivant probably did not consider himself a gentleman; but there is no mistaking who was the more efficient at his work. Mr Smoothington is too fearful of damaging his position with the duke to speak candidly to him. Mr Bullivant bothers less about people's feelings; he relies on his reputation for experience and astuteness to attract and retain his clients.

Superior to lawyers in the social scale were the doctors. They were the more genteel representatives of what was still in the early part of the century an ill-defined and unorganized profession. Apothecaries, who retailed drugs, ranked as mere tradesmen. Surgeons were practitioners in a bloody and brutal craft. Physicians, on the other hand, regarded themselves as members of a learned body. The élite of the profession normally took a first degree at Oxford or Cambridge and were proud of their ability to toss Latin tags about with a deftness which proclaimed a classical education. It was only after graduation that they proceeded to a more systematic acquirement of medical knowledge in some Scottish or Continental university. On return to England they could take a medical degree without examination and qualify for admission to the Royal College of Physicians. As a rule only those who had graduated at one of the two ancient English universities were admitted as full fellows, others became licentiates. The college's fellowship examination was conducted in Latin and it is clear that classical learning and a gentlemanly appearance were points to which examiners attached considerable importance. The Royal College, however, represented only a small minority of the profession, mainly practising in London, a few large cities, and fashionable health resorts. In the year of Victoria's accession the College membership consisted of 127 fellows, a further twenty-eight candidates for a fellowship, and some 300 licentiates: in all, about 460. This figure may be compared with the 1841 census total for England and Wales of 18,400 physicians and surgeons, the great majority of whom would have been provincial doctors.

Fortunately for the British public, there were other ways of entering the medical profession. Early Victorian doctors were a diverse group: graduates of the Edinburgh and Glasgow medical schools, Army and Navy doctors discharged after Waterloo, former assistants and demonstrators in the London hospitals, druggists' apprentices ambitious for higher things, sons of doctors who had been trained in the family practice, those who had purchased a medical degree without examination from St Andrews and Aberdeen Universities. In the last resort anyone could put up a brass plate and begin to practise, since there was no legal requirement that a doctor should have a professional qualification. It was, however, an increasingly competitive trade and training was becoming more professional and expensive. The unorganized but comprehensive medical education carried on by physicians and surgeons in London on a personal rather than an institutional basis was taking a more systematic form even before the foundation of the medical teaching schools in the two colleges of London University in the 1830s.

Nevertheless, the movement towards higher standards and more closely defined qualifications, visible in medicine as in other professions, was beset by internal feuds and general suspicion of legislative interference. The two Royal Colleges of Physicians and Surgeons were jealous of their privileges; general practitioners in the provinces, while anxious to restrict the profession to qualified men, feared dictatorship from London and any system of formal registration and standardized training. A provincial Medical and Surgical Association (the forerunner of the British Medical Association) was set up in 1832; but it was not until 1858, after several failures, that an Act was passed establishing an official register of medical practitioners and a medical council empowered to strike names off the register. Even so, it was still not an offence in law for an unregistered person to practise; only to claim that he was registered when he was not. The legislature preferred to leave it to the public and ordinary market forces to eliminate the inefficient and unqualified.

However qualified, there existed by the 1830s a large body of general practitioners (as they were becoming known), occupying a middle position between the fashionable physicians in the capital, who might end up with a fortune and a baronetcy, and the humbler apothecaries and itinerant purveyors of pills and medicines who travelled round villages, markets, and fairs. Even for ordinary practitioners the rewards varied greatly, with incomes ranging from £200 to £1,000 and above. It was symptomatic of the haphazard nature of the profession that local authorities were able to offer miserable salaries for medical appointments under the new Poor Law of 1834, some as low as £40 per annum, which was less than the wages of a skilled artisan. Poor Law Union doctors were the medical equivalent of curates in the Church of England—ill-paid and socially inferior. Yet there seemed no lack of applications for these posts, either from young men entering the profession or struggling practitioners glad to add to their scanty income.

Surtees' novels reflect the variety of the contemporary medical scene in the provinces. In the opening chapter of *Handley Cross* there is a glimpse of the older generation of country doctor in the person of Stephen Dumpling, the occupant of the only four-windowed house on the village green. He is a follower of the hounds and makes his appearance on such occasions mounted on his dun-coloured pony and clad in professional black with powdered wig and pigtail. At Hillingdon there is Dr Claudius Sacker with his white house and green rails, polished brass plate, and night-bell on the doorpost to proclaim both his profession and his respectability. In *Mr Romford* there is a derisive vignette of a Union doctor, little Tommy Squirt, who thinks that by turning out to hunt in a red coat and astride a brute of a horse he will pass for a great man, though in reality he is only making himself a figure of fun. There is mention of another Union doctor, that despised race, in *Tom Hall*. Old Doctor Bolus joins Major Guineafowle's harriers riding an ill-favoured hack and clad in a mackintosh and waterproof leggings. Surtees describes him as being 'like most country doctors . . . humble and meek, for he had a terrible rival in Mr Digitalis, the union one, who charged

less than himself'. Still, if his horse and his clothes suggest a far from prosperous practice, Dr Bolus' mild con-
ciliatory manner is a distinct recommendation to the
pompous Major Guineafowle, who agrees that he is a
highly respectable man and a very useful one in the
country—'people can get on much better without lawyers than they can without doctors'.

The classic full-length portraits of medicos in Surtees
are, of course, the two rival practitioners at Handley
Cross, Drs Swizzle and Mello. It is a nice piece of social
observation. Roger Swizzle is a bluff red-faced plebeian,
a former apothecary who having worked in a London
hospital set up as a country doctor only to find himself
in the common professional predicament of having too
many rivals and too few patients. He seizes on the opportunity offered by the Handley Cross mineral spring
to improve his position, having (as Surtees unkindly says)
'every requisite for a great experimental (qv. quack)
practitioner—assurance, a wife and large family, and
scarcely anything to keep them on'. Self-assurance and
common sense are his chief assets. He knows that the
ailments of the upper classes are mainly caused by a
combination of over-eating and under-exercise. His
standard prescription therefore is to drink the spa waters,
cut down on food (though not to an unreasonable extent),
and take regular exercise. In this common-sense approach
he mixes a little practical psychology. With middle-class
men he is bluff and direct; with hypochondriacs he is
firm and resourceful; with the wealthy and the really ill
he is ceremonious and tactful. The knowledge he picks
up from local gossip shapes his diagnosis and strengthens
his reputation. If a patient does happen to die on his
hands, he declares that he was as good as dead when he
came for treatment. Under his sensible regimen, however,
most of his patients soon begin to feel better; and his
fame (and fees) grew with the growth of Handley Cross
Spa.

Dr Sebastian Mello, on the other hand, is the genteel
type of physician who affects all the mystique of his
profession. Thin, intellectual (in appearance at least), with

flowing poetic locks, he dresses stylishly in sombre clothes with frilled shirt and snowy wrist-bands. An antique ring adorns his hand and an auburn hair-chain and small German watch his waistcoat. Where Roger Swizzle trudges round on foot or uses a common gig, Dr Mello drives around the countryside in a fashionable claret-coloured carriage drawn by matching ponies. Popular among the ladies, he flatters them with that most subtle of all female flatteries, compliments on their intelligence. By adapting himself to their individual temperaments and predilections, he convinces them of his talent and insight. With men he is reserved and mysterious, making elaborate notes in his large quarto casebook and writing out complicated prescriptions in Latin for the chemist. He recommends a different spring of water from that favoured by Dr Swizzle; and by diluting it with Epsom Salts he is able to prescribe a separate regimen for his patients. Through the medium of a spurious debate carried on in the correspondence columns of a London newspaper (for which he supplied all the letters), he was able to claim a professional victory for his treatment and useful publicity for himself.

Both doctors had their adherents; both their detractors. Their rivalry added to the gaiety of the community and the growing fame of Handley Cross. If their medical knowledge was not remarkable, they both understood human nature and neither (it is probable) did his patients much harm.

IV

The third great profession encountered in the countryside were the clergy of the Church of England. More prominent than either doctors or lawyers, their calling set them above and apart from their secular colleagues. Some of them were younger sons of the aristocracy; many were comparatively wealthy men with either a valuable living or a private income; and since almost by definition they were graduates of Oxford or Cambridge, they were all stamped with that hallmark of an English gentleman, a classical education. Their status as clerics put them on a moral if not social equality with the highest in the land; and, more practically, once inducted to a living, they were virtually irremovable.

It was the first step, securing a benefice, which was crucial. Poor men, lacking the opportunity to distinguish themselves, lacking family connections or aristocratic patronage, might languish for years as penniless curates. The more fortunate, with money or influence, even perhaps a family living to step into, might find a comfortable niche for life at an early age. Where there was no resident squire, the parish clergyman took his place as leader of his little community and the universal authority to whom all could appeal. Where there was no resident doctor, the parson of the parish might also act as physician, dispensing medicine and justice alike from his study. Fewer perhaps, like Sydney Smith in Somerset, kept a set of surgical instruments for minor operations or, like Charles Kingsley, sat up all night with cholera-stricken cottagers. Presiding over their congregations on Sundays, rebuking drunkards and wife-beaters during the week, the more well-to-do clergy, in their large rectories full of children and servants, formed one of the pillars of English country society.

In view of their numbers and influence, Surtees has comparatively few clerical characters in his novels. This could hardly be due to the circumstance that County Durham, for historical reasons, had fewer parishes and therefore fewer clergy in proportion to its size and population than the southern counties of England. It is more probable that a certain respect for the cloth, and for the susceptibilities of his readers, curbed his natural tendency to satire. There is one passage which even hints at a certain envy of their position. 'We never get into a parsonage house', he observes in *Hawbuck Grange* (ch. xiii), 'without thinking if it wasn't for writing the weary sermons, we'd like to be a parson ourself. They are always so snug, and have such capital port wine!' Such mundane considerations would hardly have won the approval of a reforming bishop; but they might not have been absent from the calculations of the less devout candidates for ordination. Coming from a country landowner, the compliment at least argued an acceptance of the clergy as social equals. It is difficult to imagine Surtees making the same remark about doctors or lawyers.

Certainly when Surtees was young, the Church was a perfectly respectable career for a gentleman. It provided a certain status in society; the prospect, given the right circumstances, of material comfort and personal independence; and required little in the way of specialized training. Fortunately too, its patronage was largely in the hands of lay or semi-secular authorities. In the generation after Waterloo half the presentations to its ten thousand or so benefices were made by lay patrons; another seven hundred by Oxford and Cambridge colleges, who usually appointed from among their own members. In default of patronage there was always the purse. Advowsons could be legally bought and sold like other forms of property and there was a steady trade in livings which continued for most of the nineteenth century. The rest of the livings were in the gift of the Crown, municipal corporations, bishops and cathedral chapters; and were the objects of much interested solicitation and not altogether disinterested bestowal. Good family connections counted for much; to the extent that the Church seemed to disgruntled critics almost an extension of the aristocratic system. George IV linked orthodoxy and a connection with the peerage as the two prime considerations for promotions to the episcopacy, since he thought it essential for Church and State to buttress each other. If this was an extreme view, it remained true that the Church in the early Victorian period was still a profession for those who had the right social qualifications rather than a vocation which demanded certain moral or spiritual qualities.

In such circumstances a body of some 14,000 clergy at the start of Victoria's reign, rising to over 19,000 by 1861, exhibited an almost infinite variety of types, including

more than a few eccentrics. There was, to take some extreme cases, the Revd Peter William Pegus, Lady Charlotte Guest's stepfather, who tried to marry off her
mentally deficient brother to a lady of doubtful virtue,
dispatching them to Brighton for a fortnight to bring
about the desired outcome. There was the lonely parson,
known to Mozley in Northamptonshire, who on his
regular walk from parsonage to church collected sticks
which he took back home. At his death nearly two
thousand faggots were found, neatly arranged by size,
filling a complete room. One would think that Surtees had
heard of him when he drew his character of Jogglebury
Crowdey in *Mr Sponge*—were it not that we know that
Crowdey was based on Surtees' own schoolmaster, the
Revd James Birkett, who collected thousands of saplings
during his life to carve into walking-sticks which filled
his attic and were never given away. A more traditional
type of cleric was Goldwin Smith's neighbour near
Mortimer, Berkshire, who took his churchwarden up to
Oxford for a college feast and was by the same churchwarden put to bed in his boots dead drunk. Then there
were the clerical tuft-hunters, the hangers-on of the
aristocracy, like the parson described disgustedly by
George Osbaldeston who recited some 'most fulsome
and ridiculously complimentary verses' in honour of Lord
Middleton and his pack of hounds after supper at the
end of a day's run.[3] Peel mentioned a similar cleric when
describing to his wife the company he met at Apethorpe,
Lord Westmorland's seat, in 1833. 'A clergyman, a Dr
Bunney, who performs all the duties of the Groom of the
Chambers, and some of those of the housemaid. His
civility in showing *little conveniences* to the guests is
amazing.'

More representative, and, to men like Surtees, more
congenial, were the sporting parsons. One of the grandest
was Lord Frederick Beauclerk, younger son of the duke
of St Albans, clerk in holy orders, Vicar of Radbourne,
Hertfordshire, who died in 1850. At his marriage in 1813
he was described as an expert cricket player, racehorse
owner, and knowledgeable betting man, 'has a living of

800 a year in Hertfordshire . . . and a very pretty parsonage'. Since his income of £1,000 per annum was doubled
by his marriage to a daughter of Lord Dillon, he could
clearly afford his sporting pursuits. A brilliant and (it
must be said) unscrupulous player, he was the most
famous clerical cricketer of the century. Another, but not
so well-known sportsman was the Revd William Cotton,
brother of the Peninsula general Lord Combermere, and
celebrated in Cheshire as 'a good farmer, a cock-fighter,
and horse-racer', whom General Dyott met in 1831. The
most famous racing parson, probably, was the Revd John
King who inscribed his name in the annals of racing by
winning the 1,000 Guineas in 1856 with Manganese and
following up that success with an even better horse, the
filly Apology, which won both the 1,000 Guineas and
the Oaks. Another well-known sportsman of the mid-
Victorian era was the Revd William Karslake in Devonshire, an Oriel College friend of Mozley, who described
him as a 'hunting, shooting and yachting man'—activities which did not hinder his becoming chairman
of Quarter Sessions, vice-chairman of the Board of
Guardians, Rural Dean, and later Prebendary.

Devonshire, in fact, was a nest of sporting clergy. In
the time of the Revd Jack Russell (the man who gave his
name to the breed of terriers), it was said that there were
a score of parsons in the Exeter diocese who had packs
of their own. Yet Devon was not unique. Bishop Blomfield
complained that in Cheshire fox-hunting was almost a
religion in itself. It is indicative that advertisements of
advowsons for sale were not uncommonly accompanied
by statements of the local sporting facilities. In some parts
of the country participation in the hunt was almost a
social necessity for the clergy. When Mozley went to his
living at Cholderton in Wiltshire in 1836, he was told by
another parson who turned out with Assheton Smith's
hounds that, unless he went to the meet occasionally, his
range of acquaintances in the county would be restricted
to a few clergy.

The new breed of bishops who were beginning to
arrive on the episcopal bench after 1830—less aristocratic,

more conscientious, more sensitive to public opinion—
did not approve of these secular activities and sometimes
tried to prevent them. Henry Phillpotts, the disciplinarian bishop of Exeter from 1831 to 1869, had a number
of brushes with his hunting parsons, who usually gave
as good as they got. A parson's freehold was not easily
encroached upon; and bishops were not universally
popular. Lay opinion in the rural areas was on the side
of the unregenerate clergy in such matters. It was also
observably true that addiction to fox-hunting did not
necessarily indicate neglect of pastoral duties. Mozley's
friend Karslake declared that after fifty years' hunting he
could solemnly affirm that he had never sacrificed either
public or parish duties to a day's sport. The Revd Jack
Russell himself was an excellent parish priest, a good
preacher, and an active worker in various Devonshire
charitable causes. Charles Kingsley, whose sporting instincts were never far below the clerical surface, was
through circumstances more self-denying. In his early
years at Eversley he not only could not afford to go out
with Sir John Cope's (now the Garth) Hunt at nearby
Bramshill, but felt that he should not allow himself the
distraction. Since he also thought that shooting would
cause trouble in his notoriously poaching parish, he
contented himself with Izaak Walton's quieter recreation
of angling. In later years, however, he would turn up at
meets on one of his cheaply acquired elderly horses and
he boasted that he knew every fox in the district. 'Ain't
they my parishioners?' Whatever the foxes may have
thought, he had few more devoted admirers than the
grooms and huntsmen of the Bramshill estate.

Nevertheless, pressure was slowly mounting against
clergy who appeared too conspicuously worldly in their
habits and appearance. The Revd Baptist Noel's public
attack on sporting, dancing, and card-playing parsons
in the middle of the century could be dismissed as the
peevish exaggeration of a puritanical cleric who had
seceded from the Church of England to become a Dissenter. The bishops of the Establishment themselves,
however, were setting their faces against even the lesser

frivolities. Old Bishop Barrington of Durham as early as 1820 counselled new clergy against playing cards as setting a bad example to their flock. Bishop Phillpotts was known to indicate his disapproval to clergymen who appeared in white trousers. Evangelicalism was itself producing a stricter type of clergyman. They were not always popular in country districts. Harriet Martineau in 1866 mentioned a Low Church parson in the Lake District who preached every year against the local race-meetings. His reward was to be teased by the more unregenerate younger gentry with requests for race subscriptions and grumbling by the lower classes against a man who, with a comfortable house, servants, and carriages, sought to deprive the poor not only of their beer and tobacco but of their annual amusement as well.[4]

Surtees has nothing to say about the larger questions affecting the Church of England; no bishop graces his pages. His incidental comments about the clergy as a body are both few and unsurprising. We are told, for example, that curates count for nothing in the matrimonial stakes; that Whig parsons are scarce; and that a clergyman is 'a sort of necessary appendage at a great man's table'. Nevertheless, scattered through the novels there is a fair representation of the different types of clergy to be met with in his day. The one notable omission is a Tractarian clergyman. Surtees might have had much fun with vestments, incense, and genuflexions; but perhaps the spread of eager young Oxford curates, imbued with the gospel of the beauty of holiness, came too late to make much impression on his consciousness. He probably did not approve of the Oxford Movement; he certainly disliked the more extreme evangelical clergy. There is a sketch of one of them in *Hillingdon Hall* (ch. xviii) which is not far removed from Harriet Martineau's Lakeland parson. He is James Blake, 'one of those desperately over-righteous, cushion-thumping, jump-Jim-Crow breed of parsons, so sanctified that he could hardly suffer the light of heaven to shine upon him, and he ate cold roast potatoes to save his servant the sin of cooking on Sunday'. The contemptuous description continues.

Blake is weak in character and therefore violent in opinion. He preaches hell-fire sermons, astonishing the easy-
going members of his audience but enrapturing all the
servant girls. But then, Surtees concludes with a shrug,
'common people like to be d——d in heaps'.

Blake's part in the plot is an inglorious one. An admirer
of Emma Flather, though she has no intention of grati-
fying him, he is brought in as what, in sporting terms,
might be described as a 'teaser', to stimulate the marquis
of Bray's lagging ardour. The Revd James is not insensible
to female charms—'stiff-backed parsons are but flesh and
blood', observes Surtees cynically, 'notwithstanding all
their thunder, sulphur, and pretension'. Nor is he above
sartorial vanity. To impress Emma he attires himself—
not in white trousers certainly but—in 'a stiff white
starcher, his best black coat and waistcoat, Wellington
boots, Sunday hat, and—we blush to add—a pair of
lavender-coloured gloves. Altogether he was a very
passable swell.'

Hillingdon Hall contains another cleric whom Surtees
equally dislikes. This is the Revd Mr Prosey Slooman, 'a
little, bristly-headed, badger-pyed, pedantic, radical
schoolmaster, who farmed his own glebe, and managed
matters somewhat in the style of the celebrated Wackford
Squeers, frequently recreating the boys with a little work
on the farm'. At the dinner at the St Boswell's Agricultural Association Show he is one of several orators who
inflict themselves on the restive company, giving them a
long-winded account of his experiments with the effect
of guano on Swedish turnips. Obsequious with his social
superiors, peremptory with his inferiors, Mr Slooman
presents a distressing combination of Low-Church sentiments and pedagogic conceit. Another schoolmaster-
parson, more briefly but more sympathetically sketched,
appears in *Handley Cross*. He has the redeeming merit,
denied to the radical Slooman, of being a sportsman and
a good rider. His name, one of Surtees' innumerable
facetious inventions, is the Revd Titus Cramcub, described
approvingly by Mr Jorrocks to Pomponius Ego as

a learned man like yourself—reads Lord Bacon's works, and eats fat bacon for breakfast. He teaches the young idea 'ow to shoot, but prefers 'unting himself, and as soon as 'ounds 'ave shaken off the crowd, and settled to a run, he drops into the front rank, and goes as if he couldn't 'elp himself.

Much may be forgiven to a schoolmaster, apparently, if he is a bold follower of the chase.

There are three more figures in Surtees' gallery of clerical portraits, all mentioned with approval, all apparently hunting men. In *Hawbuck Grange* is the Revd Timothy Goodman, rector of Swillingford, chaplain, secretary, and chronicler of the Goose and Dumpling Harriers. We are to presume that he also turned out in their remarkable costume of long, bottle-green frock-coats, striped waistcoats, patent cords, and broad-brimmed hairy hats. Living in a secluded part of the kingdom, far from roads and railways, the Harriers were no doubt rarely troubled by visits by eminent strangers; but even the bishop of the diocese might have failed to recognize a brother-cleric in that attire. More orthodox in dress, though no more likely to earn episcopal approval, is the Revd Mr Teacher in *Mr Romford*. He is the local vicar who makes up the party of four which the bachelor Mr Sterling had assembled to dine, drink port, and play whist, on the evening before the meet. We are not expressly told that he turns out with Mr Romford's hounds the following morning; but clearly a clergyman who dines with three fox-hunters (and plays cards with them even if it is only for moderate stakes) is a man with his heart in the right place.

There is lastly Parson Blossomnose of the Scamperdale Hunt, who, despite his Falstaffian surname, earns the highest commendation of all. He is one of the regulars in the field when Mr Sponge first makes his appearance with those celebrated hounds and is on the select list of those described as the 'great guns' of the Scamperdale Hunt—'the men who ride *to* hounds, and not *after* them'. This, in a field ruled by Lord Scamperdale, is distinction in itself; but he receives a further accolade from that not easily impressed critic, Mr Sponge himself, who singles him out together with Lord Scamperdale and Jack Spraggon for scrutiny. He describes him afterwards to Mr Jawleyford as 'a tall man in black, on a good-looking young brown horse, rather rash at his fences, but a fine style of goer'. We are told further that he was dressed on that occasion in a serviceable costume of drab cords and jack-boots, a hat with the brim turned upwards, and a double ribbon as hat-string. Though Jawleyford, from whose dinner the previous evening the parson had basely excused himself at the last moment, grumbled that it would have been more to his credit if he had stayed at home and attended to his parish, we are not expected to pay much attention to that sulky criticism. Indeed, Mr Blossomnose is the nearest we come to the experienced hunting parson who follows the hunt in orthodox black and takes care that he has a horse that will enable him to keep up with the best. He was clearly a cleric who would have been welcomed by Assheton Smith as fit for any gentlemanly company.

As the century wore on, there were fewer of them. As early as 1854, Bishop Pepys of Worcester could remark with satisfaction that the sporting clergyman, once so common, was now rarely encountered. A generation later the species was almost extinct. An article on 'The Sporting Parson' in the *Daily Telegraph* of 4 April 1888 acknowledged with nostalgic regret their passing. Even so, it reminded its readers, they had shown great powers of survival. The Revd Philip Honeywood in Essex, Parson Bullen in the Belvoir country, had kept up the tradition into the 1880s, while 'of existing masters of foxhounds one is a clergyman, though far be it from us to mention his name'. The Revd Jack Russell was still hunting the fox in the 1870s and the hare in the 1880s. Nor was he the only Devonshire parson to carry the old habits into the final decades of the century. In November 1882 Mrs Oliphant's Oxonian son, reading Greek philosophy with a Devonshire vicar, described to his mother how on the day of the meeting of the Dartmoor hounds, his host and tutor (it being All Saints' Day) held an early service before breakfast—'a sort of hunting mass'—after which he breakfasted hastily in his cassock, disappeared for a few minutes, then reappeared in full hunting garb, 'entirely transmogrified from the priest of the sanctuary to the sportsman eager for the chase ... such a fine sportsmanlike appearance that he might have been taken for Mr Mildmay's underkeeper'. Young Oliphant's Balliol superciliousness was also perhaps a sign of the times.[5]

5

LANDOWNERS AND FARMERS

I

The purchase of land in Surtees' day was a social rather than an economic speculation. A landowner would be fortunate if his purely agricultural rents yielded as much as 5 per cent on the capital value. Professor Thompson suggests 3.3 per cent as a typical return in the earlier part of this period, declining to $2\frac{1}{2}$ per cent in the 1860s as a result of increased competition for land. The general picture in the novels confirms that estimate. Mr Jorrocks, looking at it with a businessman's eye, thought that 'landownin's a *werry* poor trade'. It was true that the standard $3\frac{1}{2}$ or 3 per cent government stock offered no better return; but, as the same authority observed, 'money i' the funds may pay small interest; but blow me tight, funds pay punctual, and the gates never want repairin'. He was not the only new landowner in the novels to make that discovery. In *Ask Mamma* the first thing that struck Sir Moses Mainchance when he became a landowner was how little interest he got on investment. In the City he had scorned any transaction that would not pay him 10 per cent; as a novice proprietor he found he could hardly recover 3 per cent from his acres. That cautious banker, old Mr Hall, making (on his own statement) from 15 to 20 per cent from his business, not surprisingly showed little enthusiasm for acquiring land. As Surtees philosophically observed in another place, land was like family plate, valuable to sell, but unprofitable to keep.

The problem of owning land was to a large extent the problem of finding good tenants. Like proverbial wives, landlords found it impossible to get on without them, and difficult to get on with them. Farmers were a race of grumblers. When harvests were good, prices fell; when they were poor, prices rose but there was not much to sell. In bad times farmers wanted their rents reduced and had a habit of falling into arrears if that was not granted. In good times there was usually something they wanted done at the landlord's expense—fences repaired, roofs made watertight, or farm buildings extended. They needed watching to be sure that they did not, by over-ploughing or overstocking, extract more out of the soil than they put in: and though a steward or agent could take that off an owner's shoulders, this not only meant another salary to be paid but a further degree of invigilation over the steward himself in case he connived with the tenants to fleece the landlord or made money on the side by way of commission. There was no worse sign for a landlord, Surtees recorded in his unpublished papers, than when his departing agent got a testimonial from the tenants: it meant that he had let them do much as they liked.

In *Hillingdon Hall* (ch. xxxii) there is a passage in which Jorrocks and James Pigg compare experiences of the complaining habits of farmers. Pigg quotes his cousin Deavilboger as saying that no man was fit to be called a farmer who was not a good grumbler. Pigg himself has various recipes for dealing with importunate tenants. They range from invading their farmyards 'ramin' and swearin' and blawin' everybody up' to going round with an armful of plans for the complete rebuilding of the farm premises. The craggy James Pigg had no illusions and few scruples. The country squire, if he had outgrown the first, could not afford to dispense with the second. For social as well as economic reasons an outwardly decent relationship with his tenants was always desirable; and since both sides were dependent on each other, compromises had to be found. On larger estates the image presented to the outer world was often one of almost feudal solidarity. Cavalcades of mounted tenants rode to the hustings at general elections to cast their vote for the candidates approved by their landlord and formed guards of honour at weddings and funerals. Such occasions, and periodic hospitality, with roast beef, strong ale, and sentimental speeches, were no doubt useful in making individual tenants feel identified with the interests of the whole estate in a general paternalistic relationship.

There was another side to the medal. In 1836 Sir John (later Lord) Wrottesley's tenants in Staffordshire presented him with a document which they had all signed to the effect that because of the fall in agricultural prices they were unable to continue on their farms. The indignant baronet summoned them to his presence, told them he would not be blackmailed, and that they might quit their farms if they thought fit.[1] The Wrottesley estate (as recorded in 1873) was nearly 6,000 acres with a rent-roll of £11,000, one of the largest in the county, which made this example of collective tenant resistance of wider significance. Capitulation by larger landowners had consequences for the smaller. Indeed, it was usually the bigger estates which came off best in internal conflicts with tenants. Good farms with generous (which was as much as to say wealthier) landlords attracted the best tenants in good times; in bad times the large, well-organized estates could afford if necessary to take over the direct management of individual farms rather than submit to an unreasonable demand for rent reduction. In times of deep agricultural depression, as in 1834–5 and 1850–1, it was the smaller landowner who was at the greatest disadvantage.

Such men were usually heavily dependent on their agricultural rents. For them tenant pressure, less dramatically conveyed, was a commonplace experience; and not only in the exceptionally bad years. Agriculture had been suffering for a long time. The great war with France had brought prosperity and expansion, with high prices, large capital investment, and the cultivation of much marginal land. Peace in 1814 threatened the collapse of demand at home and dangerous competition from abroad. To ease the apprehensions of farmers and landowners, the government sponsored the notorious corn bill of 1815 which prohibited the import of foreign wheat until a ceiling-price of 80s. a quarter was reached. In the event this high degree of protection proved economically delusive and politically unpopular. By 1830 most of the country gentry in the House of Commons were beginning to realize that in an age of general tariff reductions it would be impossible to maintain indefinitely high protection exclusively for agriculture. The question was always more complicated than farmers seemed to think; since what predominantly decided the level of food prices was not the corn tariff but the weather. As a class farmers looked to legislative protection, easy credit, and inflationary money policy for their salvation. The more intelligent landowners believed that improvements in farming methods, leading to greater productivity, offered the only escape from the stagnation into which British agriculture had fallen in the post-war era.

The Royal Agricultural Society, founded in 1838, was expressly designed to spread the gospel of scientific stockbreeding, drainage, and artificial fertilizers. Under the inspiration of influential peers like Spencer (the Society's first president), Richmond, Fitzwilliam, Exeter, and Ripon, and eminent commoners like Peel, Graham, William Long, and Philip Pusey, the new society proclaimed itself completely non-political, dedicated solely to the principle embodied in its motto 'Practice with Science'. The Royal Society gave national leadership at a critical time in farming history. The overriding need for systematic drainage, for example, for both arable and pasture, had been recognized and experiments made with various materials and types of drains. Smith of Deanston's famous book on *Draining and Deep Ploughing* had appeared in 1831. In the 1840s the great drainage experts were Josiah Parkes and J. J. Mechi. In 1840 the German chemist Liebig's book on the effects of chemical substances on plant nutrition and soil composition was published in England with an introduction by the young Scottish scientist Lyon Playfair. Attention was also being given to substitutes for farmyard manure. Experiments with nitrate of soda (Jorrocks' 'nitrate of sober') began in the 1830s; and the first cargo of guano from Peru arrived two years before Victoria came to the throne. In the longer future the invention of the steam engine offered the possibility of adding mechanical energy to the wind and water, horse and human power, on which farming had immemorially depended. A new age of scientific agriculture had dawned.

It was not, however, a dawn which brought immediate illumination to the great body of English farmers. Conservative in their habits, with little intellectual training, reluctant to experiment and in any case with little capital, most of them regarded the new school of scientific farming with distrust and sometimes hostility. At the foundation meeting of the Royal Agricultural Society itself there had been a challenge from a group of farmers who accused the gentry of betraying their interests by diverting attention from the fundamental principle of legislative protection. The local agricultural societies and farmers' clubs which sprang up in the 1830s under the encouragement of reforming gentry too often became little more than social meeting-places for disgruntled protectionist tenants. In spite of the good intentions of promoters of these meetings, wrote the biographer of John Grey of Dilston, a leading agricultural reformer of the time, 'there was a tendency to degenerate to purposes of eating, drinking and flattering after-dinner speeches'.[2] Worse still in the eyes of some conservative squires, such assemblages gave farmers ideas above their station. The racy account of the foundation of the Agricultural Association in *Hillingdon Hall* (chs. xvi–xvii)—president marquis of Bray, vice-president John Jorrocks—catches the actual lineaments of such assemblies.

Whatever their shortcomings, the farmers were a large and influential class who because of their property qualifications made up a high proportion of the county electorate. Spackman calculated on the basis of the 1841 census that the number of farmers and graziers in England and Wales was nearly 250,000. Naturally they varied in wealth and importance and, it is a fair presumption, in intelligence, honesty, and industriousness. Some large tenants, especially in moorland and sheep-grazing districts, might farm four or five hundred acres; at the other extreme were smallholdings worked by a single family without hired help. Though there was little uniformity over the country as a whole, or even in individual regions, most farms were over a hundred acres, which was large by Continental standards. In Surtees' own county of Durham they tended to be on the small side compared with the national average; most were between fifty and a hundred and fifty acres.

Surtees' sketches of farmers are rarely flattering. Witness, for example, the three tenant farmers in *Ask Mamma* (ch. xxix) who appear before Sir Moses Mainchance on his annual rent-day. First comes Mr Brown, who with his brother had obtained their run-down farm by offering more rent than they could afford or it produce. Next to appear is Jacky Hindmarch, who went round his fields in tattered clothes and crownless hat, looking more like a scarecrow than a farmer. He farms seventy acres with no other assistance than his wife's, is always behindhand with his work, and consequently his rent. Having an obstinate temper and a smattering of law, however, he is usually able to hold his own against any landlord. Finally, there is the meek Mr Turnbull, who does not come in person but sends a more than adequate deputy in the mountainous and formidable person of Mrs Turnbull. A match for any man in the county either with her tongue or her fists, she fairly drives Sir Moses out of the room. Surtees makes it plain that in describing this remarkable trio he is singling out the most useless class of small tenant—shifty, dishonest, impermanent, ready to take any farm at any rent since they have no intention of keeping their side of the agreement and little expectation of staying for more than a year or two. 'There is', he says later in the book, 'a regular rolling stock of bad farmers in every country, who pass from district to district, exercising their ingenuity in extracting whatever little good their predecessors have left in the land.' Bad landowners attract bad tenants. Sir Moses, being only concerned to screw money out of his estate, is perhaps

justly rewarded with tenants who are leagued against
him in a kind of mutual-aid association to deprive him of
its proceeds.

Other farmers in the novels are not quite on this
debased level. In *Hillingdon Hall* (ch. xiv) we are presented with Mr Goodheart, described as one of the old-
fashioned, stay-at-home farmers who sells his produce
locally, knows nothing of the 'guano, nitrate o'sober, or
gypsy manure' advocated by Mr Jorrocks, but consistently improves his farm in small affordable ways,
draining, manuring, and repairing. Yet even this
praiseworthy man is turned into a figure of fun. His
knowledge of public affairs is derived from a Cornish
county newspaper which an old friend sends up to him
by wagon in yearly instalments. Since Willy Goodheart
takes another year to get through a consignment, he is
always a couple of years or so behindhand in his comments on national events. We learn less about Jorrocks'
other tenants, farmers Wopstraw and Heavytail, other
than that they are slow and simple in everything outside
their immediate interests, and are generally resistant to
new ideas. He has kinder things to say about farmers as
a class in his *Analysis of the Hunting Field*; but though
the satire is absent, the journalistic effusiveness which
colours that book makes what he says less persuasive.
He rightly draws attention to the gulf which separates
the men who scratch out a living on a starve-acre holding
from the great graziers of Northamptonshire or the sheep-
farmers of Lincolnshire with an annual turnover of £3,000
in wool; but when he dilates on the 'quiet, respectable
loyalty that pervades the whole class' of farmers, 'one of
the mainstays of the country', a certain disbelief creeps
in. This is more the language of an audit-dinner than a
considered personal statement.

In this sentimental vein, however, it is something of a
back-handed compliment for Surtees to say that the worst
accusation that can be brought against the farming
community is that they are doltish and stupid. Certainly
the general reputation of farmers in the age of protection was one of backwardness, inefficiency, and lack of

education. Mozley, in sadness rather than contempt, concluded from personal experience as parish priest that the ignorance of farmers on ordinary affairs was so profound and universal that it was prudent for a clergyman to take it for granted they knew nothing until he found otherwise. One of the worst consequences of this, he observed, was that the gentry were accustomed to joke about farmers and despise them as a class, thus perpetuating a social divide which neither side wished to cross. The severest criticism was a lack of skill even in their own profession. Sir Thomas Acland, the Peelite MP for Somerset, who after losing his seat in 1847 studied agricultural chemistry at London University and won a prize from the Royal Agricultural Society for an essay on farming in Somerset, wrote of the farmers there that 'the more I see of them, the more I see the wretched state of their farming'. Another writer in the *Journal* of the RAS, reviewing the progress of agriculture in the quarter of a century since 1838, affirmed that 'it is scarcely an exaggeration to say that the thorough-bred British farmer of that day despised science as much as he feared Free Trade, and that the only things which commanded his entire confidence were his father's experience and his own skill'.

Those traditional resources were not to be despised. It would be absurd to assume, as Surtees himself pointed out in *Hillingdon Hall* (ch. xv), that before the 1830s all was darkness on the agricultural scene and that nothing existed to enlighten the British farmer on the secrets of his art. To illustrate the point Surtees listed from his own shelves some eighteen different works on farming, flanked by twenty volumes of the *Farmers' Magazine* and innumerable pamphlets. It is true that some of them dated back to the middle of the eighteenth century. Even so they must have embodied a great deal of practical wisdom. Whether the average tenant-farmer in the county possessed a similar library of farming books is more doubtful. Yet there had clearly been a considerable expansion of farming knowledge during the reign of George III. Those two great agricultural reformers Arthur Young

and Sir John Sinclair flourished during the Napoleonic
Wars. Pitt had founded the Board of Agriculture in 1793
and the series of county reports which it elicited form
the first reliable survey of modern English farming. The
interest, the scientific approach, and gradually the knowledge, were there before 1815; the problem was how to
bridge the gap between the theoretical reformer and the
working farmer.

That was not easily done. It was a question not merely
of ignorance and prejudice but also of lack of capital and
incentive. After 1830, at all events, few farmers could
have been oblivious to the new wave of agricultural
doctrine. It was dinned into their ears from all sides—
from local agricultural societies, from the Royal Society,
from scientific experts, MPs, and reforming landlords,
from newspapers and magazines. Even the great Nimrod
in 1841 contributed an article on 'Agriculture' to the
Sporting Oracle and Almanack of Rural Life in which he
warned farmers that sooner or later the duties on foreign
corn would be reduced and the British agriculturalist
obliged to find his salvation in improved cultivation and
diminished expenditure. 'To be an economical farmer,
indeed,' he wrote severely, 'a man must of necessity know
something of chemistry, or receive instruction from those
who do.' Wopstraw as a chemist requires a certain effort
of imagination. It would not be surprising if many farmers
were daunted or confused by this flood of exhortation
and advice. Even Surtees is not without some sympathy
for their predicament. One of the aims of *Hillingdon Hall*,
as the preface makes clear, was to poke fun at the excesses
of the theoretical and over-enthusiastic agricultural
reformers.

Jorrocks, though not the only one, is the prime example
in the novel of the zealous and uncritical apostle of the
new farming religion. On first arrival at Hillingdon he
writes to Bill Bowker about his plans (ch. v).

I means to take a hundred or a hundred and fifty acres in hand
and try all the new experiments on a liberal scale—guano,
nitrate o'soder, bone manure, hashes [ashes] and manure
mexed, soot, salt, sand, everything in fact; shall lector on

agriculture, and correspond with the Royal Society, and so on—Mr Jorrocks on buck wheat, Mr Jorrocks on clover, Mr Jorrocks on long 'orns, Mr Jorrocks on short 'orns.

This is light-hearted caricature. Yet even the more knowledgeable and serious reformers did not—in Surtees' view—exercise sufficient judgement in their advice to farmers. 'They do far more harm than good, for farmers get confused; and, frightened at their own ignorance, despair of coming up to the mark, and so remain as they were; or else attempt fanciful experiments, which, after endless expense, they find unsuited to their climate or soil, or unproductive of the anticipated ends.'

There was some point in this criticism. As the early volumes of the *Journal of the Royal Agricultural Society* illustrate, experiments by different persons with different crops and soils yielded diverse results. Philip Pusey confessed in 1842 that over the preceding four years 'we have learnt many of the chemical principles on which manures act, but we do not yet know how to apply those principles to the daily work of the farm'. His own trials with nitrate of soda and sulphate of ammonia, for example, had been failures. Others found that the cost of some artificial manures outweighed the additional profit derived from the higher yield. When experts expressed such doubts, plain farmers could be excused for remaining passive. For all the intensity of debate on scientific farming in the 1840s, the practical effects on British farming were only marginal. When making his classic survey of English agriculture in 1850–1, James Caird found that old-fashioned methods still predominated in most parts of the country. Surtees considered that 'the great difficulty under which farming labours' was lack of capital, and wondered why agriculture should be regarded as somehow an exception to all other trades in this respect.

The logical conclusion from this was that the small farmer with insufficient means was an encumbrance to the whole industry. Surtees' prescription was a drastic one. Whatever he had written as a journalist, there was no real place in his utilitarian mind for the romantic myth of the sturdy English yeoman. His solution was to get rid of the backward and inefficient tenants altogether. In chapter xxx of *Ask Mamma*, entitled challengingly 'Commerce and Agriculture', he pointed once more to the contrast between the economic practices of the two different worlds and the shortcomings of the small farmers. 'In these accelerated days, when even the very street waggon horses trot, they are the only beings whose pace has not been improved . . . a pitchfork at their backs would fail to push some of these fellows into prosperity.' The course he favoured was to consolidate the smaller farms into large profitable units, leaving those previous occupiers who had neither capital, courage nor capacity to sink down into the ranks of the ordinary labourer.

Any doubt whether this outburst in his novel went beyond his settled opinion is dispelled by what he wrote a few years later in an essay on farming in Durham. Though unpublished, it seems to have been intended for publication, since it survived among his papers in the form of a printer's proof. In it he makes the point that such reforms as had taken place over the previous ten or fifteen years were ascribable to the great landowners; the spirit of improvement had as yet hardly penetrated through to the mass of small proprietors. Against the tenant farmers he levels a catalogue of charges: wilfully ignoring the terms of their leases, cheating on the allowances given for purchase of lime and manure, a fixed prejudice in favour of arable over grassland, and an inherent unwillingness to contribute anything to the improvement of their farms. In general, the mass of small occupiers did not have enough capital and farmed badly. It would, he concludes trenchantly, be a real kindness to get rid of the whole race of small, capital-less, Durham farmers. The essay in fact is one of the clearest demonstrations that the opinions Surtees expressed in his novels represented his own personal convictions.[3]

One may still ask, however, how far these opinions even though genuine were reliable. An answer is fortunately to hand in the shape of an essay on 'Agriculture in the County of Durham' by Thomas George Bell which

won the prize offered by the RAS in 1854 and was published in volume xvii of its *Journal*. Bell's family had long
been connected with the north-east, and his findings,
though more sedately expressed, bear out the substance
of Surtees' criticisms. Farming in the county was generally backward, he wrote, because of the poverty of
the soil, the prevalence of common land, the competition from mining, and the smallness of the farms. Little
drainage had been carried out until very recently and
much remained to be done. Farm buildings generally
were in a bad state. Durham farming, in fact, had been
styled 'the worst in the kingdom'. The remedies Bell recommended were for the most part technical; but he
confirmed that a large portion of the county was held in
small properties; that many of them frequently changed
hands; and that even on the larger estates the actual
farms were usually small. He tells us that the question of
enlarging the farms of the county had often been discussed, but on the radical solution advocated by Surtees
he prudently avoids taking sides. Opinion was divided,
he said, whether large farms, though likely to be better
managed and more productive, would attract men with
capital. Nevertheless, he agrees that small farms were
one of the reasons for the 'backward condition of agriculture in Durham' and that their tenants were deficient
in the capital required for new and improved methods of
management. Though blander in tone, there is nothing
in this independent survey that seriously conflicts with
Surtees' more outspoken assessment.

II

County Durham was beyond doubt an extreme case and
this perhaps coloured Surtees' general view of farmers.
Even so, the state of English agriculture as a whole, and
the experimental nature of the movement for scientific
farming, make it easier to understand why in the 1840s
farmers for the most part preferred the easier and more

traditional safeguards of legislative protection. They found themselves, however, in a political world in which the tide of public opinion was setting decisively against them.

The great industrial depression which began in 1836 and lasted until 1843 was accompanied in 1838–40 by bad harvests and higher prices for bread than had been known for twenty years. The activities of the Anti-Corn Law League and the tentative tariff proposals of the struggling Whig government ensured that 'cheap bread' became one of the battle-cries of the 1841 general election which brought Peel and the Conservative Party to power. Both main parties accepted the principle of some protection for agriculture, and the difference between the Whig proposal for a fixed duty on corn and the Conservative adherence to a sliding scale was largely technical, even though passion and propaganda portrayed the issue in much starker terms. It was beyond dispute that the modified tariff of the 1828 Act had failed to give farmers and consumers the steady level of prices both needed; and it was generally anticipated that Peel, when prime minister, would bring in a new corn bill. Once in office, however, he used the new device of a peacetime income tax to finance a sweeping reduction in tariffs on a wide range of imports, including a drastic lowering of the duty on imports of wheat and other cereals. With better harvests, and a sharp fall in the price of wheat which continued for five years, agricultural unease began to grow.

The first organized opposition to government policy came in 1843 over the bill to allow free entry to Canadian corn. In the same year a fresh irritant was injected when the Anti-Corn Law League carried its crusade into the rural districts. The League's naïve assumption that tenant farmers were the helpless victims of class selfishness and landlord oppression; and their violent propaganda, vituperative beyond even the generous latitude of Victorian public debate, produced a sharp reaction. This was not surprising. When the League newspapers and lecturers talked of 'tyrannical, brutal, and unfeeling landlords', 'monsters of impiety', 'relentless demons', 'rapacious harpies', and 'merciless footpads', it was not a picture that was readily recognizable in the country-side. When League journalists turned their invective against the farmers themselves, describing them as going 'cap in hand, crawling and sneaking to their land-lords' and calling them 'deluded slaves', 'Clodpoles', 'chawbacons', and 'hawbucks', it was hardly calculated to win their hearts and minds. When finally a League newspaper went so far as to give veiled encouragement to incendiarism by aggrieved agricultural labourers (in an article entitled 'Swing versus the Corn Laws'),[4] there seemed some justification for the charge (which the government itself for a time half-suspected) that the League was prepared to promote crime and disorder to get its way. The accumulation of such evidence presented to audiences of farmers, had a powerful effect.

The League, of course, had other, more respectable arguments at its disposal: Bright's attack on the game laws, for example, or the familiar case for more scientific rather than protected farming. But it never made the headway with farmers which it had hoped for, and claimed to have achieved. It is probable also that the violence of the League's rhetoric, by inflaming feeling on both sides, decreased the chances of securing a peaceful political solution of the corn-law controversy. The effort to win over farmers and farm labourers was in the end counter-productive. In their mutual hostility Leaguers and Protectionists both contributed to the great parliamentary and party crisis of 1846.

The League, in fact, created an 'anti-League'. The immediate response to the campaign in the country dis-tricts was the formation of a network of agricultural protection societies designed to mobilize feeling against the repeal of the corn laws. On the initiative of Robert Baker, a local tenant farmer, the Essex Agricultural Protection Society was formed in December 1843. This was the signal for a hundred such organizations to start up over the next few months, mainly in southern and eastern England. The impetus came mainly from below, from farmers and freeholders; but in February 1844 a

Central Agricultural Protection Society was set up in London by a number of protectionist landowners and politicians, headed by the dukes of Richmond and Buckingham. Their object was probably to retain some control over a movement that threatened to become an independent political force; but though ostensibly nonpolitical, and less vociferous than the provincial associations, the Central Society offered an important measure of respectability and leadership. Peel disliked the protectionist societies for the same reason that he disliked the Anti-Corn Law League—the limitation they sought to impose on the independent judgement of members of parliament; but there was little he could do about it.

To the liberal middle classes of the late-Victorian generation, Cobden and Bright were venerated public figures who in 1846 had put right a great social wrong. The more disreputable side of the League's activities was forgotten, or dismissed as the propaganda of their opponents. To many contemporaries, however, the League appeared at the time an unpleasant, unscrupulous, and dangerous organization. Even among those sympathetic to its aims, there was some disgust at its methods. Tom Hughes, then a young and idealistic undergraduate, returned from a trip to northern England an ardent free trader. When his more staid elder brother told him to consider the actual relations between a dozen landlords known to them in Berkshire and their tenants and labourers, and ask himself whether the League's accusations were not utterly untrue in their case and in the county they were familiar with, and probably untrue of counties elsewhere, he was forced to wonder whether 'a cause which needed such libels to support it could be a just one'. An older liberal came to that conclusion on his own account. The Quaker philanthropist J. J. Gurney could not square it with his conscience to subscribe to the League. Though he had no doubt that the principle of free trade was a Christian principle, 'yet [he confided to his journal in 1844] evil must not be done that good may come; and at present I doubt the working of the machine'.[5]

Being neither a young man nor what passed as a liberal one, Surtees was able to express his opinions with fewer reservations. *Hillingdon Hall* was written during the heat of the League's invasion of the farming world, appearing in monthly parts in the *New Sporting Magazine* in 1843–4. Though its main purpose was to satirize the movement for scientific agricultural reform, with all its illusions and pretended experts, the secondary theme was provided by the county by-election and the arrival of Mr Bowker as an Anti-Corn Law League candidate. This enables Surtees to present a picture of the League's objects and agents which may have struck readers at the end of the century as absurdly biased and far-fetched. To farmers and landowners at the time it would hardly have seemed so.

It was, writes Surtees sardonically, a fortunate day for the League when they enlisted Mr Bowker as one of their lecturers, for they thereby gained the services of 'an able and most unscrupulous coadjutor'. By a lord out of a lady's maid, the former clerk of a recently deceased conveyancer, keeper of a seedy tobacconist's shop and an alcoholic wife, Bill Bowker lived by his wits and above his station; a kind of Cockney equivalent of Soapey Sponge and Facey Romford. He is recruited to the cause by a broken-down actor of his acquaintance who himself had become a League lecturer under the resounding alias of Mr St Julian Sinclair. Rafferty (that being his real name) easily sweeps aside Bowker's protestations of ignorance on the grand subject of the corn laws. 'You've a quick apprehension and a ready tongue—lots of jaw—and *that's* what the League want.' For eight guineas a week and expenses, Mr Bowker joins one of the itinerant teams of lecturers equipped with a van painted with slogans and suitable literature for distribution, their laudable purpose being to 'enlighten the lower orders on the monstrous iniquity of the bread tax, and the great advantages of a free trade in corn'. Or, in the more cynical language of Mr Jorrocks, to further the interests of the League while feathering their own nests.

As stated in their official publications, the kind of men

the League sought to recruit were rather different. When launching their campaign in the agricultural districts, their newspapers advertised for

gentlemen of education and character, and possessing the requisite powers of eloquence . . . knowledge of farming, although not indispensable, might be advantageous. The Council would especially PREFER the services of those who are strongly convinced of the *immoral* and *irreligious* character of the Corn Laws, and who could, CONSCIENTIOUSLY, advocate its total and immediate *repeal*, as a *Christian* duty.

Life being what it is, the League lecturers fell a trifle short of this ideal, being in fact rather closer to Bill Bowker and Rafferty in the social scale than the gentlemen of education and character specified in the advertisement. This was hardly surprising. Contemporary society regarded hired propagandists with some disfavour; and the financial rewards for the lecturers (usually £200 per annum with travelling expenses), though attractive to those with few visible means of support, were hardly likely to tempt the respectable. In reality the League lecturers and journalists were a decidedly mixed bag. One of their most loyal and long-serving agents, James Acland, was in constant difficulties over money, had seen the inside of a gaol, and was not over-honest in his personal affairs. Among the others, Paulton was a vehement young ex-medical student; Greig an ex-trooper of the Blues who specialized in violent abuse of the aristocracy; Somerville and Roberts drunkards who disappeared on drinking bouts for days at a time. W. J. Fox certainly fell into the category of religious enthusiasts, but his brand of sanctimonious piety, while popular with certain audiences, repelled more moderate supporters; even Cobden disliked him. They were not all like this; but the League never solved the problem of its lecturers and was often embarrassed by them. When a judicious modern historian of the League can write that some of its employees were 'of questionable character or downright disreputable',[6] it may be accepted that in Bowker and Mr St Julian Sinclair the author was not exceeding the bounds of reasonable satire.

With Bowker's entry as candidate in the county by-election, Surtees turns to another aspect of the League's activities in 1843–4—its ambitious policy of fighting every parliamentary by-election and its practical difficulties in finding respectable candidates. Local men were unwilling to stand as proclaimed nominees of the League; and, in an age which still prized political independence in an MP, to put up their own paid agents was to invite derision and defeat. When in August 1844 the League nominated its treasurer William Rawson to fight the borough of Dudley in Worcestershire, he secured fewer votes than any previous Liberal candidate had done in the five elections that had taken place there since the Reform Act. They had one electoral success in Bright's much-trumpeted victory in the city of Durham in 1843, but this was primarily due to the capricious support of Lord Londonderry, who had quarrelled with the orthodox local Conservatives. Elsewhere the League met with a string of defeats which impoverished their finances and strained their relations with the Whigs. The *Hillingdon Hall* by-election is, in fact, a fair reflection of the contemporary electoral tensions. Although the League claimed success in setting up local organizations in the agricultural constituencies, most of them were houses of straw without weight or durability. The type of men they recruited instanced by Professor McCord—a tobacconist, as chairman, for the Gainsborough Association, a druggist, a grocer, and a printer as officers of the Boston Association—bear a strong family resemblance to Mr Bowker's election committee, which was made up of a bankrupt baker, an insolvent painter, a radical schoolmaster, and a sold-up farmer.

The outcome of this fictional by-election is a remarkable anticipation by Surtees of actual events. When the marquis of Bray is left in possession of the field as a moderate free-trader (Mr Bowker having pocketed his bribe and departed), the indignant farmers put Jorrocks up as protectionist candidate and carry their man to victory against the traditional influence of the duke of Donkeyton. In the winter of 1845–6, when first rumours and then confirmation came of Peel's determination to

end the corn laws, angry protectionist meetings were
held all over England to protest against the government's change of policy and to obtain pledges from
local Conservative MPs to vote against it. Faced with this
outburst of feeling in the provinces, the Central Agricultural Protection Society in London abandoned its rule of
non-intervention in politics and called on its members to
bring pressure to bear on their parliamentary representatives. Several free-trade Peelite MPs resigned their
seats during the crisis because of the views of their
constituents. Lord Lincoln, in a by-election created in
South Nottinghamshire by his appointment as Chief
Secretary for Ireland, was heavily defeated by a protectionist in a constituency which he had held unchal-
lenged for fourteen years. Some wavering Conservative
members, who in other circumstances might have supported the prime minister, succumbed to pressure from
below and joined the new Protectionist party in the
Commons. There can be little doubt that the activity of
the county protectionist societies in the constituencies
played a decisive part during the early months of 1846 in
the defection of some two-thirds of the Conservative Party
and Peel's retirement from office once the corn laws were
repealed.

It requires, perhaps, some effort of the imagination to
picture Mr Jorrocks taking his place at Westminster in
the party led by those two patricians, Lord Stanley and
Lord George Bentinck. The Conservative Party generally
had always been socially more exclusive and homogeneous than its opponents. There had been the occasional
MP of eccentric origin in the House of Commons during
the previous decade—John Gully the former prize-fighter,
Cobbett a former ploughboy turned farmer and radical
journalist—but they had sat among the more diverse
liberal-radical members on the other side of the House.
Nevertheless, the farmers'-club meeting in Sellborough,
when the indignant Heavytails, Wopstraws, Haycocks,
Clotworthys, and Grumbletons resolved to invite Jorrocks
to stand, was prophetic warning of what was going to
happen in some English counties only a year after the
novel was published in book-form.

III

It is doubtful whether Surtees himself, as landlord and farmer on his own account, was ever a violent protectionist. At any rate he adapted himself without difficulty to the momentous economic and political changes of 1846. Two years earlier he had joined the committee formed in Durham to counteract the propaganda of the Anti-Corn Law League and had become a member of the Northumberland Society for the Protection of British Agriculture. With the repeal of the corn laws, however, his efforts were directed to healing rather than perpetuating political enmities. 'I so fully agree', he wrote in May 1847, 'in the absurdity of retaining the old names of Whigs and Tories that on the accession of the present Ministry [i.e. the Liberal free-trade government of Lord John Russell], I wrote to withdraw from the Conservative Association of this division . . . So far, therefore, as any little influence I have goes, it is decidedly in favour of the Ministry.'[7]

Any prospect of restoring the corn laws was, in his opinion, illusory. He refused to stand as parliamentary candidate in support of Lord Stanley's minority and still ostensibly protectionist government in 1852, even though he would not have been pledged personally to vote for a return to protectionism. In the years immediately after repeal, good harvests at home and imports from abroad had brought prices down and driven farmers into a panic. Surtees' private opinion was that not one in fifty of them really understood the question. In 1850, at the annual meeting of the Derwent and Shotley Bridge Agricultural Society, he sought to enlighten them. It was an interesting speech because it constituted what was probably the most explicit public statement of his views on agricultural policy. He told his audience bluntly that they were as likely to go to the moon as get protection back, and that over the kingdom as a whole landlords and tenants were occupying more land than they could put to good effect. It was not acreage but proper management that made farming profitable. He praised Peel's recent Drainage Act—'it was impossible to overrate the advantages of draining'—and cited as proof the example of some great landowners who were already making use of it. Farmers must change their methods, he said, and landlords must encourage and assist them. They could not compete with the foreigners in corn during ordinary years but they could in cattle. The golden rule therefore should be 'plough less and pasture more'. Farmers, he repeated, must abandon all idea of protection and address themselves energetically to the task of improvement unaided by the legislature, though with the prospect of earning the approval of their landlords. Six months later he declined an invitation to attend a meeting of the Durham County Protection Society with a laconic message: 'Dear Sir, No more agitation for yours very truly, R. S. Surtees.'

What he preached to others, he was already practising himself. During the 1840s he had undertaken systematic drainage on his own home farm and a notebook survives with elaborate details of the size of pipes he used and the depth of the trenches in which they were laid. In this, as in his public advice to farmers, Surtees was taking his place among the more active and sensible landlords of his day. Drainage, in fact, was at that time the greatest single need of British agriculture, both for arable and pasture; and it was during these years that the longest and most sustained draining campaign was being carried out. The initial obstacle had been its expense. Special tile-making machinery, developed in the 1840s, reduced the cost to a minimum of £3 or £4 an acre and this was soon followed by the production of tile-laying machinery. Even so, the expense was a considerable burden for many tenants and small landowners. The practical way round this barrier came with the Public Money Drainage Act of 1846, to which Surtees had referred in his 1850 speech. It was one of Peel's several, though at the time undervalued, compensations to the landed interest for the repeal of the corn laws. It authorized the advance from public funds of, initially, £2 million in Britain and £1 million in Ireland, to finance draining works undertaken by private landlords. The loans were offered at $3\frac{1}{2}$ per cent interest (lower than commercially available), repayable over 22 years; and applications had to be approved by the existing Enclosure Commissioners. It was this Act, more than anything else, which stirred owners and land-agents into action. The success was immediate, some £2½ million being borrowed in the first eight years of its existence. So heavy was the demand from landowners that within a few years private improvement loan socie-ties were established by special Acts of parliament with wider charters and more flexible rules, though still under the supervision of the Enclosure Commissioners. Fifteen years later a new Land Drainage Act encouraged landowners to form local drainage boards to co-ordinate work over a whole area. By 1866 over £8 million had been issued in improvement loans, public and private, under the supervision of the Enclosure Commissioners;[8] by 1878 this figure had risen to £12 million, not counting a large but unknown amount that had been expended by landowners from their own pockets. The significance of this investment may be judged by the fact that, except in the period of the Crimean War, the entire annual yield of the Income Tax had never during Surtees' life reached £12 million and in the year of his death had fallen back to £9 million.

Not all landowners, particularly the wealthier and more enterprising, saw a profitable return from the vast sums used in agricultural improvements during the middle decades of the century. Nevertheless, the years from 1850 to 1860 proved a golden age for British farming. It was not entirely the result of draining, artificial fertilizers, and mechanization. The Crimean War gave a useful stimulus to consumption at a critical time; the spread of railways provided cheap and quick transport to urban mar-kets. Sustaining it all was the steady development of British society—the headlong and apparently unstop-pable growth of population, accompanied by rising consumption and a higher standard of living. It was this which enabled the farmer to flourish despite the rising imports of foreign grain from North America: imports which in fact tended to keep prices stable rather than depressed. A report published by the Royal Agricultural Society in 1864 suggested that the previous quarter of a

century had seen greater improvements in British agriculture than in any equivalent previous period. Farmers
were better educated and more ready to learn; in possession of resources, both scientific and mechanical,
beyond the dreams of their forefathers; facing a demand
for their products that had never been known before. No
doubt there were still Wopstraws and Heavytails to be
found in the countryside; but the kind of antediluvian
farmer instanced by Surtees in 1861, who had objected
to draining because, as he told a drainage commissioner,
he did not want the 'sap taken out of his land', was probably a vanishing species even in County Durham.

Though in *Hillingdon Hall* Surtees had exploited almost to exhaustion the topics of scientific agriculture and
protectionism, he continued to air his views on farming
policy in the later novels. In *Hawbuck Grange* he goes to
the trouble of inserting a footnote in praise of the great
drainage authority J. J. Mechi, the London cutler who,
having made a fortune with his 'magic razor strop', turned
to farming and writing. In the same novel (ch. xvi) Mr
Bluff, the fox-preserving and therefore praiseworthy
farmer, receives Tom Scott 'with the now common accompaniment of a country gentleman, a draining-pipe in
his hand'. In *Ask Mamma* (ch. xv) there is an approving
passage describing how Major Yammerton regained his
prosperity instead of succumbing to the disastrous fall
in rents he had to submit to after the repeal of the corn
laws. 'Just when things were at their worst, the first
sensible sunbeam of simplicity that ever shone upon land,
appeared in the shape of the practical easy-working
Drainage Act, an act which has advanced agriculture
more than all previous inventions and legislation put together.' Ignoring the scepticism of his agent and the
resistance of his tenants, the gallant major used his intelligence and energy to save him from financial ruin. He
took out a government loan and 'soon scared all the
snipes and half the tenants off his estate'. Draining his
land, working it well, cleaning it well, and manuring it
well, he found he could make as much on one acre as his
tenants had done on three; and instead of becoming a

bankrupt, he was able to set himself up in a second-hand coach large enough to accommodate both himself and his three crinolined and marriageable daughters. He was even granted the ultimate satisfaction of reading in the local newspaper that a neighbour who had previously scoffed at draining was applying to the Lands Improvement Company for a sum of £4,000 for that very purpose. This, incidentally, was an actual company, incorporated by an Act of 1853; Surtees was nothing if not topical.

The eminently moral tale of Major Yammerton nicely illustrates two of Surtees' basic convictions about farming: the superior profitability of pasture over arable, and the indispensable role of landlords as pioneers of agricultural improvement. Though in *Hillingdon Hall* he had poked fun at the duke of Donkeyton's model farm and derided gentlemen farmers as a class, it was only because their aim was so often ostentation rather than profit. For a sensible reforming landowner he had only approval. One of the great virtues of the 'ruthless repeal of the Corn Laws', he says in *Plain or Ringlets* (ch. li), was that it made the country gentry more businesslike in their habits and more commercially minded in their attitude to the land. Once they had been brought to that receptive state, 'squires will find no safer or better speculation than in draining and improving their own land. We do not advocate their teaching the farmers their trade, but we like to see them dispel the prejudices of habit by their example and superior intelligence.' Conservative though he was in many matters, Surtees had a robust and essentially Victorian approach to the question of making money. That draining and converting to pasture also produced better hunting country—larger fields, firmer ground, trimmer hedges, better gates—was an additional but uncovenanted reward.

PART TWO
Domestic Interiors

WOMAN AND THE PURSUIT OF MAN

I

In her book *How I Managed My Children*, published in 1865, Mrs Warren propounded two axioms, that 'married life is a woman's profession' and that 'it is the concealed hope of all girls to marry'. As propositions they were neither new nor peculiar to her time. By most middle- and upper-class families it was taken for granted that a girl's probable destiny was marriage and that it was only prudent for parents to guide their daughters towards a suitable match. Exceptions are not difficult to find. There were girls who did not wish to marry; girls who defied their parents and married for love; parents who neglected their responsibilities for safeguarding their daughters' future, or more culpably kept them at home to act as unpaid companions and nurses. Yet, when the exceptions are noted and proper reservations made, the characteristic quality of young women in the early Victorian period seems to have been the realism with which they, as well as their parents, confronted the problem of matrimony.

There were practical as well as emotional reasons why young middle-class women should take seriously the question of finding a husband. What else had they to look forward to? For most of them there was no alternative to matrimony other than financial dependence as a spinster in another woman's household. A girl from a middle-class family was unlikely to have much money of her own; there were few occupations that would afford her a living and not many were attractive. Poverty and

propriety closed her in on both sides. Among the working classes (the adjective here has a particular significance), women had more economic freedom, even if it
was only freedom to earn low wages, for long hours, in
bad conditions. Work on farms, in cottage industries, in
cotton mills and other manufactures, above all, as a
servant in a private house, was freely available for the
girl from a poor family while she was waiting for marriage. Spackman calculated that in the England of 1814
there were more women than men engaged in manufacture; more than three times as many women as men in
domestic service. Work for women was not lacking in
Victorian Britain; only that kind of work which was
compatible with social respectability.

In the Bohemian world of the capital, from which
Surtees took his more lively female characters, class
divisions were less distinct and notions of respectability
more elastic. As a result there was a variety of ways in
which an unmarried girl of resource could keep herself
in tolerable comfort. When Lucy Sponge, deserted by
her scapegrace husband, asked Mr Romford despairingly
what she was to do, he observed expansively, 'set up a
register-office, start a school, teach dancing, give lessons
in riding, return to the stage—a hundred ways of making money in this great, rich metropolis'. Even though
some of these occupations needed some talent or capital,
he was probably right in thinking that the means were
there for a certain kind of woman to support herself in
London without sinking too low in the social scale. One
of Lucy's own friends, Betsy Shannon, at the age of 25,
made a passable living, we are told, by singing, dancing, and modelling. Yet these, particularly the last, were
scarcely genteel employments. More respectable and
utilitarian occupations, such as in shops and offices, were
by custom a masculine monopoly. Sarah Ellis, the author
of the widely read *Women of England*, published in 1838,
observed that 'it is a curious anomaly in the structure
of modern society that gentlemen may employ their
hours of business in almost any degrading occupation . . .
while, if a lady does but touch any article, no matter how

delicate, in the way of trade, she loses caste and ceases to be a lady'. Her own modest but practical proposals for enlarging the scope of respectable employment for women included millinery, engraving, and pattern-designing.

A dozen years after she made these suggestions the situation seemed no better. In 1853 the intellectual Margaretta Grey, sister of John Grey of Dilston and aunt of Josephine Butler, examined in her own rigorous fashion the historical reasons for the limited range of opportunities open to middle-class women. She attributed it mainly to the growth in the nation's wealth and population, which had resulted in 'a spurious refinement that cramps the energy and circumscribes the usefulness of women in the upper classes of society'. A lady, she observed sarcastically, to be such, must be only a lady. She was victim of prosperity and snobbery. The increase in servants debarred her from the kitchen, garden, dairy, still-room, and poultry-yard. The greater numbers and professionalism of doctors had diminished the traditional female responsibilities for nursing, physicking, and mid-wifery, which once had been carried out as a matter of course by middle-class housewives and their daughters. In the commercial sphere she thought that the opportunities open to women had also declined. 'Retail businesses that in my early years were managed, in whole or in part, by women' had been taken over by men. In proportion as the business and mercantile classes had grown in wealth and status, they themselves had erected social barriers against the participation of their womenfolk in work which produced that wealth.[1]

Surtees agreed with both these ladies. Like Miss Grey he considered that there had been an actual deterioration in the general domestic competence of middle-class women since the eighteenth and early nineteenth centuries. In this earlier period, he once argued, girls from such families had at least learned practical household management. Even if their interests were confined to 'domesticity, pickling, preserving, and pressing people to eat' and their conversation apt to run on 'corded petticoats and patent mangles', these at any rate were all useful matters. Since then 'a new era sprang up, which banished everything in the shape of utilitarianism, and taught the then rising generation that the less they knew of domestic matters, the finer ladies they would be'. It is true that by the time he wrote *Ask Mamma*, in which these reflections appear, there was beginning to emerge an altered attitude among the public at large to what Lord Stanley in 1856 called women's 'claim for more extended freedom of action'. His remark was prompted by the national interest in the work of Florence Nightingale during the Crimean War. Despite the remarkable publicity given to her achievements, however, the practical consequences of her example were slow in coming. Even the celebrity of one unusual woman was not enough to change immediately the prejudices and practices of generations.

The conventional education provided for middle-class girls did little to equip them for economic independence. The defect seized on by most critics was its haphazard, shallow nature. There was no framework of knowledge; no intellectual rigour. The best education, probably, was that received by girls like Emily Shore and Florence Nightingale, taught at home by a scholarly father in the company of their brothers. In the nature of things, such parents were rare. The mere presence of a liberal-minded, intellectual father was not in itself a guarantee of an enlightened education. The upbringing of Mary Gladstone, the prime minister's daughter, was cruelly described by Lucy Masterman. 'Her mind was kept like a kind of domestic pet, to be fed upon literary tit-bits.' Surtees does not attempt to portray a girls' school from within, but his comments on the products of such schools show that he shared the opinion of contemporary critics. The Yammerton girls in *Ask Mamma*, for example,

were very pretty, and very highly educated—that is to say, they could do anything that is useless—play, draw, sing, dance, make wax flowers, bead-stands, do decorative gilding and crochet work; but as to knowing how many ounces there are to a pound of tea, or how many pounds of meat a person should eat in a day, they were utterly, entirely, and most elegantly, ignorant.

They could all, he adds contemptuously, reel off the dates of every British royal reign and name the chief towns in the kingdom, but none of them could write a letter without a copy or were reliable in their spelling.

It is almost as though he were writing with Mrs Ellis's book open in front of him at page 336 where she says that 'our young ladies are made acquainted while at school, with the dates of most of the leading events in history, with the years when certain kings began to reign, and the precise time of their holding the reins of government'. Her criticisms, however, were that these facts were merely imprinted on the adolescent memory by a variety of ingenious methods, 'without the mind being in any way enlarged, or enlightened by the reception of them'. Yet despite the critics and the existence of a few good schools, conventional middle-class education for girls continued largely unchanged during Surtees' lifetime. The parents who paid for that education must have believed in its value for preparing their girls for entry into society since the demand seemed to be increasing. Day schools for girls being comparatively rare, the effect was mainly seen in the multiplication of boarding schools, especially in towns claiming to be particularly smart or salubrious. It is said that in 1836 there were at least a hundred private schools for girls in Brighton alone. Whatever their worth, and inevitably they varied in quality, they were not cheap. Surtees makes Major Yammerton send his girls to a finishing school at Westbourne Grove kept by the celebrated Miss Featherey, who for £200 a year, or as near £200 as she could get, 'taught them all the airs and graces'. The major had his three daughters charged as two. Even so, £400 per annum was a good middle-class income for a whole family. Major Guineafowle's three daughters went to a seminary in Maida Vale which charged 50 guineas a year with extras that might amount to as much again. Twenty years earlier, the cost of sending Belinda Jorrocks to a school in Bromley was at the Featherey level—£200 per annum 'and upward'—though whether the difference was due to a decline in the living expenses between the 1830s and 1850s or the superiority of the Bromley establishment is not clear. As far as one can judge, these fictional examples from the novels give a realistic indication of the range of school fees a parent would have to meet in this period. Extras, however, could be costly, and the more pretentious the school, or possibly the lower the basic fee, the more onerous they were likely to be. An article in the *Ladies' Journal* for 5 June 1847, for instance, assumes a figure of 150 guineas per annum for pupils at 'a first-rate establishment' with extras amounting to a further £50. In spite of all that the critics said, the British middle classes were clearly prepared to spend an increasing amount on their daughters' education. For many families it must have represented a considerable burden.

It was probably financial considerations that made a private governess more attractive than a boarding school. Where there were three or four girls to be educated, a governess at a salary between £25 and £50 per annum, even allowing for the cost of her board and lodging, represented a substantial saving. It seems generally agreed by social historians that it was more usual at this period even for middle-class girls to be educated at home rather than sent away to school. The daughters of the aristocracy were almost invariably kept at home and probably those of the gentry too. The great Nimrod, in a sketch of 'The Sporting Gentleman', wrote in his customary authoritative style that the daughters of such a man would be educated at home by a governess and other instructors, meaning presumably the occasional tutor brought in from outside for specialized subjects. The father, he continued ominously, 'is too good a judge to send them to a boarding-school, having been let into some of the proceedings of those seminaries as they are called—and not inaptly, inasmuch as they are the seed-plots of vice—by his wife'. What vices he had in mind he did not reveal; one must assume that it was something more than the spitefulness and bullying from which even family life is not exempt.[2]

Whether in school or at the hands of a private governess, however, the education given was likely to be equally
shallow, since the greater personal attention which a
governess could give was offset by her inability to teach
effectively all the subjects which her employer was likely
to expect. For who were the teachers and governesses?
For the most part products of the same system who had
failed to get married and had to support themselves
in some other way. It is true that a growing number of
women were making a good income for themselves by
writing. Some, like the Countess of Blessington and Caroline Norton, owed their literary reputation to their social
position; others, like Charlotte Yonge, Margaret Oliphant,
and Frances Trollope, to their native talent, industry, and
determination. Besides the fashionable and the gifted
were many forgotten female hacks who supplied the expanding market for popular fiction of the Gothic horror
or sentimental description. Yet authorship was not, any
more than today, a profession in the sense of a remu-
nerative occupation needing only preliminary training
and reasonable application. A relatively small number of
women, through luck or perseverance, found a profitable
niche in literature, but for the rest 'the only field at present
open for what is considered lady-like employment', wrote
Mrs Ellis, 'is that of educating the young'.

In effect, conventional middle-class education fitted
girls for only two things—finding a husband or teaching
other girls. As long as the undiscriminating demand from
parents for the current superficial girls' education was
more than matched by the supply of superficially educated young women offering themselves as teachers, little
educational improvement could be expected. It was a
desperately over-crowded and ill-paid profession. To call
it a profession at all is an exaggeration. Teaching girls
was an employment for amateurs; and not very gifted
ones at that. From this came its other deplorable features—low wages, low status, and lack of security. The
private governess was a stock figure for pity or contempt
in Victorian society. There was indeed a fortunate minority: governesses in wealthy households who formed

their own little society in London and often remained on lifelong terms of friendship with their former charges, governesses who married their widowed employers or bachelor friends of the family. Yet nobody in his senses would have held out these rare examples as inducements to enter the teaching profession. Becoming a governess usually reduced a girl's chances of getting married to a point where it could no longer be a reasonable expectation. As an occupation it was not so much an acceptable alternative to matrimony as an awful reminder of what might happen if she did not get married. To become a governess was for the ordinary middle-class girl a species of social emigration.

II

Given that there was no satisfactory alternative, husband-hunting in the social classes which Surtees describes in his novels was a serious business. Given also that social conventions limited the freedom of contact between the sexes, it was a business which needed the assistance of older people. Surtees' interest in the subject runs through all his fictional writing; and his comments are all of a piece. Woman is the hunter; man the prey. At the head of chapter xcvi in *Plain or Ringlets* there is a vignette by Leech which is perhaps the most cynical of his many illustrations to the Surtees novels. It shows a lady in riding habit holding a small body aloft in the traditional attitude of a huntsman at the scene of the kill, when he displays the limp corpse of the fox before casting it down to the hounds. The tiny body, however, is not a fox but a young man. The bridal orange-blossom, explains the author in the text alongside, is the fox's brush of female life.

He generalizes on this theme in innumerable other passages. It is a sport in which the game is plentiful, the hunters numerous and not too particular. There is nothing, he observes (*Tom Hall*, ch. xxix), in the shape of a man that is not acceptable to some woman; and few women are without allies in their pursuit of their quarry. One might as well, runs another dictum, try to restrain a cat from mousing as woman from match-making. Women have a real pleasure in the chase and, ominously for the other sex, they will always combine to catch a man. Their passion for the sport is so intense that they play at mentally appropriating men, even though they know their chances are remote—'it is their castle-building in the air'. Appropriation, however, indicates rivalry; and the art of the huntress is not only in running down the victim but heading off the rest of the pack. The competitive instinct affects even minor social relations. The overpowering Mrs Flummocks in *Handley Cross*, known irreverently as the Crusher, adjusts her degrees of courtesies according to the presence or absence of danger for her three marriageable (but so far unmarried) daughters. To the Bowerbanks, who also had nubile female offspring, she simply inclines her head. To little, old Miss Gaby, who could in no way interfere with her matrimonial plans, she graciously extends her fingertips.

There are endless little touches like these, as though the subject was one of universal observation. Ladies who eye a man with secret favour run him down in public in order to depreciate his market-value in the estimation of other women. If the quarry is a really rare and valuable prize, the chase is kept up even when, in sporting language, all is over bar shouting. The experienced Mrs Blunt of *Tom Hall* encourages Lord Heartycheer's infatuation with her daughter Angelena even after she arrives at a firm understanding with young Tom, on the sage principle that it is always advisable to have a second string in the field. She knows her own sex and fears that 'such an unwonted prize as Tom Hall would be fought for even up to the very church door'. On the other hand, it is clearly the duty of prudent parents to discourage suitors with neither present means nor hopeful prospects. Miss Watkins, to further whose virginal aspirations Mr Romford was invited to Dalberry Lees, had up to that point only received 'two or three indifferent offers—a curate, a cornet, and a nibble from a count, or a person who called himself one—though some said he was only a courier'. Two young men on the lowest rung of their careers and a dubious foreigner could only be regarded, from a common-sense point of view, as non-starters in the matrimonial stakes.

Surtees had proffered a similar list of undesirable suitors in an article he had written a few years earlier for *Ainsworth's Magazine* entitled 'Thoughts on Fortune Hunting'. Though no more than an amusing pot-boiler, it contains some characteristic reflections and phrases. Among what he styled 'detrimentals of all sorts', namely young men who were obviously ineligible but kept dangling to allure higher game, he singled out 'foot-soldiers, curates, sucking lawyers'. The presence of curates in both lists confirms their position at the bottom of the matrimonial field. Contemporaries would have endorsed Surtees' selection. In a lively sketch written in 1841, the famous authoress Mrs Gore depicts a débutante mentally assessing the marital value of a strange young man who is about to ask her to dance. He is probably, she thinks pessimistically, either a plain John Smith, or an ensign in an infantry regiment, or a bank clerk, or a clergyman's younger son. For a young woman without such powers of instant penetration and lacking a mother to give her guidance, the presence of a chaperone was invaluable. An experienced chaperone, according to Mrs Gore, was a diligent reader of the *Peerage*, the *Baronetage*, and *Burke's Landed Gentry*, learned in family histories and genealogies, replete with society gossip, and furnished with means of her own for discovering the incomes and expectations of every young man who came near her charge. In return for these indispensable services, the chaperone enjoyed a modest addition to her income, a respectable position in society, and a pleasant round of social engagements.[3]

At the top of the list of eligible young men were, of course, heirs to titles and estates. The English system of primogeniture, which elevated the elder son at the cost of depressing both the fortunes and social status of his brothers and sisters, contributed to the cut-throat nature of the marriage market. Elder sons were necessarily few in number compared with the serried ranks of unmarried daughters. In 1835 the puritanical mind of Professor Raumer was shocked by the perusal of a pamphlet on primogeniture which depicted in stark terms the corrosive effect of this institution on relations within English society as a result of

the competition for high prizes in marriage; the intrigues and manoeuvres of mothers to catch elder sons and to keep younger sons at a distance from their daughters . . . Hence arises the noble science of husband-catching. The more generous and amiable half of the human race is transformed into baits with which to catch heirs.

He was sensible enough, however, to see that this picture was too highly coloured to be totally convincing. Radical critics of primogeniture had an interest in ascribing a multitude of evils to that aristocratic institution. There were many other reasons, social as well as economic, why the problem of finding suitable husbands for their daughters occupied the minds of Victorian parents.

As with other game, it was well known that some venues were likely to yield better results than others. London enjoyed a position of acknowledged supremacy in this respect. Annually during the London season crowds of young people from good families were on parade. London was where girls 'came out' and young men came into society. Yet even here there were limitations. London, opined the knowledgeable Mrs Pringle in *Ask Mamma* (ch. xxvi), is 'only the cover for finding the game in; and the country the place for running it down'. The sentiment is clearly Surtees' own since he repeats it in his own person in the first chapter of *Plain or Ringlets*. 'London is a capital cover to find the game in; but the country is the place to run it down.' London was too big; too distracting; it offered too many possibilities and too many rivals. In the country there was more leisure; more opportunity to concentrate on the individual of one's choice; more favourable surroundings in which to bring matters to a head. Spas and watering places combined the advantages of both town and country. Just as useful as the country, Surtees observes at the start of *Plain or Ringlets*, are the 'sauntering, simpering watering-places' where young people could not help meeting each other and where an attachment must either lead on to a formal engagement or be ended by one of the parties leaving the field for fear of being caught. This was not a peculiar view. Dickens in *Sketches by Boz* was evidently of the same mind. The two unfortunate Misses Maplesones (*Tales*, ch. i) 'had been at different watering-places for four seasons; they had gambled at libraries, read books in balconies, sold at fancy fairs, danced at assemblies, talked sentiment—in short, they had done all that industrious girls could do —and all to no purpose'. That indefatigable publicist for spas, Dr Granville, wrote with typical early-Victorian lack of reticence, of their special fitness 'to promote and forward matrimonial schemes', and authoritatively advised that 'prudent mammas, who are anxious to see their daughters speedily and well settled in the world, had better look to "the Spas of England" '.

Such places seemed designed by nature and by man to promote the biological scheme of things; which was perhaps the reason why they were increasing so rapidly in the early nineteenth century. A small society, congregated for mutual entertainment in one spot, following a common round of leisure activities, made incidental encounters inevitable and social informality an obligation. The Victorian vogue for picnics, for example, encouraged a delightfully unceremonious mingling of the sexes. Surtees has two picnics in *Plain or Ringlets* and devotes a chapter to each. Balls and dances could bring to a conclusion what had been started in more alfresco surroundings. When Mrs Somerville (alias Lucy Glitters) declared on one occasion that 'everyone knows that the real business of a ball is either to look out for a wife, to look after a wife, or to look after somebody else's wife', she was only expressing with her usual candour a sentiment which applied equally with the role of the sexes reversed.

There were of course dangers in popular resorts. Matrimony was a two-handed game, and spas and watering places by their nature attracted that well-known species of male predator, the fortune-hunter. At Cheltenham, according to Grantley Berkeley, strange men frequently put in an appearance in this period with more resounding social claims and even more hollow antecedents than the unfortunate William Heveland ADC who created such a flutter among the ladies of Handley Cross; until it was discovered that the impressive initials stood for Assistant Drainage Commissioner. Those who came to such resorts to seek a wife however, were not all rogues and impostors; or at least, only to some extent. Most were simply men with not quite enough to live on comfortably who were on the look-out for a wife who could assist them in attaining the standard of comfort to which they would like to become accustomed. Facey Romford, who had at least one eye cocked for a likely heiress, declared that 'a thousand a year will draw men from all the corners of the earth'. The novels contain several others of this particular species. The most amiable, perhaps, is Admiration Jack, otherwise Mr Bunting, in *Plain or Ringlets*. He is young, gay, and handsome, with a disarming faculty for imagining himself in love, and his only serious blemish is a tendency to represent his unproductive scrublands and dilapidated shooting-box in Renfrewshire as a baronial Scottish estate complete with castle.

A more elderly and shabbier specimen is Major Guineafowle in *Tom Hall*, who, having been left a widower at an early age, is determined to try his luck a second time— 'passing for a bachelor or otherwise, as circumstances might favour'. Packing his three daughters off to boarding school, he goes the rounds 'from watering-place to bathing-place, and from bathing-place back to watering-place . . . always keeping his weather eye open for an heiress or a widow'. As a rule the characteristic inquisitiveness of the female sex uncovered the existence of his daughters and the non-existence of his landed wealth in time to upset his successive courtships; but in the end he is successful in catching, on the rebound from yet another disappointing affair, 'the once capital but then slightly waning beauty, Miss Longmaide, with her fortune of sixty thousand pounds'. The fortune turns out to be only an estimated share of an estate firmly under the control of trustees. Yet at least the major knew this beforehand, whereas his fond bride did not learn that she was acquiring three stepdaughters until after the wedding. For the cynical Surtees such deceits and stratagems were all part of the game.

The story of the second Mrs Guineafowle also illustrates the convention that where there are several daughters to be disposed of, the rule of seniority—almost, one might say, a female version of the law of primogeniture —enjoyed a certain status. Mrs Guineafowle, as much from self-interest as from magnanimity, took charge of her stepdaughters as soon as they were out of school, resolved to marry them off before the first of her own rapidly appearing brood came on the market. Having had a good deal of personal experience in such matters, and having been taken in once herself, she proves dextrous in mustering a strong field of candidates, bringing them to the declaratory stage, and rigorously scrutinizing their material prospects. Only the high, not to say excessive, standards demanded by her snobbish husband foil her efforts. When, therefore, the eldest of her own dark-haired beauties is old enough to enter the field, she warns the three blonde daughters of the first marriage that having had their opportunities, 'they must not interfere with Laura'.

The presence of several unmarried elder sisters was a decided handicap to a girl. Not only did they constitute possible rivals but their mere existence cast doubts on the ability of her father to come down with something handsome for the younger girls. On the other hand, it was not in human nature for the junior ladies to wait indefinitely. The head-start allowed by convention to the eldest daughter might be very short indeed. When the returned Australian convict Peter Corcoran, alias Granby Fitzgerald, in *Mr Romford*, invites Willy Watkins to his home, 'the eldest and most presuming of his daughters' was given only two clear days in which to capture him: a feat which she accomplishes with ease. Less unscrupulous families with less presuming daughters no doubt gave a more reasonable latitude.

III

In Surtees' novels the theme of husband-hunting is recurrent to the point of monotony. It is not an elevating subject even when one remembers that he was an inveterate satirist. Yet it is difficult to believe that he was doing much more than treating a well-known aspect of society in a way that would be amusing as well as recognizable for his readers. Courtship ending in marriage is the stuff of most novels. The conventional emphasis is on the active role of the male. Surtees simply inverts the convention and points, with a total lack of sentiment or idealism, to the active role of the female. Perhaps for that reason *Ask Mamma* and *Plain or Ringlets*, novels which are devoted almost exclusively to this theme, are more appreciated by women than by men. In such matters they are the more realistic sex.

Surtees was at least consistent in his views. In his article on 'Fortune Hunting', written some fifteen years earlier, he expressed in a more explicit manner the same views that emerge more pervasively in these two 'society' novels. Women, he argues, are quite as mercenary as men, though more devious; and marriages arranged by them are as calculating as in any other society in Europe.

We laugh at the French for their method of conducting matrimonial affairs by the mutual arrangement of parents: but really we think it infinitely better than the English . . . In England we do exactly the same thing as the French, with the hypocritical pretence that the girl has free choice. We all know that, with the exception of the daughters of labourers and those who live by the sweat of their brow, all girls, at least all girls worth catching, are regularly drilled and tutored on the subject of matrimony.

He does not go so far as to assert that all marriages are
concluded on the market basis of accepting the wealthiest bidder. His contention is that girls were trained to
look upon marriage as an enterprise in which calculation
was at least as important as affection.

It may be objected that this insistence on the predatory nature of women is at variance with the traditional
stereotype of the early-Victorian girl as an innocent,
submissive creature—'a pure ethereal being', in Surtees'
mocking description, 'a sort of compound of love, sentiment, and omelette *soufflée'*. One may doubt whether
the paradox is more than the discrepancy that usually
exists between the accepted ideals of society and the
unregenerate behaviour of the human beings who
compose it. The ideal of submissive selflessness was
certainly present. The burden of Mrs Ellis's book on the
Women of England is that girls should be kind and considerate inside and outside the family circle; they should
obtain their influence through unselfish devotion rather
than by assertion of their personality. It would argue a
singular faith in the power of moral exhortation to think
that this, or any other improving work, had much effect
on the actions of young Victorian women. Even when
accepted intellectually, ideals are apt to break down when
interests and passions are involved.

Undoubtedly, when compared with Continental society, English girls had a reputation for being puritanical
and unsophisticated, or, in more discourteous language,
for prudery and lack of polish. There was wide agreement
that French women, for example, were more vivacious
and more adept in the art of pleasing men. At the
Congress of Vienna, according to Lady Shelley, English
women were mocked for their prudery and vulgarity.
Their habit of discouraging elaborate compliments from
men, which at home gained them respect, at Vienna
seemed merely ridiculous. Despite Lady Shelley's fear
that exposure to Continental ways after 1815 would corrupt English womanhood, the same differences were
being noted twenty years later. Professor Raumer observed in 1835 that Englishwomen were less affected,

less concerned with their clothes and general appearance, than their Continental sisters in Germany and France. One sign of the growing vogue for simplicity and artlessness was the decline in the use of cosmetics since the early years of the century. Cyrus Redding could remember the innumerable varieties of cosmetics, including not only rouge but a heavy white face-paint, which had been popular in smart English society up to about 1805 but fifty years later had been almost entirely forgotten. By the middle of the century the use of rouge by young women, though not unknown, was an expedient to be employed with the greatest discretion. That terrible coquette Miss Hazey, for example, wishing to make a particular impression on Facey Romford at the breakfast table, endeavoured to counteract the yellowish pallor in her cheeks which she had observed on waking, by applying 'the slightest possible touch of rouge'. Judging from advertisements in women's magazines, the more conventional aids to beauty were oil for the hair, 'pearl dentifrice' for the teeth, rosewater, lavender water, and a variety of patent preparations, for the complexion.

Behind the fashionable simplicity and maidenliness which were the marks of a lady, there were certain artifices. A small appetite was held to be a sign of refinement. To Mrs Flather in *Hillingdon Hall*, for example, it was an article of faith that men disliked 'guzzling girls'. Young ladies dining in company therefore were counselled to make a hearty lunch at midday so that they could appear fragile and ethereal in the evening, able to deploy their powers of entertainment while their coarser male companions addressed themselves to the food. Other qualities regarded as suitable for young women were an excessive sensibility to the pathetic and the picturesque, and a readiness to be shocked by whatever was thought to require such a reaction. Neither was a difficult accomplishment: it is always easier to simulate emotions than to conceal them. Lady Dorothy Nevill at the end of her long life wrote scathingly of the affectations of feminine weakness and sensitivity which prevailed when she was a girl in the 1830s and 1840s.

'Nevertheless, in spite of this pose, they were much the same then as today in the essential qualities of their sex. Then, as now, man was their quarry.'[4]

There are obvious contrasts of dress, speech, and manners between the early-Victorian period and the generations which preceded and followed; but there is little to suggest that women at that time, young or old, had fundamentally different natures. The normal human instincts and emotions were there, even though convention required their concealment. Mrs Ellis let slip more perhaps than she intended when she wrote concerning women that 'it is seldom regarded as consistent with that delicacy which forms so great a charm in their nature, that they should act out to their full extent all the deep feelings of which they are capable'. Some of those feelings are indicated by what Florence Nightingale wrote during the rebellious period of her girlhood in 1850:

Women go about maudling to each other and preaching to their daughters that 'women have no passions' . . . If the young girls of the 'higher classes' who never commit a false step, whose justly earned reputations were never sullied . . . were to speak and say what are their thoughts employed on, their *thoughts* which alone are free, what would they say? They seek a companion for their every thought . . . they see themselves engaged with him in stirring events . . . fancy compensates itself by endless interviews and sympathies . . . and you say 'she is not susceptible, women have no passion'.

Frances Grenfell, on her own confession, went further than this. She lay in bed in Nice thinking of Charles Kingsley, whom she already called husband, and imagining 'delicious nightery' in each other's arms. Miss Nightingale herself, though she came to despise the emotionalism of women and the notion of romantic love, was honest enough to recognize that she too possessed what she called a 'passional nature' which would have been satisfied by marriage.[5]

When emotions as strong as these were frustrated, the effect could be physically obvious. Frances Grenfell and Charles Kingsley fell in love soon after they first met in 1839. The marriage did not take place for another four years, mainly because of the opposition from her family. Sent abroad to keep her apart from her penniless under-graduate lover, Miss Grenfell not only poured out her emotions in a series of passionate, unposted letters (which she kept for the rest of her life) but fell victim to a variety of nervous symptoms including hysteria, headaches, palpitations, and alarming loss of weight. Only when her family became frightened for her health did they finally give way. Looking at the photographs of the middle-aged Mrs Kingsley, heavy-featured, forbiddingly clad in voluminous dark clothes up to her neck, stiffly posed, it is not easy to imagine the vulnerable, emotional creature she was in the 1840s. Victorian photography hides as much as it reveals. Yet any preconception that Victorian women 'had no passion' can hardly survive much read-ing of the period.

Surtees, being primarily an observer of manners rather than an analyst of emotions, never attempted to describe the feelings of a woman in love. Belinda Jorrocks' resist-ance to her aunt's desire that she should marry Captain Doleful is a creditable display of firmness and loyalty but that is all. The one good and attractive girl in the novels genuinely in love with her future husband, she is never-theless—apart from this one brief episode—a colourless figure. Surtees is never tired, on the other hand, of re-counting the little artifices, known if not practised by all women, which their sex employs to catch the eye of the impressionable male. Victorian dress, both in what it concealed and what it revealed, lent itself admirably to this purpose. There are frequent allusions in his books to the deliberate displays of legs and lingerie when women are getting into a carriage or out of a railway compart-ment, descending a staircase, or even merely seating themselves in a chair. Emma Flather, for example, 'had a good foot and ankle, pulled her stockings well up, and didn't mind showing her legs a little'. Fancy-dress balls, which gave temporary licence for showing even more, were (we are given to understand) welcomed by young ladies conscious of possessing neat legs and feet. The abbreviated knee-length skirts, which were the traditional stage-garb of gypsy girls and Swiss shepherdesses, were particularly popular. There were, after all, professional examples of the attractions of the well-formed leg in the sketches of famous ballet dancers in a variety of lively poses and exiguous costumes which frequently appeared in women's illustrated journals. Even in the more restricted surroundings of the drawing-room, there was room for a little opportunistic dexterity. When the Empress of Morocco (the tanner's wife in *Tom Hall*) has her tête-à-tête with Lord Heartycheer (ch. xvi), she 'placed her beautiful foot on the broad fender' and slightly raised her velvet dress as though innocently enjoying the warmth of the fire. A 'polished steel fender' was similarly exploited by that ambitious lady's maid, Miss Willing, to ensnare Mr Pringle senior in *Ask Mamma*.

Fugitive glimpses of what was below were balanced by more lavish revelations of what was above. Few Victorian girls could have been unconscious of the attractions to the male eye of their shoulders and breasts; and Victorian evening toilette was not illiberal in the opportunities it afforded them. Of Emma Flather in *Hillingdon Hall*, for example, we are told that, when in her evening toilette, she exposed so much of her admittedly presentable shoulders 'as to make bystanders fear she might be enacting Mrs Eve'. From Leech's illustrations to the novels it is clear that she was not alone in this dangerous degree of exposure. When low-cut dresses were fashionable, it would have required considerable self-denial on the part of well-endowed young ladies not to have made the most of their physical assets. Lucy Glitters, to take another of Surtees' handsome young girls, knew perfectly well that gentlemen would admire her figure 'not the less for being finely developed'. It may be objected that Lucy is not only an imaginary character but depicted as an experienced woman of the world. Yet in real life Frances Grenfell, an innocent, well-brought-up young woman from a good family who at one time contemplated entering a religious order, was distressed by her increasing thinness as she pined for her lover, because 'I know men like a nice round figure'.

Surtees, writing mainly for a masculine readership, is disarmingly frank on such matters. According to Nimrod, sporting country gentlemen usually had handsome wives since, being accustomed to look out for the 'points of the brute creation', they did not ignore them when selecting a wife from the females of the higher species. Surtees' verbal portraits of women bear this out. He is as attentive to 'the points' of attractive women as he is to the details of their dress. Of Emma Flather he tells us that 'she was a fine girl—straight as a milkmaid, fine drooping shoulders . . . splendid bust, tolerably small waist, and good feet and ankles'. Rosa McDermott in *Plain or Ringlets* (ch. ii) is described as being 'in the full bloom of womanhood, of medium height, plump and fair' with a 'rather prematurely developed form' that suggested she was a couple of years older than she really was. In the *Analysis of the Hunting Field*, the three 'blooming, buxom' Cottonwool daughters are 'fine, full-grown, full-limbed, ripe, luscious-looking, fair-haired girls'. A man did not need to be a fox-hunter to appreciate their attributes; and they on their side were aware of the effect they made on the males, since they had 'all the accomplishments of ogling, worsted-making, dancing and flirting'.

What nature withheld, the dressmaker could supply. As Surtees mused in chapter x of *Hillingdon Hall*, 'It's wonderful what miracles dress accomplishes. We have seen girls who were really quite plain, expand into beauties under the hands of a good milliner. "*Expand*" we may well say, for they generally make them look about half as big again as they are.' Emma Flather, whose appearance at Donkeyton Castle prompts this reflection, did not need filling up—'fining down would have been more to the purpose with her'. Even so, she gives an extra tug to her stays and reduces her waist by an inch or so to emphasize what was above. Similarly, Mrs Guineafowle, anxious to ensure that Laura makes a suitable impression on young Tom Hall, orders a special dress from London with the bodice made tight, 'setting off to advantage Laura's beautiful figure'. To make her even more alluring, she arranges for her three younger sisters to come to the dinner table 'in various coloured rather shabby merinos'.

In the presence of these sartorial gins and mantraps, it is understandable that the duke of Donkeyton took the precaution of presenting his own son with a copy of Lord Chesterfield's *Letters to His Son*, having previously underlined in red ink the passage recommending young men to attach themselves to married women rather than their daughters. Yet it would be a mistake to read into Surtees' satire a strain of positive antifeminism. The writer who could create such characters as Lucy Glitters and Miss de Glancey was hardly a misogynist. With four sisters, a wife, and two daughters, Surtees had more than enough material at hand for studying women, and his general attitude is more one of admiration for their shrewdness and skill in the conduct of life. His novels are merely sermons at large on a text he puts into the mouth of that sagacious woman Mrs Pringle in *Ask Mamma*.

The stupidest woman that ever was born, is better than the cleverest man in love-affairs. In fact, no man is a match for a woman until he's married—not all even then. The worst of young men is, they never know their worth until it is too late—they think the girls are difficult to catch, whereas there is nothing so easy.

With their constant emphasis on the superiority of the opposite sex, the novels might have been designed as educational manuals for young men. Whether in his day they read them in that spirit, or would have taken any notice of them if they had, is another question. Surtees dedicated *Plain or Ringlets* to his only son Anthony, then 13 years old. A curious choice, one might think—unless it was silently proffered to him as a repository of worldly wisdom, a kind of latter-day Chesterfield's *Letters*, as he grew to manhood.

Had the younger Surtees extended his reading by looking at his father's 1843 article on 'Fortune Hunting', he would not have received much more illumination than was already afforded by the novels. Despite the title, that article dwelt on the difficulties rather than the opportunities confronting the young man who sought this way of setting himself up in life. Women, he would have read, were as shrewd as men and more unscrupulous. Their 'fortunes' were rarely as substantial in reality as they were held out to be in prospect. Landed jointures tended to be tied up and encumbered with other burdens. Real money was more likely to be found among merchants and City people. A wealthy widow might seem a tempting target since she was more likely to be mistress of her own fortune. As against that, she was likely to be too worldly-wise and experienced to be easily caught. 'Widows without doubt are the noblest and wildest game.' In general, Surtees continued unhopefully, what was needed for successful fortune-hunting was impudence and a knowledge of human nature; but these were qualities which could not be taught. They were accomplishments that had little to do with ordinary scholastic attainments. The unspoken verdict was that in the battle of the sexes a young man entered the lists inadequately armed and needed time and experience before he could fight on level terms.

IV

It followed from this robust view of women that marriage would not necessarily be a one-sided relationship in which all the advantages were on the side of the man. Certainly the law gave the husband a paramount position in such matters as control of property and custody of children. Such statutory modifications as took place in this period—the Infant Custody Act of 1839 and the Divorce Act of 1857—were few in number and limited in effect. The real question, however, was how far the inequality of the law was softened in practice by the good sense of the parties concerned and the changing attitudes of public opinion. The legal structure of marriage was not, after all, a middle-class invention; it had evolved primarily under aristocratic and clerical influences. It is one of the paradoxes of Victorian social history that while the middle classes regarded themselves as the defenders of family values, it was liberal middle-class opinion that secured the reforms in the marriage laws, the improvements in girls' education, and the opening-up of careers for women, which were to undermine the whole institution of marriage.

On the other hand, the failure of the movement for women's rights to make much headway in this period suggests that dissatisfaction with that institution was less prevalent than is sometimes suggested. Most of the prominent and influential women of the time were opposed to an active campaign for legislation on such matters. Harriet Martineau repudiated the doctrine of abstract rights and thought progress would best be made through the example set by women of ability and character. Florence Nightingale wrote in 1858 that she was 'brutally indifferent to the wrongs or the rights of my sex' and in her *Notes on Nursing* (1859) attacked the jargon about the 'rights of women'. If it is objected that these two ladies were spinsters (though that has never acted as a bar to feminist agitation), there is the example of the authoress and society celebrity Caroline Norton in the earlier and of Mrs Oliphant, the novelist, in the later part of the period, who both accepted that nature had given women a different role to that of men. Miss Nightingale thought that the secret of a successful marriage was for the wife to be treated as a person in her own right. That many Victorian husbands did treat their wives as 'persons' is amply illustrated by the biographies and letters of the period.

If, as some contemporary critics suggested, the activities of young middle-class women in such public causes as the anti-slavery campaign, the Anti-Corn Law League, the Temperance movement, and Chartism, not to say parish visiting, charitable bazaars, and attending scientific and philosophical meetings, were an indication as much of boredom with their ordinary life as of philanthropic or religious zeal, at least the energy was there.

Marriage for many, perhaps most girls, was a release from a restricted existence within the family circle. 'Ah, I've a *happy* home', sighed Angelena Blunt in *Tom Hall* (ch. xix), 'clasping her hands, and thinking with upturned eyes, what she would give to be away from it'. Marriage put a woman at the head of a household, and gave her a higher status in society. In her new sexual role she was more advantageously placed to manage her relationship with her husband than she had previously been, as a daughter, with her father and mother. Surtees put the matter with his usual cynicism. 'Most men—real men, we mean in contradistinction to boys—marry for quiet, whereas nine girls out of ten marry for the sake of being their own mistresses, and beginning to *racket.*' Whatever the law might say, marriage was a private and personal relationship in which character counted for more than anything else. The realities of Victorian marriages were decided in the last resort by human nature. One must presume that the proportion of strong-minded wives and complaisant husbands was much the same as in any other period; and Charles Kingsley could not have been the only one to think that 'wherever man and wife are really happy together, it is by ignoring and despising, not by asserting, the subordination of women to men, which they hold in theory'.

The stereotypes of the domineering Victorian husband and submissive wife find little support in the pages of Surtees. A long procession of middle-class married couples pass through his novels, and while the women vary considerably in temperament, they are all individuals and most of them more than a match for their husbands. Their world may be thought a narrow one. They are usually housewives with grown-up children and their business in life is the humdrum one of running their households, entertaining guests, managing their husbands, and marrying off their daughters. For most people, however, life is made up of little things; and within that confined sphere they led active and not altogether unsatisfactory—or unsatisfying—lives. Ennui may have afflicted their daughters; it does not seem to have been a characteristic of the mothers. Miss Nightingale and Miss

Martineau would not have been content with their existence; but fortunately for the stability of society and the
propagation of the race, most Victorian women did not
aspire to their peculiar eminence.

Some of Surtees' women are decidedly domineering.
In *Mr Romford* there are two such characters: Mrs Gilroy,
relict of 'me Oncle Gilroy', who is a virago able to strike
terror even into the redoubtable Facey, and Mrs Willy
Watkins, 'fair and stout, with a commanding presence,
and a very determined look about her—pushing, self-
asserting, doubtful sort of woman, who would push her
way if she could'. In *Hillingdon Hall* there is the overpowering Mrs Trotter who battles with Mrs Flather for
second place in the hierarchy of local society, first place
belonging as of right to the inhabitants of the Hall. 'Mrs
Trotter was of the masculine order: a great, tall, stout,
upstanding, black-eyed, black-haired woman, with a
strong, unturnable resolution; and a poor, little, hen-
pecked Jerry Sneak of a husband, who was of no more
account in the house than if no such being existed.' Her
forte was public life. She was a member of the Ladies
Anti-Corn Association, the Book Club, and the Ship-
wrecked Mariners Association; she presented prizes at
the local Sunday School; and acted as self-appointed
invigilator over the morals of the lower orders.

Another married woman who turned her energies into
public activities was, surprisingly, Mrs Jorrocks. In the
earlier Jorrocks novels she is painted in uniformly unpleasant colours, almost as though Surtees wants to
engage our sympathies for her unfortunate spouse. Her
pedigree being, in the language of the stud and kennel,
by a gentleman usher out of a lady's maid, she is cursed
with pretensions to, and a certain smattering of, gentility.
She has no children of her own, and all she does for her
niece Belinda is to try to force her into marriage with the
odious Captain Doleful. She is vain, selfish, jealous, and
bad-tempered; even Jorrocks, so great a man in both the
City and the hunting-field, is not master in his own house.
Yet this unpromising creature is not without certain
philanthropic instincts, even if they are not unmixed with

personal vainglory. Not content with modernizing and embellishing Hillingdon Hall and its grounds, according to her notions of what is smart, she takes in hand the village school. Her chief objection is to the dowdiness of the girls' dress, and with the aid of her London friend, Miss Slummers, she introduces a new school uniform of white jacket, scarlet petticoat, and black stockings with accessories in the form of horsehair bustles and beribboned straw hats. The effect may have been startling, but the intention is laudable—and all at her own expense, or at least that of her husband.

Another strong-minded woman, who briefly appears in *Ask Mamma*, is Mrs Rocket Larkspur, the fast wife of a 'good slow sort of gentleman-farmer'. She is all fire and bustle, wanting to manage everybody's affairs. Her husband had married her, it was supposed locally, 'out of sheer submission, because she had made a dead set at him'. In the same novel, and not far behind her in authoritativeness, is Mrs Yammerton, formerly the beautiful but impecunious Miss Winnington, who had snapped up Yammerton as soon as he had succeeded to his grandfather's estate. Different from these two only in the greater flexibility of her tactics is Mrs Jogglebury Crowdey, 'a fine, bustling, managing woman with large family for whom she exerted all her energies to procure desirable god-papas and mammas'. To forward these innocent aspirations she persuades her husband to take up hunting and will not let him abandon it, though he would much prefer to be wandering along hedgerows looking for saplings suitable for turning into walking-sticks.

Other wives are distinguished for the sly artfulness with which they triumph in any matrimonial clash of wills. Mrs Blunt, spouse of the formidable Colonel in *Tom Hall*, is one of them, though he is not an easy husband to manage since he possesses, along with his ruffian force of character, a certain rogue's shrewdness. Mrs Guineafowle in the same novel is another adept in man-management, besides enjoying undoubted physical advantages. She is tall and elegant while Mr G. is a dumpy little turkey-cock of a man. Even the more placid married ladies are not without spirit when provoked—witness plummy Mrs Bowderoukins in *Plain or Ringlets* when her husband brings home two hungry fox-hunters in the middle of her preparations for a grand dinner, or the obsequious spouse of the great Marmaduke Muleygrubs JP of Cockolorum Hall, when she is obliged to listen to the outrageous conversation of Mr Jorrocks.

Then there is Surtees' collection of widows, who more than bear out Mr Weller's advice to Sam. The most formidable is Mrs Brantinghame, who makes an unforgettable appearance in the final chapters of *Handley Cross*. As resourceful, experienced, and flinty-hearted as an old lawyer, she plays the suspicious Captain Doleful as though he were a fat trout, gently at first and then with increasing pressure until he lies gasping and terrified on the bank. The hooking of the dreadful Doleful is as cynically amusing an episode as any in all Surtees' novels. A second is Mrs Flather, the great rival of Mrs Trotter at Hillingdon, 'the undespairing widow of a clergyman' who is that dangerous creature, an apparently stupid and simple woman who is really cunning and deceitful. Finally there is Mrs McDermott, the youthful blonde who patrols the background of *Plain or Ringlets* with coolness and dexterity. She is the astute chaperone of her daughter, matching one suitor against another and eventually guiding her Rosa into what seems the most lucrative match. That done, she keeps her hand in by enticing Mr Boyston to the altar on her own account. Once remarried, moreover, she makes it cruelly clear who is going to rule the matrimonial roost. She cuts down on his drinking (not, it must be admitted, before time), improves his sartorial habits, and even threatens to borrow his hard-mouthed hunter to pull the coalcart. By the end of the book poor Jug's predicament seems hopeless.

Surtees' assemblage of wives and widows are not distinguished by either learning, wit, or charm. Any affection that may once have existed between them and their husbands has settled down into the jogtrot of middle age. They do not command our respect or invite our sympathy; they arouse no emotion other than occasional amusement. Yet some items stand to their credit. They are faithful to their husbands after their own fashion; they do their duty by their daughters; they have character and personality; and they have acquired a certain shrewdness in the affairs of life. In any matrimonial differences they usually contrive to get their own way. What they do not appear to be is meek, exploited, or oppressed.

THE MIRROR OF SOCIETY

I

While Surtees forfeits any claim to be ranked among the 'social novelists' of the period by what (to borrow Miss Nightingale's phrase) could be called his brutal indifference to the wrongs and rights of the poor, he deserves perhaps a cautious mention for the attention he gives to the domestic servant. After all, they were, as he pointed out, part of the working classes. They possibly did not regard themselves in that light and they are not alone in this. Socio-political historians too have generally neglected them in favour of the industrial proletariat of the towns. It is easy to see why. They did not form a separate political interest; they did not burn down their employers' houses, riot on the streets, petition parliament, join trade unions, or go on strike. Yet though they were politically quiescent, their social importance is considerable. Their sheer numbers are impressive. In England and Wales in 1841 they totalled 999,000: the second largest occupational group after agriculture, being slightly more than all those employed in manufacture and mining put together, and a third more than the fourth largest group, the general labourers. Indeed, if from the crude figure of $1\frac{1}{2}$ million for the agricultural industry as a whole are deducted farmers, graziers, gardeners, gamekeepers, and land-agents, the basic work-force of agricultural labourers numbered only 965,371. On this calculation the domestic servants in the middle of the century formed the largest distinct class of worker.

Their significance is not merely in their numbers. Alone of the labouring classes they lived and worked in their employers' household, in permanent and familiar contact with the classes to whom they ministered. This in itself casts a certain doubt on any concept of early-Victorian Britain as divided into two nations, the rich and the poor. It could scarcely have been irrelevant to the social history of the period that a million of the labouring classes were eating and sleeping in the houses of the well-to-do. Servants reflected the variety and complexity of the classes which employed them. There were enormous contrasts of wealth and status between the major-domo of a ducal establishment and an over-worked slavey in a London back-street. Servants aped the pretensions, imitated the social gradations, and copied the habits of those above them. Just as the domestic comforts of the prosperous depended on the existence of servants, so the life of servants was shaped by the households which employed them. In effect, they were a mirror-image of Victorian society.

A novelist of the period would have found it difficult to ignore them entirely. Jane Austen in her novels contrived to make them almost invisible; we know they are there but we scarcely ever catch a glimpse of them. Such cool indifference was becoming less common in the following generation. Everybody who was anybody had servants. They were a topic of universal interest—the problems of having them, the inconvenience of being without them, the difficulty of getting good ones, their many sins, their seldom virtues. It was a subject on which most well-to-do people had views because most of them had personal experience. For a satiric writer like Surtees it would have been a positive sacrifice to have abstained from such a topic. The sacrifice would have been even greater since he had little love for servants and took pleasure, one suspects, in dwelling on their defects. Mr Jorrocks' household presents in miniature his unflattering portrayal of the whole race. The boy Benjamin was a Cockney guttersnipe who would have been a useful recruit for Fagin's gang in *Oliver Twist*. Sharp, idle, and mischievous, he cheats and plunders his master at every turn, pilfers his food, reads his letters, rides his horse without leave, and in the country adds poaching to his town-bred vices. Betsy, the cook and general factotum (though she has a girl under her too lowly for further mention), contrives in the course of two novels to have a couple of illegitimate children. James Pigg, who fathers them, is a drunken, obstinate, rough-tongued north-countryman with no respect for his master or anybody else. His redeeming features (but these considerable in Surtees' eyes) are his practical sagacity, his independence, and his skill as a huntsman. He is entertaining as a character but hardly a model servant.

Prejudice apart, Surtees seems to have thought that the quality of servants was largely decided by market forces: the wealthier employers obtained the best, the less affluent had to be content with the leavings. The rich had no idea, he observes in *Handley Cross* (ch. xix), what the middle classes had to put up with in the way of servants. Even at this lower level, however, he distinguishes between the mediocre, the unsatisfactory, and the utterly incompetent. Fortunately for the misfits, unfortunately for their employers, people were always ready to recommend to others servants whom they would not dream of employing themselves. Newly-wed couples, he observes elsewhere, were particularly liable to be landed with domestics whom their friends had long been waiting to get rid of. For those unable or reluctant to make use of personal recommendations, there were two other courses open. They could advertise or apply to a domestic registry; both were daunting prospects. A provincial registry-office was a gossip-shop which gave the manageress a fund of information about the private habits of local families, thus enabling her to plant out her clients in positions best suited to their peculiar needs. It was in this way that Mrs Chatterbox, who was herself a cook before becoming the head of the registry office in *Tom Hall*, was able to foist the inebriated Mrs Hogslard on the unsuspecting Guineafowle household, she being one of those incompetents whom everybody had had once and nobody ever kept. The alternative was to advertise the vacancy. When Jorrocks tries to find a huntsman in this way he merely elicits a flood of illiterate and useless replies. Surtees amuses himself by offering us half a dozen choice samples. Nobody who had not had the experience could conceive, he observes, the kind of person that applied for any situation that was going, regardless of their suitability for it. Ploughmen would offer themselves as butlers; men who could not ride as coachmen.

Surtees' lash is wielded almost indiscriminately. Servants were unreliable; they got drunk; they stole; they betrayed confidences. It was useless to bribe them to secrecy; they kept the money and passed on the secret. Above all, they were lazy; and the higher their status, the less they did. In large establishments much of their time was spent in getting others to do their work. Most of them, he suggests, could do twice as much if only they were paid for it. Major Yammerton, who had a certain shrewdness in money matters, was a rare example of a middle-class employer who had decided that it was 'cheaper to pay one man the wages of one-and-a-half to do the work of two'. The only comparable character is Martha, the maid of all work of that formidable widow Mrs Brantinghame. 'For the wages of one servant and a half she did the work of three, eating only the victuals of one.' When dressed up in Miss Louisa's cast-off silk dresses, she could even play the part of an upper servant. Employers sufficiently hard-headed to be able to calculate so precisely the ratio of wages to work are, however, not conspicuous in the novels. Most of them fall into one of two categories. There are those who think that they can economize by paying low wages—and are indifferently served in consequence; and there are those who seem to regard servants primarily as an extension of their social status—and are even worse served. In Sir Harry Scattercash's notoriously slack household, for example, all the servants procured deputies to do the rough work; even the under-housemaid had an assistant. 'Lady Scattercash was a real lady and liked to have the credit of the house maintained, which of course can only be done by letting the upper servants do nothing.' She was, of course, only a would-be lady, being before her marriage Miss Spangles of the Theatre Royal.

In the *Analysis of the Hunting Field,* where he is writing seriously rather than satirically, Surtees modifies some of these views. 'It has long been a settled opinion of ours that high wages do not necessarily procure good servants.' Wealthy men could certainly outbid others, he explains, but they were not always good judges of character or in enough control of their establishments to know when they were being well served. That is a reasonable observation, but there is a touch of prejudice in the further suggestion that 'a place in a country Squire's house is generally looked upon by servants as the best situation'. Although in such households there was likely to be a stricter supervision by the master, he argues that this was something that 'no really honest servant will ever object to'. The compensation was that there was no need in such circumstances for underlings to curry favour with the upper servants as in large establishments. This no doubt was regrettable, but often true. Yet Surtees himself makes it clear that not all servants were honest or hard-working. Those who were not may well have preferred the idleness and favouritism of great households to the industriousness and integrity of the small. Perhaps the real moral was that bad employers made bad servants. Surtees' prejudice against the great aristocracy was certainly sweeping enough to include their retainers. Willing servants, he observed, were only to be found in small establishments; in the large the strict demarcation of duties, the universal dislike of doing anything that could be deemed another's work, the 'sacred right' of idleness 'that each newcomer is bound to preserve inviolate', all the restrictive practices of the upper servants, meant that the guest of a duke was likely to be less well served than the guest of a squire. In the households of the great, something not unlike a form of trade-unionism flourished unchecked.

One type of servant which incurred Surtees' particular dislike was the valet, the 'gentleman's gentleman' as they styled themselves. Clearly, to take one's own servant when visiting or travelling was a convenience in that it ensured personal service. It was also calculated to procure respect from the other domestics at inns and private houses. As the sapient Mrs Pringle observed to her hopeful offspring:

A valet is absolutely indispensable for a young gentleman. Bless you! you would be thought nothing of among the servants if you hadn't one. They are their masters' trumpeters. A valet, especially a French one, putting on two clean shirts a day, and calling for Burgundy after your cheese, are about the most imposing things in the lower regions.

There were other advantages in having a valet besides impressing the vulgar. Like a lady's maid, a valet on confidential terms with his employer could be an invaluable source of information about other families picked up in that gossip centre, the servants' hall. At an even higher level, an understanding between a valet and the lady's maid offered great advantages in any courtship. To quote Mrs Pringle again, in such a fortunate conjuncture, 'no man with an efficient, properly trained valet, need ever be catspawed or jilted, because the lady's maid would feel it a point of honour to let the valet know how the land lay, a compliment he would return under similar circumstances'. A valet, therefore, was a creature floating dextrously between two worlds, a little lower than his master but vastly superior, in his own eyes, to the common run of domestics.

Surtees, who disliked pretentiousness in anyone and thought that familiarity by a master bred insolence in a servant, called a valet's position 'the laziest of all lazy lives'. The two valets to whom he gives some space in the novels are both unsavoury characters. Each in his own way is a rogue exploiting the ignorance and inexperience of his youthful master. John Branfoote, nicknamed Tights, was 'a slangy, saucy Londoner': a sort of inferior and less amusing Sam Weller, who acts as groom and valet and is 'up to all the bad practices of both services'. Before being taken on by Tom Hall he had been in and out of innumerable situations, never amending his ways and never abashed by his inability to stay long in any employment. There was an even more disreputable history attached to the other valet. Born Jack Rogers, he had been first a circus hand and then a postboy. Seized with a desire to see the world, he sold his employer's horses and with the proceeds went off to the safety of France, where he learnt the language and grew a profusion of hair and whiskers. Returning ultimately to his native land in the guise of Jean Rougier, courier and valet, he was engaged by Mrs Pringle, who fondly imagined that his apparently incomplete command of English would be a barrier to any serious indiscretion while in her son's service.

Consequently, in discussing what he calls 'servitude' (an old-fashioned term that few other writers would have employed to indicate the state of being a servant), Surtees offers disciplinarian counsel. Masters, he says severely in *Mr Romford* (ch. xiv), should not give way to their men; and men should not presume on their masters. As it was, he admits, servants presumed a great deal. Though only some went so far as to be openly impertinent to their employers, 'few are totally free from it, and talk of their masters and mistresses as though they were something inferior to themselves'. Given the opportunity, some servants would tyrannize over the very people who provided them with a living. What a humiliation, he exclaims in *Mr Sponge* (ch. xxxvi), to pay a man £80 or £100 a year and find him in house, coals, and candles, only to be bullied by him, as poor Puffington was by his huntsman Richard Bragg and, added Surtees sadly, as most owners were who kept hounds. Almost as bad, though less detectable, was the maliciousness which servants sometimes showed when they wanted to revenge themselves for real or fancied slights. They would deny callers the house, spill soup or wine over their clothes when waiting at table, or play other tricks. Jean Rougier, for example, in a memorable scene in *Ask Mamma*, hid under the bed in his master's room in order to overhear the conversation of the inquisitive Misses Yammerton, and afterwards cruelly embarrassed Miss Clara by returning her dropped glove in the drawing-room, announcing at the top of his voice where he had

found it. Partridge, Mrs Brantinghame's borrowed butler in *Handley Cross* (ch. lxxix), puts a strong purgative
in the luncheon wine with distressing effects on Captain
Doleful's bowels at a critical point in his courtship. Compared with such spitefulness, little habits like maids' trying
on their mistresses' dresses, reading their love-letters, or
spying through the keyhole when they received callers,
seem almost forgivable.

Actual stealing by servants was a less amiable practice,
though one, if the novels are to be trusted, which was
widespread. Ruth Mustard, 'Dirtiest of the Dirty' in *Mr
Romford*, was an incorrigible thief, unblushing even when
detected; Mrs Holdsworthy in *Tom Hall* equally systematically though more carefully pilfers from the duke
of Gormanstone while employed as his housekeeper, and
is so adroit in evading suspicion that she is able to marry
the butler and retire to one of the duke's farms when her
service is over. Burlinson, the Watkins' butler in *Mr
Romford*, had once been in a noble household until the
pressure of his racing debts induced him to pawn his
master's plate—an excessive liberty which earned him a
period of incarceration in gaol. If we believe what Surtees
says in *Hillingdon Hall* (ch. xiv), even estate stewards
frequently took illicit commissions from tenants when
arranging a renewal of their leases.

Women servants, denied some of the usual perquisites
of men, had ways of their own for redressing the balance.
A lady's maid, we learn in *Ask Mamma* (ch. iv), could earn
a commission from dressmakers for guiding her mistress's custom to one establishment rather than another.
There were other, more adventitious opportunities of
making additional money. Though Surtees was inevitably less explicit on this point, the suggestion is clearly
present in the novels that young and pretty women
servants were not above exploiting their sex. Certainly,
if we may judge from Charley Stobb's flirtatious advances
to the little chambermaid in chapter xxvii of *Handley
Cross* and a similar episode between Soapey Sponge and
the Jawleyfords' housemaid (ch. xxx), presentable female
servants, in establishments where male guests were

common, lacked neither opportunity nor temptation. Over the morals of Mrs Mansell in *Tom Hall*, whose youthful beauty had secured her promotion from dairymaid to housekeeper with that confirmed womanizer Lord Heartycheer, and Mrs Markham, Sir Archy Depecarde's comely housekeeper in *Handley Cross*, who agrees to visit Jorrocks in his bedroom when the rest of the household had retired, Surtees leaves no room for uncertainty, in the minds of his male readers at least.

When not cataloguing their shortcomings or hinting at their frailties, Surtees also lets fall much incidental information about servant life in general. For all his dislike of the higher aristocracy, we get an occasional glimpse of the splendour of their domestic establishments. At Lord Lazytong's seat Dawdle Court in *Hawbuck Grange* (ch. v), there is a groom of the chambers, Mr Lampoil, who appears resplendent in pumps, pantaloons, and a cataract of white lace and is supported in his dignity by a bevy of bedizened flunkeys. Lord Heartycheer's household in *Tom Hall* boasted both a senior and junior groom of the chambers in addition to his lordship's valet and the usual complement of footmen (ch. xlvii). At the ducal seat of Donkeyton Castle in *Hillingdon Hall* (ch. x) there was a staff of a dozen gardeners under the direction of Mr Tuliptree, and a wall-garden of five or six acres with glass-houses and other horticultural buildings. One tiny detail which conveys the size and complexity of even a moderate establishment is the casual mention in *Mr Romford* of the 'girl in charge of the numbers' at Dalberry Lees whose sole job it was to watch the board and identify each bell that rang in the servants' hall, calling out the room number to the other servants for appropriate action.

There is also some mention of wages. Mr Smoothington, the duke of Donkeyton's lawyer, we are told with a touch of condescension, 'would have commanded five-and-forty or fifty pounds as a butler'. An ex-Meltonian groom, on the strength of a brief and questionable association with that fashionable centre, is overpaid, with £80 per annum and a house, by the snobbish and gullible

Mr Watkins. At the bottom of the servant scale, Mrs Mustard accepted 6s. a week with her keep to work as housekeeper, partly because Lord Lovetin, her employer, was short of cash, partly because she had a slightly damaged reputation. Most people who knew her would not have taken her on at any price. Proudlock, the keeper in the same establishment, earned twice as much—12s. a week with house, coal, and free rabbits. He too had been obtained cheaply, being an ex-poacher who had appeared before magistrates. In London an odd-job man in a stable who slept in the hayloft would be given as much. Excessive economy, however, could be self-defeating. Major Guineafowle in *Tom Hall* took boys straight from the workhouse at £8 for the first year and £10 thereafter; but since they were apt during training to eat as though making up for lost years, smashed an inordinate amount of crockery, and when trained promptly took themselves off to better-paid situations, the net saving on this system, as Surtees observed, was hardly commensurate with the trouble.

While servants' wages were low, a counterbalancing item was the expense of their clothes. Surtees gives us some idea of what they were like, though he does not cost them. At Tergiversation Castle the footmen wore powdered wigs and gorgeous plum-coloured livery with silver lace. Partridge, Sir Archy Depecarde's butler, on loan to Mrs Brantinghame for the purpose of impressing Captain Doleful, turns out in 'a rich blue, green, yellow, red, all the colours of the rainbow reflecting, cut velvet vest, set off with steel buttons', a splendid velvet-collared blue coat, and superfine drab trousers with broad brown stripes down the sides. The impressionable Captain accepts this finery as a sign of wealth since it was a form of social display not uncommon among the more affluent and snobbish middle classes of London. In the villas around Croydon, a fashionable residential district for metropolitan professional and business families, Surtees records elsewhere the sight of 'footmen in jackets, and in yellow, red and green plush breeches', who emerge to watch the Surrey Hunt go past. Not to be outdone in

sartorial splendour, the female side of such establishments also took such opportunities as came their way to
cut a dash, even if they had to contrive the means themselves. Cheap materials and the rage for being in fashion, Surtees thought, had revolutionized the appearance
of congregations in country churches.

The housemaid now dresses better—finer at all events—than
her mistress did twenty years ago, and it is almost impossible
to recognise working people when in their Sunday dresses.
Gauze bonnets, Marabout feathers, lace scarfs, and silk gowns
usurp the place of straw and cotton print . . . There is a medium
in all things, but the mania for dress has got far beyond the
bounds of either prudence or propriety.

The Dirtiest of the Dirty, having become the Cleanest of
the Clean under Lucy Somerville's tuition, was hurt
because she was not allowed to wear a low-necked dress
on the occasion of her mistress's At Home. 'There should
be a distinction made', she said with new-found hauteur,
'in favour of upper servants.' Rebecca Mary, the pretty
maid at Mr Bunting's temporary quarters at Burton St
Leger, walked out on Sundays dressed like a duchess
with bonnet, parasol, and hooped skirt. In real life the
radical Alexander Somerville made a similar comment
after attending a service in Wilton Church in the early
1840s. Lady Ashley and other ladies, he noted, 'in the
exceeding plainness of their dresses, shewed very hum-
bly in contrast with the more expensively decorated wives
of the upper servants'. The aristocracy, he moralized,
could afford to dress plainly because nobody doubted
their wealth, 'but poorer people's pride must not hazard
a suspicion'. Possibly rivalry among the servants themselves, or a female desire to look attractive, had as much
to do with it as pride.[1]
    How young women in service were able to afford such
displays is not altogether clear. Cast-off dresses from
their mistresses would account for some of it; and also
set a standard. Certainly the market was there for mass-
produced, cheap, but modish clothes. It was further
stimulated by the fashion-plates in women's journals

which were no doubt eagerly studied in the servants' hall as well as the drawing-room. The new textile machinery of Lancashire, and the sweated industry of the London clothing factories, were putting articles within the reach of housemaids which their mothers could never have afforded. With their board and lodging found for them, it would have only been human for the younger women servants to spend the greater part of their spare cash on clothes; and no doubt tips from visitors were often used to increase their wardrobe. The custom of tipping was long-established, and in households where guests were frequent may have represented an appreciable addition to the minute yearly wage. For Soapey Sponge, that inveterate sleeper in other people's beds, gratuities posed a problem. 'He could only counterbalance the extravagance of inns by the rigid rule of giving nothing to servants in private houses.' Such a self-denying resolution could scarcely add to a guest's popularity below stairs or his comfort above. Though the organized and onerous system of 'vails' (a kind of fee paid by visitors to all the servants of a household according to their rank), prevalent in the eighteenth century, had largely died out, it was universally accepted that the additional burden placed on domestic staff by the presence of guests required suitable financial recognition.

Surtees also mentions certain non-financial perquisites which helped to make life more agreeable if not more lucrative for many kinds of servants. They could entertain their friends at their employer's expense, though it was prudent not to do it too openly. The staff of large establishments had a reputation for making visiting servants tipsy down below while their employers were being entertained above; a practice which must have made the journey home sometimes hazardous. Some form of more modest refreshment open to all was a hospitable feature of many houses. J. J. Gurney, who brewed his own ale, at first made a supply of drink available not only to his domestic staff but to all the labourers on his estate. Being converted to teetotalism in the 1840s, he took the unpopular decision to discontinue the free beer and in its place to open what he called 'a coffee tap' in his hall where there was a plentiful supply of hot coffee and bread for all who chose to partake. 'Now I can leave home for two or three months', he reflected piously, 'without care and anxiety, knowing that one great source of evil is stopped.'[2] Upper servants in large establishments could expect rather grander privileges, including the right of dining at their own table and being waited on by other servants. On the duke of Donkeyton's estate there was even a special wood, known as the 'valet covert', for the exclusive use of the sporting members of that domestic élite. Did Surtees invent this unusual feature, one wonders, or were there such things in real life? Among indoor recreations we are given a glimpse in Lord Heartycheer's establishment of the butler playing billiards with my lord's gentleman at a time when both could consider themselves, in their master's absence, as off-duty. A lavish standard of food and drink was a standard feature of such households. From Tantivy Castle Billy Pringle reported back to his knowledgeable mother that 'the servants here seem to live like fighting cocks . . . they sit down, ten or a dozen at the second table, and about thirty or so in the hall'. The upper servants had wine at table and punch in the evening. It is hardly surprising that when writing in his own person in the *Analysis* (ch. xi) Surtees remarks that 'there are no people under the sun so well done by as gentlemen's servants. They live on the fat of the land, have no cares, no anxieties, and are paid out of all proportion to their labouring brethren.'

He was referring presumably to those who served the aristocracy rather than ordinary country gentlemen like himself. Lower down the social scale the life of servants was apt to become less luxurious; but meanness in an employer was still held to be a cardinal sin. Mr Jogglebury Crowdey kept his servants to a set menu for their meals—roast beef on Sunday, fried beef on Monday, mutton on Wednesday—and rationed their consumption of beer to $1\frac{1}{2}$ pints a day for men and 1 pint for

the women. It was not a regime that recommended itself
to visiting servants, though it would have constituted
positive luxury to an agricultural labourer at that time.
Servants, however, tended to pitch their standards high.
As Mrs Pringle, a former lady's maid, sagaciously observed in *Ask Mamma* (ch. xiv), they judged everything
by the best establishments they had ever seen and were
discontented with everything that fell short of that. The
moral of this was never to take one's servant when visiting
a great house in case he became corrupted. According
to Surtees (*Mr Romford*, ch. xxxix), women were as bad
as men in this respect. Ladies' maids—'those most elegant
and sensitive creatures'—were notorious for being more
difficult to please at house parties than their mistresses.

What Surtees most lamented was the disappearance
of the old-fashioned domestic who stayed with one family
all his life, was satisfied with his lot, and was prepared
to do any job in any capacity. Major Guineafowle in *Tom
Hall* had such a paragon in Jonathan Falconer, 'one of a
class of servants now nearly extinct—an honest, industrious, painstaking man—who was always doing something, and could turn his hand to anything, never standing
upon this not being his work or that not being his place'.
He acted as groom, huntsman, gardener, game- and cow-
keeper, and occasionally second footman. An almost
identical character is old Solomon, Major Yammerton's
servant, who was coachman, shepherd, groom, and
game-keeper, as well as a huntsman. He put on a cocked
hat to drive the family coach, waited at table on state
occasions, and in the summer months turned his hand to
fishing, gardening, and haymaking. The major had at
least the virtue of paying this Admirable Crichton above
the regular wage. Even so, we are treated to the same
mournful remark that he was one of the old breed, now
almost vanished, who remained in one family and did
whatever he was asked. Since Solomon is clearly a
reworked Jonathan, the two should more properly be
regarded as Surtees' single exception to his general
indictment of the servant race.

Otherwise nothing in the novels suggests any real

warmth of feeling in the relationship between master and employer. There is a homely middle-class flavour about the little episode in *Tom Hall* (ch. xv) when Mrs Hall summons Sarah the maid, Martha the cook, and Jane the housemaid, to see and admire Tom in the glory of his first appearance in full hunting kit; but there is not much more to be inferred from this except the usual interest in such small households about every detail of the family's life. There was very little that servants did not know, Surtees observes later in the same book, about the affairs of the people they served. An illustration of this is the constant discussion among servants about the progress of the various courtships that form the plot of several of the novels. Another is the use of the collective 'we' by upper servants. Dicky Thorndyke, Lord Heartycheer's trusted henchman in the pursuit of the fox and the fair, invariably replies to an enquiry about his master's health, 'well, sir, I really think that we are very well, indeed I think we are better than we have been for some time'.

II

The question is how far we are entitled to take Surtees' picture of servant life as accurate. On some matters there can be little dispute. Take, for instance, the hierarchy of servants in the larger establishments. At Lord Radnor's house in 1835 de Tocqueville noted the careful order of precedence observed by the domestics when they filed in for prayers. The steward led the way, followed by the male indoor staff, with the grooms coming at the tail; while among the women the governess came in ahead of the housekeeper, the chambermaids, and the other females. Lord Belgrave, heir to the wealthy earl Grosvenor, maintained at Motcombe, his house in Dorset, what was regarded as a modest household for a man of his standing. He had a valet, his wife a French maid. A coachman and a footman made up the male side of the establishment while the female staff comprised a cook-housekeeper, two kitchen-maids, two housemaids, and two of those indispensable workers, the laundresses. The children (thirteen were born between 1820 and 1840 though not all survived infancy) were supervised by what was virtually a separate staff—two governesses and two nursery maids. In all, fifteen servants existed to serve a married couple with a family which at no time numbered more than thirteen.[3]

This comfortable establishment may be compared with Sydney Smith's household at Foston a decade earlier where he, his wife, and their four children were attended by a lady's maid, a cook, a housemaid, a laundry-maid, a girl, and a man of all work. This was for a clergyman in receipt of a comparatively generous stipend of £500 per annum together with the proceeds of occasional literary reviewing. Twenty years later, when Charles Kingsley and his wife set up house at Eversley in 1844 on their joint income of £670 per annum, they limited themselves to a more frugal establishment—a maid, a cook, and a man who doubled, or rather trebled, as groom, gardener, and butler. It was not only young clergymen at the outset of their married life who were in need of Surtees' favourite domestic, the man who could turn a hand to anything. Members of the aristocracy, not all of whom were blessed with abundant means, were capable of similar economies. Acland in 1845 reported that the two coach-horses of Lady Emily Pusey, wife of the celebrated agricultural reformer, were regularly used for ploughing. When the team was needed for the family coach, the same man that had trudged behind them in the field donned livery and mounted the box. Though a household name in agricultural circles, Philip Pusey, a modest country squire, had perhaps as much occasion for ploughing as for carriage-visiting.

The level of wages quoted in the novels is also in broad agreement with historical evidence. Everything confirms Surtees' view that the larger the establishment, the less the amount of work, the higher the remuneration, and the more chance of supplementing it with tips. The

Grosvenors' housekeeper was paid £50 per annum, a
salary which reflected her employers' status as well as
the fact that she was also responsible for the cooking.
When the middle-class Edward Pease had to reorganize
his household, following his daughter's marriage in 1838,
he engaged a Quaker, Abigail Thorpe, as his housekeeper
at £40 per annum. She became the head of a staff of four,
the others being a man and two women. The man was
paid £20 per annum with an allowance of two new suits,
two hats, and a 'morning jacket' each year and an upper
coat every two years. A widower presumably would
expect to pay more for a housekeeper than when there
was a wife to direct operations.[4] The Kingsleys paid their
three servants an impartial £25 per annum each. Mrs
Carlyle, more economically, gave her girl £12 with
£1. 10s. 0d. extra as beer-money. Miss Martineau in the
1860s, living in rural isolation at Ambleside, was only
able to offer a new maid a starting wage of £9 with beer-
and tea-money; but even on that scanty sum, her mistress
reported, she felt rich. 'She saves the beer & she will rise
rapidly to the £12 wh. is my limit.' This was not an exceptionally low wage for an inexperienced girl. A maid
of all work in a small London house where no other
servant was kept might get £10 or less. That, with justice,
could be termed servitude.

In her *Book of Household Management* which appeared in 1861 Mrs Beeton gave a table of wages which
do not differ substantially from these samples from a
slightly earlier period. Men, according to their station,
ranged from £100 for a steward or £60 for a butler down
to a stable boy at £6. A housekeeper could earn up to
£50, a cook £45, a lady's maid £25. What is also interesting
is the proportion of total income which was deemed
necessary to spend on servants' wages. An earlier manual,
quoted by Marion Lochhead in her book on *The Victorian Household*, which had been compiled by two ex-
servants, Samuel and Sarah Adams, suggested that an
employer should devote as much as a quarter of his
income to that purpose. However, it was admitted that
this proportion would diminish for lower incomes until

at about £100, for instance, a widow or spinster would have to make do with a girl at £10 or less. Even with this reservation, however, to recommend spending a quarter of one's income on servants' wages seems unrealistic. No doubt ex-servants had a professional interest in magnifying the importance of their order; they did not after all have to foot the bills. When to wages are added the inescapable additional costs of board, lodging, laundry, light, and heating, with occasional extras like board-wages, livery, and the government tax on men-servants, it would have required a very wealthy or a very foolish person to come up to the Adams' conception of a suitable establishment. Mrs Beeton's own indications of an appropriate staff for people on different levels of income imply that something based on 10 per cent of total income was nearer the mark.

The aristocracy, which might have been expected to spend more on staff, for reasons of social display if not actual necessity, often seem to have been as economical in relation to their means as the middle classes. The various examples cited by F. M. L. Thompson, taken from the middle decades of the century, suggest that the upper classes may even have spent a smaller proportion of their incomes on servants' wages than middle-class families. It is evident from his figures that on an income of £3,000, for example, less than a tenth was usually sufficient to cover domestic wages. This is not altogether surprising There was no need for the aristocracy to pay grossly inflated wages to their servants since the employment they offered was obviously more attractive than in smaller households. The larger the staff, the easier it was to effect economics. In a small household the difference between having three domestics and making do with two was considerable. Middle-class employers were more likely to save on this section of their domestic budget by having only women servants and spending less on clothes and diet.

There was another side to middle-class households which distinguished them from the grander establishments. Though they did not ensure, at least they provided the opportunity for, warmer personal relationships. In a very large aristocratic house the gulf separating the titled employer from the lower servants might be startlingly wide. For a busy, absentee, or lazy proprietor it was easy to sink into reliance on the upper echelon of domestics—the steward, the valet, the housekeeper, the lady's maid—for the smooth running of the household. There is a nice anecdote about the fifth earl Fitzwilliam, who succeeded to the title in 1833. Urged by his wife to take more interest in the management of Wentworth Woodhouse and not allow himself to be entirely in the hands of the upper servants, he one day made a visit of exploration to the lower regions of that vast mansion. Discovering a boy all alone in one of the rooms, he asked him who he was. 'Why,' came the retort, 'I am the boy who does all the work in this 'ere 'ouse, and who the devil are you?' Since the story was related by Lady Fitzwilliam in 1858, it has a certain authenticity.[5]

In a small house with only one or two servants, it was obviously easier for closer ties than this to develop. Surtees' general portrayal of servants is not only one-sided in that he virtually ignores the existence of good servants but cynical in that he also ignores the possibility of genuinely affectionate relationships between employers and their domestics. The nearest he comes to it is in the rough masculine familiarity, bordering on equality and not without a reluctant mutual regard, between Jorrocks and James Pigg. Jorrocks, however, is too inefficient a manager of his domestic staff to win their respect, and too coarse-grained and egotistical to need their friendship. The gentler approach is seen, for example, in John Grey of Dilston as he sat with the maids as they sewed in the evening, reading aloud to them from the novels of Walter Scott; or in Harriet Martineau during the Crimean War, when she gathered her maids together after the evening post to explain to 'these intelligent girls' the latest state of the fighting with the aid of maps and globe. These were clearly conscious attempts on the part of two humane employers both to educate and to establish warmer relationships with their domestics. It was, if not

exclusively, at least a characteristically middle-class phenomenon and owed something perhaps to a lack of any
inherited sense of class distinction and a greater religious
and moral sensitivity than was likely to be encountered
among the aristocracy.

In so far as Surtees was aware of it, he did not apparently think it an English trait. When comparing
English and Scotch servants in the *Analysis* (ch. vi), he
wrote that 'the Scotch, we believe, are kinder—more
attentive at least—to their servants than the English. They
treat them more as friends and companions.' The contrast
he noted was the result probably of the greater egalit-
arianism of Scottish employers. Yet possibly a change
was taking place even among the class-ridden English,
though not perhaps the English with whom Surtees
habitually mixed. As a child in an old-fashioned Unitarian
family at Norwich during the Napoleonic War, Harriet
Martineau instinctively disliked 'the imposition of passive
obedience and silence' on the servants in her parents'
house and was about in the kitchen often enough to know
something of the resentful feelings it caused. Another
middle-class literary figure of her generation, Henry
Crabb Robinson, showed a similar sensibility even at the
age of 68, when the springs of human sympathy are apt
to run dry. On learning that Mrs Wordsworth had lost
her servant Jane, he wrote to her in October 1843:

the death of an old and attached servant of her description is
one of a very serious character indeed, and I fear, in a degree,
irreparable. It shows the vanity of our artificial classifications
of society. How indignant you would feel were anyone to say,
by way of consolation or remark on your sorrow, that she was
only your servant![6]

This is a different attitude to the benevolent paternalism
displayed by the aristocracy when they feasted their staff
on roast beef and plum pudding at family celebrations
or put in an appearance at the servants' ball at Christ-
mas to dance with the cook or the laundress. Mrs Ellis
reveals something of the origin of this greater social
sensibility when she urges ladies to respect the common

humanity of their servants and recall that when they spoke offensively to them, they were themselves guilty of a moral offence. Most servants, she thought, were able to appreciate kindness, 'and the slight effort required to obtain their confidence, is almost invariably repaid by a double share of affectionate and faithful service'.

Women, perhaps, were better at making friends with their servants than men: partly because of their quicker emotions, partly because they saw more of them during the day while their husbands were at work. Single women were particularly likely to appreciate the companionship of a good and trustworthy servant of their own sex. Florence Nightingale, for example, became deeply attached to Temperance Hatcher, her maid for many years, who eventually married one of her Crimean protégés. For the rest of her life she corresponded with them, sent presents to their children, and remembered them in her will. Miss Martineau wrote of one of her maids, Martha, that she was 'beloved like a daughter by me, and honoured by all who knew her'. When, as good maids often did, she left to get married, Miss Martineau invited her to stay as guest in her house before the wedding. She appeared at the dining-table and in the drawing-room— 'a more graceful lady I never saw'. After a few years her mistress found another treasure in Mary Anne, a Nottingham laceworker of 16, whom she taught spelling and arithmetic. In her last years 'Marianne' became her personal attendant and trusted friend to whom the Martineau family wrote when they wanted news of the invalid. The faithful Martha wrote of her mistress after her death that she was 'one of my dearest and best friends' and Marianne that 'it has been a privilege to be with such a noble woman'.

Women servants, no doubt deservedly, had the reputation of being more loyal, harder working, and more neat-handed than men. Jorrocks' preference for being waited on by women is well known to Surtees readers, but there were many like him in real life. Grey of Dilston, according to his daughter, disliked having men servants in the house, where he thought they were apt to expect the women to wait on them. When Colonel Berkeley dined with Lord and Lady Tavistock about the year 1830, the company of four were waited on by a butler and two maids. The service, he wrote many years later, was 'attentive, noiseless and quick, as it ever is when the work is done by girls'. A similar preference was expressed more boisterously by Richard Milnes senior in the 1850s when he wrote that 'I wish the whole generation of London Butlers and Valets was extinguish'd, & to be attended only by women-slaves from Circassia'. In default of such exotic and alluring females, he made do at Fryston with a cook, a maid, and a boy from the village, even though this meant that the kitchen-maid often had to come out to hold the horse's head when a visitor arrived.[7] In middle-class homes the presence of a man-servant might indicate no more than a desire to outshine neighbours, or at least to keep up with them in social pretentiousness. Surtees believed that women in particular were prone to this form of snobbery. 'Where is the lady', he asks in *Mr Romford* (ch. liv), 'who will submit to be tended by one of her own sex, if she can possibly help it?'

For girls from poor families, domestic service offered an escape from poverty and squalor into a cleaner and more civilized world. Sydney Smith has left a characteristic account of how he 'caught up a little garden-girl, made like a milestone, christened her Bunch, put a napkin in her hand, and made her my butler'. When Bunch was promoted to cook (accompanying the family when they migrated to Somerset and eventually marrying the coachman), he took another little girl as his personal attendant. The necessary business of finding and training girls for domestic service was not always as casual as this. George Nicholls, one of the leading poor-law administrators of the time, in an article published in 1846 on the state of the agricultural poor, mentioned with approval that 'many ladies take a lively interest in the education of the young females in their neighbourhood, and superintend the training and preparing them for service and other occupations'. He instanced one lady who had established a kind of training establishment for girls of 14 and above, chosen from the local schools. Some were taught dressmaking, others household work. Some she took into her own house, where they learned the various duties of chambermaid, housemaid, kitchen-maid, and laundress; and when trained they were found positions in other households. Even conceding that there may have been an element of self-interest in such schemes, it would be cynical to deny them any merit.[8]

In exceptional circumstances servants might rise to even higher spheres. Bessy Barnet, who was taken on as servant by the Carlyles for a few months despite the admonitions of their friend Mrs Montagu, later became the wife of a successful doctor and the mistress of a fine mansion at St Leonards. Though she refused to go out into society, as she 'does not choose to be patronised', she had (noted the sharp-eyed Jane Carlyle) 'the completest silken dominion' over her husband. Another true-life Samuel Smiles story of worldly success was that of Luff, a footman with Lady Charlotte Guest who became successively butler, house steward, estate agent, and mayor of Blandford: and lived to see his son marry a general's daughter. It is one of life's gentler ironies that the Dorset immortalized by the greatest tragic novelist of the century perversely produced such an eminently Victorian and optimistic version of the *Mayor of Casterbridge*. Less dramatic, though possibly equally pleasing to the Victorian conscience, was the history of Wordsworth's servant James Dixon. A workhouse boy, turned out upon the world at the age of 9 with a couple of shillings, he learned to read, write, and play the accordion, developed a taste for drawing, and became a respectable tailor. A great favourite with the family, Mrs Wordsworth even gave up her pony and trap after her husband's death so that he could continue in her service. Dixon answered the Surtees ideal of the old-fashioned domestic, especially in his satisfaction with his lot in life. 'I have often said,' he told Crabb Robinson, 'I consider myself as a favourite of fortune.'

There can be little doubt that when treated with

kindness and respect many Victorian servants did respond with loyalty and long service. Common as it was
for contemporaries like Surtees to mourn the passing of
the traditional family retainer, one may suspect that this
was no more than the universal tendency of elderly
mankind to praise an imagined past at the expense of an
imperfect present. There are plenty of instances of long
service in a single family among Victorian servants.
Sydney Smith's domestics, his daughter recorded, usually parted from him only on marriage or death. J. J.
Gurney's old nurse occupied a cottage in the grounds
for eighty years up to the time of her death in 1846. The
elder Nightingales' housekeeper remained in the family
twenty-five years and her death in 1872 left an almost
irreparable gap in the organization of the household. In
the middle decades of the century, Goldwin Smith's
parents at Mortimer in Berkshire had five upper-servants
whose individual years of service with either his father
or his stepmother averaged forty-six. 'They thoroughly
identified themselves with the family and its interests,'
wrote the son, 'and when the household was broken up,
took their pensions and went into no other service.' The
old coachman who had been fifty years with his father
could neither read nor write, but for all that was not
without a certain quaint delicacy of feeling. When his
mistress was dying he sent her up a rose as his farewell.
In turn his employers, who seldom left home, 'treated
the domestics not as servants, but as members of a
household'.[9]

The habit among servants of identifying themselves at
least verbally with their employers was not uncommon.
'Sir Robert looks quite well,' said Peel's porter to a visitor
at the prime minister's house during a difficult period in
the parliamentary session of 1845. 'We carry it with a high
hand!' Smaller households could be more demonstra-
tive. Charles Dickens' domestics dressed the house with
flags to greet him on his return from the triumphal
reading-tour of the USA in 1868. In an even more spontaneous gesture of sympathy the maids at Cheyne Row
clapped their hands in delight when the telegram arrived

announcing the enthusiastic reception of Carlyle's
Rectorial address at Edinburgh University in 1866.

This was one side to Victorian servant-life; there were
others. Surtees' cynicism was not so much ill-founded as
selective. Servants were many and human; they exhibited as many shades of behaviour and character as their
employers. Some were loyal and upright; some faithless
and dishonest; the majority, no doubt, were ordinary
imperfect mortals like the rest of humanity. Much depended on the employer. Those who regarded servants
merely as servants were hardly capable of bringing out
the best in their natures. Indifferent employers made for
indifferent service. There were disciplinarians who ex-
acted as much work as possible from their domestic staff;
snobs who ignored their existence as human beings. In
such households even conscientious servants were likely
to do no more than their contractual duties with little
sense of loyalty or gratitude. The diary of William Tayler,
a footman employed by a wealthy widow living in the
Marylebone district of London in 1837, may not be typical
but is at least revealing. He had a comfortable, well-paid
position with considerable leisure; there were three maids
in the house to do the hard work. Yet clearly he had little
affection or respect for his mistress, her relatives, and
the friends to whose middle-class chatter he listened as
he silently waited at table.[10] It was not unnatural in such
circumstances for the occupational drawbacks of domestic service—restricted personal liberty and enforced
outward deference—to give rise to an occasional emotional resentment or even, as in Tayler's case, a flicker of
class-hostility. Given the vast numbers of people who
sought employment in domestic service, it is probable
that many were temperamentally unsuited to its peculiar
demands. It would in any case be unreasonable to expect
a higher standard of behaviour among servants than
obtained generally among the class of population from
which they were recruited. If Surtees was right, there
was a greater sense of criticism if not actual antagonism
among servants than was usually realized by employers.

There could have been few employers, however, who did not from time to time make disconcerting discoveries. General Dyott, having engaged a keeper on the strength of excellent references, learned in the course of 1839 that he was not only systematically depleting the estate of game in collusion with a local poacher but had seduced the general's cook. Charles Dickens on one occasion found out that in the family's absence the cook, in a lady's habit, and his groom, in a dress coat (both presumably borrowed from the employers' wardrobes), had amused themselves by careering over the countryside on his and his daughter's horses. Thackeray's servants repaid a kind and over-lenient master with insolence and petty theft. One manservant insisted on having another to keep him company and on his departure left behind a pregnant housemaid. When the newly married Froudes took up residence at Plas Gwynant in Snowdonia in 1850, the young historian, in the intervals of contemplating the catalogue of men's follies and crimes in Tudor England, found human frailties to distract him in Victorian Wales. The nurse they brought from London took to drink and in a fit of delirium tremens tried to float down a waterfall. A replacement from a fashionable metropolitan household had a nervous system that required green tea, breakfast in bed, and cake instead of bread—a genteel line which became slightly less convincing when it transpired that she was separated from her husband and had a lover. That the Froudes suffered as employers from youth and inexperience is probable. Neither seems to have been a good judge of people or a good manager of domestic staff. Charlotte Froude, of wealthy family, intellectual, and religious-minded, had received no household training. 'Her knowledge of what servants and kitchen apparatus she possesses', wrote her fiancé ruefully on the eve of their wedding, 'extending no further than that she has her dinner daily.' In Devonshire six years later things were no better. Servants flowed through the house in a steady stream, all spoiled, according to Froude, by what he called

his wife's 'consideration and care', though one may suspect that in reality it was weak good-nature and an
undiscriminating desire to please.[11]

That we know so much about the domestic trials of
Victorian literary figures is perhaps not so much a reflection of their ineptitude as employers as a result of their
itch for putting down their experiences on paper. Few
households, for example, have provided us with such a
compendious catalogue of servant tribulations as that of
the Carlyles. No doubt they were not the easiest of
employers any more than they were the most tranquil of
married couples. Yet in their thirty-two years at Cheyne
Row Mrs Carlyle kept one servant twelve years and
another six. Others, however, came and went in a picturesque procession of incompetents and misfits that
would probably have been familiar to many similar but
less articulate London households. There was 'Thornhill
Nancy' who blunted Carlyle's razors by shaving with
them herself, and 'Lancaster Jane', amiable, intelligent,
and ineffective, who read her master's books in his study
instead of cleaning the grate. A maid who had moved
from an establishment where eight servants were kept
threw up her job after six days complaining of loneliness.
The formerly exemplary Helen Mitchell from Kirkcaldy
was re-engaged only for the Carlyles to discover that in
the interval she had become an alcoholic. Another listened at doors and read her employers' letters; a third,
who claimed to be the genteel daughter of a half-pay
naval lieutenant, turned out to be an Irish impostor who
lied, stole, and finally absconded during the night after
less than three weeks. An alleged 'Treasure' of over 70
proved an arrant fraud who could not cook and stole
eight bottles of ale. Then came Charlotte and Sarah who
joined forces to bully their mistress, followed by Mary
and Flo who quarrelled incessantly with each other.
Finally calmer waters were reached with Mrs Warren, a
respectable widow of 50 who cooked, and Fanny, young,
modest, and intelligent, as maid.

Mrs Carlyle's defects as mistress of a household have
been blamed by Alexander Carlyle as the chief reason

for this chequered domestic history. No doubt her alternate petting and scolding was not the best way to command affection and respect. Yet it would probably be a mistake to assume that her difficulties were exceptional just because they have been exceptionally well chronicled. Even the calmer and more practical Miss Martineau had a run of unsatisfactory maids at The Knoll in the last decade of her life. One was incorrigibly idle, a second always in debt, a third had no underclothes, and a fourth was given to crude practical jokes. What is of interest are the lessons Mrs Carlyle extracted from her experiences. In the first place, it was never to take a servant from a larger establishment because she would miss the company of other domestics. Next, never to trust a pretty face, a plausible manner, or a show of religion; in particular never to take a Scotch girl who was a devout member of a Free Church congregation since she would be both independent and censorious. Finally, never to pay a high wage in the hope of getting better service, because it would only lead to a demand for better accommodation than was physically possible; for greater assistance in the house than was financially affordable; and, in the case of a cook, for more frequent opportunities to show off her skills than a frugal middle-class family could possibly provide. A general servant at £12 to £14 a year who could do plain cooking became her modest ideal.

With all or much of this Surtees would have been in full agreement. There is, for example, his passing reference to the Watkins' woman Lubbins in *Mr Romford* (ch. xxxviii)—a 'show-off cook' who required the stimulus of brandy and formal dinners, and was above the humdrum preparation of mere family meals. It is possible that the Carlyles' experience was no more than a microcosm of Victorian servant life in a big city. Indeed, since Mrs Carlyle was too wise or too economical to have a manservant in her house, she was spared one particular problem which plagued other employers. Professor Raumer thought that, unlike Berlin, where cooks and housemaids in private houses frequently carried on a private trade in prostitution, the same class in London were undoubtedly more chaste and decorous. On the evidence available, the danger to the morals of Victorian female servants seems to have come from fellow domestics rather than men of a higher social class. Followers were not usually encouraged by employers; and if tolerated were carefully supervised. Extra-marital pregnancies usually resulted in dismissal. In Berlin, if Raumer is to be believed, such supervision and discipline would have been impracticable. Employers there feigned ignorance of their servants' behaviour because there was no reason to believe that any replacements would behave any better.

Dangerous as it is to generalize about Victorian servants, it is difficult to avoid the impression that, as a class, they were neither oppressed nor submissive. They seem to have possessed spirit and independence; they had their own methods of self-protection; and, at any rate, middle-class employers, who statistically must have provided the greatest number of households with servants, were often perplexed to know how to manage them. For all that, servants were an indispensable part of middle-class life. Indeed, it would not be unreasonable to suggest that the continued growth of middle-class comfort, self-confidence, political power, and moral influence was largely made possible by the existence of a large, cheap servant force.

It is beyond dispute that, as the century wore on, the middle classes began to occupy more and more of the social territory once largely the monopoly of the landed gentry and aristocracy. This was not without a wider political and cultural significance. In a sermon on 'English Education for the Middle Classes', preached at the opening of Hurstpierpoint School in 1850, Bishop Thirlwall made the observation that it was the privileged, more wealthy, and more leisured section of the population 'which affords the true measure of the national intelligence, which exhibits the genuine stamp of the national character, and is the legitimate organ of the national mind and will'. In so far as the Victorian middle classes (and

Thirlwall clearly had them in mind) justified this description—and it would not be easy to dispute that claim at this half-way point in the century—they owed perhaps almost as much to the servant class which underpinned their social life as the manufacturers owed to the industrial workers who made possible their economic strength. In an age when machines, labour-saving devices, and artificial sources of energy were still for the most part confined to industry and long-distance transport, the work of the domestic household was almost entirely dependent on human hands and muscles. If it did nothing else, the source of abundant cheap labour represented by the great army of Victorian servants provided the middle classes with a higher standard of living, a greater degree of luxury and leisure, and a wider opportunity to devote their energies to interests outside home and office. The large place occupied by servants in Surtees' novels is a just, if perhaps unconscious, recognition of their indispensable function in Victorian middle-class society.

PART THREE
Manners and Morals

8

MANNERS

I

That in the course of the nineteenth century English society had become quieter, more orderly, more disciplined, and more humane was never doubted by educated Victorians. To explain why it had happened was more difficult. Many influences had been at work and many of them had started long before Victoria ascended the throne. Eighteenth-century rationalism, Benthamite utilitarianism, humanitarianism, political fears and aspirations, had all played their part. What they had in common was a more serious attitude towards social problems; and at the heart of this greater moral seriousness was evangelical religion. From its origins in the Methodist movement of George II's reign, Evangelicalism had, during the age of the French Revolution and the post-Waterloo period, filtered into every class of English society. The various Churches which made up the collective religiosity of early Victorian England were not all Evangelical in the narrower meaning of the term but they shared the Evangelical emphasis on personal behaviour and sensitivity to moral issues in national affairs.

The high-tide of the Evangelical movement proper came in the 1830s and 1840s with the campaign for stricter Sabbatarian legislation. Had it succeeded, English society would have been placed under a social discipline reminiscent of Calvin's Geneva or the Cromwellian Commonwealth. In the event the only parliamentary success came in 1854 in partnership with the powerful Temperance movement when an Act was secured further limiting the hours on Sunday in which public houses could open. The Sabbatarians significantly failed to

prevent Sunday deliveries and collections in the reformed
postal service or Sunday trains on the new railways.
When it came to a decision in parliament, dislike of undue
state interference, a reluctance to pass measures which
would be unpopular with the poorer classes, and a
healthy suspicion that the proposed laws might prove
unenforceable, combined to frustrate the moral reformers. As it was, Sabbatarianism had made enough progress for another kind of criticism to be voiced. To the
new puritanism was ascribed, for example, the general
drunkenness which was particularly marked on that day.
Since public houses and gin-shops were able to remain
open while theatres, concert halls, and dance rooms were
closed, the consumption of alcohol seemed the one
popular recreation that was left for the great unwashed.
Mrs Ellis attested in her book to the crowds of idle young
men and women, apprentices and shop assistants, who
thronged the streets on Sundays for lack of anything
better to do. One by-product, in fact, of the Sabbatarian
movement was a search by the more sensible reformers
for some respectable amusements and recreations which
could be provided for the Sunday leisure of the poorer
classes.

What the whole Sabbatarian campaign demonstrated
was that though it enjoyed some aristocratic and Dissenting support, the organized movement itself was essentially Anglican and middle-class. 'It was', writes the
historian of the movement, 'strongest in the respectable
middle class of the small towns and suburbs in the south
of England.'[1] It was the programme of a relatively small
though influential organization of zealots that had been
rejected, not the wider attitude on which it had been
based. As in other spheres of Victorian life, the voluntary
principle had been preferred to the compulsory principle.
Social Sabbatarianism remained strong, even though
legislative Sabbatarianism failed to find a place on the
statute book. It was in the diffusion of their principles
rather than in the imposition of their practices that the
Sabbatarians enjoyed their real success. By argument,

example, and propaganda, by appealing to the sympathies of a religious-minded society and taking advantage of the traditional character of Sunday as a day of
rest, they gradually succeeded in bringing about what
became known to posterity as the 'Victorian Sunday'. It
was, after all, the day appointed not only for public
worship but for a cessation of toil by the great mass of
people who had no other means of earning their daily
bread. Among the poorer, and largely non-church-going,
classes, Sunday was at least observed by dressing in their
best clothes, eating their best meal of the week, and
walking abroad—the women and girls to show off their
finery, the men and boys with sticks and dogs in search
of sport, gambling, or less innocent pastimes. During
the middle decades of the century the pressure of religious organizations, masters, and employers was a
powerful influence on the classes both above and below
them in bringing about further refinements.

'It is astonishing', the duke of Wellington once observed, when discussing this subject, 'how much power
may be obtained by any body of people in this country
who have a good end in view, and persevere in working
together.' There was a certain amount of mortification in
the remark since he had been obliged to adapt his own
social habits to the new climate of opinion. In the early
part of the century Sunday had been a favourite day for
giving large dinner-parties, even among the clergy. It
was (if Lady Shelley is right in her chronology) after the
passage of the reform bill, and the blow to aristocratic
prestige it entailed, that public opinion turned against
any such displays of opulence and secular frivolity among
the upper classes in the metropolis. 'We are grown so
good', wrote the duke sarcastically in May 1835, when
inviting her to a strictly family meal, 'that we don't give
dinners on Sundays!' He explained to Lady Salisbury a
few years later that he could not give formal dinners
on that day without being attacked by anonymous
letters, and that if he dined out himself, he went in a cab
to avoid observation.[2] Mrs Villiers, Lord Clarendon's

mother, who died in 1856 at the age of 80, said that no
change had taken place in her lifetime more remarkable
than in the observance of the Sabbath. She could remember how George III's queen held drawing-rooms on
Sundays after divine service and ladies went into the
Chapel Royal beforehand in full Court dress. Everybody
used to give dinners on that day and many played at
cards.

In surrendering to what some of the more unregenerate members of the aristocracy called the Judaization
of Sunday, the upper classes were showing the same
prudent conformity with middle-class ethics that they
did on other issues. By the middle of the century the
stricter observance of the Sabbath in the form of regular
attendance at church services, sometimes twice on the
one day, abstention from purely social visits or entertainments, avoidance of travel, walking if necessary instead of bringing out horses and carriage, consumption
of cold meals in order to give servants less work, restriction of reading to serious books, was becoming
common among middle-class families. Though in Surtees'
novels religion is largely conspicuous for its absence,
reflections of the new morality can be found even here.
His characters, though hardly religious, have for the most
part a sound idea of the conventions it is useful to observe
in an age of religiosity. There is, for instance, the ingenious stratagem of Haimes the saddler who follows
Mr Jorrocks' hounds. Since his customers include many
evangelicals who disapprove on principle of such sports,
he named his horse 'Business' so that, when he was out
hunting, his foreman could always explain that this was
what his master was away on. Again, when Mr and Mrs
Hazey in *Mr Romford* wish to establish an early acquaintanceship with the new arrivals at Beldon Hall, a
preliminary reconnaissance is made on Sunday by the
gentlemen but Mrs Hazey is banned from accompanying them since 'Mrs Somerville may be serious, and not
like to be called upon on a Sunday'. For her part Mrs
Somerville, who, if not serious (that is to say religious),
is anxious to be regarded as 'respectable', arranges to be

discovered by her unexpected callers seated on a sofa
'in a half recumbent attitude, with a volume of "Blair's
Sermons" in her hand'. Since Hugh Blair, the famous
eighteenth-century divine, academic, and literary lion,
had published no less than five volumes of sermons,
Lucy's choice could hardly have been more impressive;
though perhaps it was lost on Mr Hazey.

Mr Jessop and his faithful Jug had perhaps a more
genuine sense of what constituted the social and religious duties of the Sabbath. For them it was a *dies non*
as far as their customary sartorial, drinking, and eating
habits were concerned. They put on Sunday clothes of
the plain orthodox kind, and punctiliously performed their
duties as both employers and parishioners.

The Jug always inaugurated a pair of clean nankins in which,
regardless of the weather, with a large Boyston Park prayer-
book, wrapped up in a red cotton kerchief, he stumped perseveringly to church, accompanied by Mr Jessop, and such of
his servants as liked his leading. The clergyman dined at the
Hall, and there was a sermon for the establishment and the
neighbourhood in the evening. So Mr Jessop commenced
the week well, and prospered in the course of it, as he deserved to do.

This was an example of social Sabbatarianism in action
of which, if we may judge from the last sentence, Surtees
himself approved.

Good works could be carried too far, however, and a
parade of outward virtuousness was something which
Surtees instinctively suspected. Jerry Pringle in *Ask
Mamma* is the typical hypocrite engendered by every
age in which religion is fashionable. 'A fawning, sanctified, smooth-spoken, plausible, plump little man, who
seemed to be swelling with the milk of human kindness,
anxious only to pour it out upon some deserving object.'
Being also a rich man, he lived in an elegant villa in
Peckham Rye. 'Here he passed for quite a model man,
twice to church every Sunday, and to the lecture in the
evening, and would not profane the sanctity of the day
by having a hot potato to eat with his cold meat.' This

'ripe rogue' is the Pecksniff of the Surtees novels, less memorable only because he is given such a minor role.

II

One effect of the growing ascendancy of morality was the stricter conventions governing the printed word and polite conversation. The process which gained for Dr Thomas Bowdler literary immortality with the publication of his expurgated *Family Shakespeare* in 1818 was being applied in a more diffused way to the language as a whole. Leigh Hunt in the 1830s was already ridiculing the delicacy of booksellers who banned the use of the word 'shift' for a woman's undergarment and thought even the French term 'chemise' an inadequate disguise. Mrs Brookfield, who was by no means a prude, still thought it advisable when writing to her husband in 1848 to apologize for her use of the expression 'in a cold sweat' by adding defensively in brackets 'to be coarse'. When Guizot, dining at that centre of sceptical thought Holland House, cited the proverb about hell being paved with good intentions, his hostess Lady Holland whispered across the table, 'we never use the word *hell* here, unless in quoting from Milton; high poetry is the only excuse'. Similarly, 'devil' was avoided in respectable conversation and publications other than the Prayer Book and other professionally licensed writings. Even Surtees, when quoting that other common expression about work for idle hands, employs the more colourless and poetic term 'Satan'. He is equally circumspect in his use of swear-words. The picturesque expletives of Lord Scamperdale and Mr Jorrocks in the hunting-field, though original and amusing, are also literary substitutes for the more earthy language of reality. When he has to make a direct reference to swearing he employs the standard camouflage of the initial letter. 'Everybody was sick of Willy Watkins. It was—oh, "D" Willy Watkins! and "B" Willy Watkins!', where presumably 'damn' and 'blast' are to be understood.

Much of this was of course mere affectation. People pretended to be shocked because it was conventional to be shocked. Mrs Ellis, however, defended the primness of women in mixed company with the argument that it was better that they 'should be guarded by a wall of scruples' against even the suggestion of loose language than that they should unconsciously become 'less worthy, and less efficient supporters of the country's moral worth'. Propriety of language, in other words, was the outer defence of propriety in thought and conduct. It was not only women who were affected. There is much evidence that there was a decline in the masculine habit of swearing in the course of the century. Algernon West was sufficiently surprised to make a note of it when in 1860 he heard a cabinet minister, Sir Charles Wood, say to a colleague on the India Council (to quote West's censored version), 'D——n your eyes, my dear Perry'. Charles Kingsley remarked in 1857 that even at the covertside or in fast company 'I never hear an oath, and that, too, is a sign of self-restraint'. The restraint in all probability only lasted until he was out of earshot; but earlier generations would not have shown such respect for the cloth when out hunting.

It was on the subject of sex that middle-class sanctions asserted themselves most strongly. This is not surprising. It is a topic of universal and timeless interest; and as a physiological fact had given rise to a large vocabulary of coarse descriptions and vulgar witticisms. Much of it had been recorded for Victorian posterity by the assiduous antiquarian Francis Grose, whose *Classical Dictionary of the Vulgar Tongue* had gone through several editions since its original publication in 1785. For middle-class moralists it was a cause of profound satisfaction that, unlike the allegedly profligate societies of the Continent, the English were conspicuous for their reserve on this subject. That this confidence would hardly have survived prolonged contact with certain classes in the community need hardly be argued. Yet the contention that this was not only a middle-class but to a degree a more national characteristic was justified. It was observable before the start of Victoria's reign and among people who had no

obvious reason for being nice in such matters. Puritanism in English society has long and extensive roots. One
of William Cobbett's biographers, for example, has drawn
attention to his sexual prudery. Yet Cobbett was brought
up in the country and had served in the army. George
Holyoake, who came from an impoverished industrial
background, was a free-thinker in religion, and a radical
in politics, said of sexual reticence that 'it is a sentiment
of civilisation, and means moral refinement'. He criticized
Americans for their lack of it and blamed even Scotland
for its deficiencies in this respect. 'I have heard', he wrote
in 1841, 'at public assemblies there things said before
a mixed audience, by educated persons, which no class
in England could anywhere be found to utter.'[3] Prudishness on such matters was the crowning item in the list
of English qualities given by Mr Podsnap in Dickens'
Our Mutual Friend: 'There is in the Englishman a combination of qualities, a modesty, an independence, a responsibility, a repose, combined with an absence of
anything calculated to bring a blush into the cheek of a
young person, which one would seek in vain among the
Nations of the Earth.' Podsnappery was certainly to be
found in abundance in Surtees' England. Even Jorrocks,
though a shameless reprobate in sexual matters, showed
a streak of puritanism on the subject of behaviour in
mixed company. It was he who quelled ribald interjec-
tions at a music-hall in Margate by majestically reciting
the couplet written by that more quoted than identified
seventeenth-century poet the fourth earl of Roscommon:

> Immodest words admit of no defence,
> For want of decency is want of sense.

There is no reason to suppose that the sexual emotions of the Victorians, both men and women, were any
different from those of their ancestors or their descendants; it is simply that they were reluctant to discuss
them in public. Such topics as religion, sin, death, duty,
patriotism, and honour (some of which were to be found
embarrassing by their grandchildren) were acceptable;
sexual emotions were not. It was a restriction which

irked many individuals. Charles Kingsley, for example, noticeably outspoken for a clergyman, commented to Mrs Gaskell in 1857 on 'the prudery of a not over cleanly, though carefully white-washed age'. He was himself posthumously subjected to the whitewashing process by his own wife when she edited his letters and other writings for publication. In her biography of her husband she left their passionate courtship in an obscurity where it remained for another hundred years. Her editorial ban extended even to what, to a modern mind, would be harmless expressions of physical affection, such as a reference (in a letter, moreover, to his small daughter) to kissing his wife's feet. Yet from what we know of Mrs Kingsley's own temperament, it is unlikely that she objected to such demonstrations from her adoring husband when he was alive. The simplest explanation is that she felt she had a right to guard the privacy of their relationship against the public even if it did involve the scholarly sin of mutilating and rephrasing her husband's letters.

There is a tendency to interpret Victorian reticence as prudishness and prudishness as indicating shame or disgust. It is an odd conception of human nature to believe that a reluctance to talk of private emotions is a sign of absence of warmth and passion; it may in fact signify the reverse. Part at any rate of Victorian reticence on sexual matters may be credited to a natural desire for privacy. To give one example, in 1853 George Hughes, the solid, unacademic, landowning elder brother of the author of *Tom Brown's Schooldays*, told the lady to whom he had just become engaged that though he was keeping a journal, her name did not appear in it once. 'It may be absurd, but I consider my feelings towards you so sacred, that I should not like to parade them even to my nearest relations.' Still less, one must conclude, before a nameless posterity. Another instance is the Indian civil servant John Beames. Singularly outspoken on other matters, when he came in his memoirs to record his marriage in 1860, he contented himself with the observation that 'I could write much about the perfect happiness of my married life and of my dear wife's many excellencies, but such things are too sacred to be written about. In the words of Tennyson

> ... not easily forgiven
> Are those, who setting wide the doors, that bar
> The secret bridal chambers of the heart,
> Let in the day.'[4]

The feeling is not unnatural; nor is it peculiar to the Victorian age. It was, however, so much taken for granted in that society that not many people writing their biographies would even have thought it necessary to allude to it. Perhaps, to the standard list of Victorian values, should be added a respect for personal privacy.

III

Victorian respectability was largely the creation of the middle classes; but Victorian society was a heterogeneous mass and there were always observable gaps between conventional standards and actual conduct. The barrister William Johnston, discussing in 1851 the manners and conventions of his time, made the observation that the greatest reserve and formal politeness were to be found among the middle classes. The aristocracy were characterized more by blunt speech, indifference to the feelings of others, and considerable informality of manners.[5] Even among their women there was far less affectation and far more freedom of speech and behaviour. That was one contrast; another was between private talk among equals and more formal conversation in mixed company. It would argue a remarkable transformation had there not been profanity and indelicacy in the speech of undergraduates in college, officers in the mess, politicians in the corridors of Westminster, or journalists in the coffee houses of Fleet Street. It is not unreasonable either to suppose that women in the drawing-room before they were joined by the men, or in the privacy of each other's bedrooms, and girls at boarding school behind the backs of the mistresses, indulged in franker speech than they would have permitted themselves in public. Florence Nightingale said that she had heard far more indecencies from the daughters of her mother's evangelical friends when she had to entertain them in the nursery than she ever encountered later in hospitals.

There was also the contrast of generations. Young men, and young women too, were less likely than their parents to conform to the accepted view of what was permissible. Marianne Darbishire, aged 22, daughter of a prosperous Unitarian solicitor, indulged in long cross-country rides with her young tutor, James Froude. A great excitement, she confided to her younger sister, was fording a river 'with habit gathered up in a graceful bunch on my knees, I sitting like a Turkish Sultana or English tailor cross-legged on the saddle'. At the same age, though already married, Lady Charlotte Guest in 1834 thought it 'a lark' to go off with her weak-minded younger brother one Saturday evening to visit the beer-gardens and gin-palaces of the not very salubrious district of Pentonville. 'My greatest ambition was to go inside a gin shop'; but though they peered inside several, the squalid appearance of their customers always deterred them. Twenty-four years on it was a different story. Visiting a fairground at Wimborne in Dorset, she firmly suppressed a passing inclination to go inside one of the travelling caravans because 'it would have been deemed anything but decorous to have entered, and of course was not seriously thought of'. Times had changed and Lady Charlotte had grown older. Young blood, however, was still young. When earlier that year she rebuked her 21-year-old daughter after a ball for dancing three times with the same man, there was a violent scene which 'unnerved me completely, and made me quite ill'.[6]

As her gin-shop expedition had demonstrated, while young women could be shielded against the coarser side of life, they could not be entirely isolated from it. Marion Lochhead remarks, when discussing the upbringing of Canon Wordsworth's daughters at Stanford in the Vale

in Berkshire during the 1850s, that between parish visiting and reading the Old Testament, Victorian girls could
scarcely have been as ignorant or as innocent as posterity
supposes. As in most rural parishes, the inhabitants of
Stanford were highly immoral by conventional standards;
which is a way of saying that they went on much as rural
people had always gone on. 'We learned a good deal',
wrote Elizabeth Wordsworth, who was to become later
the first principal of Lady Margaret Hall, 'by visiting the
poor, of the ordinary facts of practical life.' A decade
earlier Miss Nightingale had gone through a similar
period of enlightenment when doing parish work at
Holloway in Derbyshire and in the Hampshire village of
East Welland. Among the weavers of Holloway, she
observed drunkenness, overcrowding, and brutality; at
Welland, during an epidemic in 1845, she was present at
two deaths and one difficult confinement. The state of
the poor was much the same everywhere. When the Revd
Charles Kingsley senior took up his living in Chelsea in
1836, he and his wife began an energetic programme of
parish visiting in that recently urbanized and crowded
district. Their youthful son, the future novelist, was
shocked to discover that the respectable young women
who volunteered their services were being sent to
'abominable scenes of wretchedness, indecency and filth,
in order to read the Bible to the degraded people who
live in these slums'. Against what might seem the undue
emphasis of the middle classes on decorum, cleanliness,
and respectability must be set the often forgotten fact
that they had, as it were, under their own eyes and often
in close proximity to their homes masses of their fellow-
countrymen who were distinguished by none of these
things. Even if she did not penetrate into their dwellings,
no Victorian woman equipped with eyes, ears, and a sense
of smell needed much further instruction to teach her
about the more sordid aspects of society.

Surtees had no interest in slums or parish visiting; and
in common with other contemporary novelists did not
follow his couples into the bedroom. For the most part
he accepted the conventions of the publishing trade in

his plots and dialogues. He had, nevertheless, a more casual attitude to speech and behaviour than strict propriety would altogether have approved, and one may suspect that in this regard he came nearer to life than many of his contemporary fiction-writers. He had in any case little patience with affectations of modesty. Miss Willing, the future Mrs Pringle in *Ask Mamma*, gave up her first post, we are told, because, she said, 'master would come into the missis's room with nothing but his night-shirt and spectacles on', but in reality, observes Surtees drily, because the missis had some of her dresses cut down for her children instead of passing them on intact to Miss Willing. Other females in the novels show no squeamishness at seeing gentlemen in various stages of undress. Miss Jelly, the dressmaker in *Handley Cross*, assists her lodger Captain Doleful in the privacy of his bedroom to put on the Oriental costume she had devised for the fancy-dress ball. Mrs Jorrocks similarly helps the marquis of Bray to dress himself up as a girl in some of Belinda's clothes for the Harvest Home in *Hillingdon Hall*. Later on, when he turns up wet and bedraggled at Mrs Flather's house, he changes into Emma's second-best dressing-gown while Emma in her smartest one is left to entertain him in the small hours of the morning. Young ladies on their own are equally indiscreet. Sophy Ferguson in *Tom Hall* contrives clandestine meetings with her adorer Captain Mattyfat whom her father had forbidden the house. Angelena Blunt, delighted by an unexpected visit from Lord Heartycheer, not only tells him (untruthfully) that her parents are out but allows the old rake, with only the merest of maidenly protests, first to give her a vigorous embrace and then, under the pretence of repairing the disorder this causes to her dress, to pass his experienced hands under her chemisette 'as adroitly as a lady's-maid'.

In his conversation-pieces there are two or three occasions when Surtees goes to the limit of what was allowable by the publishing conventions of his time, notably in the leering suggestiveness of Lord Heartycheer's flirtations with Angelena and the smart indecencies of the set of theatrical ladies and fast young bucks who gather round Sir Harry Scattercash in *Mr Sponge*. In one scene Miss Howard and Miss Glitters are discussing the imminent arrival of Soapey when Sir Harry mentions that he is to be put up in the chamber above the billiard-room. Miss Howard protests that she already occupies it. 'Oh, it'll hold two well enough,' observes Miss Glitters. 'Then you can be the second,' retorts the other lady.

There is more indelicate banter in the following chapter when the same party is surprised while at breakfast by the sight of schoolboys arriving for the New Year's meet of the Scattercash hounds. Miss Glitters' suggestion that they were 'some of the little Sponges come to see their pa' is applauded by the gentlemen as a delightfully humorous reflection on that absent bachelor. Then, when another group appears in the drive:

'Who's sliding-scale of children is that, I wonder!' exclaimed Miss Howard, contemplating the varying sizes of their chubby faces through the plate-glass window.

['They must be on their way to the Great Exhibition of National Industry to show against the prince's little people,' observed Miss Glitters, eyeing them.

'There you are again, Miss G.!' exclaimed Captain Cutitfat.

'I said nothing,' replied the young lady, looking quite innocent.

'O-o-oh no!' replied the captain putting his thumb to his nose, and making a fan of his fingers.]

Mr Sponge's Sporting Tour appeared first in the *New Monthly Magazine* between January 1848 and April 1851. The long-awaited 'Great Exhibition of the Works of Industry of All Nations' (to give it its full title) opened at the Crystal Palace in May 1851, with Prince Albert as President of the Commissioners. By that date he and Victoria had produced seven children since their wedding in 1840, a rate of reproduction which had attracted much comment from the British public, partly ribald at their prolificness, partly indignant at the cost to the British taxpayer of their fast-expanding family. The *double entendre* of Miss Glitters' allusion to Prince Albert's industry, though easily comprehensible at the time, must have been thought on reflection too *risqué* a witticism to be given a permanent place in the novel. When the Bradbury and Evans issue in thirteen monthly parts (1852–3) and the 1853 first one-volume edition appeared, the words enclosed here in square brackets were omitted and the phrase 'sliding-scale of children' softened to 'sliding scale of innocence'.

The whole scene, with the thinly veiled indelicacy of the women and the oafish delight of their male companions, has an air of authenticity. More positive confirmation is hard to come by since those familiar with such conversations were not likely to write them down for the enlightenment of posterity. A few hints can be found in Victorian literature, however, which suggest that Surtees' fictional representation of fast language was if anything toned down rather than exaggerated. Lady Ashburton in the middle of the century commented with a certain impatience on the contrast between the sedate language she had to employ when entertaining her middle-class literary protégés and the 'gross conversation that goes on in our class both with men and women'. She gave as an illustration the remark made to her by Lady Sidney concerning another titled lady that 'she popped two chicks before she married'.[7]

Rosina Wheeler, the wife of Bulwer Lytton, stood socially about half-way between the world of Lady Ashburton and that of Lucy Glitters. She had a rackety upbringing, lived with Bulwer for a year before they were married, and behaved sufficiently reprehensibly after their separation to make him withdraw their children from her care. Her accidentally preserved correspondence with a woman friend, Mary Greene, is generally decorous: not surprisingly since Miss Greene, we are told, was not only unmarried but of a straitlaced disposition. Yet even to such a person Mrs Bulwer allowed herself one or two touches that would have gone down well at Nonsuch House. For example, in a letter from Italy in 1833 she mentioned the re-interment of Raphael's coffin beneath a statue of the Virgin Mary—'many were the indecorous jests that flew about, purporting that had Raphael been alive he would have chosen his position *vice versa*. (I hope Mr Wilkinson is not within ten miles!).[8] Who was the delicate-minded Mr Wilkinson is not revealed; but this is a more coolly deliberate witticism than the exasperated rejoinder put in the mouth of Mr Jorrocks on the occasion when he was riding back through Handley Cross in deplorable plight, having been deposited by his horse into a muddy ditch. He is assailed by the jeers of children and the audible comments of housewives gossiping at doorways, one of whom calls out, 'old fatty's had a fall', to which her neighbour replies, 'he's always on his back, that old feller'. The angry Jorrocks, forgetting all the moral advice of the earl of Roscommon, is stung into retorting, 'not 'alf so often as you are, old gal!'.

IV

The gradual refinement of language and behaviour in nineteenth-century England was a slow and uneven process. Many influences were at work at different levels of society, from Prince Albert at the slightly raffish court of the young Queen Victoria down to humble Methodist Sunday schools in the industrial midlands. It was inevitably accompanied by a measure of pretence and hypocrisy. These are features of most societies dominated by one particular system of politics or religious observance. In the latter years of Victoria's reign the gap between the conventional standards which the respectable classes affected and the opinions and conduct which characterized them in private seems to have been unusually wide. The early Victorians, however, are to be judged not so much by the kind of society which they had helped to bring about as by the nature of the society in their own time which they were trying to improve. Both Guizot and Raumer agreed at the start of the reign that, while the forces of moral reform were gaining the upper hand, they had much to do before victory could be assured. No society of fifteen or twenty million can change its habits and outlook in a single generation, and there was much in the England of the young Queen Victoria more characteristic of the cartoons of Hogarth and Rowlandson than the gentler Victorian productions of Doyle and Tenniel. Middle-class morality was only part of a general campaign to improve a society still in speech and manners not far removed from the eighteenth century. That the moralism of the middle classes was sometimes narrow, prudish, and intolerant is in the circumstances not altogether surprising.

At the bottom of the social scale there were more vigorous and intractable survivals. Little seemed to have changed since the Gordon riots of 1780. On every occasion of hardship, food shortage, unemployment, and political agitation, the response of the English people was invariably disorder and violence. The wartime Ludditcs in the manufacturing midlands, the agrarian rioters in East Anglia in 1816, the popular demonstrations in London at the time of the queen's funeral in 1821, the machine-breakers of the southern counties in 1830, the reform bill riots at Nottingham, Derby, and Bristol in 1831, the Chartist rising at Newport in 1839, the 'Plug Plot' riots of 1842, were only the larger and more notorious manifcstations of what seemed to many a permanent anarchic element in English society. There was in a sense some truth in this. The natural consequences of a decentralized, unpoliced state and a strong-willed, emotional, and predominantly youthful population were a casual indifference to authority and a roughness of behaviour among both crowds and individuals. The disorderliness and uproar that attended popular politics, for example, often made inexperienced foreigners believe that they were witnessing the beginnings of a revolution. 'We quiet continentals cannot understand the noisy and public life of this country', wrote Raumer in 1835. What in the disciplined states of Prussia and France would have signified a collapse of law and order, in the looser libertarian society of England was no more than the habitual physical exuberance of the free and independent 'sovereign people'.

Part of the rowdiness of English crowds in this period could undoubtedly be attributed to the drunken habits of the working classes. It was not the result of poverty only; there was general agreement that the better-paid workmen—miners, journeymen, and skilled artisans —drank more heavily than the others. James Burn, who served his apprenticeship as a journeyman-hatter in the north-east of England, thought intemperance was the leading vice of the profession. Though popular drunkenness was no worse than in Scotland or Ireland, it was regarded even before Victoria's reign as a national scandal. In several towns after 1830, clergy, businessmen, and other well-meaning members of the middle classes were promoting the establishment of Temperance Societies in the hope of abating the evil. The date 1830 is significant in this context because in that year was passed the notorious Sale of Beer Act designed to improve the quality of beer, discourage the growth of tied houses, and halt the decline in local and domestic brewing. Though passed with the best of intentions by the government, by permitting anybody to open a beer-shop on payment of a two-guinea licence without further reference to the magistrates, it removed a traditional check on the number of beerhouses and the personal character of those who kept them. At the same time the duty on beer was abolished and was not restored for another half-century. The result was what has been called 'a beer-shop explosion' all over the country which in turn was followed by a determined and largely successful effort by the big brewers to offset their losses on beer by encouraging the sale of spirits and making the premises where they were consumed—the so-called gin-palaces—more alluring to the poorer members of the public. Not until the Wine and Beerhouses Acts of 1869 and 1870 were beerhouses brought back once more under the supervision of the licensing JPs. The 1830 Act, which the duke of Wellington considered as one of the most beneficial of his short administration, made the early-Victorian period a halcyon era for drinkers when beer was cheaper, more widely available, and less controlled, than at any other time in modern British history.

Excessive drinking, however, while it may have stimulated, did not cause the ingrained love of fighting and destruction that characterized the poorer classes. Roughness and brutality could be found everywhere. It was not only gypsies, poachers, racecourse gangs, and the followers of professional prize-fights who constituted the disorderly element in the population. Men in regular trades and occupations were equally notorious for their lawless habits. Osbaldeston described a stand-up fight at the Pytchley Hunt races in Northamptonshire about the time of the 1832 Reform Act between himself, his hunt servants, and some local farmers on one side, and a crowd of Northampton shoemakers on the other. When Master of the Quorn in the 1820s he had experienced similar trouble with the stocking-makers and weavers of Leicestershire who used to assemble in crowds at the covertside on hunt days. Though judicious bribery helped to diminish this particular nuisance, ill-feeling persisted as a consequence of attempts by Osbaldeston to stop their other practice of hunting the Quorn coverts with curs and terriers on Sundays, when ordinary sport was barred by law. On one occasion he was returning at the end of a day's hunting with only a couple of companions when the hounds were attacked as they went through a village. A fight followed in the course of which the horse of his whipper-in had an eye knocked out. Race meetings and prize-fights were magnets for a different kind of men, the organized gangs of pickpockets, touts, and bookmakers' assistants. At the St Leger meeting at Doncaster in 1830 there was a pitched battle between a party of gentlemen headed by Lord Wharncliffe and a set of gambling people who had been driven off the course the previous day by Earl Fitzwilliam's grooms. Even simpler local festivals, where games and competitions were the main attraction, often led to disorder. Many forms of popular sport were, of course, rough enough in themselves. The annual Shrove Tuesday football match at

Derby in the post-Waterloo period usually produced much destruction of property and one or two deaths among the mass of contestants as the battle raged backwards and forwards through the town from noon until dusk.

Some glimpses of this underside of Victorian society are provided by the famous circus-proprietor 'Lord' George Sanger in his book *Seventy Years a Showman*. As a small boy in 1833 he was caught up in the great fight between two rival circuses, Wombwells and Hiltons, when he and his brother were nearly burnt alive in their caravan. In a later incident he records, about 1840–1, a notorious gang of roughs from Bath under cover of darkness smashed and looted the stalls at Lansdowne Fair. As the tired and drunken rioters returned home in the small hours, they were intercepted by the vengeful showmen, who managed to capture a dozen, including their ringleader, a red-haired virago called Carroty Kate. The men were first ducked in a pond, then tied to the wagon-wheels and horsewhipped. Kate was handed over to a couple of brawny show-girls for her flogging. The only intervention by authorities was when the remnants of the gang were intercepted by police on their return to Bath and a number arrested after more fighting. 'The authorities', observed Sanger reminiscently, 'in those "good old times" were a much more easy-going, non-interfering lot than they are today, and a rougher-mannered population took advantage of the fact.'

Though Surtees does not describe this level of English society, he was well acquainted with it. There is a minor episode in *Mr Sponge*, for example, which is an exact parallel to Osbaldeston's experiences when MFH. The occasion is the meet of the Puffington hounds (ch. xli) when at the first cover they draw they are confronted by 'all the Swillingford snobs, all the tinkers, and tailors, and cobblers, and poachers, and sheep stealers, all the scowling, rotten-fustianed, baggy-pocketed scamps of the country ranged round the cover, some with dogs, some with guns, some with snares, and all with sticks or staffs'. Like Osbaldeston, Mr Puffington prefers discretion to

valour and tries to bribe the crowd away by offering
them free ale if they go down to his house. This they do,
abstracting a couple of dozen silver forks behind the back
of the footman while they are there. Another passage
in the same book complements Mrs Ellis's description of
the idle young men and girls who paraded the streets on
the Sabbath. When Leather, Mr Sponge's groom, arrives
at Laverick Wells with his two horses, dusk is falling,
respectable young ladies have gone home, and, deprived
of their restraining company, 'licentious youths linked
arms, and bore down on the broad *pavé*, quizzing this
person, laughing at that, and staring the pin-stickers and
strawchippers out of countenance'—the last-named objects of their attentions being, one imagines, the milliners' assistants and shop-girls still lingering on the
streets.

If Surtees and Mrs Ellis were right, loutish behaviour,
even though stopping well short of the excesses of the
true English mob, was not uncommon among the
younger male members of the lower middle classes.
Given a certain amount of drink, and the bravado engendered by being an anonymous member of a group;
university undergraduates and army subalterns were
probably not much better. At Haileybury, the training
school for the Indian Civil Service, Beames has described
the 'uproar of oaths, songs, indecent jokes and horse-
play' in the 1850s when the young men gathered after
dinner to give their breakfast orders to the two 'modest,
quiet, hard-working girls' who presided at the buttery.
'One hopes', he added, 'they did not understand the
meaning of half that was said.'

V

A less frequently observed feature of Victorian society is
a certain quality of hardness which characterized the
governing classes as a whole. It was a quality reinforced
by their dealings with the mass of their poorer fellow-
countrymen, inculcated by their own sports and pastimes,

and for many of them inseparable from their own early upbringing. English public schools were barbaric places in which flogging by masters was sometimes matched by unmerciful tormenting by older boys. The evidence of this is strong and almost universal. Mozley spoke of the 'immense amount of cruelty, and worse wickedness' at Charterhouse during his schoolboy years there in the 1820s. Froude, who was a colleger at Westminster for three and a half years (1830–4), afterwards referred to the place as a 'den of horrors'. His sufferings were mainly at the hands of older boys. They made him drunk for their own amusement; he was flogged, half-starved, had his breeches set alight to make him dance, and was woken at night by glowing cigar ends pressed against his cheek. A son of Admiral Beresford who went to Eton in William IV's reign recorded that though there was not much bullying by his seniors, floggings by the headmaster, Dr Hawtrey, though less expertly delivered than those by his celebrated predecessor Dr Keate, were of frequent occurrence. The junior master in charge of the lower school also enjoyed the privilege of birching and used it freely even for trivial offences. Beresford was once flogged three times in one day. At Merchant Taylors' the under-masters habitually carried long canes which they used for the slightest fault. Their special technique was to grasp a boy by his hair, pull him down into a bending posture, and lash him on his back. John Beames, who was there from 1847 to 1855, said that he often went home at night 'with my shirt sticking to my back with blood which had congealed on it'. The well-known Victorian barrister Serjeant Ballantine, who was at St Paul's in the 1820s, described the three under-masters (he never encountered the head) as 'all tyrants—cruel, cold-blooded, unsympathetic tyrants'. They flogged continually, one with grave attention to his task, another with witty levity, and the third with savage anger. Compared with the 'halo of terror' which surrounded them, he added, bullying by other boys was regarded as no more than a minor nuisance.

This physical brutality of the educational system in most

public schools at this time is a phenomenon which is difficult to explain entirely. It had a long tradition behind it; perhaps too it was aggravated by the peculiarities of the teaching profession. Assistant masters, with the conspicuous exception of those at Eton, Rugby, and Harrow, were generally ill-paid. Most of them were clergymen who had failed to get a living and often perhaps felt a degree of embitterment as a result. Mozley thought that the one thing all schoolmasters had in common was a hatred of their profession; some in consequence vented their resentment on the boys who were its largest feature. Others had been confronted at the start of their career by too many undisciplined and defiant adolescents. Once acquired in self-defence, the use of the cane became a habit and sometimes an addiction. These can only be partial explanations. What is incontrovertible is that learning through the rod was a time-honoured practice and by no means confined to the public schools. The numerous but more ephemeral private schools varied perhaps more widely in character, since what chiefly counted here was the personality of the schoolmaster and his wife. Some were pleasant and efficient institutions, others as bad as the worst public schools. For this, too, reasons could be advanced. The smaller and more financially precarious the school, the more difficult it was to refuse any paying pupil. Private schools, therefore, were often the depositories for boys thrown out elsewhere. The institutions which specialized in taking orphans and other unwanted boys, while stimulating Dickens' fervid imagination to invent Dotheboys Hall, were not necessarily worse than many more conventional private and public establishments.

The harshness of school discipline in general was something against which public opinion was remarkably slow to make any effective protest. *Nicholas Nickleby* in 1838 made a brief stir about the Yorkshire schools but nobody wrote against the fashionable public schools. *Tom Brown's Schooldays* was not published until 1857; and that famous work of romantic fiction, besides setting a fashion, chiefly served to gain for Arnold's Rugby a greater reputation than it altogether deserved. It was designed as a best-seller, not as a piece of sociological criticism. What also protected the system was the immemorial instinct of the schoolboy not to 'blab' to his parents or be thought, in the early-Victorian vernacular, to be a 'sawney', otherwise soft. Often parents could have had little idea of what was going on in the schools to which they trustingly sent their sons. In any case, there were always defenders of the system. It discouraged pretentiousness; squires' sons and dukes' sons were equal under the lash. It enforced order and discipline on what were often rebellious and high-spirited young adolescents. It taught stoicism and endurance. For Surtees, if we may judge from his acid comments about the marquis of Bray in *Hillingdon Hall* (chs. xi, xxii), there were two main benefits of a public-school education. The first was that it knocked boys into shape and fitted them for the society of their equals. The son and heir of the duke of Donkeyton was a cautionary example of one who had escaped that salutary experience.

The Marquis, having had the unspeakable misfortune of being brought up at home, had conceived the not at all unnatural idea that the world was chiefly made for him, and that he might do as he liked with impunity. No greater misfortune surely can befall a young man than such an education; and lucky it is that so few of them get it. Eton knocks and Eton kicks save many a 'terrible high-bred' lad (as the Epsom race-list sellers describe the horses) from ruin.

The other advantage was that at a formative stage of his life a boy would make the right kind of friends. Again the contrast is with the unfortunate marquis of Bray—'a homebred youth, reared at his mother's apron strings, he had none of the suitable-aged companions a public school and college enable a youth to select'.

Surtees was praising a system of which he was not a product. His own education had been at a private boarding school, followed by one year at a grammar school; and he finished with schooling at an age when public schoolboys were barely launched on theirs. He

must have met many former public men in after years
and presumably learned to respect their qualities. One
wonders also whether he did not regret having missed
the social advantages which public school and university
might have brought him. Nimrod had at least been at
Rugby. The views Surtees was expressing about public-
school education were in any case those held by the
majority of fathers who sent their sons to those institutions. If they had uncomfortable recollections of their
own school experiences they could always comfort
themselves with the reflection that times had changed
and things were probably better than in their time.
Certainly the expansion of the public schools which was
a feature of the early-Victorian period was undertaken
not to alter their character but simply to widen their
intake. Arnold at Rugby from 1828 to 1842, Thring at
Uppingham after 1852, were ambitious men with firm
ideas about education who transformed their small
provincial institutions into schools with a national
reputation. The new Woodard foundations in the middle
of the century were designed to capture the cream of the
middle classes for the Anglican Church. There was no
conscious intent to create a more humanitarian type of
public school; and once established they bore a close
resemblance to the older institutions. Most of the famous
headmasters of the Victorian age—Arnold, H. M. Butler,
Benson—were industrious floggers; and the individual
histories of public schools to the end of the century indicate that heavy punishments and vicious bullying
survived along with, in many cases, the systematic homo-
sexual abuses to which Victorian memoirs darkly allude.

Only gradually were the worst features of public-school
life eliminated or reduced, mainly by depriving the boys
of the unfettered freedom they enjoyed outside the
classroom in the earlier part of the century and subject-
ing them to the discipline of organized team-games and
stricter supervision of their other recreations. Conformity
and uniformity replaced the old anarchic spirit of the
larger public schools. When George Hughes revisited
Rugby, thirty years after he had been a pupil there

under Arnold, what he chiefly noticed was that 'the boys
are much more accurately dressed, less rollicking, and
more decorous. The exceeding quiet of the town and
playground struck me particularly. I should like to have
seen a little more running about, and to have heard a
little more shouting.'

Well into Victoria's reign the sardonic claim could still
be made that any young man who had survived an
English public-school education had nothing more to fear
in the world. As Sydney Smith put it, with memories of
his time at Winchester when he and his brother had
been beaten, starved, and otherwise neglected, 'the world,
bad as it is, has nothing half so bad'. What the effect was
on Victorian men of such an upbringing can only be a
matter of speculation; but effects there must have been.
One of the many paradoxes of Victorian life is that the
qualities inculcated by both the old aristocratic and the
new middle-class public schools were the same: a certain
repressiveness of emotion, respect for physical prowess,
self-reliance, stoicism, and indifference to others. It is
significant that the quality singled out by the defenders
of the system as distinguishing the boarding-school
upbringing from that of day boys was the hardening of
the character that resulted rather than any moral or intellectual superiority. Though many middle-class intel-
lectuals were jealous of the aristocracy and regarded the
new public schools as gateways to the power and influence in the state previously monopolized by birth and
connection, the effect on their sons was to make them
not less but more like the aristocracy in manners, outlook,
and taste.

The hardness of the aristocracy and gentry was seen
most conspicuously in their attitude to sport. When they
competed, it was with the object of winning. Games-
manship was more evident than any desire to play the
game. In hunting there was little compassion either for
the quarry or for the horses and hounds which made the
pursuit possible. Horses were often ridden to exhaustion
both in the field and on the race-track. Instances of
animals foundering or dropping dead during long runs

were far more frequent than in the following century.[9] The fate of Tom Hall's unlucky purchase from Major Fibs, when out with Lord Heartycheer's hounds, was something which happened to more knowledgeable riders. When money was involved, as it was in most forms of physical competition, many sportsmen were similar to Tom in 'having no more feeling and sympathy for a horse than he had for a steam-engine'. In the great cross-country race between Osbaldeston's Clasher and Captain Ross's Clinker for £1,000, much of the five-mile course consisted of stiff, undulating ploughland, and both horses finished in a state of complete exhaustion. Clinker, who fell at the last fence, 'could not get up for twenty minutes, he lay groaning, and staling all round him'. Incidents like these gave rise to growing protests during the 1830s against the cruelty of the sport. Many people felt that horses, as Nimrod concisely put it, 'could not have been intended to go four miles, at their full speed, over ground of every description, intersected with fences, and this under much more than common racing weights'. The criticism was the stronger since already, from a conviction that they placed too great a strain on horses, four-mile heats on the flat had been almost entirely discontinued. As Nimrod also pointed out, horses intended for steeplechasing needed a very special form of preparation, and it was to the lack of it that he attributed the number of good animals whose lives had been sacrificed in this particular sport. Grimaldi, one of the best steeplechasers of his day, eventually dropped dead under his rider Mr Becher just after finishing a race; Vivian, another outstanding horse, had a similar end.

Nevertheless, a number of well-known riders continued to patronize this form of racing, and any improvements in the conditions under which steeplechases were held were slow in coming. At the Daventry Steeplechase in 1838 one horse was drowned, and another died from exhaustion immediately afterwards. This is not far short of the casualty list in Surtees' Grand Aristocratic Steeplechase described in *Mr Sponge* when one man was killed, one horse drowned, another broke its back, and a third 'cut all to pieces' on a stone wall. Surtees, like many fox-hunters, disliked steeplechases. Writing in 1853, he alleged that they had been taken up by innkeepers as a substitute for the vanishing prize-fights as a means of attracting custom and providing betting opportunities for their public. The betting element and the amount of chicanery it led to was regarded by Nimrod as a further objection to the sport. On the racecourse, where money was all-important, horses could be equally pressed to the limits of endurance. Lord George Bentinck, the 'Leviathan of the Turf' in the 1830s and early 1840s, was exceptionally hard on even his best animals. At the 1845 Goodwood meeting he raced his famous filly Miss Elis on two successive days over distances in excess of two miles and then again on the final day when she finished last in a field of nineteen and was never successful again. Bentinck would even race a horse twice on the same day.

Surtees had more respect for horses, and even showed some compassion for the hunted hare, though none for the fox. Many of his fellow sportsmen, however, showed a callousness which reads oddly today. The famous Captain Ross, celebrated for his skill with a pistol, not only kept his eye in by shooting cats (a schoolboy practice over many generations) but won money by backing himself to hit swallows on the wing with the same weapon. This he achieved by taking his stand beneath their nests on the walls of his residence, Rossie Castle near Montrose, and shooting the birds as they momentarily hovered at the entrance to the nests when returning with food for their young. While some of his contemporaries praised his marksmanship and others smiled at his astuteness in honouring the letter but evading the intent of the wager, none apparently spared a thought for the fate of the nestlings.

Shooting swallows on the wing with the more conventional shotgun was generally regarded as useful training for the more serious business of bringing down pheasants and partridges. Though the practice was deprecated by some purists, this was not on humanitarian but technical grounds since the flight of swallows differs markedly from that of game birds. A more thoughtful piece of advice to the aspiring shot was to use sparrows and similar small birds, released into the air with pieces of white paper fastened round their necks.

By this device, the flight of the bird is rendered less rapid, and more regular, and at the same time presents a much better mark for practice. It also affords excellent diversion in seasons when game cannot be pursued, or in wet weather, from underneath the shelter of a shed, or barn-door. Some of the first shots in England have been perfected by this mode.[10]

The traditional Continental indifference to the casual slaughter of songbirds was clearly shared by the early-Victorian sportsman.

It is true that a more humane attitude towards animals in general was already being advocated. A campaign led by Richard Martin, MP for Galway, 'Humanity Dick' as he was somewhat derisively known, secured an Act against the ill-treatment of cattle as early as 1822. This was followed two years later by the foundation of the Society for the Prevention of Cruelty to Animals. After his death, though largely because of his earlier unsuccessful efforts, parliament in 1835 prohibited bull- and bear-baiting and in 1849 cock-fighting as well. Legislation, however, was not the same as implementation. Many ordinary and by no means inhumane people thought that a degree of cruelty was inseparable from field sports and that in any case the rich should not deprive the poor of their pleasures while preserving their own. In time the grosser and more public blood-sports like bull- and bear-baiting gradually died out; other more easily concealed activities like dog-fighting and badger-baiting probably never completely disappeared.

Surtees in *Handley Cross* (ch. xxiv) gives a contemptuous account of these more furtive popular amusements sampled by Jorrocks and his friends in an unsavoury establishment in High Holborn; but his distaste is clearly for the disreputable public which they attracted rather than the cruelty which they involved.

A vast concourse of ruffianly spectators occupied the benches rising gradually from the pit towards the rafters, along which some were carelessly stretched, lost in ecstasy at the scene below.

Ponderous draymen, in coloured plush breeches . . . Smithfield drovers, with their badges and knotty clubs; huge coated hackney coachmen; coatless butchers' boys; dingy dustmen, with their great sou'westers; sailors, with their pipes; and Jews, with oranges, were mingled with Cyprians of the lowest order, dissolute boys, swell pickpockets, and a few simple countrymen.

The arrival of the comparatively respectable figures of Jorrocks, Charley Stobbs, and Mr Bowker was greeted with jeers and catcalls until Bowker's friend Billy Slender restored order.

Cock-fighting was regarded as a more gentlemanly sport and at the start of Victoria's reign was patronized by gentry and aristocracy all over the kingdom. Many bred their own birds, and there was a store of scientific literature in existence on their training and management. Though the Revd Jack Russell in Devonshire held aloof from what he regarded as a fierce and savage sport, many of his friends in the squirearchy of that county staged annual tournaments in their own houses with cocks of the finest strain taking part.

This element of hardness among the upper classes explains much about Victorian society which otherwise seems anomalous. Though progressive liberal and press opinion generally championed a gentler, more humanitarian outlook, there was a solid, if less vocal, resistance to it in governing circles, among the aristocracy generally, and even in many of the middle classes. In a different context these conflicting attitudes can be seen in the controversies of the 1850s over Sir James Brooke's attempted extirpation of the head-hunting Dyak pirates of Borneo or Governor Eyre's suppression of the Negro rising on Jamaica in the 1860s which was followed by over 400 judicial executions. Brooke was recalled, but a royal commission set up to investigate the charges against him came to no definite conclusions. Eyre's conduct was also examined by a royal commission and its report criticized both the governor and some naval and army officers for their part in punishing the mutinous Negro population. Yet though Eyre was promptly brought home, he arrived to a hero's welcome. Kingsley and Carlyle became his champions; Tennyson, Charles Dickens, and Ruskin subscribed to his defence fund. The government declined taking any further action, but private prosecutions were started against Eyre and some of his officers. The magistrates in Shropshire, where he was living, refused to commit him for trial; and separate proceedings in the Queen's Bench revealed differences of opinion even among the judges. In the end Eyre was discharged once more, this time by a Grand Jury. Finally in 1872 his legal expenses resulting from the prosecutions were reimbursed (by a Liberal government) and two years later his official pension as retired colonial governor was restored.

To Kingsley the increasingly humanitarian susceptibilities of the Victorian public were the result of what he called in 1868 'the effeminacy of the middle class, which never having in its life felt bodily pain (unless it has the toothache) looks on such pain as the worst of all evils'. The reference, as he made clear, was to the lower middle class—'the shop-keeping class' who, according to him, shrank from 'fatigue, danger and pain, which would be considered as sport by an average public schoolboy'. He appealed to history and theology to support his argument. 'Read history,' he wrote to Ludlow at the time of the Brooke controversy, 'look at the world and see whether God values mere physical existence . . . Physical death is no evil. It may be a blessing to the survivors.' To a later, more materialistic, generation this doctrine, especially when couched with Kingsley's customary vehemence, may seem hard to the point of brutality. Yet in his refusal on principle to make life an end in itself, he had sound Christian and Anglican authority behind him. It was the great seventeenth-century bishop of Down and Connor, Jeremy Taylor, who in his *Holy Living* wrote austerely that 'no man can be a slave but he that fears pain, or fears to die'.

Kingsley certainly saw no contradiction between the
teachings of Christianity and the disciplinary needs of
secular society. In 1855 he dedicated his most successful
novel, *Westward Ho!*, jointly to Rajah Sir James Brooke
and G. A. Selwyn, the distinguished and successful first
bishop of New Zealand, in order (as he phrased it in the
dedication) to express his 'admiration and reverence for
their characters' as types of English virtue not inferior to
the Elizabethan heroes. Between Brooke's peremptory
suppression of the Dyak pirates and Selwyn's sensitive
and tolerant handling of the Maori tribes there may seem
little obvious resemblance. Yet by coupling their names
together in this fashion Kingsley was clearly drawing
attention to the need to reconcile two differing aspects
of a larger truth than was contained in the conventional
liberal philosophy of the period.

A more surprising defender of the harder attitude to
life and death was Florence Nightingale. In 1899, on the
eve of the South African War, she wrote that

few men and fewer women have seen so much of the horrors
of war as I have. Yet I cannot say that war seems to me an
unmitigated evil. The soldier in war is a *man*; devoted to his
duty, giving his life for his comrade, his country, his God.

It was a sentiment which bound her, the clerical Charles
Kingsley, and the mass of sporting gentry (of which
Surtees was one) to the lower classes in both town and
country who produced the infantrymen of the Crimean
War. Of these last she had written at the time that they
'bear pain and mutilation with an unshrinking heroism
which is really superhuman, and die, or are cut up without
a complaint'. If much of Victorian society was rough and
brutal, there were at least some compensating qualities.

9
MORALS

I

In 1856 Lady Charlotte Schreiber received a letter from her 21-year-old son who had just sat his final degree examination at Cambridge. It announced that he was going to Paris for a few days with some friends. 'God grant,' she wrote anxiously in her journal, 'he come out safe from that hotbed of iniquity.' In all probability, like most mothers, she was thinking of sexual iniquity; and with over 50,000 prostitutes registered there in 1854, there was some foundation for her opinion of the French capital. Any doubts about the equal claims of London, however, must have been extinguished by the publication in 1862 of the fourth volume of Mayhew's *London Labour and the London Poor*, which dealt with prostitutes, thieves and swindlers, and beggars. The section on the first of these categories, written mainly by one of Mayhew's collaborators, the journalist Bracebridge Hemyng, was by far the largest of the three.

The problem of prostitution in London was an ancient one. What was new in Mayhew's study was the scale and thoroughness of the research, the use of personal interviews as well as official statistics, and the objective tone of discussion. With some imperfections, it is still the first great and largely reliable survey of the subject. Even so, some obscurities remain. Unlike France, there was no registration or regulation of prostitutes in London. Those known to the police in the middle decades of the century numbered between seven and eight thousand; but this was recognized to be far short of the real total. Estimates of that ran as high as ten times the known number. The majority of these were poor and wretched

women plying their trade on the street; but in the profession as a whole there was as wide a variety of social
ranks as in society at large, from the elderly hags who
haunted the alleys of Wapping for sailors, to the beautiful creatures who drove their light carriages in Hyde
Park attended by a bevy of admirers. There were full-
time professionals operating in their own apartments;
part-time amateurs eking out the exiguous wages they
earned as shop-girls or seamstresses. There were semi-
permanent mistresses residing in neat suburban villas;
others who confined their favours to a small circle of
selected clients. Most investigators agreed that poverty
was the chief reason for entering the profession; and
that for most women in this class it was not easy to
escape. Yet many could hope to lay by enough money to
retire to a more respectable mode of living; others made
their exit through marriage; some even married well.

Raumer thought that prostitution was no worse in
London than in Paris; but it was still a large and palpable
activity which had long been recognized as a serious
social problem. The evangelical conscience of English
society was reflected in the number of religious and
charitable organizations that worked to diminish it. If
London was the 'emporium of crime', one earnest clergyman observed, it was also the 'palladium of Christianity';
and the metropolis was therefore the 'great arena of
conflict between the powers of darkness and the ministry of heaven . . . the two antagonistic principles of good
and evil'. The Georgian Society for the Suppression of
Vice, founded in 1802 to halt the spread of atheism and
blasphemy, had increasingly turned its attention to the
suppression of brothels and the rehabilitation of their
inmates. A Reformatory and Refuge Union established
in 1856 ran a special mission for work among street-
walkers. In 1860, in fact, there were no less than twenty-
three institutions dedicated to the rescue and shelter of
'fallen women'. In the 1840s and 1850s leading newspapers like *The Times* and intellectual magazines like the
Westminster Review and *The Quarterly* from time to time
published articles calling attention to the subject. Where

general social problems were concerned there was no
desire to gloss over the truth, though of course these
publications were primarily addressed to an intelligent
masculine readership; which accounts for both their
explicitness and their usually objective tone. There was
general recognition, too, that, though a social nuisance,
prostitution also served a social function. It was the price
paid for the chastity of middle-class women and the
prevalence of late, prudential marriages.

Writing for a male, predominantly sporting, hard-
headed public, Surtees could hardly have avoided
touching on the subject in the course of his novels.
Whenever he did, he said enough to make it perfectly
clear to that kind of reader what he was talking about.
When, for example, a delicate pink visiting-card, with
blue borders and a gilt edge, inscribed 'Miss Juliana
Granville, John-Street, Waterloo-Road', is discovered in
Mr Jorrocks' coat-pocket, we do not need to enquire the
lady's profession. There is slightly more ambiguity perhaps about 'me Oncle Gilroy's' establishment in the sylvan
recesses of St John's Wood; but the reference to a 'left-
handed wife' (*Mr Sponge*, ch. lxi) suggests that Mr Gilroy
had prudently avoided the legal entanglement of marriage
even while, unknown to his nephew, rearing a covey of
little Gilroys. There can be little doubt either as to the
relationship between the Misses Glitters and Howard and
the sporting gentlemen at Nonsuch House, since their
hostess, Lady Scattercash, who in a different social mi-
lieu might have acted as chaperone, hailed from the same
profession as themselves. The little boy who explained
that he had been forbidden by his mother to enter the
house because it was 'full of trumpets' testified at least
to what the neighbours thought. The equivocal history
of the 'tolerably virtuous' Lucy is made plain by Lady
Scattercash herself when, on hearing of Lucy's engagement to Soapey Sponge, she gives her some worldly
advice about her conduct. She must forget about 'Harry
Dacre and Charley Brown, and the swell in the Blues.
Must be prudent for future. Mr Sponge would never
know anything of the past.'

The theatrical world to which Lucy belonged was in fact notorious for the laxity of its morals. Until late in the Victorian period the word 'actress' still carried its traditional connotation of doubtful respectability; and not without some reason. The social level of the profession was not high; the work irregular and poorly paid; the temptation to indulge in casual liaisons very great. The good looks and vivacity usually required of the female recruits to the profession were an attraction to men of all ages. Their greater freedom of manners and conversation provided callow youths and bored middle-aged husbands with a welcome contrast to the restraints and dullness of respectable society. In certain circles to have an actress 'friend' carried a social cachet. When Sam Spring at Newmarket was describing to Jorrocks the various members of a group of racegoers in the ring, he ends by saying, 'each has a first-rate house, horses and carriages, and a play-actress among them'. In drawing on the theatrical world for his most engaging and high-spirited women characters, Surtees was probably reflecting the taste of many men of his class, even perhaps his own. The association of fox-hunters and fast women was certainly not uncommon in real life. In his last year as Master of the Pytchley (1833–4), George Osbaldeston became very friendly with another well-known sportsman, George Payne, who was later to take over the same pack. Payne's residence was Sulby Hall where he lived with his mother and an unmarried sister of pious evangelical views. On the occasion of Osbaldeston's visit he found that Payne had engaged a number of 'young females' to entertain his fox-hunting guests. With a proper regard for the feelings of his mother and sister, however, Payne had installed them in a small house which he had furnished, distant about three-quarters of a mile from the Hall. Osbaldeston himself, who did not marry until late in life, led a far from celibate existence, leaving at least one illegitimate child. In this he seemed typical rather than otherwise of the sporting set of which he was so famous a member. All that was expected of them was a modicum of discretion and a reasonable consideration for the views of others in their own class.

Middle-class opinion, though it could not prevent, at least set its face against overt promiscuity. The disapproval extended beyond the offender to those who even appeared to condone the offence. When Mrs Buller, the mother of the politician Charles, took into her house about 1839 the illegitimate daughter of another son, Arthur, and admitted in confidence the fact of the parentage, her lady friends began to look askance at her: a circumstance which helped to bring about her retirement from London to the privacy of Leatherhead.[1] There was similar silent disapproval for Osbaldeston when he smashed his leg in the hunting-field and was taken to the house of a gentleman who was also a Dissenter. His host, who generously put his house at Osbaldeston's service for the duration of his convalescence, at first visited him daily to enquire after his progress. These visits stopped abruptly when he learned that Osbaldeston's current mistress was being regularly smuggled in to see him by the nurse and his personal servant. It was in the circumstances generous of him to allow Osbaldeston to remain in his house for the full eight weeks that were needed before he was fit to go home. Since the world is not unmoved by sublunary considerations, rank and wealth tended perhaps to have a certain blunting effect even on Dissenting susceptibilities. That at least is Surtees' cynical suggestion in *Tom Hall* when describing the reactions of county society to the wicked Lord Heartycheer when he held an open day at the castle on the first day of the hunting season. On such occasions 'the morality of the country' divided into three classes. The first were the 'desperately improper ones' who did not mind what people said and boldly entered in to feed on the sumptuous fare provided and eye the voluptuous paintings and statues which adorned the walls and corridors. The second group were the moderate Laodicean folk, 'the second class morality mongers' whose sense of propriety only permitted them to partake of refreshment at the door without actually penetrating the profane castle walls. Finally there were the prudish ones who refused even to enter the park though they might casually drive out in that direction on the off-chance of catching a glimpse of the company.

To women, even among the aristocracy, rather less charity was extended. Miss de Horsey in 1857, on her own confession, scandalized society by riding and driving in public with Lord Cardigan, a married man with an unfaithful wife. The scandal redoubled when, as a result of a quarrel with her father over the association, she left the paternal roof and set up a separate establishment in Park Lane—a step which cost her the loss of many of her friends. Cardigan's wife died in 1858 and a few months later he married Miss de Horsey at Gibraltar where they had gone on his yacht. Even so, when she returned to England as Countess of Cardigan, she remained under the displeasure of Queen Victoria and, Lady Dorothy Nevill alleged and Lord Clarendon confirmed, of many other members of fashionable society. Even stronger disapproval was shown of Lady Lincoln, the neurotic, promiscuous wife of the Peelite politician, who eloped to Germany in 1848 to join her latest lover, the profligate Lord Horatio Walpole. This escapade led eventually to one of the more notorious divorce cases of the century. Shunned in London society, in 1860 Lady Lincoln finally married her Belgian courier and lived permanently abroad until, some time in the 1880s, she retired to Sussex to pass her last few years in complete obscurity. Though its own laxity of morals prevented the Victorian aristocracy from taking a puritanical view of sexual vagaries, it increasingly required from its womenfolk a reasonable respect for outward propriety. If it involved a measure of hypocrisy, that was unavoidable. As Edward Bulwer wrote pessimistically to his son in 1853, 'the world must be turned topsy turvey before the relationship between the sexes can be adjusted to any harmonious ethics that reconcile virtue with the passions of the senses'.[2]

Bulwer was concerned to warn his son against the personal danger of entanglement with predatory women. For those in the middle classes of society, equally exposed to the observation of their equals and with more to fear from their censure, respectability was a social necessity. Even Mr Facey Romford, a brazen rogue in many other respects, needed the cover of outward morality for his peculiar mode of life. When Lucy Glitters, abandoned by Mr Sponge, threw herself on his protection, his first instinct was to keep her at a safe distance. 'He was a very moral man, especially when it was his interest to be so, and was not going to prejudice his chances of getting an heiress by—even the semblance of an illicit connection.' It was only his anxiety to make his horse-dealing more profitable that overcame his fear of scandal and persuaded him to allow Lucy to take up residence in his house, duly chaperoned by her mother, for the practical purpose of assisting with his hounds and showing off his horses. Lucy Glitters was therefore metamorphosed into Mrs Somerville, widow of an Indian Army officer, and 'sister by courtesy' to Facey Romford; an arrangement which technically satisfied social convention even if it did not entirely still the voice of gossip. There is no indication from Surtees, however, that the relationship was other than a business arrangement.

II

Seductive and expensive women were not the only social danger to which young Victorian males were exposed. There was a whole class of men who made a living from the follies of their own sex. In an article, which seems to have been overlooked by his biographers, contributed to Douglas Jerrold's social study *Heads of the People* in 1840, Thackeray sketched a vivid (and, one need hardly doubt, authentic) picture of the gentlemen of fortune who battened on the simple and wealthy youth of the day. It was entitled 'Captain Rook and Mr Pigeon', a subject on which the author was well qualified to write since he had personal experience, when an undergraduate at Cambridge and later in London, of being a pigeon himself. What is striking is that he thought England peculiarly productive of such adventurers. 'There is no cheat like an English cheat,' he wrote. 'Our society produces them in the greatest numbers as well as of the greatest excellence. We supply all Europe with them.' Captain Rook (his authority for the title is left conveniently obscure) is

not interested in women; he cultivates the society of men,
especially young men. His place of action is not the club
or the gambling saloon but the private apartment where
the downy pigeon can be plucked at leisure and un-
observed. He is often in the company of a fine-looking
woman, a 'pro-temporaneous Mrs Rook, very likely, in
an establishment near the Regent's Park', to which she
brings the young man and then innocently suggests a
game of cards for, of course, trifling stakes.

The Captain had been a pigeon himself once and as a
result had ruined his chances of finding a respectable
career. He had finally graduated into his profession by
going abroad, learning the skills of cards, dice, and
billiards, and turning himself into a fashionable man of
the world, with a valet, a confederate, a carriage, and
case of pistols. Yet it was a precarious and rootless way
of life. Thackeray estimated that to maintain the social
position necessary for his work, the professional rook
needed an annual income of £1,600, all of which had to
be extracted as a rule from his victims. Since age and
declining powers overtake all, even the Captain Rooks
of this world, his ultimate end was likely to be a debtor's
prison or at best shabby exile at Calais or Boulogne.

The archetypal Captain Rook in Surtees' novels is, of
course, Johnny O'Dicey in *Plain or Ringlets*, the 'man of
fashion and youth lightener of cash' at Roseberry Rocks—
to outward view dashing, lighthearted, extravagant,
underneath skilful, patient, and remorseless once he had
his talons into a likely victim. The dinner-party described
in chapters xxviii–xxix is an exposition on how to pluck
a greenhorn. O'Dicey does without women; but his confederates—the puritanical Major Minster, the sedate Mr
Wanless, the sporting Captain Gammon, and the respectable Mr Curlew MP (ex-)—more than make up for
the absence of petticoat appeal by the artfulness with
which they play their contrasting roles in guiding
the unsuspecting and hapless Jasper Spinks towards the
catastrophe of a loss on the evening's play of £4,000.
The whole episode is so minutely described, the tactics
of the four card-sharpers so subtle, that it is hard to

believe Surtees was not drawing on his own observation.
He repeats, incidentally, one of Thackeray's character-
touches by making Captain Gammon originally a victim
of Johnny O'Dicey, who, after plucking him 'as clean
as a poulterer plucks a pullet', had converted him into
a kind of second fiddle to himself. The scene of the en-
counter too is typical. London apart, spas, seaside resorts, and universities were the favourite plucking
grounds, since at such places were to be found larger
numbers than elsewhere of foolish young men, with more
money than was good for them, and away from the
restraints of home.

The frequent references in contemporary literature to
this class of men attest to their prevalence in Victorian
society. Though of too high a social standing to be included in Mayhew's list of cheats and swindlers, they
crop up in many unexpected places. Haydon described
one of them, an old friend he had not seen for many
years whom he ran into unexpectedly in 1821. He had
served in the Napoleonic War, had been taken prisoner
and detained in France, thereby losing promotion, escaped, went to Spain, failed to get on with his superior
officer, and finally retired from active service. He was a
fine-looking man with good physique and a melodious
voice but 'a complete gambler! a man who lived by his
wits, who fired at marks for his breakfast, and gambled
at *rouge et noir* for his dinner! who could kill his man at
20 paces and make sure of him at ten! who talked of his
honour because he knew it was suspected, and passed
his life in one perpetual scene of anxiety and fret'. He
told Haydon that he always stopped when he had won
£5—a rate of profit which, earned regularly, would have
brought him in an annual income not far short of
Thackeray's estimate of what was needed for a man of
his occupation. J. G. Beresford, recalling his undergraduate days at Cambridge in the early 1840s, referred
to a certain baronet who frequented the colleges. He had
ruined his estate and his reputation but found a way to
mend his fortunes by playing cards with undergraduates,
sometimes winning as much as £500 in a single night.

Eventually he was banned from entering any college in the university. Though individuals came and went, and the *modus operandi* varied, the species was inextinguishable. Taking his freshman son up to Cambridge by train in 1861, Acland fell into conversation with a 'quiet-looking young man, like a lawyer, about thirty years of age'. He turned out to be 'a regular betting Newmarket man, a Cambridge graduate living on the turf—the quiet look being a blind to take in the fast man'. Finding that there was nothing to be gained from the Aclands, he gave them a frank disquisition on the mode of life followed by him and his confederates.

The great source of revenue being the young gentlemen with money or expectations whom they can tempt to *back* horses (i.e. bet in favour of horses they fancy), which is sure to be a losing game; and the blacklegs play a game among each other to see who can get the largest share out of the prize money made on the ruin of these poor boys.

Torn between amusement and distaste, Acland reflected that at least their cool travelling companion was an object lesson for his fledgling 18-year-old.

Acland's railway acquaintance was clearly one of those men who in the earlier part of the century had been known as 'betters-round' to distinguish them from sportsmen who made wagers among themselves on a single horse. The betters-round, later more commonly known as 'blacklegs' or simply 'legs', made a 'book' on a race by making or taking bets on any of the horses entered for it. In an age when the profession of 'book-maker' was only gradually emerging, many of these betting men mixed in good society and were only distinguished from their clients by their special devotion to the art of making money out of racehorse gambling. It demanded much time and attention, a head for figures, and a good system of intelligence. One of the greatest as well as the most aristocratic practitioners in his time was Lord George Bentinck, who used the proceeds of his systematic, large-scale gambling to finance his racing activities. In 1845, for instance, he won in prize money only £18,000 but was thought to have made nearly £100,000 in betting. The object of the professional betting man being to make money, his task was to arrange his betting in such a manner that, whatever the outcome of the race, he would be in profit. By placing his bets on particular horses at long odds early in the season, he could accept bets on them at shorter odds later on; by placing bets on other horses he insured against the failure of the horses he had previously backed; or alternatively he could place bets on them to lose. Simply to back a favourite to win was a practice he left to the amateur. His concern was to find, not a winner, but a favourite on which he could induce others to bet but which would not win.

The tendency of the gullible public to place their money on a few favoured horses to win, and the interest of the professional 'legs' in seeing that they did not win, was the principal reason for the corruption which universally prevailed in the world of the racecourse. The desired end of defeating the favourite could be brought about in a number of ways. A moderate horse, by judicious artifices such as false trials and misleading information, could be made to appear ('got up' in the contemporary phrase) a likely winner though in reality it stood no chance. Good horses could be 'nobbled' to prevent them from running to form. After Dan Dawson was executed in 1812 for poisoning a number of promising horses at Newmarket, the usual method was to administer an opiate shortly before the race. Dishonesty was not confined to bookmakers and their accomplices. Trainers could ensure that their entries were unfit to run; jockeys could hold them back in the actual race. Owners themselves were not above suspicion. They might conspire with others and agree on a winner; or the favourite could be sold, usually to a syndicate of blacklegs, on the eve of a big race, leaving them to do what was necessary. For the professional punter the great art, according to Nimrod, was to discover which was the 'book-horse', that is to say, the horse which the public had supported in their thousands but against which a substantial amount had been laid by those in the know. Such a horse was certain to lose.[3]

It is not surprising that many sportsmen were repelled by what Osbaldeston's biographer roundly described as the 'miasma of knavery' surrounding racing in the early-Victorian period. From time to time, when the blacklegs overreached themselves, there would be a public scandal. The 'Running Rein' Derby of 1844, when one of the favourites was held back by his jockey and the field included one four-year- and one five-year-old, has become a legend; but it was only one of a number of suspect races. Bloomsbury, who won the Derby in 1839 at odds of 40 to 1, was thought to be either a four-year-old, or, like Running Rein, a substitute. According to Nimrod, the results of the St Leger in 1828 and again in 1834 were fraudulent. The *New Sporting Magazine* made the uncontroverted allegation that in the Derby of 1832, won by St Giles, every horse in the race except one (Perion) was supposed to have been 'made safe', i.e. safe not to win. In 1836 Edward Ruthven, Liberal MP for County Kildare 1832–5, was found guilty by the Irish Turf Club of running two horses under false names and ages, and pocketing large sums of money as a result.

At the accession of Victoria the corruption of the Turf seemed to be getting worse than ever. For some the only remedy was to have nothing to do with racing. 'If gentlemen would associate with gentlemen', observed Baron Alderson, the judge who presided over the Running Rein case, 'and race with gentlemen, we should have no such practices. But if gentlemen will condescend to race with blackguards, they must expect to be cheated.' The difficulty was that the gentlemen themselves were sometimes cheats; and those who were not were unable to change the system. Even a sporting journalist, who might have been more disposed to sympathy than Mr Justice Alderson, was moved to write in 1842 that

without doubt there are many noblemen and gentlemen of high honour yet on the turf; but the great preponderating number of mere adventurers, and regular 'legs', has driven almost all chance of success by fair betting off the course; and, in the language of trade, has brought the best judgement to a discount. Desperate characters, without money, and void of principle, bet largely on a concocted race ... There is little dependence now to be placed on the goodness of any horse, or on the fair conducting of our modern races.[4]

Appearing in a sporting periodical which addressed itself particularly to the country gentry, there could hardly have been a more devastating judgement.

It is understandable, therefore, that fox-hunters as a class disapproved of horse-racing. Assheton Smith, one of the greatest of them, though persuaded by Bentinck to join the Jockey Club, soon resigned from it. 'He loved the straightforward honesty of a fox-hunt, but observed that the chicanery of racing was uncongenial to him.' Jack Russell, equally famous in the next generation, felt the same. On racing he always looked with a wary eye, regarding it as 'a game in which the best horse is not always the winner—very different from hunting'. Mr Jorrocks was briefer and blunter. 'Racing is only for rogues', he declared in his speech at the hunt dinner in *Handley Cross*. This was not the only occasion on which he expressed his feelings. In his third sporting lecture he made a more sustained attack, lamenting that the noblest of animals should be soiled by contamination with the 'trickey, lynx-eyed circumwentin' knaves wot would rob their own fathers if they could, and who set hup to bet thousands with a farthin' capital'. Surtees makes it clear that this attitude is not to be treated as an individual prejudice. Though Captain Strider made a face on hearing Jorrocks' remark at the hunt dinner, we have already been told a few pages earlier that he was something of a blackleg himself; 'he had made money by racing—if honestly, he was a much belied man'.

Scattered through the novels are similar expressions of Surtees' own feelings about racing. In *Ask Mamma* one of Miss Willing's early employers was the Hon. Mrs Cavesson, 'whose husband was a good deal connected with the Turf, enjoying that certain road to ruin which so many have pursued'. No doubt it was the recollection of the financial crash suffered by her employer that

prompted her to warn her son later not to have anything
to do with racing. 'It's only for rogues and people who
have more money than they know what to do with.'
Mr Bullivant, the old family lawyer in *Plain or Ringlets*,
makes the same point in a more pedantic style. To the
young Jasper Goldspink, aspiring to the hand of Rosa
McDermott, he gives his view that the habit of betting
on horse-races, together with drunkenness, constitutes
an insuperable bar to matrimony. 'It is a dangerous pursuit, and draws you into low profligate company,' he
tells Jasper in the course of a long lecture on the perils
of the Turf. 'Upon this turf business I must be firm and
peremptory. I never knew any good come of it. I have
known a great deal of ill.'

Not content with crediting many of his characters with
these views, Surtees calls on higher authority. 'What
good', he quotes Thackeray as saying, 'ever came out of,
or went into, a betting book? If I could be Caliph Omar
for a week, I would pitch every one of these despicable
manuscripts into the flames'; a sentiment to which Surtees
adds a personal *Amen*, with a rider to the effect that he
was not sure that he would not hang one or two of the
'leg' or 'list' men as well. Sir Moses Mainchance is allowed
to observe that hunting was 'peculiarly the sport of
gentlemen, and about the only one that defied the insidi-
ous arts of the blackleg . . . Lord Derby was quite right in
saying that racing had got into the hands of parties who
kept horses not for sport, but as mere instruments of
gambling.' This is a topical allusion to a letter which that
well-known politician and sportsman wrote to the
stewards of the Jockey Club in which he stated categor-
ically that 'the number of men of station and fortune who
support the Turf is gradually diminishing, and that an
increasing proportion of horses in training is in the hands
of persons in an inferior position, who keep them not for
purposes of sport, but for the purposes of gambling'.
The object of Derby's letter was to lend strength to the
reform campaign launched by Admiral Rous in 1856
with his letter to *Bell's Life* on ante-post betting. Derby's

intervention was given further publicity by *The Times*, which made the comment that 'a large portion of the sporting world is identical with the vilest section of the community' and hoped that the participation in racing by 'men of station and fortune' would eventually end altogether.

In Surtees' opinion, and not his alone, the immorality of horse-racing had grown steadily worse in his lifetime as a direct result of the increase in gambling. His views are to be found in their most complete form in the chapter in *Plain or Ringlets* entitled 'The Turf', which is virtually a separate essay. In this he argued that during the previous twenty-five years the rise in popularity of horse-racing had drowned all the gentlemen and brought 'the mud of the sea to the surface'. Once gentlemen betted among themselves on a variety of sporting events; now more money was devoted to gambling in general and a larger proportion of it to horse-racing than ever before. The gentlemen had consequently been squeezed out by the legs, and tipsters had taken over. The few professional 'book-making betting-men' who used to operate on their own account had been submerged by 'a perfect myriad of middle-men' who touted for custom, victimized the innocent, and in the character of 'sporting men' usurped the place of sportsmen. They were, he concluded roundly, 'a growing and a dangerous evil, and one that completely baffles the efforts of the legislature to suppress them'. It was the corrupt state of racing that made it possible for these people to flourish, since 'betting, where parties are sure to win', needed no capital other than a pocket-book, a metallic pencil, and unlimited impudence. On races and racehorse owners, Surtees is unsparing. Half the horses, he wrote, ran under the names of false owners; jockeys were adepts in appearing to race their mounts to the limits of their abilities while yet finishing in a pre-determined order; stewards were chosen only for their value as social decoys, while the real organizers and wire-pullers remained behind the scenes. The spread of the railways had infected the small provincial meetings with the taint of the big national racecourses. Horses from anywhere in the kingdom could suddenly appear in order to make money for their owners and connections by winning or losing, since one could be as profitable as the other; and they would be accompanied by touts, bookmakers, and gambling men—'fellows from the gaming-houses, the saloons, and the stews, riotous in jewellery—who call themselves by the conveniently indefinite title of the "London gents"'—together with the more sinister hangers-on who were ready to drug and lame unfortunate animals whenever necessary.

It is a black picture; but no blacker than that painted by many others. Admiral Rous, who thought the second quarter of the nineteenth century unequalled for the amount of money gambled on the Turf, followed Lord George Bentinck in trying to reform the conduct of race-meetings; but most of what these two energetic figures in the Jockey Club were able to achieve was of a technical nature relating to the starting of races, the regulation of jockeys and their dress, the numbering of horses, and the creation of enclosures. Bentinck's set of rules, drawn up in 1844, were gradually adopted all over the country; but his simultaneous efforts to expel the undesirable elements from Epsom, Newmarket, and Goodwood were only temporarily successful. When Rous became official handicapper for the Jockey Club in 1855 he found that already standards were falling again. The Club itself was in low water financially and little regarded. Its credit had not been strengthened by the circumstance that early that year the Hon. Francis Villiers, a steward of the Jockey Club, had decamped to the Continent, leaving behind him about £100,000 of racing debts. Over a dozen years passed before Rous was able to put into effect the new list of reforms he had first put forward in 1850. To keep meetings even relatively free from the blackguard element needed perpetual vigilance; and Rous himself could not prevent a steady decline of the sport of horse-racing into an industry from which many made fortunes who had no personal interest in horses.

III

For every one who gambled on races, however, there were scores who from time to time had to embark on the business of buying a horse for their own use. No socially respectable families could do without such a means of transport; and since few were in the position of being able to breed their own, nearly all had to buy their horses, so to speak, at second-hand. Most second-hand purchases involve an element of risk; where the trade is widespread and lucrative, it also invites fraud. Even buying from a friend was no guarantee of getting a sound article, since friends were only human and had interests of their own. 'It is an unpleasant reflection,' observed Mr Jorrocks candidly in his first sporting lecture, 'and says little for the morality of the age, or the merits of the Reform Bill, that, out of London, one can hardly get rid of an 'oss without more or less doing violence to one's feelin's of integrity.' If buying and selling horses even among friends was attended by a certain absentmindedness about vices and an undue emphasis on virtues, it followed that when doing business with professional horse-dealers, a large degree of caution was advisable.

Surtees in his capacity as a satirist has much to say on the subject of horse-dealing both amateur and professional. Not much of it is edifying. Dealers falsified the names, origin, condition, and pedigree of their animals. Those who thought it was better to buy at an auction than direct from a dealer are warned that the 'rings' that had long been a feature of furniture sales now infested the sale-yard. Good horses were bought up cheap by the ring, who then held a second, private auction among themselves. Anyone who tried to break the ring would find that the horse he fancied would be bid up out of his reach. Some dealers, like the fictional Mr Francis 'Goodhearted' Green, Facey Romford's friend, specialized in buying up cheaply, and selling dearly, vicious and unmanageable horses whose defects he could mask long enough to foist them off on unwary customers. Being a generous man, however, he was also prepared to take over lazy or broken-down animals, since 'he had a happy knack of blending the useless with the dangerous' and was always ready to exchange one for the other for a suitable commission. Was this simply a caricature? Probably not. Grantley Berkeley has a story in his *Recollections* about a London dealer Tom Marsden, popular among the fashionable young men, who lent him a horse (to be paid for when convenient) who turned out to be nearly blind. It had sagacity and courage, and was perfectly safe on roads with a good rider. Across country, however, it was useless since it could not see the fences in time. Berkeley returned it as soon as he discovered the disability and 'Marsden took him back again without a word, as he very well knew that he was perfectly blind'.

There were worse rogues than this in the murky world of horse-trading: men whose stock in trade consisted of good-looking but broken-winded or otherwise useless animals. Their mode of operation was to place alluring advertisements in newspapers offering them for sale or hire with generous promises of trial rides. When it came to the actual transaction they would ask for a deposit of allegedly half, in reality double or treble, the value of the horse before letting it go out. When the potential buyer returned from his trial ride he would find both dealers and deposit had vanished. These 'horse-chaunters', as they were known in criminal slang (from 'chaunt', to publish or advertise), were familiar in Grose's day and still flourished in the London of Queen Victoria. An example of their methods features in *Plain or Ringlets* when Mr Bunting makes his ill-advised trip to Sligo Mews to obtain a loan of 'Captain Chichester's horses'. Altogether, observed Surtees, Sligo Mews and its counterparts in other districts of London were thriving enterprises—'so brisk is the trade, and so yielding the seams of British greenness and greediness'. This was not just a rhetorical flourish. In his severely practical 'Hints to Railway Travellers', published in 1851 and reprinted as a shilling booklet in 1852, Surtees gave a serious warning to provincial visitors, looking for temporary means of transport for themselves while in the capital, to be on their guard against this type of fraudulent horse-dealer. 'Horse-chaunting', he wrote, 'is a very common pursuit in London.'

Alongside the professional dealers were the amateurs. These, while not pretending to make a living out of it, sought to add to their incomes by occasional buying and selling of horses. Many of them were knowledgeable and astute, employing their own riding skill and social contacts to pave the way for more commercial transactions. A case in point is Nimrod himself, who admitted in 1835 that he had bought and sold as many as 150 horses in the course of thirty-five years. In Surtees' novels the two prime exponents of this slightly ungentlemanly activity are of course Soapey Sponge and Facey Romford. Neither of them were gentlemen in the accepted sense. Indeed, neither was even up to the Nimrod standard of respectability. Sponge was not what he seemed, since he was not actually a man of independent means sufficient to support him. Romford was not what people thought he was, since he had encouraged them to think that he was somebody else of the same name but much higher social standing. Both men lived on their wits, relying on their intelligence and impudence to supply the lack of a steady income. They were in fact a camouflaged species of rook, plucking not so much individual pigeons as society at large. Soapey, as his name indicated, made a trade of 'sponging' on casual acquaintances, thereby saving himself a great deal of expense for bed and board, not to speak of stabling and fodder for his horse. From the start none of Surtees' sporting readers could have been in any doubt about his character and mode of living. To 'sponge' was an old expression in English slang. The word appears in Grose's *Classical Dictionary* as early as 1785 and its origin is probably much older. 'To spunge', says Grose, is 'to eat and drink at another's cost'. This concisely describes Soapey's constant endeavour in life. While allowing others to maintain his style of life as a fashionable sportsman, and keeping a weather eye open for an heiress, Soapey was also interested in horse-dealing as a profitable sideline. He kept a close watch on the regular sales at Tattersalls and was well known to all the dealers and grooms of the capital. He was prepared as well to sell horses on a commission basis. The two horses selected by him at Buckram's stables to take down into the country testify to his skill in masking equine defects. The unprepossessing pair consisted of Hercules, who was powerful and vicious, and Multum in Parvo, who was hard-mouthed, pig-headed, and stupid. The arrangement was that Sponge paid a monthly sum for their hire and had the option of buying them during the season. A condition of the agreement was that Buckram's own headman Peter Leather should accompany the horses as groom, no doubt as much to safeguard Buckram's property as to serve Sponge's convenience.

Facey Romford was a man of similar character, combining horsemanship, effrontery, keen business sense, and lack of scruples, though he was of coarser fibre and operated on a slightly lower social level. Since his speciality was not so much hunting as running a pack of hounds at a profit, his need for horses was all the greater. His preferred method of business was to work as much as possible on a commission basis, thereby reducing his overheads. He would buy anything—four-legged horses, three-legged horses, two-legged horses; he would buy them for cash or without cash, more the latter than the former. He would take them on trust, buy them if he thought he could make a profit by reselling, or pay and promise so much for their use if retained. When he took over the Heavyside Hunt his first step was to visit Mr Goodhearted Green in London, who supplied him with Honest Robin, formerly The Cur, who was liable to stop dead and refuse to go on even half-way through a hunt; Brilliant, who was an inveterate savage; and the beautiful lady's horse Leotard, a picture to look at and a capricious little devil to ride. For this choice assemblage he paid £30, £20, and £10 respectively with a reversionary share to Mr Green of half of whatever price was extracted from some unfortunate purchaser. Since all three horses had

been in and out of Green's stable with a lengthening list
of complaints and a steadily shortening price, both parties
to the transaction were satisfied, 'Goodheart thinking he
had done Romford, and Romford thinking he had done
Goodheart'.

There are other, more occasional, traders in horseflesh
that appear in the novels. In *Mr Romford* mention is made
of Mr Hazey, otherwise known as Secondhand Harry,
who was always on the lookout for a horse he could buy
to sell again, though he always pretended that they were
for his own use and was forever asking his acquaintances whether they knew anything that would suit him.
Another is Major Yammerton in *Ask Mamma*, who was in
the habit of taking semi-useless horses at bargain prices
either for cash or goods, which he optimistically hoped
to palm off on somebody or other. Surtees had even
more contempt for these amateurs than for the professional rogues, since he thought them the more unscrupulous and more outrageous liars. The men who earned
their living from horse-dealing were usually too busy
and had too many animals on their books to be unduly
concerned about selling any one of them. The part-time
dealer, on the other hand, was more anxious to make
good profit on each of his paltry two or three horses and
had greater leisure and incentive to concoct elaborate
deceptions. What made matters worse was that the
amateur moved in better society, knew the weaknesses
of his potential clients, and had more opportunities to
make a sale.

What both classes enjoyed was comparative immunity
against legal retribution for their chicanery. This was
partly because few men liked to admit that they were so
ignorant of horses that they could be overreached in a
bargain; partly because going to law about a horse-sale
was generally recognized to be a fool's game. Horses are
notoriously delicate creatures, susceptible to sudden ill-
nesses and prone to unforeseen accidents. Experts could
easily be procured to give evidence on either side; while
no dealer in his senses would ever give an unconditional
warranty, though he would be full of ingenious reasons

for not doing so. Cheating on horses, Surtees once observed, had become a science; and part of the science
was to make it almost impossible to prove in a court of
law. Any verdict there was likely, therefore, to depend
on the unpredictable prejudices of judge and jury. The
great suit of *Doleful* v. *Jorrocks*, related at length in
Handley Cross, was a warning in itself of the hazards of
seeking redress from the law. On that all the experts
were agreed. 'Never go to law about a hos' was the advice
given by the anonymous journalist 'Rough Rider' in his
'Hints to Young Sportsmen' published in the 1840 *Almanac for Sportsmen and Country Gentlemen*, 'for if you
"do", ten chances to one that you'll be "done"'. He was
kind enough to explain why. Every previous owner of
the horse would swear that when he sold it, it was in
sound condition; and the only unbiased witness, the
animal itself, could not be put in the witness-box.

IV

On violent crime as distinct from fraud and dishonesty
Surtees has less to say. This is understandable. Violence
is hardly a subject for satire; and any treatment of crime
that detracted from its social seriousness was unlikely
to win the approval of his readers. His references to it
therefore are slight and incidental. There is a mention in
Handley Cross of the experiences of old Stobbs and his
son, fresh up from Yorkshire and provincial innocence,
who on their visit to London to place young Stobbs with
Mr Twister, the conveyancer, both have their pockets
picked half-a-dozen times while staring into shop-
windows. There are stray references to the tinkers and
'muggers' who pasture their horses overnight in other
people's fields, and to gypsies—those 'swarthy ringletted
people' who tell fortunes at the Roseberry Rocks
picnic and come up before Mr Jorrocks and his fellow-
magistrates in *Hillingdon Hall* for stealing poultry. For all
these contemporary social nuisances there is ample contemporary evidence. The *Report* of the 1839 Commission

appointed to inquire into the best means of establishing
an efficient county constabulary no doubt exaggerated
the extent of rural crime because it wished to make a
case for such a force. Yet it is difficult to ignore entirely
the evidence it produced for the existence of much petty
theft, of pickpocketing, robbery, and assault, of tramps
and gypsies living off the countryside, of roving gangs
of beggars intimidating the inhabitants of lonely houses,
and of disreputable beerhouses that were haunts of
prostitutes and thieves. The conclusion of the Commission was that there was little large-scale organized crime
but a vast amount of minor criminality, the effects of
which were felt more by the poor and lower middle
classes than the rich.

Among the lesser offences, pickpocketing was almost
universal wherever there were sufficient numbers of
people to make the crime easy and detection difficult—
in London and the larger towns, at races and other
outdoor sporting occasions, at fairs and markets. Even
in church one could not feel safe. In the London of the
1830s, Mozley recalled, evening services were not favoured by the stricter clergy of the Establishment, partly
because they were common among Dissenting congregations, partly because they encouraged flirtations among
young people, but partly also because they facilitated
the activities of pickpockets who found attentive wor-
shippers in dimly lit pews and galleries ideal for their
purposes.[5] In the countryside one of the commonest
crimes was poaching, which was perhaps a kind of rural
equivalent to pickpocketing in towns. On this subject
Surtees had a good deal to say. 'Poacher', he remarks
testily in Mr Sponge (ch. xxxv), 'is only a mild term for a
"thief".' At Swillingford it was the principal trade of the
place, and Mr Puffington, when he took up residence
nearby, made the cardinal error of refusing to prosecute
the first poachers caught on his land. The rest took the
hint and began a systematic clearance of his estate, first
getting rid of his hares, partridges, and pheasants, then
proceeding to take his fish, and finally his sheep.

On the other hand, Surtees had no love for the obsessive preservation of game, with armies of gamekeepers,

beaters, and markers to provide periodic *battues* for the amusement of fashionable 'sportsmen' down from London. The introduction of the light, double-barrelled shotgun in the early years of the century, the practice of hand-rearing pheasants, and the technique of driving game towards stationary guns, had almost put an end to the old-fashioned method of shooting in which one or two men went out with their dogs and walked up to their game in fields and moorlands. Apart from discouraging the skills of shooters and dogs, the new system provoked expensive rivalry between estate-owners to produce the biggest bags. Worse still, the concentration of game attracted the professional poachers and led occasionally to murderous clashes. In less well-preserved districts 'where men shoot instead of slaughter' organized poaching gangs did not operate because it did not pay. Such poaching as existed was done in a small way by local men who were usually well known and easily detected. Intensive game-preservation, he thought, should be discouraged and 'the slaughter of the *battue* censured and despised'.

Surtees was not the only one to criticize the growth of big shooting-estates as destructive of good neighbourliness and an incitement to rural crime. The Revd Henry Horsley, a country vicar who published a book on *Juvenile Depravity* in 1849,[6] believed that there had been an actual increase in class hostility in rural districts. The old regular mingling of local residents of all classes in country pursuits was diminishing and many landowners only visited their estates for the shooting season. Freed from the restraining influence of resident proprietors, beershops multiplied and crime increased. He believed that offences against the game laws made up the greater part of rural crime. Surtees would have agreed with the diagnosis but had little sympathy for the depravity of the offender, juvenile or otherwise. For him all poachers were tarred with the same brush. They were generally 'the very scum and scourings of the country, men whose least crime is that of poaching; for if a respectable man has a real turn for the trigger, he is speedily engaged as a keeper'. The last observation may strike a more tolerant critic as a piece of special pleading. Few small-time poachers used guns. Snares, birdlime, nets, and a well-trained lurcher were the tools of their trade. Guns were noisy, expensive, and easily detectable. Moreover, there was a great difference between a country labourer in employment who occasionally poached for food or amusement, and the professionals who worked in association with others to supply game for poulterers' shops in neighbouring towns or even distant London. Poaching for the pot has never been regarded as a crime by the poorer class of country people. In their minds it is something quite different from stealing. No doubt there was always the risk that a man convicted for poaching might find it difficult to get employment with farmers and landowners in his district and so be forced into more serious crime. Surtees' sweeping condemnation, however, went further than would have been approved by many of his class.

Poachers did not often discuss their art with parliamentary committees, but one did before the Nottingham Election Petition Committee of 1843. Though a record of several prosecutions for poaching might have strained his credibility as a witness on electoral corruption, he was questioned good-humouredly enough by the gentlemen of the committee, who included a number of landowners, as well, incidentally, as Benjamin Disraeli. The man was a framework knitter by trade and told the committee that 'I do not make it a common practice to go poaching; I am very fond of the sport, and I go when I think I like to have a bit of sport'. His usual method, he explained, was to go out on a dark night with a chosen companion ('I am very particular who I go with') and drag the fields with a net. This was a kind of poacher with whom any sportsman might feel an instinctive sympathy. Others might have reasons of their own for not bearing too hardly on such men. General Dyott in Staffordshire in 1841 thought it best not to react too strongly to the occasional visits to his estate by the inhabitants of Lichfield because he did not wish to jeopardize his son's chances of election for that borough at the next parliamentary election. That was the more magnanimous since the game on his land was getting remarkably thin that year; but, as he observed philosophically in 1843, poaching had become so profitable that unless a landowner could afford to hire a battalion of keepers to protect his estate, he must be prepared to put up with his losses.

Mozley, from the scholarly vantage-point of a country clergyman, thought both gamekeepers and poachers an interesting study for social and even ethnological enquiry. 'They represent the hunting-man of the prehistoric age.' He knew of more than one in Northamptonshire in the 1830s who on occasions assumed the role of poacher turned gamekeeper not so much to harass their former associates as to gain social respectability and learn more of the secrets of the coverts and preserves for use later on. In Wiltshire some years later he had to deal with a notorious poacher who, driven from one habitation to another in the surrounding district, eventually took refuge with his wife and four children in the porch of Mozley's parish church: to the great scandal and even greater inconvenience of the congregation. In the end Mozley persuaded the man that he was unlikely to establish a permanent right of occupation in that cold and draughty shelter, and raised between £20 and £30 in the parish to finance the emigration of the whole family to Canada. Subsequently he received several letters from the cheerful and unrepentant *émigré*, declaring that Mozley had been the making of him, that he was never without his gun, had shot a few bears, and had never encountered a single (expletive) policeman.[7]

The worst features of poaching were the occasional pitched battles that took place when gangs of poachers clashed with groups of keepers. The reform of the old harsh game-laws in 1832 had taken away the monopoly of the landowning class and made the right to kill game a matter of arrangement between landlord and tenant. At the same time, however, stiffer fines had been imposed for the offence of poaching by day; and poaching by

night had been made a crime punishable by imprison-
ment or transportation, as also was trespassing with
intent and resisting arrest with weapons. Nevertheless,
the profit to be made by supplying game to towns, especially the metropolitan market, ensured that large-scale,
organized poaching continued on well-stocked, accessible
estates. In 1851, for example, there were numerous
reports of such activities. 'The newspapers teemed',
according to the *Annual Register* for that year, 'with
accounts of desperate affrays between the keepers and
poachers in all parts of the kingdom, some of them very
serious.' Near Mansfield there was a regular battle in
which ten keepers of the earl of Scarborough, Lord-
Lieutenant of the county, were involved. One of them was
killed, several seriously injured, a number of poachers
captured, and 570 yards of netting seized. Round Norwich parties of poachers were particularly bold, some
times gathering outside the house of the head-keeper
and discharging their guns in a show of defiance. One
night in December, when police and keepers made a
number of arrests, shots were fired at them in real earnest
and two policemen severely wounded. The same month
there was a desperate and more one-sided fight between
three keepers and a band of what were estimated to be
some forty poachers on the estate of Sir Arthur Clifton
at Barton Wood in Nottinghamshire. A mastiff belonging to the estate was stabbed to death and the keepers
overpowered and beaten up. Other encounters were
reported at Bagley Wood near Oxford, where lime was
flung in the faces of the keepers; in Wiltshire; and on
Lord Ravensworth's[8] estates in County Durham.

Where professional criminals were concerned, especially house-breakers, the Victorian public believed in
meeting force with force. As the spate of attacks on
country houses in the Home Counties by the notorious
Frimley gang in 1850 demonstrated, pistols and blunder-
busses were to be found in most such residences and
their owners were prepared to use them in defence
of their property. Even in suburban London, during the
scare created by a wave of burglaries in the Notting Hill

district in 1856, householders began to arm themselves. While there was no sentimentality about criminals, however, there was undoubtedly an almost morbid interest in crime. In 1845 there was a brutal murder in a field near Haverstock Hill in Hampstead, which attracted unusual attention, partly because of the social position of the victim, James Delarue, a professor of music. Londoners in their thousands streamed out to visit the scene of the crime. On the first Sunday after the news broke, Hampstead was thronged from daybreak to dusk with crowds anxious, in the disapproving words of *The Times*, 'to gratify their morbid taste for the horrible'. Among them was Haydon, who confessed to 'a natural craving to witness the scene of Crime' and even drew a sketch of the fatal spot in his journal.

The most popular outlet for this macabre curiosity was, of course, the public executions. The hangings outside Newgate were among the regular entertainments of the metropolis, and even in the provinces the last moments of those who for one reason or another had attracted special publicity were watched by large crowds.

They often came from considerable distances, sometimes on cheap excursion trains run for the event by enterprising railway companies. To execute malefactors in public as a deterrent was an ancient principle of English judicial administration, as historically in most countries; and the practice continued in Victoria's reign until after Surtees' death. In 1864, however, a royal commission recommended that they should be carried out in private and this was made law in 1868. In the eighteenth century the legislature had endeavoured to compensate for the deficiency of police by multiplying the number of offences for which the penalty was death. In the early nineteenth century, growing liberal and humanitarian feeling brought about a series of legal reforms between 1822 and 1837 which in practice restricted capital punishment to the single offence of murder; and not even then in every case. With this the great majority of Victorians seemed satisfied; a life for a life was for most a principle of natural justice. The decision to end public executions was in no sense an indication of softening attitudes towards the criminal classes in general. Only just previously, in 1862–3, a sudden rise in violent street robberies, in London and elsewhere, the so-called 'garotting' epidemic, had been answered by a sharp increase in the number of executions and the passage of an Act restoring flogging as a judicial punishment for certain crimes of violence.

Yet, while executions remained public ceremonies, they exercised a peculiar spell. Those in London were regularly attended, besides the usual horde of street idlers, petty criminals, and prostitutes, by respectable members of the public, fashionable swells, even women and schoolboys. Writers and artists, professionally concerned with emotions and sensations, found it difficult to refrain from being present at least on one occasion. In 1840 Thackeray and Monckton Milnes made up a party to see the execution of Courvoisier, a Swiss valet who had gained notoriety by murdering his employer, the aged nobleman Lord William Russell. Among the other 20,000 spectators were Charles Dickens, five peers of the realm, and several MPs, together with a large number of menservants, apparently demonstrating in this practical way a sense of professional loyalty—though whether to the valet or his master is not easy to determine. Thackeray relieved his horrified feelings by giving a detailed description of the event in *Fraser's Magazine*. Dickens, who was almost a regular attender at executions, after seeing the double hanging of Mr and Mrs Manning for the murder of the wife's lover in 1849, wrote to *The Times* to deplore the wicked levity of the onlookers and demand an end to public executions. Not all men of letters shared their sensitivities. One may doubt, for instance, whether in 1840 Milnes, who collected *memorabilia* of murders and hangmen, was as much revolted as his novelist companions. That organ of the respectable middle classes, *The Times*, devoted four closely packed columns to a description of the Mannings' execution; and among the estimated 30,000 spectators were what in social terms would be classed as ladies and gentlemen, who had paid two or three guineas for a comfortable seat at a window of one of the nearby houses and watched the proceedings through opera-glasses.

Dickens' slightly obsessive interest in executions (he went to witness them abroad as well as at home) might prompt a comment from a psychologist. Surtees himself, soon after his arrival in London in the spring of 1825, yielded to the lure which such spectacles seem to have had for literary men. A rogue called Probert, who had been implicated in a well-known murder, that of Mr Weare in 1823, but saved himself from the gallows by turning king's evidence, was later convicted of horse-stealing and executed—to the great delight of the criminal class who disliked informers on principle. 'I am half ashamed to say,' wrote Surtees long afterwards, 'I went to see him meet his fate.' His brief account of the experience, perhaps because it was put down when it could only have been a distant memory, is more restrained and objective than those of his two more illustrious novelist contemporaries some twenty years earlier. He had no difficulty in securing a place in front of the gallows outside the Old Bailey. There were some rough elements in the crowd but the majority were ordinary work-people and respectable citizens. He remembered as an unforgettable detail the four white night-caps carried by Calcraft, the executioner, which were later pulled down over the faces of the four condemned felons after they had been pinioned. 'A thrill ran through the crowd as those four white-covered heads assumed the same sideways attitude as they were launched into eternity.' There is little sympathy in this, only sharp observation.[9]

10

THE LIMITS OF PRUDERY

I

Of all Surtees' satirical remarks on the foibles of his society, perhaps the most startling comes in chapter xiv of *Plain or Ringlets*. In giving an account of the swimming race at the Roseberry Rocks Regatta, he describes how a score of hobbledehoys strip off their clothes in a boat lying offshore, in full view of the spectators on the beach, 'in a way that but at the seaside would have a very embarrassing effect'. He then talks about sea-bathing in general and reflects how circumstances affect conventions of modesty in women.

It is wonderful what a difference the locality makes in these Apollo Belvidere matters. If those great naked men we now see proceeding so leisurely from Underdown Cliff to the sea, were to exhibit themselves in that way in a secluded wood in the country, there would be such a running and shrieking . . . But because they come down upon the open coast, with a grand sea before them, people think nothing of it; and these fair ladies in the mushroom hats, with their back hair spread upon their shoulders, sit on unconcernedly by as so many dowagers in a statue gallery.

If, as Surtees says, the sight of naked men bathing from seaside beaches was familiar to Victorian women, our notions of Victorian prudery ought perhaps to be revised. What is odd is that this deliberately provocative observation of Surtees has received no attention from commentators.

It is clear that at the beginning of the century the notion of putting on an item of clothing in order to enter the water would have seemed artificial. As Surtees, with his usual common sense, remarked when Jorrocks on his excursion to Margate went for a dip in the sea, his first action was 'to do what all people of either sex agree upon in such cases—namely to divest himself of his garments'. On this particular occasion Mr Jorrocks, who was in some respects a man of uncommon modesty, observed some females on the cliffs above. He therefore retained his stocking-net pantaloons until he reached the water's edge, where he left them—only to have them washed away by the incoming tide while he disported himself in the water. The unfortunate grocer had to return to his hotel, pursued by the jeers and laughter of a mob of children, with his nether half inadequately concealed by the tail of his shirt weighted down by pebbles knotted into the corners. This species of social contretemps was not perhaps uncommon at the seaside; it was certainly a stock subject for popular humour. A contemporary street ballad, 'The One Horse Shay', recounted the misadventure of a Cockney couple, Mrs Bubb, 'fair, fat and forty-three', and her spouse, who drove down to Brighton for a stay at the seaside. Dismayed by the extortionate charge of 1s. 6d. for a bathing machine, they elected to undress in the open and leave their clothes in their one-horse chaise. Unfortunately, while they were in the sea, some marauding children made off with their garments and they were forced to make their way back to their lodgings in a state of nature only partially concealed from onlookers by the apron of their vehicle.

If not many women had the hardihood—or simplicity—of Mrs Bubb, at least it was normal practice in Georgian times for both sexes to bathe without any sort of costume. It is true that a contemporary physical training manual, P. H. Clias's *Gymnastic Exercises* (1823), had illustrations which show boys diving and swimming in a kind of bathing-drawers; but this almost certainly was an artifice simply to comply with the conventions of publishing. By a social paradox the depiction of complete male nudity was avoided in art, though tolerated in real life; while female nudity, though not respectable in real life, was a standard feature of painting and sculpture. Dr Granville, for example, included a print of the bathing beach at

Tynemouth, thronged with bathers, but in such small detail that their bodies appear only as white streaks. Benjamin West's picture of 'The Bathing Place at Ramsgate', showing a group of boys running down to the water, is more explicit in its nudity; but West, who died in 1820, flourished in a more broad-minded age. A Victorian painter would have been more discreet. There is a well-known painting by William Mulready, who exhibited constantly up to 1862, entitled 'Bathers Surprised', in which the central figure is a plump and naked young woman seated on a rock, doing her hair, while in the background her companions are hurrying out of the water with alarm. To have exhibited a similar study of men bathers at that time would have been out of the question. When it came to the actualities of life, however, the artistic conventions were irrelevant. Dickens, writing from Broadstairs in 1843, gave a lively description of himself at his midday swim, splashing about in the ocean like 'a kind of salmon-coloured porpoise'. That strong-minded woman Mrs Carlyle in 1846 was even more direct in her language to her husband. Having listed the attractions of Speke Hall near Liverpool, where she was convalescing, she added, 'such beautiful bathing, too! You might run naked out of your bed into the sea, under cover of tall, mournful trees.'[1]

Almost to the end of the century—to the 1870s when Kilvert bathed at Weston super Mare, to the 1880s when Kipling swam at Westward Ho, even to the 1890s when boatloads of Cambridge ladies and gentlemen passed through the bathing pool at Sheep's Green, 'pink with boys, as naked as God made them, for bathing drawers did not exist then, or, at least, not on Sheep's Green'[2]—the time-honoured practice was for men and boys to bathe without a costume. Only in mixed bathing at the seaside had a change come about. Inland, at certain traditional spots, the practice never died out. On the Thames at Reading, for instance, about three miles below Caversham Bridge, there was a bathing place in the 1920s much frequented by the boys of the town. It consisted of a small shallow bay where beginners could stand

in safety and a miniature headland from which the more
expert could dive into deep water. It was often crowded
in the summer months and hardly any of the boys and
young men who used it wore costumes. Those from
poorer homes often brought a bar of soap as well as a
towel and lathered themselves all over before plunging
into the current. When ladies strolled by, as often happened on sunny afternoons, they made a slight detour
round the spot so as to keep at a decent distance.[3]

There is a good deal of evidence to suggest, moreover,
that swimming was a favourite recreation even in the
eighteenth and early nineteenth centuries before the rise
of popular seaside resorts and the cult of organized games
at schools. It went on not only in the countryside but in
the crowded metropolis. Perhaps because there were
in fact so few other opportunities for physical activities,
bathing seems to have been a particular addiction of the
poorer London boys during the summer months. Along
Millbank in the 1780s, then a willow-lined stretch of the
river where shingly beaches in those pre-embankment
days provided a storage-space for timber, hundreds of
boys could be seen in warm weather bathing in the
Thames, having left their clothes on the piles of logs.
According to Francis Place, who in his time had been
one of them, almost every boy who had reached the age
of 11 could swim, some even younger. Another favoured
spot was Islington. When that curious Victorian rogue
Renton Nicholson was a boy in the post-Waterloo years,
this little township on the northern fringe of London
constituted 'the Brighton, Margate, and Ramsgate of
the boys of the adjoining localities'. At holiday time in
the summer they swarmed out to the bathing spots
of the 'Sisters', High Bank, Sluice House, and Hornsey
Wood, camping out in fields and woods near the water.
These traditional sites were used by one generation of
London boys after another until the tide of bricks and
mortar eventually swallowed them up. Even in Dickens'
time Millbank was still a popular bathing place for the
'sportive youth' of the capital, despite the menacing
presence of the new Penitentiary which reared its geo-
metrical bulk on what is now the site of the Tate Gallery.

It was not only the children of the London poor who found pleasure in the water. The boys of the big public schools still embedded in the heart of the City also went swimming when they could during term. This perhaps was partly for hygienic reasons as well as recreation. There were no bathrooms at public schools in those days, or even at Oxford and Cambridge colleges, though they were being introduced into some country houses. Certainly there were none at Charterhouse when Mozley was there at the start of George IV's reign. He used to go sometimes with other boys to a 'Bagnio' or private bath, off Newgate Street; but such establishments cost money and were beyond the means of most impecunious schoolboys. For them, as well as the poor London families, hot water and soap counted as luxuries. The waters of the Thames, though becoming increasingly polluted, offered a cheaper cleansing agency. Mozley used to patronize a large floating swimming-bath moored west of Blackfriars Bridge where, as he remembered it, 'the water was greenish, but nothing worse'.

There was another recognized bathing place in the early years of the century at the eastern end of Westminster Bridge which even boasted a bathing machine. Dressing himself on its steps one day, Leigh Hunt saw Byron swimming in the river for a wager against another man. That was about 1809; a decade earlier, when a boy at Christ's Hospital, Hunt used to go out with his friend Thomas Barnes, the future editor of The Times, to swim at Nicholson's old haunt, the New River at Islington, and at other places along the Thames. On one occasion a party of them were tempted by the hot weather to take a dip in the river from private grounds near Hammersmith. They were caught flagrante delicto by a smart lady in riding habit and feathered hat, who gave them a lecture on the impropriety not of their nakedness but of their trespass on her property. Discovering later that the land in question belonged to a house inhabited by the Margravine of Anspach, they firmly believed that their unconventional 'admonitrix' was her Serene Highness in person.[4]

There is no reason to suppose that bathing in the

country districts in rivers and ponds was any less popular than in the capital, given the greater opportunity and
wider choice of places to swim. When Mozley and his
brothers were young, their parents discouraged them
from mixing with other boys and their chief amusement
was rambling over the countryside and bathing in the
summer. In consequence, despite a weak leg (the result
of an accident in 1819), he became an unusually powerful
swimmer, able to cover up to a mile in the River Derwent.
There were at that time, he wrote in the 1880s, a dozen
places within easy reach of Derby 'where any one could
bathe in something like seclusion. I doubt if there is one
now.' For the same reasons schools in the country were
more likely than their London counterparts to encourage
this form of exercise. At Harrow there was a school
swimming-pool known as Duckpuddle where Peel and
Byron once splashed and swam. From Eton the young
Leveson Gower wrote to his sister in May 1829 that he
bathed nearly every morning before breakfast. 'I hope
Susan [another sister] won't die of envy, but perhaps she
may still think it cold for that.' At that time the school
possessed in Henry Dupuis a master who was a positive
enthusiast for swimming. He looked out for suitable spots
along the Thames and did much to organize swimming
as a regular school sport. Goldwin Smith, who was in
the school then, had the impression that all boys at Eton
were required to learn to swim. By 1840, at any rate,
when boating was officially recognized, there was a rule
that no boy should row until he could swim. Professional
watermen were engaged to teach the younger boys at
special school bathing places on the river.

Whether Mr Dupuis' enthusiasm went so far as to join
the boys in the water is not recorded; but it would not
have been surprising had he done so. In the 1820s, before he went as headmaster to Rugby, Dr Arnold kept a
small coaching establishment at Laleham on the Thames
near Staines at which some seven or eight young men
were prepared for the universities. In addition to their
more bookish studies, he prescribed gymnastics and
swimming in the Thames in which he himself participated

as often as he could. 'The youths used to go with me, and I felt completely for the first time a boy as they were.' Fifty years later, when Stalky and Co. were engaged on their nefarious activities at Westward Ho, masters as well as boys bathed off the beach. 'We enjoyed ourselves in the water and in the sunshine', wrote G. C. Beresford, the original of M'Turk, 'wearing the costume of the early days of Eden, which was the invariable garb of both masters and boys, even when bathing from the sands or the Pebble Ridge.'[5] It was, after all, a sensible precaution to supervise boys when they were swimming in deep water; and the greatest security was to have one or two adults actually in the water with them. This was certainly the case on a tragic occasion at Sunderland in October 1845 when some twenty or thirty boys from Dr Cowan's private school had obtained permission to bathe in the sea near the village of Hendon. They were accompanied by four masters, two of whom went into the water with them while the other two watched from the beach. Caught in an unsuspected offshore current, several of the boys were swept out to sea and drowned. One of the masters swimming with them was also lost in trying to save them.

Habits formed at school continued at university. Bathing in the Thames frequently figures in accounts of the outdoor activities of Oxford undergraduates both in the first half of the nineteenth century and earlier. Asshcton Smith, though more renowned even in his student days as a rider and cricketer, was also remembered as a 'fearless swimmer'. The Quaker Gurney, taking private tuition there at the start of the new century, devoted his one allotted hour of afternoon recreation to walking or bathing. Acland, an undergraduate at Christ Church in 1827–31, like Arnold's young men took his exercise in the form of gymnastics and swimming. His contemporary Francis Doyle, being neither a good horseman nor fond of boat-racing, used to scull leisurely down to one of the 'lashers' on the Thames for a bathe. This was also one of Mozley's pleasures when he was at Oriel in the 1820s. 'Taking headers into the pool under

the floodgates below Sandford Lasher', he recalled, 'was
one of the most delightful of my Oxford enjoyments.' It
was an enjoyment not unmixed with a thrill of danger,
for more than one life had been lost at that spot. In June
1843 there was a notable Oxford tragedy when the son
of Dean Gaisford and the son of Dr Phillimore, Regius
Professor of Civil Law, were both drowned when on a
bathing party with two other Christ Church men at that
same place, the old Lock Pool at Sandford where a torrent
of water poured into a deep pool.

To Oxford men of a later vintage it may seem odd that
none of these early nineteenth-century reminiscences
mentions Parsons Pleasure. Nevertheless, this famous site
on the River Cherwell was already a traditional bathing
place. It had been known in the seventeenth century as
Paten's Pleasure and in the nineteenth was called for a
long time Loggerhead. The land belonged to Merton
College, which sold it to the University in 1854 as part of
the area eventually laid out for the Parks in 1864. In 1868
it was leased to a private manager for use as a bathing
place and it is probable that it was at this time that it
was first screened off for greater decorum from the
footpath that runs beside it. By that date, if not earlier, it
was the main bathing spot for Oxford undergraduates.
According to one piece of oral testimony, the deep water
at that point was popular with the public-school men
who came up already good swimmers; the town boys,
less proficient, preferred the shallower side-channels.[6]

Even when he had left school and university behind
him bathing remained one of the Englishman's recreations. The bored officers of Ensign Keppel's brigade, in
cantonments on the River Dender before the battle of
Waterloo, amused themselves by swimming in its waters;
though not apparently their men, who spent their leisure
in helping the peasants on whom they had been billeted
with their farm-work. In the Ionian Islands a year later
Keppel and his brother officers, thrown on their own
resources by the Oriental seclusion of the local ladies,
found distraction in sailing and swimming.[7] Acland, in
camp at Sidmouth with his yeomanry regiment thirty

years later, when he was 36, used to bathe every morning in the sea. An even more aristocratic figure, Lord Belgrave, when in his forties still bathed regularly in the chilly waters of the North Sea when he stayed at his wife's family seat of Dunrobin Castle on the Dornoch Firth; he even taught his son to swim there. He was a passionate swimmer himself and even after he succeeded, at the age of 50, as Marquess of Westminster in 1845, he used to take a house at Bournemouth each autumn for the sake of the sea-bathing.

Even graver and more venerable pillars of society could be found disporting themselves in the ocean. When Dr Granville visited Wells in 1840 he was disappointed in his hope of seeing the bishop, the aged George Henry Law, 'he being absent for the benefit of sea-bathing at Weymouth': and that at the age of nearly 80. His purpose was no doubt purely medicinal; but that cannot be said of another well-known Victorian cleric, H. P. Liddon, canon of St Paul's. Uninterested in games but a splendid swimmer, his favourite exercise at Oxford in the 1840s was 'long country walks, including a bathe, if possible'. His skill in the water was not without service to the wider world of scholarship and the Church. When on a reading-party in Wales, during his last long vacation as an undergraduate, he saving from drowning his tutor and fellow-bather Mr William Stubbs, later to become Bishop of Oxford and historian of the medieval English constitution but then simply a fellow of Trinity College. Another Anglican lover of water was Charles Kingsley, who used to bathe in the little streams of his parish of Eversley and seems to have taken every opportunity to swim when on holiday at the seaside or among the Welsh mountains. Addiction to bathing was not, however, a peculiarity of the Establishment. Seaton in County Durham was so popular a bathing place with Quakers that Edward Pease in 1841 paid for the erection and furnishing of a meeting-house there to ensure that the spiritual as well as the carnal enjoyments of the more athletic Friends were provided for.

Among secular figures two notable early-Victorian

zealots for open-air bathing were Haydon and Carlyle.
For Haydon it was the sheer sensuous contact with the
elements that he enjoyed. In September 1814 he recorded
swimming in the sea at Hastings when it was blowing
a half-gale. Almost suffocated by the foaming breakers
and tossed up and down by the waves, 'I felt like a God'.
In September 1826, after a hard summer of painting in
London, he took coach to Brighton on a sudden impulse.
'I rolled in the Sea, shouted like a Savage, and laved my
sides like a Bull in a June meadow.' He used the same
forceful simile when describing a trip to Gravesend in
August 1834 when he 'dived, swam, bathed and revelled,
like a bull in June'. Later that year he was at Sandgate,
where he was seized with cramp in front of a beach
crowded with spectators and nearly drowned. Undeterred
by this experience, he was down at Dover in July 1844,
swimming and diving and shouting like a boy at the age
of 58.

The less boisterous Carlyle also loved to swim when
on holiday—at Scotsbrig in Dumfriesshire, at Kirkcaldy
on the Firth of Forth, and off Tynemouth in the North
Sea. At the cottage he took for the summer of 1841 at
Newby on the Solway Firth he was only ten yards from
the beach where he took his daily swim. On a trip to
Ostend the following year he discovered that the broad-
minded habits of the British were not to the taste of the
puritanical Belgian authorities. Having submitted to the
hire of a bathing machine, he made a few preliminary
dives into the warm but shallow waters and then struck
out seaward—only to be pursued by the attendant on a
horse, waving his hat and vociferating in unintelligible
but urgent accents. Returning to his machine he discovered that among the bathing equipment it contained were
not only towels but a jacket and breeches of blue gingham
designed to cover his nakedness: a Continental refinement
which, though he was not ordinarily given to hilarity,
made him burst into laughter.

There was a marked unselfconsciousness in the way in
which men in early nineteenth-century Britain were ready
to strip in the open whether at the seaside or inland. The

journalist Cyrus Redding described a meeting with the two Haydons and the Scottish painter Wilkie at a dinner at Plymouth in 1810 to celebrate the jubilee of George III. On the spur of the moment the younger Haydon invited their new acquaintance to make up a bathing party the following morning when he proposed to fulfil a promise to teach Wilkie to swim: a plan put into effect at the appointed time when they all bathed from a boat in Plymouth Sound. Redding figured in another impromptu bathe, this time on Dartmoor, when he accompanied a number of visitors, including some barristers of the Western Circuit, on an expedition to the Devil's Bridge near Lydford. Foiled in their first attempt to follow the course of the stream through a chasm in the rocks, 'two or three of us stripped, determined to get up the bed of the torrent, as far as the bridge': a boyish exploit in which they succeeded despite the gloom and iciness of the water in the pools across which they had to swim. Presumably there were no ladies in the party. Half a century later Acland, now nearly 60, was on a walking tour in the same district with a friend. They stopped the night at Lydford and next morning he settled down to sketch the view of the church and castle, while his companion, a respectable civil servant, D. A. Fearon, Assistant Commissioner on the Schools Inquiry Commission (of which Acland was a member), took off his clothes and enjoyed himself in the water.

Even hunting men could swim when put to it; a useful accomplishment in view of the hazards of the chase. Colonel Berkeley had a story about himself, when master of the Oakley Hunt in Bedfordshire in the 1830s, which showed that MFHs out of season could appreciate the gentler side of Nature. He had gone down with his rod to fish in the Ouse, but was so tempted by the sparkle of the water, the warmth of the sun, and the wild flowers in the meadow beyond, that without having had any previous intention of doing so, he 'undressed and bathed in, and swam the river to get on the other side'. An incident with rather less Arcadian tranquillity happened to a friend of his, the famous sportsman Jack Musters, about the time of Waterloo. Going down to the Trent to do some fishing, Musters discerned in the field beyond a troop of yeomanry at exercise. Wishing to see this martial display at close quarters, he promptly undressed, swam the river, carrying his clothes in a bundle on his head, and in the rapid current was swept about a hundred yards downstream before he could find a landing spot. There he encountered a bargeman who subjected him to what Musters thought was an impertinent scrutiny and refused to go away when ordered. Musters dried himself with his handkerchief, calmly got into his clothes, and then in the best traditions of the Regency buck, gave the bargee a thrashing with his fists.

Fragmentary and anecdotal as some of this evidence is, it suggests that the sight of men and boys bathing in inland rivers and at the seaside could not have been an uncommon one in the first half of the century. Indeed, the prevalence of the habit among men of good social position may help to explain why there was so much reluctance later on to submit to any restrictions on their traditional recreation. How women were supposed to react to the spectacle depended partly on their own background. Among the poor the matter must have been largely one of indifference. In Lancashire, for example, there was a working-class custom, dating from the eighteenth century, of an annual descent on the seaside which took on almost the air of a popular festival. Whole families—men, women, and children—went off in carts, gigs, and wagons to enjoy the pleasures of sandy beaches and salt water. These 'padjamers', as they were known at Blackpool, bathed naked with no separation of sexes, imbibed great quantities of spirits, and often slept rough in lofts, outhouses, or even on the beach. Working life in the early industrial revolution did not make for niceties of convention; and the mill-girls of Lancashire were never renowned for the delicacy of their manners. Attitudes among the rural poor, in their crowded and insanitary cottages, were probably no different. To moral and social reformers this indifference to middle-class standards of decency was often taken as a proof of ignorance and immorality. In a speech in the House of Lords in 1867 on the subject of agricultural gangs, that great, good, but not very worldly philanthropist Lord Shaftesbury quoted the evidence of a Dr Morris who had been in practice at Spalding in Lincolnshire for a quarter of a century. 'I have also seen', reported the medical man with evident horror, 'boys bathing in the brooks and girls between 13 and 19 looking on from the bank.' Whether the peers on the benches around him were equally shocked or even surprised by this disclosure is open to question.

Respectable opinion, however, required women when they came across such sights either to show disapproval or at least to pretend not to notice. Dickens, in one of his *Boz* sketches, portrayed the embarrassment of mixed boating parties on the Thames in London when, after a pleasant and flirtatious outing, they had to return, because of the incoming tide, along the Millbank with its customary swarm of naked bathers.

When you are obliged to keep inshore coming home, and the young ladies will colour up, and look perseveringly the other way, while the married dittoes cough slightly and stare very hard at the water, you feel awkward—especially if you happen to have been attempting the most distant approach to sentimentality, for an hour or two previously.

That was written a couple of years before Victoria came to the throne. Sixty years later there was little change. Gwen Raverat recalled similar, though slightly more composed, behaviour in such trying circumstances. Here she is describing the passage of Cambridge boating parties past the men's bathing place at Sheep's Green. 'These dangerous straits were taken in silence, and at full speed . . . Each Lady unfurled a parasol, and, like an ostrich, buried her head in it, and gazed earnestly into its silky depths, until the crisis was past, and the river was decent again.'[8] Modesty, however, did not apparently prevent ladies from regularly participating in such expeditions, despite the shock to their moral sensibilities. Repetition perhaps made it easier to affect the right reactions without undue disturbance to the emotions.

We are entitled to doubt at least whether all women were shocked who pretended to be, or did not use their eyes when feigning interest elsewhere. More vulgar souls than the ladies of Miss Raverat's childhood may have been more honest. In another of Dickens' sketches, 'The Tuggs at Ramsgate', a Cockney family settle themselves into their beach-chairs to watch the spectacle, rarely seen in their native Southwark, of bathers of both sexes emerging from their machines to plunge into the water. Mr Tugg is struck with astonishment, and possibly other unexpressed emotions, by the sight of four young ladies bouncing out into the sea in four successive splashes. Mrs Tugg is no less observant of the other sex. 'Why, here's some gentlemen a-going in on this side', she exclaims in a tone of horror. The reasons for Mr Tugg's amazement and Mrs Tugg's horror hardly needed to be explained to Dickens' readers. Ramsgate, possibly because it was so popular with Londoners, enjoyed some notoriety in the middle of the century for the freedom of its beach behaviour. One later critic accused visitors there of leaving their manners and modesty behind in their lodgings, and both the bathers in the sea and the spectators who lined the beach with opera-glasses and telescopes of having no more sense of decency than Pacific islanders.[9]

II

Women were naturally more self-conscious than men about exposing their bodies to fresh air, water, and the gaze of the curious. To take casual dips in the ocean or yield to sudden impulses on the banks of rivers was not something they could safely indulge in; though for some at least it was a matter of regret that the vulnerability of their sex placed such delights out of reach. Miss Weeton the governess, who was, on her own admission, 'passionately fond of water', was greatly tempted one hot day in 1825, while walking on a lonely Welsh beach as the tide was coming in. She was then 48.

I should have been so glad to have bathed; modesty prevented me, for I must have taken off all my cloaths. Not a human being was to be seen, but some one *might* appear, when I should least be prepared to *receive company*. Yet, as I approached the rocks, I saw many a snug aperture amongst them, which would have served for both bath and dressing room, and I cast many a wistful eye on the tide as it flowed amongst them.[10]

Not many ladies, and certainly no governesses, were in a position to exercise the seigneurial authority to preserve their privacy which the unfortunate Lady Munro of Fowlis was able to do when she bathed from the beach in the Bay of Cromarty early in the century. Her custom was to take some of her maids with her down to the water and post a male servant at a distance away to prevent anyone from passing along the beach. One tragic day in August 1803 she and all three of her attendant maids got into difficulty. A passer-by, hearing cries for help, tried to reach the spot but was turned away by the vigilant manservant, who thought that the distant shrieking was only from his mistress and her companions ducking and splashing each other. By the time a boat was procured and taken round to the spot, all except one of the maids had drowned.

Reports of fatalities such as this are a useful supplement to the scanty evidence we have on the bathing habits of women in the earlier part of the century. We learn, for example (though not from her *Journal*), that Mrs Arbuthnot, when she visited the Duke of Wellington at Walmer in 1832, took a daily dip in the sea. 'The weather is charming, and I enjoy the sea air beyond measure.' But what of more obscure figures bent on pleasure rather than supposed medicinal benefits? In August 1800 four young ladies were drowned in the River Ettrick near Selkirk. Their parents being away from home, the two daughters of the house, together with two friends staying with them, had decided to bathe in the river which ran at the bottom of the garden, leaving their clothes on the bank and not telling the servants. In 1802 three maids from Deal Castle, tempted by the warmth of a late October evening, went secretly to bathe from the beach after

nine o'clock at night when it would have been quite dark.
Two of them, getting out of their depth off the steeply
shelving beach, lost their lives. The circumstances of both
these fatal accidents suggest that they were the consequence of a sudden impulse by girls who had no great
experience of deep water. It is reasonable to suppose
that in general girls tended to be worse swimmers than
boys because of their more restricted opportunities.

This was not the only difficulty of bathing for girls. It
is probable that on all these occasions, as the case of
Lady Munro most vividly indicates, the bathers were
naked and the privacy they naturally tried to secure
for themselves was itself an added risk. This was
clearly illustrated by a case of drowning in May 1842 at
Milnthorpe in Morecambe Bay. A lady on holiday took
her daughters and two female servants about a mile along
the beach to a secluded spot where the girls could bathe.
One of the maids went into the water with them. She,
and the elder girl, floundered unexpectedly into a deep
pool with some twelve feet of water. There was a panic
attempt at rescue by the rest of the party who all went
into the water after them. In the event both daughters
were drowned together with their nurse. The mother,
with the other servant, was rescued by a small boat which
providentially happened to be passing soon after the
accident. Privacy on a bathing expedition, when none of
those present was a good swimmer, could be a dangerous luxury round the treacherous coasts of Britain. Much
safer were the casual bathing opportunities afforded by
the shallow pools of Palestine where Harriet Martineau
travelled with a group of friends in 1846–7. Whenever she
came to a pool or stream she seems to have taken a
bathe; but in that empty region she was able to indulge
her wishes without risking either safety or modesty. This
is her picturesque description of one such occasion.

Miss —— and I stole away to bathe. We found each a drooping tree, which made a close drawing room . . . I found a pool
chin-deep; and there in that quiet spot, we bathed . . . It was
dusk when we came out, and a lustrous planet hung over the
nearest hill.

From the fact that the ladies bathed separately it appears that neither made use of a bathing dress.

Bathing on the crowded beaches of English holiday resorts clearly needed more defences to modesty than a drooping tree. Colonel Berkeley, who in the middle decades of the century had a house at Christ Church in Hampshire, with grounds stretching down to the beach, used to put up a tent for the use of those of his lady visitors who wished to bathe. Such private facilities were not for everyone. The publicly available equivalent at established seaside resorts was the bathing machine. These were a long-standing institution, having made their appearance in the first half of the eighteenth century. They existed at Scarborough as early as 1736; and similar contraptions, known as bathing chariots or carriages, were to be found in the middle of the century at Margate and Brighton. In an age when women still habitually bathed naked and immersion in the sea as well as drinking sea-water was medically recommended for invalids and cripples, some such device was obviously desirable. In 1796, for instance, when a special building was erected at Margate for poor people for whom sea-bathing had been prescribed, a bathing machine was built for their exclusive use.

A bathing machine, however, could not go much more than axle-deep into the water otherwise the floorboards would have been awash. The amount of cover it provided was therefore only partial; and between leaving its shelter and sinking modestly below the water there was always a moment of exposure. The waves, too, had a habit of suddenly retreating in a disconcerting manner. A contemporary cartoon depicting 'Summer Amusements at Margate 1813' shows a group of gentlemen furnished with a variety of optical aids, spying on the naked females floundering about in the shallows in front of their machines. Canvas screens each side of the steps, or better still a kind of extending canvas hood leading down into the water (the invention of the ingenious Margate Quaker Mr Beales), offered more secure protection against such intrusive male spectators. By no means all resorts, however, provided these refinements. Dr Granville noted with disapproval at the start of Victoria's reign that neither at Brighton nor at Hastings did the bathing machines have hoods. Gentlemen at Brighton at times made themselves as much objects of curiosity as women bathers. 'Many lacking courage after they have stripped to the skin, will stand on the outer steps of the machine, shivering and hesitating, their persons in the meanwhile wholly exposed, owing to the want of hood that ought to project over the steps.'

At some seaside resorts further methods were employed to preserve a modicum of public decency. As at Brighton, the bathing machines for the two sexes could be sited in different places. Alternatively hours could be reserved for ladies only. Men could be forbidden to go on that part of the beach where women were bathing; boats banned from approaching too near on the seaward side. It is noticeable, however, that there never seemed to be any complementary prohibition on ladies from strolling where men bathed and they seemed to take full advantage of this freedom. As the popularity of the seaside increased and beaches became more crowded, it became difficult to maintain these regulations. A more reliable protection for female modesty was the bathing costume. Miss Weeton possessed one as early as 1810, described by her as a 'blue flannel bathing dress'. In this she could boldly emerge from her cottage on the sandy shores of the Mersey just north of Liverpool and walk down to the water a few yards away. Lady Elizabeth Grosvenor bathed from a machine at Hoylake in 1831, assisted by one of the maids from her hotel who was a good swimmer and cheerfully waded about up to her neck in water in 'a large blue flannel surtout'. Whether Lady Elizabeth wore anything in the water seems doubtful. On a cold windy August day at Ayr in 1839 Mrs Carlyle entered the sea clad in a flannel gown, having undressed on the beach under the protection of her mother. Afterwards she took a reviving gulp of brandy and ran back to her house, only three or four minutes away, in her wet costume 'with little regard to appearances'.

This early form of 'bathing gown' seems to have been as voluminous as an ordinary dressing-gown; an elegant variety of it had long been used at Bath in the indoor hot baths where both sexes mingled in cheerful contiguity. Though completely answering the purpose of covering the wearer, it could not have been suitable for anything more active than ducking down into the water. Its advantage was that it could also serve for walking down the beach from a hut, tent, or cottage after undressing, even if spectators were present. To Surtees, however, this was only another illustration of his doctrine that conventions of female modesty depended largely on time and place.

What lady would traverse the passages of a house with nothing on but bathing gown and slippers? . . . If she should happen to meet a man she would never get over it. Yet here in the broad face of day, with myriads of gazers and regiments of telescopes, they come out with the greatest coolness and deliberation, and walk unconcernedly into the sea! So much for a 'pure mind in a pure body' as the advertisement says.

Nor, he might have added, did modesty prevent young ladies from accepting with enjoyment the embrace of the strong-armed male attendants who were frequently hired to carry them out to the bathing machines when the state of the beach or the tide left them far out in the water. At Brighton that severe moralist Dr Granville noted that though elderly women were usually at hand to assist, the ladies who patronized the machines at Kemptown 'seemed to prefer being carried to their distant, and almost floating *cabinet des bains*, in the brawny arms of stout, broad-shouldered fellows employed for that purpose'.

A more exotic, flesh-coloured costume was apparently worn by Lady Hastings, who in the 1830s used to bathe from the sands near Lymington on the Solent. Her custom was to ride down to the beach on her pony, undress in the open, and leave her clothes in the crutch of her saddle. With a sensible distrust of the elements, however, she used to tie herself to one end of a long cord, the other end of which was held by a female companion who also had charge of the pony. On one memorable occasion the poor attendant found herself the centre of a tug of war between Lady Hastings who was battling against a strong ebb-tide and a wayward pony who started to back up the beach. In the end she chose to let go of the reins, whereupon the animal trotted off. Emerging from the water, Lady Hastings energetically pursued her disappearing clothes along the sands, leaving her companion, encumbered by skirts, toiling in her rear. Fortunately an elderly coastguard, who had been watching the bathing party through his telescope, intercepted the pony and insisted on accompanying her back to her friend, 'peeping at the peach-coloured dress of the lady in intense but respectful admiration'.

Among more plebeian folk such garments would have seemed a superfluous luxury. Among Colonel Berkeley's neighbours at Christ Church was Sir G. H. Rose, an elderly retired diplomat given to writing religious pamphlets, who tried to enforce more seemly customs for bathing on the part of the beach he owned near Mudeford. His puritanical zeal was encouraged by the local proprietress of the bathing machines, a Mrs Jane West, who considered that any casual swimming from the beach deprived her of her lawful income. Once, when a male bather ignored a peremptory order to come out of the water, the pious landowner told his servant to remove the man's clothes. He then rode leisurely back towards his house, obediently followed by his servant holding the garments, and at a longer interval by the naked and indignant bather. Not until the procession reached a part of the beach occupied by ladies, maids, flocks of small children, and grinning donkey-boys did Sir George suddenly become aware of the even greater affront to decency he himself had created.

Another of Colonel Berkeley's recollections of the Christ Church beach concerned a rustic couple who objected to paying for the *two* machines which Mrs West's sense of decorum (or business) insisted on their using. Instead they retreated to a more secluded spot under the cliffs from which they presently emerged, walking hand in hand down to the sea like a rather stout version of Adam and Eve before the fall. To men like Berkeley the restrictions which Sir George Rose tried to impose on his stretch of beach appeared excessively prudish. Nudity that was proper and natural, as when a man bathed off a quiet seashore, did not strike him as being in any sense indecent.[11] Many other educated people clearly felt the same way. The distinction between natural actions and artificial conventions was still an important one. De Tocqueville observed that in Ireland, where the poorer classes were notably chaste, neither sex showed much repugnance at exposing themselves. 'I have seen young girls bathing in the sea at a short distance from young men.' The sight prompted him to reflect on the nature of modesty. 'Does not what we call "decency"', he asked, 'derive rather from the state of civilisation than from that of morals?'

Civilization, however, in the form of crowded seaside resorts, continued to extend its domain. As bathing dresses for women became the rule on the beaches, they began to evolve into something less primitive, more practical, and more attractive. After the middle of the century there was a noticeable change from the early shapeless and utilitarian 'bathing gown', which must have been a severe handicap to swimming, to a more manageable two-piece costume of blouse and bloomer. In this more coquettish outfit a woman could dive from the roof or wheels of her bathing machine, or more precariously from the side of a rowing-boat. An early follower of the new fashion was Lady Galway, Monckton Milnes' sister, who visited the French resort of Trouville on the Normandy coast in 1857 and bathed in 'trousers and a bloomer petticoat to her knees'. The 'Mermaids' of John Leech's 1854 sketch seem to be already wearing such a dress; those in his similar 'Diving Belles' of 1862 undoubtedly are. An advertisement in 1867 described as 'new' a bathing dress for ladies which offered 'perfect liberty of action without exposure of the figure'. It consisted of a short tunic with wide trousers fastened at the ankles, made of blue and white striped flannel. The

newness could only have been in minor details. Indeed,
it sounds very much like the attire of the 'blue and
white clad sea-nymphs' described by Surtees as dancing, splashing, and generally enjoying themselves in the
water on sunny mornings at Roseberry Rocks some eight
years earlier. Clearly the new form of bathing dress was
designed not only for greater freedom but also for its
effect on the beholder. It was more civilized, in de
Tocqueville's sense, than Miss Weeton's old blue flannel
gown, and a little less innocent.

Civilization was also threatening the male bather. At
first it took the form only of occasional local regulations
forbidding bathing from the open beach. 'I am afraid
you would not be permitted to bathe here naked,' wrote
Mrs Carlyle to her husband from Merseyside in August
1845, 'but there are nice machines, constructed for the
purpose, to be had at a short distance.' By 1860 were
beginning to be heard the first demands that male bathers, as was generally the rule at Continental seaside resorts, should wear some kind of covering. That many
women apparently did not object to the existing practice
was held to be a criticism of themselves. 'The present
indecency', wrote a certain Dr Thomson sternly in 1860,
'is not diminished by the blushing intrusiveness of the
fairer sex.' There does not seem in fact to have been any
widespread disapproval among women. When certain
ladies at Brighton at one period tried to embarrass male
bathers by taking up position on camp-stools to interrupt
their passage back up the beach from the water, they
were protesting against bathing on the Sabbath, not at
bathing without a costume. Attempts at Scarborough, in
1866, to make bathing-drawers compulsory for men met
with stout resistance on behalf of their clients from the
bathing-machine proprietors, who argued that good-class
visitors objected to this regulation. Nevertheless, the
practice slowly spread, despite its unpopularity with men.
Readers of Kilvert's *Diary* will remember his surprise,
when bathing from a machine at Seaton in 1873, at finding
on his return that one of the pieces of cloth with which
he had been provided was not, as he had assumed, a

towel but a pair of short red-and-white striped drawers. However, despite his unwitting flouting of the convention, 'the young ladies who were strolling near seemed to have no objection'. It is worth noting, moreover, that his own sister Dora had come down with him and was sitting on the beach while he bathed. The following year at Shanklin on the Isle of Wight he again came up against 'the detestable custom of bathing in drawers'. Though he obediently put them on, they promptly slipped down to his ankles in the rough waves and in that hobbled condition he was thrown down on sharp shingle and rose streaming with blood. Smarting mentally and physically he disentangled himself from 'the wretched and dangerous rag' only to find when he came out of the water that 'of course there were some ladies looking on'.

Until well after Surtees' death, therefore, there was little change in the unconcerned bathing habits of the English male or the unconcerned tolerance of the English female. Use and wont are powerful influences on social conventions. As far as can be judged, most Victorian women were not particularly shocked by what they occasionally saw. Whether they approved or disapproved, they were accustomed to it; and custom breeds tolerance. Miss Weeton in the early part of the century was something of a prude who objected even to undressing a girl of 7 for a bath in front of her younger brothers and sisters. Yet, sitting in August 1809 at her bedroom window at Beacon's Gutter, from which she could see crowds of naked people bathing in the River Mersey, she observed to a woman friend that

the latter is not the most delicate sight; but I am now so accustomed to it, that really I do not feel so much shocked as I ought to do. It appears to me as a mere thing of course, and I think no more now of the objects in the water, nor notice them any more than I should passengers in the street. How much custom reconciles some people to—almost anything.

Alongside this philosophical reflection may be set, as a kind of male counterpoint, the exasperated comment of the Revd Francis Kilvert sixty years later, following his

mishap at Shanklin. 'If Ladies don't like to see men naked, why don't they keep away from the sight?' With
both attitudes, one suspects, Surtees would have had
some sympathy. All his observation led him to believe
that the women of his society had tougher fibre and less
acute sensibilities than the conventions of the time appeared to assume.

PART FOUR
The Changing Years

11

THE DECLINE OF ELEGANCE

I

To Surtees one of the great social changes in his lifetime
was the increase in comfort at the expense of elegance.
To a historian it might seem a natural development in
which national prosperity, a wider distribution of wealth,
the growth of technology, and the popularity of utilitarian ideas all played a part. Surtees was less inclined to
analyse the causes than to criticize the consequences;
in particular the vulgarity which permeated much of
Victorian culture. It was observable most clearly perhaps
in the fine arts: in architecture the collapse of a coherent
native tradition, in design the emphasis on decoration
rather than form, in painting the vogue for realistic detail
and literary subjects. Surtees never showed much interest
in those fields, but he was a keen and minute recorder
of costume; and it was here that he chiefly noted the
decline of style. Take, for example, his reference to the
vanished days when Mr Puffington was a young swell in
London, a period which can be approximately placed in
the 1820s.

In those days great people went about like great people, in
handsome hammer-clothed, arms-emblazoned coaches, with
plethoric three-corner-hatted coachmen, and gigantic, lace-
bedizened, quivering-calved Johnnies, instead of rumbling
along like apothecaries in pill-boxes, with a handle inside to
let themselves out. Young men, too, dressed as if they were
dressed—as if they were got up with some care and attention
instead of wearing the loose careless, flowing, sack-like garments they do now.

These observations were made about 1850. Three years
later, in *Tom Hall* (ch. l) he returned to the charge.

There never was a time when so little care or taste was exhibited in dress generally, or when such ugly, misfitting garments
were allowed to pass as coats. What would have been thought
in the dandy, swallow-tailed days of George IV—when coats
were made to fit like wax, and the slightest wrinkle was cut
out and fine drawn—of the baggy, sack-like things of the
present day, with sleeves that look like trousers put in by
mistake?

For the elderly and the conservative-minded it was
tempting to regard the sartorial changes which took place
between Waterloo and the Crimean War as evidence of
moral degeneracy. More impartial observers might conclude that they were symptoms of larger developments
in English society.

Historians of men's dress in the nineteenth century
are familiar with the process whereby the ordinary clothes
of one generation became the formal wear of the next,
and its casual dress promoted to the status of standard
attire. What is interesting is that this was the first time
such a development was discernible. Previously fashion
had merely succeeded fashion; now style in clothes was
moving in a specific direction—towards greater comfort,
utility, and economy. Surtees' dislike of what was happening owed something perhaps to a feeling that it was
the consequence of social tendencies even more regrettable. His comments on dress-changes in his lifetime have
therefore a certain deeper significance.

The most obvious mark of the new era in men's clothes
was the victory of trousers over breeches. At the start of
the century the usual costume of the gentry was the
traditional wide-lapped coat in a variety of colours (blue
often affected by Whigs, red sometimes by Tories), drab
waistcoat, breeches commonly of leather, and top-boots;
for evening wear knee-breeches, stockings, and pumps.
Fashionable day-wear in town already included, however,
pantaloons shaped to the leg, worn with calf-length boots.
Though the lady patronesses of Almacks were still in-
sisting in 1814 that no gentleman should appear at their
assemblies unless in knee-breeches, this was already
regarded as rather tyrannical. The duke of Wellington,

fresh from his Peninsular campaign, innocently turned up one evening in black trousers and was turned away by a vigilant attendant—or so Gronow says. After Waterloo, however, low shoes became common, and in the 1820s the tight pantaloons were broadening out into what are unmistakably trousers, often kept in place by a strap passing under the instep. By the reign of William IV the majority of upper-class men had adopted the new mode. The trousers, fashionably white, were of broadcloth in winter and linen in summer, worn with a frock-coat or swallow-tail of contrasting colour. The fullness of the trouser-leg depended on the taste of the wearer. In the late 1840s Soapey Sponge, who was of a conservative turn of mind in clothes, was still wearing trousers shaped to the leg 'as soft and as supple as a lady's glove' and almost as tight-fitting.

Surtees takes care, however, to point out that in this Sponge was adhering to 'the close-fitting costume of former days'. Most men, more concerned with comfort, less disposed to spend time and money on the refinements of the tailor's art, were content with the broad-legged trouser with the fullness at the bottom obscuring half the shoe. The confining under-strap had disappeared and in another ten years the modern 'turn-up' made its appearance. At first this was simply a practical device against dirt and wet. Later it became a tailoring convention to embody a turn-up in all trousers other than for evening wear. It is a mark of Surtees' fidelity to detail that even this minor change finds a place in his novels. Carroty Kebbel in *Ask Mamma* had his trousers 'turned up at the bottoms to avoid the mud'. Willy Watkins in *Mr Romford* wore on occasions 'white flannel-looking trousers, turned up at the ancles to show his red stockings and Balmoral boots'—the latter being ones that laced up in front.

Changes in fashion, of course, are rarely instantaneous or universal. Economical men went on wearing garments inherited from their fathers. Conservative men clung to the fashions of their youth. Country squires still went around in a sporting costume of breeches and top-boots.

When General Dyott was on a country visit in 1837 he observed that his host followed 'the old system of dress. Leather breeches in a morning, and breeches again in an evening.' But this was clearly unusual enough to warrant a mention. Dyott himself had been wearing trousers for many years. In April 1830, for example, he was grumbling that the unseasonable cold weather had forced him to give up his recently assumed white linen pantaloons and revert to 'cloth and woollen stockings'. As late as the 1850s Surtees describes the guests at Sir Moses Mainchance's hunt-dinner as exhibiting every variety of coat from the tight, short-waisted swallow-tails of George IV's reign to the 'sack-like garment of the present day'.

In fashionable town-society, however, the movement towards plainness and uniformity was unmistakable. It was most marked in evening-wear, with black becoming the prevailing colour. This in itself was a minor revolution. Until almost the middle of the century a black dress indicated either a clergyman or somebody in mourning. Yet by the end of Surtees' life male evening dress had been drained of all bright colouring. In the 1870s Lord Albemarle could write that a black coat was 'now a gentleman's stereotyped dinner dress'. But there were other details of men's dress that illustrated the steady drift towards a quieter and simpler appearance. Shirts had become less ornate; frills down the front had declined; wrist-ruffles had disappeared; the high, starched wings or 'gills' to collars, popular in the 1840s, gradually subsided. The cravat, wound several times round the neck with a complicated bow in front, gave way during the 1860s to the modern style of a thin, knotted tie worn under a narrow, turn-down collar. Meanwhile, knee-breeches, along with stockings and buckled shoes, were relegated to that last refuge of superannuated fashion, formal occasions at Court. Several of these changes are recorded for posterity in Surtees' later novels. Mr Bunting in *Plain or Ringlets*, a London swell hoping to make an impression in the provinces, puts on a purple and black tie and 'careful collar'. In *Mr Romford* the decline of the high, enveloping cravat enables the Hon. Lovetin Lonnergan to display the full amplitude of his sallow face and looming chin above 'the turn-down collar and diminutive neck-string of the day'.

At the start of Victoria's reign, however, there were still eccentrics and dandies. The supreme contemporary example of the dandy was the Count d'Orsay, leader of fashion in both London and Paris, emulated by many, admired by all, even though his taste in clothes was more exotic than would have been tolerated in anyone else. Gronow compared him to a gorgeous dragon-fly; to the bourgeois Haydon, whom he once visited at home in 1839, he was like a vision from another planet—'such dress—white great coat, blue satin cravat, hair oily and curly, hat of the primest curve and purest water, gloves [scented with] eau de Cologne or eau de jasmine, primrose in tint, skin in tightness'.

Eccentrics and dandies appear in Surtees' novels too, perhaps in more abundance than they occurred in real life. Lord Scamperdale and his crony Jack Spraggon, when dining at home, outdo Henry Brougham by appearing in 'flaming, large-checked red-and-yellow tartans' with black and white Shetland hose and red slippers. The would-be elegants are more numerous still. The resourceful Mr Bowker launches his Anti-Corn Law campaign in Sellborough clad in a mulberry-coloured frock-coat with a velvet collar, a velvet waistcoat of even brighter hue, flowered satin cravat, fawn leather breeches, and Hessian boots. There could have been few League candidates in reality who attained that pitch of sartorial splendour; yet the marquis of Bray in the same novel outshone even this. His morning dress on one occasion consisted of a pea-green coat, white trousers, pink-striped shirt, matching stockings, and buckled shoes. For evening wear he is described as turning out in a blue coat, white cravat, frilled shirt, blue satin waistcoat, pink silk stockings, and shoes. The heir to the Donkeyton dukedom evidently had more money than taste. Soapey Sponge had a smaller income but better dress-sense. When he wishes to make an impression at Jawleyford

Court, he dresses for dinner in a blue coat, white waist-coat, fancy-fronted shirt with a tendency to pink, stiff high collar, black tights, and patent leather pumps. Twelve years later, and under the moderating influence of Lucy Glitters, Facey Romford goes off to an interview for the mastership of the Larkspur Hunt in what Surtees calls a becoming sporting attire—single-breasted grey morning-coat, striped buff waistcoat, cord trousers, and buttoned boots.

In the middle of the century the trend was towards more comfortable as well as more sober clothes. One sign of this was the growing popularity of tweeds. Here at least Surtees was prepared to welcome innovation. 'How we pity people', he remarks in *Hawbuck Grange*, 'who lived before "tweeds", railways, and writing directions on newspapers, were invented!' That was in the mid-1840s, and the quotation marks testify to the novelty of even the name. The word was said to be a trade term based on a misreading of the Scottish term 'tweel' or twill, and the reference in *Hawbuck Grange* (1847) is possibly the first, certainly a very early, use of the word in English literature. Being a twilled woollen cloth of rough texture, tweed did not lend itself to elegant tailoring. What it offered was warmth and comfort. When, for example, Jenkins Jones, Mr Scott's involuntary host at Down House, got out of his hunting kit at the end of the day, he put on a comfortable suit of plaid for the evening. Tweeds, moreover, could be adapted to a variety of purposes by those indifferent to fashion. Mr Jawleyford rides to a meet of the Scamperdale Hunt with his nether man encased, we are told, in rhubarb-coloured, tweed pantaloons of the newest make, a material (adds Surtees drily) 'extremely soft and comfortable to wear, but not so well adapted for roughing it across country'. That unenthusiastic sportsman Mr Jogglebury Crowdey went to visit Mr Sponge in a black frock-coat and fine cinnamon-coloured tweed trousers with broad blue stripes down the sides.

As these examples show, the introduction of tweeds counteracted the tendency towards quieter fashions in men's formal wear. A striking visual illustration of this is provided by Leech's print of the scene when Facey Romford entertains Soapey Sponge to a little music on his flute. It shows his burly figure, clad in a startling suit of tartan tweed—coat, waistcoat, and trousers—towering over the thin, fashionably dressed Soapey seated in a chair with his crossed legs elegantly encased in skin-tight pantaloons strapped under his shoes. There are more tweeds in *Ask Mamma*, bearing witness to the continued popularity of the material in the following decade. Sir Moses Mainchance changes into a suit of dingy old tweeds for the utilitarian purpose of pursuing an absconding tenant. Mr Kebbel, the peripatetic attorney who prefers lightness and convenience to smartness and fashion in his clothes, travels in a suit of 'black-grounded tweed' with purple dots. The thick weave of tweed traditionally lent itself to a multiplicity of colours and patterns and in its first period as a favourite men's suiting it went to remarkable extremes of garishness and vulgarity. There is no reason to think that Surtees was exaggerating in his descriptions. Looking back to the 1860s Lady Dorothy Nevill remembered it as a time when there was a perfect craze for 'large and loud checks and plaids'. The introduction of aniline dyes in the late 1850s possibly added a peculiarly strident character to men's tweeds, as they did for a time to the colours of women's clothes.

The new vocabulary which accompanied these sartorial changes itself hinted at a different attitude. Surtees records some examples. Aeneas M'Quirter, the editor of the *Swillingford Patriot*, refers to his trousers, for example, as 'slacks'. This was the slang term originally applied to the full-length, loose garment that came in during the 1820s. Even more revealing is the phrase Surtees uses when he describes Facey Romford as getting up in the morning and hastily donning 'his lounging-suit of grey tweed'. Whether he coined the expression or made use of one already current is not easy to discover. In either case it is only a short step from this to the modern 'lounge suit' which Partridge ascribes to tailor's jargon of the

early twentieth century. Slacks and lounge suits were
the products of a very different world of fashion than
that represented by the Count d'Orsay. Appropriately
that last great champion of the age of elegance had already disappeared from the London scene. Driven by
debts to take refuge in France in 1849, he died only three
years later at the early age of 51.

II

Clothes were not the only contrast between Regency male
society and their mid-Victorian successors. Equally
striking was the increasing disuse of the razor. Apart
from a certain latitude in the matter of side-whiskers, it
was customary at the start of Victoria's reign for gentlemen to be clean-shaven. Only officers in the Hussar
regiments and the cavalry of the Household Brigade were
traditionally permitted to wear moustaches. In the political cartoons of HB, the royal duke of Cumberland, as
General of Hussars, is easily distinguished from other
public characters of the time by his luxuriant whiskers.
The Crimean War is credited with popularizing beards;
and this is at least a convenient date for marking the
change. A decade earlier a beard would have stamped
a member of the upper classes as either a crank or an
artist. In the parliament of 1841–7, for example, G. F.
Muntz, the Liberal MP for Birmingham, was conspicuous
as the only member who had a beard. Though this gave
him a certain distinction within the House, it was apt to
cause irreverent comment outside. In Birmingham the
only other men in local public life who sported beards
were the followers of the eccentric Joanna Southcott.
Muntz was a big, powerful man, however, and habitually
carried a thick malacca cane when he went out with
which to answer any insults he encountered on the
streets. For some censorious people beards signified not
only social but intellectual heterodoxy. When, in the early
1850s, the Revd E. R. Larken was bold enough to appear
in the pulpit with a small, dark beard under his chin, it

was held to indicate a serious laxity in his theological principles.[1] On similar grounds the Christian Socialists of the same period earned a reputation for dangerous political heresies because they included among their followers some bearded figures as well as a few vegetarians and phrenologists.

Whether the subsequent Victorian fashion for facial hairiness was a form of compensation for the increasing sobriety of their formal dress or a subconscious assertion of their masculinity is a question which may be left to psychologists. It was not, however, a development viewed uncritically even by their own sex. Colonel Berkeley in the 1860s thought that while 'quiet and unostentatiousness in dress characterize the gentleman' of that period, 'the assailable points in his get-up are usually his hair, beard, and whiskers'. The returning veterans of the Crimean winter no doubt helped to make beards fashionable. Surtees himself in *Ask Mamma* refers to the 'Crimean-bearded' Mr Kebbel. Yet the war could only have accelerated, not caused, the revolution of fashion seen at the end of Surtees' life. There was a vogue for increasingly long, luxuriant side-whiskers long before the outbreak of the Crimean War. Mr Scott in *Hawbuck Grange* is shown in the illustrations as possessing them. So too do half the circle of gentlemanly toadies who gather round Lord Lazytongs, though it is true that we are told in the text that several of them were army officers. The face of the noble lord himself is framed in a great, rope-like fringe of hair which descends from his ears to his chin. Earlier still, in *Handley Cross*, though Jorrocks himself is clean-shaven, many of the gentlemen present at his lectures are adorned with side-whiskers. The Crimean beard was merely the final stage of a development which had been growing in popularity over the previous decade.

To Surtees, as to Berkeley, the fashion was a regrettable one. In an article on 'Fox Hunting in Past and Present Times', written in 1848–9, he shows a degree of contempt for what he clearly regarded as a vulgar innovation. Describing his ideal fox-hunter, he says approvingly, 'there is a neat, quiet, easy manner about him; he is properly shaved and wears neither beard nor chin-wig (those shop-hand appendages!)'. Though there are plenty of hirsute characters in the later novels, not many of them are gentlemen and few are dealt with charitably. Mr Sponge, though his hair is at least closely cropped, has 'carefully tended whiskers, reaching the corners of a well-formed mouth, and thence descending in semicircles into a vast expanse of hair beneath the chin'. These appendages are at any rate well groomed and carefully shaped. Those of Facey Romford constitute an unpruned, straggling growth in which Nature has been allowed a free hand. The effect on the beholder of his 'large backward-growing-all-round-the-chin-gingery-whiskered face' is not improved by his habit of tugging at his whiskers in moments of perplexity until wisps of hair come away in his hand. Even more repulsive, though mercifully briefer, is Surtees' description in the same novel of the beard belonging to Mr Bonus, once of the Stock Exchange—'a skewbald fan beard formed of alternate tufts of yellow and white hair, just like the fringe of a kettle-holder'.

After the Crimean War the fashion for side-whiskers, moustaches, fringes, and beards of all descriptions, was unstoppable. So much did they determine the normal appearance of the Victorian male that the hairless countenance of young Billy Pringle, in the illustrations to *Ask Mamma*, the first of Surtees' post-Crimea novels, creates by itself an impression of youthful gullibility. One of the attractions, perhaps, of the new hirsute style was precisely that it conveyed an air of masculinity and maturity in those who without it might not have felt so confident of possessing these qualities. There was even, apparently, among those who wished to seem older and wiser than their years, a habit of bleaching their hair to give a preternatural appearance of advancing age. While older men resorted to the dye-bottle to hide the ravages of time, some younger men, including reputedly members of the clerical profession, used toiletry to conceal their youth. 'For some time past,' wrote Grantley Berkeley satirically, 'people have wondered at the vast increase of venerable-looking young men, patriarchs of thirty, and Methuselahs of twenty-five, with flowing locks and hirsute appendages *white as snow*.'

Those for whom growing their own hair in sufficient quantity was a problem in itself could resort to the other artificial aids available at London hairdressers. The tyranny of fashion and the vanity of men were never more cruelly satirized in Surtees' novels than in the ludicrous episode when Captain Doleful yields to the skilful salesmanship of his Holborn hairdresser and purchases the false scalp and 'invisible spring d'Orsay whiskers'. It was true that d'Orsay affected from an early age a thick, curly fringe of hair growing down the sides and under the chin, like a wreath of foliage surrounding his distinguished aquiline countenance. It was a style which, though a trifle precious, suited his uncommonly handsome features. The great, horse-collar roll of hair which was named after him, however, was a travesty of his style. Colonel Berkeley regarded the later version of this fashion as 'the most ridiculous appendages to the cheeks of men'. They were known to the irreverent Cockneys as 'Piccadilly weepers'. Berkeley tells with relish the anecdote of a street urchin who, kicked aside by a swell thus adorned, called out to a companion, 'my eyes, Jemmy, look here! if here ain't a chap what 'as killed and swallowed 'is grandmother's cats and got their tails a-hanging out on either side his kissers'. It was perhaps this kind of ridicule that helped to bring about the end of this particular fashion.

Though Captain Doleful may have been right in thinking that ladies liked men with whiskers, not all their sex relished the hairy exuberance of the mid-Victorian male. Large unkempt beards had disadvantages more obvious to the spectator than to the wearer. They retained the smell of tobacco, and, in the case of careless eaters, traces of food. Lady Morley, renowned in London society for her sharp tongue, said of the Duke of Newcastle that 'I can always know how many courses he has eaten at dinner by looking at his beard'.[2] Newcastle was one of many who qualify chronologically as 'Crimean-bearded'.

Content up to about 1854 with side-whiskers, by 1856 he had grown a bushy beard; and by the end of his life (he died in the same year as Surtees) he was distinguished even among contemporaries by an enormous mass of hair which hung down over his chest, obscuring most of his shirt-front. Surtees himself kept aloof from an untidy fashion he clearly disliked; his thin, spare face was innocent of beard or whiskers even in old age.

III

In the general decline in masculine elegance there was a third development which deserves notice: the habit of smoking. By the end of the eighteenth century the gentry and aristocracy had largely given up tobacco except in the refined form of snuff. Leigh Hunt, whose father used to smoke a pipe every evening before retiring, thought that he was one of the last of the gentry to retain 'the old fashion of smoking'. After Waterloo the few members of higher society who still used a pipe seem to have been those with German connections. The royal duke of Sussex, for example, who died in 1843 at the age of 70, smoked little china pipes adorned with the royal coat of arms—objects of great curiosity to English eyes. When in 1819 young Lady Jerningham visited Holkham, where the duke was also a guest, she was taken to his dressing-room by her host's daughter Miss Coke, 'to see his *Pipes*'. A year earlier another Germanic tobacco-addict, the Prince of Hesse-Homburg, had come to England to marry George III's daughter, the Princess Elizabeth. It was reported from the Court that he had been bathed several times and prevented from smoking for three days beforehand, to get him into a suitable state for his nuptials.[3]

The modish form of smoking was the Spanish cigar, introduced into England during the Peninsular War. In Spain cigar-smoking by both sexes was common in all classes and many British officers picked up the habit.

The officials and officers of the East India Company also brought back the cheroot, a southern Indian version of the cigar. Later, in the post-war garrisons of the West Indies, where cigars were plentiful and cheap, they were habitually smoked in the officers' messes. The army, in fact, seems to have played a large role in popularizing this exotic article. Until the 1820s, however, their use was still confined to a relatively small set. Haydon, though aware of the vogue in high society for what he spelled 'segars', had never sampled their delights until 1827 when he was presented with one by a 'young man of fashion' on a coach. Unwilling to show ignorance, he accepted— a piece of snobbery which proved expensive, since his officious acquaintance arranged for his own supplier, a 'whiskered German', to call on Haydon. To *keep up my Character*, the painter gave him an order for 300, consoling himself for the extravagance by the pleased reflection that the word would get round in artistic circles that 'Haydon spends his time smoking segars'! In civilian society at that date cigars clearly were the mark of fast young men and unconventional aesthetes. One never hears, for example, of the leading politicians—Liverpool, Canning, Grey, Melbourne, or Peel—using tobacco. Melbourne indeed, rather tactlessly, told the young Victoria that smoking was a dirty German habit. For their generation smoking of any kind denoted either foppery, eccentricity, or vulgarity. Poodle Byng, one of the great characters of the West End clubs and, like his contemporary Charles Greville, a confirmed snubber of the young, used to enquire when he met any of them smoking, whether he wished to be taken for an omnibus conductor.

Snobbery apart, smoking seems to have been disliked in polite society mainly because it was a noisome habit. Some also had moral doubts about what was increasingly seen to be an addictive practice. The Quaker Pease in 1838 classed an 'ardent love of tobacco', with excessive sociability and a taste for liquor, as evidence of a soul in captivity. John Grey of Dilston called people with pipes in their mouths 'sensualists'; and though his anti-smoking prejudice aroused amusement in his family, a modern psychologist might perhaps agree with him. Surtees was not given to moral or psychological judgements on his fellow-men, but he made remarks which suggest that he too had a low opinion of the craze for smoking among the younger generation. 'Young gentlemen must smoke now-a-days, whether they like it or not', he comments in *Plain or Ringlets* (ch. x), when describing, at the conclusion of the picnic lunch under canvas, the exodus of the gentlemen 'to pollute the fresh air outside with cigars'. Another slighting reference to the habit is put in the mouth of Major Yammerton in *Ask Mamma* when he puzzles over the indifference of young men to hunting— 'must be that they smoke all their energies out'. In this physiological explanation he had the support of a real-life contemporary. Henry Smith, elected professor of geometry at Oxford in 1860, ascribed the falling-off in the intellectual capacity of students which he had noticed to their habit of smoking. A more forthright condemnation of the practice comes from the mouth of Jorrocks himself, on his first appearance in court on the magisterial bench. When a witness (a woman too) mentions having smoked a pipe in her kitchen, ' "nasty stinkin' old beast", grunted Mr Jorrocks, who hated tobacco'.

Jorrocks—and Surtees—were in distinguished company as far as their own generation was concerned. The great duke of Wellington strongly disapproved of tobacco smoking. In 1845, when commander-in-chief of the army, he issued a General Order calling on commanding officers to discourage the use of pipes, cigars, and cheroots among their officers. He roundly denounced smoking as 'not only itself a species of intoxication occasioned by the fumes of tobacco, but undoubtedly, occasions drinking and tippling by those who acquire the habit'. His strictures came too late. The order secured more amusement than obedience; and for a time pipe-stoppers in the likeness of the duke became popular in military circles.

Until well past the middle of the century smoking was a gratification which could only be achieved in special circumstances and in the face of a considerable degree of social disapproval. It was peremptorily banned on the new railway trains of the 1840s. The majority of hostesses in both upper- and middle-class society forbade it in their public rooms and usually in the bedrooms as well. Their guests had to satisfy their craving for nicotine in a variety of less comfortable quarters—the servants' hall, the stables, the harness room, outdoors in the shrubbery, or at best in the conservatory. Even Mrs Carlyle did not allow her husband to smoke in his bedroom, though on occasions he was permitted to lie on her drawing-room hearth-rug in his dressing-gown and smoke up the chimney. Once he was reduced to creeping down in his night-shirt to smoke by moonlight in the backyard of his Chelsea home.

The taboo on smoking in other people's houses is taken for granted in the Surtees novels. Soapey Sponge, for example, who had some gentlemanly instincts, felt it decidedly improper to smoke in his grand bedroom at Hanby House. It is the coarser-grained Jack Spraggon who borrows a cigar off him and carelessly lights up as together they compose the famous hunting article for the *Swillingford Patriot*. At Mr Puffington's demesne Sponge more considerately chooses the stables and shrubberies in which to smoke his cigars. The more pliant Mr Bunting in *Plain or Ringlets* yields with only faint demur to the Jug's callous proposal that they should round off their meal at the Bowderoukins with a smoke— to the indignation of their hostess at having her house made to smell, as she puts it, like a pothouse. The casualness of these allusions is convincing evidence of the strength of feeling against tobacco at this period. Posterity, which once smiled at what it considered the over-refined sensibilities of Victorian hostesses, may now perhaps learn to be more sympathetic.

Nevertheless, despite its unpopularity with many men and most women, the smoking habit steadily grew. From being a private and almost illicit pleasure, it became a common spectacle. Algernon West once stated that no gentleman ever smoked in the street until after the Crimean War. Much depends on the definition of a gentleman. One evening in 1842 Haydon met 'a dandy from a party with a cigar in his mouth' walking along a street in central London; but at least the sight was sufficiently unusual for him to remark on it. On the eve of the Crimean War Leech depicted Mr Waffles sauntering along the road in Laverick Wells in broad daylight puffing at a cigar; but though a swell in his own estimation, he was hardly a gentleman in either West's or Surtees' sense of the word. Behind doors, however, smoking was by now common—and not only in regimental messes. Clubland itself had yielded to the cult. In 1845 White's Club, that haunt of dandies, opened its first smoking-room: though it was not until 1881 that smoking was permitted below the attic floor of that other exclusive club, Brooks's. Some of the larger, more heterogeneous clubs had begun to cater for smokers even before the start of Victoria's reign. When the new Reform Club building was being planned in 1837 it was decided to include a smoking-room as well as two billiard rooms. There was already one at its great rival, the Carlton, since in 1836 the committee of management ruled that, as there was a special room set aside for the purpose, smoking was not to be allowed in other apartments. Even if the institution of 'smoking-rooms' was a defensive measure, it is clear that in such gregarious, male establishments an absolute prohibition would have been unsustainable.

Prince Albert installed a smoking-room for himself at Osborne as early as 1845. This, however, was more a mark of the Germanic habits that Melbourne so deplored than one of changing English customs. Ordinary English country houses were much slower to surrender. Exceptions, however, could be found even in the 1840s. On a visit to Fryston, the Milnes' Yorkshire residence, Carlyle was positively encouraged to use his bedroom for smoking; and the same year, in the same tolerant household, Thackeray was told that Mrs Milnes would not object to a cigar in the drawing-room. At the Headingley home of the great Leeds textile manufacturers, the Marshalls, there was a real smoking-room where one of the younger brothers kept his pipes and cigars. Yet it was not until the 1860s that smoking-rooms were beginning to be generally introduced into English country houses: and, even so, there was still a measure of segregation. They were often put in towers, sometimes close to the billiard room or as an annexe to it. Their permitted existence was, nevertheless, a clear sign that the battle over smoking in private houses had been won.[4]

The outcome had been predictable, perhaps, twenty years earlier from the spread of the smoking habit among university undergraduates. Habits contracted at Oxford and Cambridge probably had a greater influence on the mid-Victorian generation than the isolated example of the not very popular Prince Consort. Goldwin Smith claimed that there was no smoking when he was at Eton and Magdalen in the 1830s and 1840s; it was forbidden at school and never happened in college. If his memory was accurate, this must have been unusual. Sir John Mowbray, who was at Oxford in the mid-1830s, confirmed that there was little or no smoking among undergraduates at that time; but he thought that he had been at the end of an era as far as smoking was concerned. When he went down in 1837 to read for the Bar in London, he found that cigars were always brought out after dinner. Only two years later the future Dean Church was writing half-humorously to his mother, complaining of his undergraduate friends who perfumed his room 'with every possible combination of tobacco smoke, scents, and pomatum'. By the 1850s the habit was so firmly entrenched at Oxford that it had even been taken up by the theological students at the new college at Cuddesdon. In 1855 there were scandalized comments about their appearance out of doors, wearing fez caps, coloured ties, and smoking clay pipes. The Principal delivered a short homily on this regrettable behaviour but it was not kindly received by his young ordinands.[5]

That the young gentlemen of Cuddesdon smoked clay pipes was perhaps an added offence. Clay pipes were undoubtedly 'low'. Surtees makes a number of references to them, usually with a touch of contempt. In *Hawbuck Grange* Mrs Trumper, when entertaining the Goose and

Dumpling Harriers, permits the production of clay pipes and a large tobacco box after she has retired from the table; but Trumper was a farmer and this was after all the Hunt Dinner when a certain laxity was traditional. Other references in the novels are more pointed. At one of the meets in *Ask Mamma* there is 'a knot of half-horse, half-pony mounted Squireen-looking gentlemen, with clay pipes in their mouths'. The motley followers of Major Yammerton's Harriers stow their clays in their breast-pockets before moving off behind the hounds. At Sir Moses Mainchance's 'sham day', Captain Luff RN breaks off with a few other thirsty souls at a public house 'to wet their whistles and light the clay pipes of gentility'. The attraction of clays to sportsmen was presumably that they were cheap and expendable; there were other more expensive and durable articles available. The artist who is shown painting the equestrian portrait of Dick Bragg, Mr Puffington's huntsman, smokes what looks like a German china or meerschaum pipe as he works. The more homespun Facey Romford, we are told, had an 'old briar-root pipe'.

For the thrifty there was a further advantage to clays; they could be easily cleaned by putting the bowl in the fire. Charles Kingsley had taken to clay pipes when he was an undergraduate at Cambridge and continued to use them for the rest of his life despite the efforts of first his mother and then his wife to wean him of the habit. A thorough addict, despite his straitened means, he bought the cheapest tobacco and kept a number of clays about the house, never allowing any of them to become foul. He claimed that, at the age of 20, tobacco had relieved him of his adolescent fits of depression. In his later life tobacco clearly acted as a sedative during the excitement of literary composition. For Kingsley smoking was not a sensual indulgence, but a boon to mankind. In *Westward Ho* (1855) he put into the mouth of Salvation Yeo the most eloquent tribute to tobacco in the English language. Literary men may, indeed, have helped to establish smoking as an acceptable social practice. Tennyson was a great smoker, credited with getting through nine pipes a day, a consumption almost double

that of the despised Prince of Hesse Homburg a generation earlier. Though Dickens seems to have smoked
mainly cigars, when he lived at Tavistock Square in the
1850s he used to entertain friends in his garden on Sunday mornings with trays of bottled stout and churchwarden pipes—reputedly his way of protesting against
the dullness of the conventional British Sabbath.[6]

Cigars, however, were the respectable form of smoking
in the middle of the century. They were, of course, a
luxury commodity which only the well-to-do could afford.
Though, at the start of Victoria's reign, they attracted
duty at three times the rate of ordinary loose Virginia
tobacco (9s. per lb. compared with 3s.), the method of
levying the tax, by weight and not value, meant that it
represented only a small part of the price paid by the
customer. To smoke cigars was the mark of a gentleman.
They were smoked out of doors by riders waiting at the
covertside, indoors after dinner in clubs and private
houses; by clergy and college dons as well as swells and
country squires. Though Jorrocks in the early 1830s
declared that 'they always make me womit', it is evident
that even then cigars, with hip-flasks and sandwiches,
were among the creature comforts that a wise hunter
carried with him in the field. Among fashionable, and
still more, perhaps, would-be fashionable young men in
London, cigar-smoking became something of a cult,
centred on the smart cigar shops or 'divans', as they were
sometimes called. These establishments offered not only
a wide range of cigars and cheroots but rooms in which
to smoke them and sometimes facilities for billiards and
other recreations. As an additional lure to the impressionable young there was usually a pretty young woman
behind the counter whose vivacious conversation encouraged her clients to stay on to sample the other attractions provided on the premises. For Dickens they
were the best place to observe the idle street-loungers of
the 1830s.

Peep through the window of a West-End cigar shop in the
evening, if you can manage to get a glimpse between the blue
curtains which interrupt the vulgar gaze, and you see them in

their only enjoyment of existence. There they are lounging about, on round tubs and pipe-boxes, in all the dignity of whiskers and gilt watch-guards; whispering soft nothings to the young lady in amber, with the large earrings, who, as she sits behind the counter in a blaze of adoration and gas-light, is the admiration of all the female servants in the neighbourhood.[7]

In this account the clients sound more like 'gents' than gentlemen, pretentious young males of the middle class rather than members of the aristocracy. Nevertheless, they had money to burn, and the ownership of such establishments offered a prospect of easy pickings for older men of no fixed profession and insufficient income. It was another version of the rooks and pigeon phenomenon.

Surtees gives a classic account of such a shop in *Mr Romford*. We are told there that when Soapey Sponge took on the burden of a wife, he tried to solve the problem of making money without having any capital by opening the 'Sponge Cigar and Betting Rooms' in Jermyn Street. The attractive Lucy presided at the front of the premises while Soapey supervised the sporting transactions at the back. When Facey Romford calls there, he finds Lucy behind the counter fetchingly dressed in a low-cut semi-evening dress with an imitation Spanish mantilla round her bare shoulders and a circle of young swells in front of her talking 'in the familiar way fools talk to women in bars and cigar rooms'. An unfeeling legislature, however, had put an end to the betting side of the establishment and all Lucy's charms were not enough to make the profits from cigars enough to support them both.

There is a close parallel in real life to this fictional episode in the contemporary career of the disreputable Renton Nicholson. An even seedier character than either Soapey or Facey Romford, he had recourse to the same expedient to keep himself afloat. Some time in the 1830s, as far as can be judged from his dateless and sprawling autobiography, he simultaneously took on a wife and a cigar shop, the latter in a turning off Regent Street. His wife was young and pretty; and behind the shop was a large room in which customers could drink and play cards. He had no licence for that purpose, but he was never particular about such things and for a time did a roaring trade. Then his impecunious past caught up with him and he was imprisoned for debt. To retrieve his fortunes he and a friend launched a flashy periodical called *The Town* and one of the first articles to appear in it was one entitled 'Cigar Shops and Pretty Women'—a subject of which Nicholson could now speak with first-hand experience.[8] The character of such establishments could only have strengthened the suspicion in many early-Victorian minds that tobacco was inextricably linked with the social vices of the age. That upholder of bourgeois morality, Mr Jorrocks, included among the temptations awaiting the provincial in London the painted Jezebels who sat behind their counters being 'fumigated by all wot buys cigars at her shop'. It could hardly have been reassuring that some cigar shops remained open all night: a circumstance which in 1861 induced the strait-laced Mr Gladstone to bring them under the operation of the Refreshment Houses Act, which entailed the payment of a licensing fee and liability to inspection by the police.

For all that, the practical convenience and social cachet of the cigar confirmed it as the fashionable form of smoking in the second half of the century. It was, of course, almost exclusively a male habit. The prejudice against women smokers was still strong. They could be found, however, in Bohemian circles where women mixed with men on terms of greater familiarity and equality than in conventional society. When, for example, Haydon dined with Belzoni, the Italian actor, traveller, and engineer, in 1821 he was taken aback when Mrs Belzoni stayed on after the meal to smoke with the men. It was true that the excuse could be made for her that she was foreign and uneducated. Nevertheless, he observed prudishly, 'it is singular, when a woman has once been admitted to a certain degree of masculine habit, she never relishes the delicate retirement of her own sex'. The same observation could be made, presumably, about the fast set of women at Nonsuch House in *Mr Sponge* a generation later. At the famous meet of Sir Harry Scattercash's hounds (ch. liii), 'Lady Scattercash, with several elegantly-dressed females, all with cigars in their mouths' converse with their gentlemen friends through the open window of the drawing-room. Later Leech portrays Lady Scattercash driving off in her phaeton, puffing at a cigar, in view of all the company.

By the time *Plain or Ringlets* appeared in book form in 1860, the prejudice against at any rate the aroma of cigar-smoke was apparently dying down. The young gentlemen strolling among the Spanish hats and floating dresses on the promenade at Roseberry Rocks are described by Surtees as 'whiffing and smoking as they walked, the ladies all declaring they liked the smell of cigars out of doors'; though perhaps it was male company they liked even better. Lady Charlotte Schreiber, though she disapproved of her sons' habit of disappearing after the evening meal to smoke outside the house, was sufficiently flattered by the opportunity of monopolizing Tennyson's company to sit with him in a conservatory until one o'clock in the morning while the poet smoked and talked. No doubt the smoker lent enchantment to the smoke. Curiosity also, perhaps, was a factor in breaking down the taboo. When Harriet Martineau was in Egypt, that highly moral spinster learned to smoke a native pipe, the chibouque, and even brought one back to England. Later on, in the 1850s, she experimented with mild cigars as a cure for her deafness. The materials for this curious remedy were supplied by her admiring young friend, James Payne; but the cigars did not prove helpful and she soon gave them up.

It was not respectable for women to smoke even the diminutive form of cigar known as the cigarette. This novelty is often said, like beards, to have come in with the Crimean War; but they were available in England at least a decade earlier. In 1844 Mrs Carlyle reported to her husband, with a mixture of impatience and incredulity, that her new literary acquaintance, Geraldine Jewsbury, having first staged a jealous, emotional scene in her bedroom, next 'sat down at my feet and—smoked a cigaretto!! with all the placidity in life! She keeps a regular supply of these little things, and smokes them before all the world. In fact I am not at all sure that she is not *going mad!*' Miss Jewsbury was not only literary but also neurotic. Mrs Carlyle's exclamation marks sufficiently indicate her astonishment at her unfeminine behaviour.

IV

Since women, in the Victorian as in other periods, had an interest in appearing attractive, there was nothing on their side comparable with the beards, tweeds, and tobacco of their menfolk. Yet perhaps it is not entirely a coincidence that the 1850s and 1860s saw two novelties in women's fashions: the bloomer and the crinoline. The first was a reaction against the current mode of dress; the second an exaggeration of it. Both were defensible up to a point on utilitarian grounds; both had grotesque features which bordered on vulgarity.

Since the irruption of the French Revolution 'natural style' at the beginning of the century, fashion in women's dress had steadily moved away from the seductive simplicity of the high-waisted, loose gown of the Jane Austen period towards fuller and more ornate styles. Waists came down to a natural level; skirts expanded. Corsets moulded the figure above; padded and stiffened petticoats swelled the circumference below. By the 1830s the fashionable lady's appearance was already large and imposing; by the 1840s it had apparently reached its physical limits. Petticoats lined with horse-hair 'deceivers', and bustles like toy bolsters tied behind the waist, were standard accessories. It seemed that the dressmaker's art could do no more. Mr Jorrocks in *Hillingdon Hall* was probably voicing the secret feelings of many men in real life when he sighed for a return to nature unalloyed 'and the habolition o' bustles and 'oss-'air pettikits'. Only the very poor and the severely religious were exceptions to the general rotundity of feminine fashion. Mrs Carlyle attended a soirée in Liverpool in

1844 where the company was mainly Unitarian—'the men with faces like a meat-axe; the women most palpably without bustles—a more unloveable set of human beings I never looked on'.

The disadvantage for husbands of the vogue for voluminous skirts and multiple petticoats was the sheer expense of the quantity of material needed; the disadvantage for women was its sheer weight. The point had been reached when it was physically burdensome to carry around the amount of dress required by current fashion. Four or five under-petticoats of flannel, surmounted by two more of starched cotton, constituted a formidable drag on movement; the more so since skirts had steadily descended until they now literally swept the ground. It was said by Paxton, not altogether in jest, that the floors of the Crystal Palace Exhibition of 1851 had been kept permanently clean with the continual brushing by ladies' skirts. Out of doors in bad weather skirts had to be lifted clear of the ground to prevent the hems being soaked with moisture or clogged with mud. Returning to the filthy streets of London in November 1850, Mrs Carlyle found it 'such a fatigue carrying up one's heavy Winter petticoats' after the clean, gravelly roads of Hampshire.

The two Victorian innovations of the bloomer and the crinoline were both designed to free women from the monstrous encumbrance which fashion had imposed on them. They appeared almost simultaneously. The bloomer costume was perhaps an aberration more than a fashion, achieving notoriety rather than popularity. Invented in America about 1850—but not by Amelia Bloomer, who merely publicized it in her women's paper—it was already attracting notice in England the following year. The intention of its designer, Mrs Miller, was to produce a rational dress for country walks. It consisted of a small jacket, a short skirt reaching to the knees, and loose trousers gathered in at the ankles. In that form it was an eminently practical, modest, and comfortable costume, though not a particularly beautiful one. It was the bottom garment, of course, which caught the eye and aroused most public comment.

Trousers for women could not be said to be unknown, since they were the usual accompaniment to a riding habit. Their function was to guard the wearer against the hazards of exposing her limbs if she were thrown from her horse or had her skirt ripped open or even torn off bodily by quickset hedges and thick undergrowth. They were made either of broadcloth or fine leather; and their use seems to have been almost universal. In 1825 Mrs Arbuthnot discussed with some women friends whether it was better to wear 'Cossack' cloth trousers or leathers. She was laughed at as a prude when she confessed that she would on no account ride with less than three petticoats under her habit. It transpired that her friends wore only 'Cossacks'. A generation later Surtees describes Lucy Glitters as wearing 'beautifully made chamois-leather trousers with black-cloth feet' when she goes out with Facey Romford's hounds. Lucy, though not a lady, took care to dress like one. The un fortunate and less sagacious Angelena Blunt, on the famous occasion when a downpour of rain washed away her chances of marrying Lord Heartycheer, had been unwise enough to wear under her riding habit 'an abundant crinoline petticoat' and her 'white silk eider down bustle'. These fragile articles offered so little protection against the elements that her habit 'stuck to her figure like a wet bathing dress'.

There is a great psychological difference, however, between garments meant to be seen and those normally concealed from view. The oddity about the bloomer costume was that it managed to combine two contradictory attributes. On the one hand it deliberately displayed what were undeniably female legs, even though these were decently encased in what were sometimes described as 'pantillettes' or 'pettiloons'. To a generation of Victorian males accustomed to skirts that descended to floor-level, hiding not only the ankles but the feet of the wearer, this was clearly a titillating sight. Many who experimented with the bloomer cult were probably only dashing young women with a zest for daring novelty; but the adoption of the costume by chambermaids, waitresses, and others whose business it was to attract male custom, strengthened its reputation as a dress for 'fast' women. Yet, on the other hand, it was designed as a rational costume and its use advocated by serious females who supported women's rights and sexual equality. Bloomer-clad lecturers, attended by acolytes in similar attire, endeavoured to demonstrate to the public the advantages of the new form of dress. They succeeded only in identifying it with the zealots and cranks of the women's movement. A fashion that was simultaneously taken up by bar-maids and bluestockings obviously possessed comprehensive qualities; but there was little prospect of permanent popularity for a garment which contrived to be both suggestive and eccentric.

In the event, the bloomer craze proved no more than a brief though memorable episode in the history of nineteenth-century women's clothes. It caught the nation's amused attention but expired with meteoric rapidity. Even the sober *Annual Register* was moved to publish a brief note on the bloomer phenomenon 'among matters which require to be chronicled, not because of their intrinsic importance, but on account of the interest they excite at the time'. What it called 'an attempted revolution in female dress' was killed, as far as can be judged, by public ridicule and male prejudice. *Punch*, for example, not as a rule an illiberal magazine, ran cartoons for several weeks on the subject, satirizing the garment and hinting broadly that if women were allowed to wear the trousers they would take over men's occupations as well. The reversal of sexual roles was also the burden of a popular street ballad 'The Bloomer Costume', which proclaimed that

> The pretty ladies one and all
> Are going to join the bloomers . . .
> The men shall wear the petticoats
> And ladies wear the trousers.

By June 1851 the *Annual Register* was already announcing that 'the absurdity died away'. It did not die entirely unlamented, even by those who were neither female emancipationists nor youthful coquettes. In 1852, at the mature age of 65, Lady Shelley climbed on foot a Dartmoor tor strewn with boulders and squelching with water. 'I regretted', she recorded half-humorously, 'that I had not worn a Bloomer costume!' There is no reason to suppose, however, that she had ever owned or worn one.

Surtees, with his eye for the ludicrous and love of topicality, caught the two conflicting aspects of the bloomer craze with great fidelity. In the new chapter entitled 'William the Conqueror; or, the ADC', which he inserted into *Handley Cross* when preparing its reissue in 1852, he introduced Constantia, daughter of the hostess of the Turtle Doves Hotel, in 'the full-blown costume of a Bloomer'. In this attire she was clearly one of the attractions of the establishment. Her outfit is described with Surtees' habitual love of detail: a 'silver-buttoned, light-blue silk vest, with a flowing jacket of a darker blue above a lavender-coloured tunic and white trousers', together with a 'cambric collarette and crimson silk necktie above her richly-figured shirt'. The impact of this vision on the susceptible males is expressively conveyed by Leech in a coloured print showing the elderly and ogling Major-General Sir Thomas Trout in his bath-chair, the unrestrained stares of admiration from the younger men, and the disdainfully aloof countenances of the other ladies present. Miss Constantia Mendlove, though highly respectable, was evidently an enthusiast for the new fashion. When she finally captures and marries her Assistant Drainage Commissioner, she not only wears her bloomer costume for the wedding ceremony but is supported by six bridesmaids similarly attired.

The other type of bloomer-devotee is featured, though more briefly, in *Mr Sponge*, which first came out serially in 1847–51 and then, with some rearrangement and re-writing, in 1852–3. This time it is a Literary Bloomer— Lucy Grimes, a lady of uncertain age, 'say liberal thirty', the daughter of Mr Grimes, the astute editor of both the *Swillingford Patriot* and the *Swillingford Guide*. She clearly had pretensions to being a bluestocking since she is described as 'a most refined, puritanical young woman, full of sentiment and elegance'. The elegance presumably was in her aspirations rather than her appearance. As portrayed by Leech she is the popular Victorian stereotype of an 'intellectual woman'—a severe face, a monocle, baggy trousers, plain tunic, a mannish jacket, and a full bow-tie beneath a Byronesque shirt-collar. One would fancy that of his two Bloomers Surtees preferred Constantia; the more so since Miss Grimes was opposed on principle to blood-sports.

The bloomer cult had hardly died down before the other great innovation of the crinoline arrived. By remaining entirely feminine it managed to stay in fashion considerably longer. Indeed, when it eventually passed away, it was by a process of evolution into the late-Victorian bustle-skirt rather than through any sudden fall from grace. Moreover, the ridicule it encountered was directed against its excesses rather than its basic principle. The crinoline in fact had some of the advantages of the bloomer costume without its eccentricity. Admittedly it allowed, encouraged even, skirts to expand even beyond the generous proportions already in fashion; but that was only an incidental feature. The primary purpose of the 'artificial crinoline' introduced in 1856 was to free the wearer from the weight of multiple petticoats and their attendant stiffeners and small bustles. The term 'crinoline' had been in use for some years, at first to describe the horse-hair employed to thicken the under-petticoats (from the French *crin*) and later as a general name for the dome-shaped dress it helped to create. The 'artificial' crinoline was a light framework of whale-bone, wire, or watch-spring, which served to distend the skirt while leaving the legs relatively unimpeded underneath. This was no small relief. Gwen Raverat's aunt, who belonged to the generation of women who had actually worn them, was emphatic on this point. 'Oh, it was delightful,' she told her niece. 'I've never been so comfortable since they went out. It kept your petticoats away from your legs, and made walking so light and easy.'

This freedom of movement made a difference to the

carriage of women when moving about which the pictures and photographs of the period were unable to capture. When in motion the crinoline swayed and dipped, giving glimpses of boot and stockinged leg above the ankle. The swaying action was one of its attractive features, though from misogynists and old-fashioned males, used to the stately progress of multi-petticoated ladies dressed in the old style, it sometimes provoked unkind comparisons. Among these must be classed Surtees himself. In *Plain or Ringlets*, which, with *Ask Mamma*, comes in the novelist's 'crinoline period', he speaks derisively of 'the peculiar dromedary sort of movement these singular encasements give them'. He is equally witty and merciless when he compares crinolined ladies caught in the open by the wind to 'peacocks with their tails up'. He had no good words at all for the fashion. When it is not the motion of the crinoline, then it is their size which he criticizes. After describing the 'wheeling, and circling, and spreading, and guiding of crinoline' at a dance, he comments sarcastically, 'wonderful fashion! We suppose we shall have the other extreme next, and dresses as scant as they are now inflatedly full.'

The characteristic swinging action of the crinoline was a dangerous as well as a piquant feature. In crowded rooms with large open hearths the crinoline was an undoubted fire-hazard. Lady Dorothy Nevill in her reminiscences of the period denounced it as 'an odious, hideous, and dangerous affair'. The second epithet is hardly justified on the evidence of an 1865 photograph which shows her wearing a charming example of the offending style. Her dislike, however, was probably because she was nearly burnt to death by one in her own drawing-room. The incident happened after dinner, but before the gentlemen had joined them, when she was pointing to a picture which hung beside the fireplace. Her crinoline caught alight and the other ladies, because of their own voluminous garments, were in no position to come to her assistance for fear of being set ablaze also. She only saved herself by rolling on the hearth-rug and beating the flames out with her hands. With flimsy materials spread out over a light, mobile framework, there was clearly a constant risk of such accidents. Colonel Berkeley might have been exaggerating, but there must have been some grounds for his assertion in 1866 that 'it is really terrible to read week after week the accounts that appear in the papers of ladies burnt to death without having the slightest hope of rescue' as a result of wearing crinolines.

The chief social disadvantage of the crinoline, however, was its increasing size. As much as eighteen yards of material might be needed to construct the dress that went over it; and Berkeley facetiously suggested that a portly husband could find sufficient healthful exercise by merely walking round his wife when she was fully arrayed. This amplitude might be ostentatiously defended by puritanical elderly ladies as keeping men at a proper distance, or secretly appreciated by younger, eligible ones as adding to the provocativeness of their charms. Coming at a time when skirts were already large, it was not so much a new fashion as an intensification by ingenious means of the old. Nevertheless, like some prehistoric monster, the crinoline soon outgrew the natural limits of its environment. Getting in and out of vehicles, passing on narrow pavements, moving around on dance-floors, and finding enough space to sit in drawing-rooms, became increasingly difficult. The men, who suffered most from the physical obstruction presented by the crinoline, were loudest in their complaints; but women too were conscious of the problems they created for themselves as well as others.

Writing to a friend in 1861, Mrs Oliphant pleaded the smallness of the rooms in her new house at Ealing and begged her 'to prepare for the dread necessity of dispensing with crinoline when you come to see me'. In the privacy of their own homes, when company was not expected, women were happy to relax in less demanding garments. Surtees' unfailing eye noted the contrast between ladies in 'dress' and 'undress' state. At Roseberry Rocks the early part of the day was given over to bathing and sauntering along the promenade. Then came luncheon and 'the exchange of easy morning robes for the rotundity of discomfort, when the inflated ladies became "at home", and sat looming on their chairs, like hens upon broods of chickens'. Mrs Bolsterworth, calling unexpectedly on Mrs Tartarman and her daughters, catches them in dishabille. The young ladies are hastily sent upstairs to exchange their limp morning dresses for 'well-distended muslin ones'. It is true that in *Ask Mamma* he makes Mrs Wotherspoon put on a crinoline for breakfast. This is no ordinary breakfast, however, but a '*déjeuner à la fourchette*' to which neighbours had been invited to meet Major Yammerton and his hounds.

When popular ridicule reinforced considerations of common sense, the decline of the crinoline was foreseeable. *Punch* never tired of publishing cartoons of crinolined maidservants threatening havoc in kitchen and drawing-room, or similarly encumbered ladies vainly trying to climb into omnibuses or out of railway carriages. The ballad-mongers too enjoyed their fun. There must have been a palpable advantage to the crinoline for Victorian women to have defied public ridicule and practical inconvenience for over a decade.

Yet there was ultimately a certain vulgarity about the crinoline. It resulted not from the basic design but from the extremes to which the fashion was taken. The physical lightness which was its chief attraction also made possible an elaboration which in the end became ludicrous—and therefore unladylike. Surtees seized on this point. The absurdity of the crinoline might be tolerated, he wrote, if it only inconvenienced the wearer, but in practice it inconvenienced everybody.

The only advantage we see in the absurdity is, that it forms a sort of graduated scale of gentility: the more extravagant a woman is in her hoops, the less inclined we are to think her a lady. It is only the vulgar who go into extremes, and make themselves look like curtains to bathing machines.

He receives support in this view from Colonel Berkeley, who in his strictures on the 'odious *crinoline*' comprehensively condemns it as ugly and dangerous, and a thorough nuisance to all the unfortunate men who have to travel with women, take them into dinner, or make conversation with them in the drawing-room.

It is impossible to imagine a more helpless object than a short man or a man even of ordinary bulk striving to make himself infinitesimally small, jammed in a corner between mountains of tarlatane and billows of satin and lace. If you see the victim's nose, it is as much as you can. He dare not move, and it is more than his life is worth to attempt a sneeze or blow his nose.

Writing about the time of Surtees' death, he was able to congratulate himself that 'ladies of the best society are leaving off crinoline, and ladies of no rank will do the same in due course'.

By 1870, in fact, the crinoline was in full retreat—literally so, since the fullness had retired to the rear of the wearer to produce that curious protuberance, the late-Victorian bustle. Surtees did not live to see the disappearance of a fashion he had consistently satirized. His novels can hardly be said, in any demonstrable sense, to have hastened its departure, but at least they are good evidence of the dislike which the crinoline evoked among many men of his generation. A style which originally was both practical and attractive disappeared because opulence and ostentation had been allowed to obliterate sense and style.

STAGE-COACHES, STEAM, AND
SPEED

I

Half-way through Surtees' life began the revolution in
transport which more than anything else separated the
Victorian age from all that had preceded it. The coming
of the railways provided the country with a cheap and
comprehensive system of moving people and goods long
distances at speeds which bore no recognizable relationship to what had previously been possible. In the space
of a few years the British public was able to travel three
times faster than it had been accustomed before. The
whole popular concept of speed was transformed. The
limitations imposed by the rate at which a horse could
gallop, oars propel a boat, or wind drive canvas, were
now irrelevant.

The contrast between old and new ideas of speed at
the start of Victoria's reign is dimly seen in the curious
and largely forgotten case of Mr Cocking in 1837. He
was an elderly landscape painter with an interest in aero-
nautics, considerable self-confidence, and an incomplete
grasp of aerodynamics. In June of that year he cut himself
loose from a balloon five thousand feet above Kent in
order to test a parachute of his own construction. At the
subsequent inquest Mr Finch, a surgeon, expressed the
opinion that death had occurred as a consequence not of
Mr Cocking's velocity through the air during his descent
but of his collision with the ground at the end of it. From
eyewitness accounts he estimated that the speed of his
fall had been only thirty miles an hour and he assured
the jury that it had been proved experimentally on the

railroads that humans could travel at sixty miles an hour without injury.

The jury could not reasonably have been expected to know, as Mr Finch evidently did, about the extraordinary speeds which George Stephenson and his engineers had attained in private trials with the locomotives. Stephenson in fact had told acquaintances a couple of years earlier that he would have no difficulty in making his engines travel faster than a bird could fly and that he believed the human frame could tolerate speeds up to 400 m.p.h.[1] Had any of the people in court been sportsmen, it might have occurred to them that on the racecourse, for example in the Derby Stakes at Epsom over $1\frac{1}{2}$ miles, jockeys travelled at more than 30 m.p.h. without any harm. The jurymen, however, as ordinary members of the public, would have been more familiar with the fact that a good stage-coach even over a short section could only average 12 or 14 m.p.h. Even to reach that velocity needed a combination of powerful horses, strong, light vehicles, and smooth, metalled roads. That such conditions existed in 1837 was itself the result of generations of human skill and ingenuity.

II

It is an irony that the railway arrived just when road travel had reached its peak of perfection. In the reign of George IV Britain had a road system that was not only better than at any time since the departure of the Romans fourteen centuries before but was the best in the world. There were nearly 100,000 miles of public highway and some 25,000 miles of turnpike maintained by private companies, many resurfaced on the principles of the Scottish engineer J. L. McAdam. Well-made roads and well-trained horses, as J. J. Gurney observed in 1831, 'of late years have been the means of so curiously compressing distances'.

Once off the great national trunk roads, of course, travellers had to adjust themselves to greatly inferior conditions. Many towns retained their cobbled streets; hard-wearing but noisy, and highly uncomfortable to passengers in vehicles. Even so, they were better than the main street of the dilapidated township of Sludgington in *Hawbuck Grange* (ch. vi), where Tom Scott spent a memorably miserable night at the Goldtrap Arms. It consisted of 'one continued bed of hard, loose, whinstone, whose roughness and sharpness was only relieved by a plentiful covering of cold, bleak-looking mud'; a combination threatening severe damage to the knees of the horse and the clothes of the rider in the event of a fall. In the open country the lanes meandered, as the early Ordnance maps show, from parish to parish with frequent twists and turnings calculated to baffle any stranger. A cross-country journey in unknown territory was still, as it had always been, a tedious and frustrating business. 'Township roads', maintained by the parish under the indifferent supervision of an amateur 'surveyor', were notorious for being dust tracks in summer and quagmires in winter, with the additional hazards of pot-holes roughly filled with large stones. These were not the only perils. When Mozley lived in Northamptonshire most of the local roads were, for economy's sake, fenced on only one side. Consequently, when he went to Northampton, Banbury, or other nearby towns, he had to open and shut some thirty field-gates: nuisance enough in daylight, at night positively dangerous. Surtees has plenty of disparaging comments in his novels on the subject. The road from Jawleyford Court to Woodmansterne in *Mr Sponge*, for instance:

where it did not lead over the tops of the highest hills, it wound round their bases, in such little, vexatious, up-and-down, wavy dips as completely to do away with all chance of expedition. The route was not along one continuous trust, but here over a bit of turnpike and there over a bit of turnpike, with ever and anon long interregnums of township roads, repaired in the usual primitive style with mud and soft field-stones, that turned up like flitches of bacon.

Between towns and larger villages there were usually
better roads with the additional merit, for the unfamiliar
traveller, of having signposts to tell him where they were
going, even if they had not yet achieved the status of a
metalled highway. Mr Sponge, to his relief, came to one
of these intermediate roads at the village of Hardington
when on his way to Bewley—'a road adorned with mile-
stones and set out with a liberal horse-track at either
side'.

To meet the various town and country needs of the
public, a large number of specialized vehicles had been
evolved by the early nineteenth century, from the huge
fourgon, used to carry luggage and servants on Continental trips, to the new dog-cart which General Dyott
dismissed as no more than a common butcher's cart when
his young officer son acquired one in 1840. Large and
wealthy households might possess as many as a dozen
different vehicles; it was a very impoverished middle-
class family which had none at all. Though relays of fresh
horses would need to be hired on long journeys, not to
travel in one's own carriage was socially demeaning. In
London the old-fashioned barouche, a capacious vehicle
driven by a coachman with two or four horses, was still
the fashionable mode of paying formal visits. For longer
journeys there was the post-chaise or, faster still, the
light, open *britzchka*, furnished with a hood. A popular
conveyance, for the owner who liked to drive himself,
was the four-wheeled phaeton. Lighter and more dashing
was the curricle, much patronized by young men in the
early part of the century for both town and country use.
Having only a single shaft for its two horses, however,
the fast curricle easily overturned. Almost as dangerous
were the Tilbury and the Stanhope, high-wheeled, lighter,
more elegant versions of the gig, named after their in-
ventors. Behind a spirited thoroughbred they were, wrote
Nimrod sardonically, the best friends that doctors and
undertakers ever had. Their main use was by fashionable
young men for getting about the countryside. On his
honeymoon in 1820 Robert Peel drove his bride round
the Staffordshire roads in one without mishap; but not

long afterwards one of his brothers had a bad accident with the same horse and vehicle—an event which made old Sir Robert implore his new daughter-in-law 'not to be carried in a gig or Tilbury drawn by a spirited hunter'. In its more utilitarian form, however, the gig— two-wheeled, one-horsed, light, and cheap—became perhaps the commonest vehicle on the road at the start of the railway age. It was the standard conveyance for commercial travellers, who found its roomy boot ideal for carrying round bulky samples. According to Surtees, gigs had the further recommendation of being capable, with the aid of a sensible horse, of taking their masters home in safety and without much assistance after an evening's heavy drinking. To the members of the Goose and Dumpling Harriers in *Hawbuck Grange* (ch. ii) their gigs were their 'drinking carts'.

Most of these vehicles were expensive to buy new; consequently there was a vast second-hand trade in them. It was more difficult to economize on upkeep. Horses ate whether they were used or not; coachmen and stablemen expected higher wages than most of the indoor servants. To travel in one's own carriage was not only a mark of status; it was a sign of wealth. Raumer stated in 1835 that in London nobody could afford to keep a carriage on an income of much less than £3,000 a year. Catering for such a wealthy clientele, coach-builders were notorious for the high prices they charged for their elegant products. Surtees had some harsh words to say about this in *Ask Mamma*. To illustrate his point he printed in full a bill from one of them which, with extras, came to nearly £400 for a single carriage. 'Sir Robert Peel was right when he said that there was no class of tradespeople whose bills wanted reforming so much as coachmakers. What ridiculous price they make wood and iron assume, and what absurd offers they make when you go to them to sell!'

Middle-class families on limited incomes resident in London, where stable accommodation was scarce and dear, had to make do with hired vehicles. In the early-Victorian years there were still hackney-coach stands with their old-fashioned vehicles licensed to carry up to six people. Four-wheeled, slow, dirty, and smelling permanently of the damp straw put down on the floor as a protection against muddy feet, they were neither cheap nor popular. Snobbish people would sometimes pay them off at the street corner and walk the rest of the way to avoid the indignity of being seen to arrive at their host's door in such a common conveyance. Those who could afford it would hire what was misleadingly known as a glass coach, cleaner, better appointed, and more respectable. For the sake of readers who in 1858 might be too young to remember them, Surtees explained in *Ask Mamma* in what their social superiority lay. They were not, he informed them, literally made of glass but comprised 'a better sort of hackney coach with a less filthy driver, which by a "beautiful fiction" of the times, used to be considered the hirer's "private carriage" '.

By the 1830s other public conveyances were beginning to compete successfully with the hackney coach. The cabriolet, a small, open, one-horse, hooded vehicle, looking not unlike a sedan-chair on wheels, with a driver perched perilously on a wing-seat, appeared on the streets about 1830. Soon after came the hansom cab, named after its designer. Originally a clumsy box-like structure with a door on either side, it was soon improved; and by 1836 a fleet of some fifty were plying for hire on the streets of central London. General Dyott noticed them as a novelty when he visited the capital in 1837. He did not entrust his person to one, however, though they struck him as 'a convenient conveyance'. When he had to make a couple of trips into the City, he went by the cheaper omnibus. These, he thought, had increased in number and popularity since his previous visit. On both occasions he had to share his journey with fourteen fellow-passengers—two more, he noted disapprovingly, than the regulations laid down. The original Shillibeer's omnibus, introduced in 1829, was a long van, drawn by three horses, with windows and facing seats in the interior. It was quickly imitated by numerous competitors. In the 1840s 'knifeboard' seats appeared, enabling another

half-dozen passengers to be carried, somewhat precariously, on the roof of omnibuses, exposed to the elements.
By the time Surtees came to write *Mr Sponge* twelve years
later, the streets of central London were thronged in the
daytime with 'buses' of different companies in their
various distinctive colours, all jostling for custom. The
knowledgeable Mr Sponge 'had a sort of "bus" pano-
rama in his head, knew the run of them all, whence they
started, where they stopped, where they watered, where
they changed, and, wonderful to relate, had never been
entrapped into a sixpenny fare when he meant to take a
threepenny one'.

In the countryside, where these metropolitan amenities
were unknown, finding transport was often difficult for
middle-class people with no vehicle of their own. At the
larger inns post-chaises could often be hired, sometimes
even gigs. Otherwise the intending traveller had to take
what he could find. When Mrs Flather in *Hillingdon
Hall* wanted to pay a ceremonial call on the Duchess
of Donkeyton, for which a carriage would clearly be required, she had to apply to the inn at Sellborough for
their one available coach—'a wretched copy of a wretched
original, a London glass coach'. This was an old landaulet,
built towards the close of the previous century, with little
left of the original structure except 'the roundabout tub-
shaped body' with low seats and high windows 'better
adapted for concealing the inmates than for surveying
the country'. Such antiquated contraptions probably
remained in use well into the Victorian age, along with
all sorts of hybrid conveyances which fitted into no
recognizable category. The vehicle which Mr Jorrocks is
described as using in the London of the 1830s, when
Jaunts and Jollities was written, he called a phaeton and
the irreverent Cockney urchins a fire-engine. It was 'a
nondescript double-bodied carriage (with lofty mail-box
seats and red wheels)'. It had a folding back-seat to
accommodate luggage and a spare pole to allow for a
pair of horses if necessary. As depicted by Alken it looks
more like a small mail-coach than anything else. Certainly
it bears little resemblance to a phaeton, which normally

had a fold-down hood and a rumble seat for a groom, as shown by Leech in chapter xxxii of *Mr Sponge*.

According to Surtees, who thought nothing of these omni-purpose vehicles, Jorrocks had picked up this curious article at a second-hand shop in exchange for £17 and an old 'cruelty-van' (otherwise known as a booby-hutch or four-wheeled chaise). By the time Jorrocks arrives at Handley Cross, some ten years later, he has progressed to 'an old, low, open, double-bodied' carriage, seating four comfortably, five at a pinch. Though Surtees also, and confusingly, describes this as looking like a fire-engine, it appears, as depicted by Leech, to be in fact a *britzchka*, a carriage which even more confusingly is mentioned as travelling on the same train as that on which the Jorrocks household make their well-publicized arrival at Handley Cross station. One can only conclude that in the extensive rewriting to which the text of *Handley Cross* was subjected before its reissue in 1853–4, Surtees mixed up what he recollected writing about Jorrocks' first vehicle with his description of the second. The Leech illustration, however, must be regarded as the authoritative statement, since it would have been approved by Surtees himself.

III

The queen of the roads was the stage-coach. It was the fastest, and for ordinary people the only practicable, method of covering long distances. The construction of the vehicle had been refined to the point where, according to that great authority Nimrod, it 'seems to have arrived at perfection'. The body was lighter and stronger; the centre of gravity lower. By the end of George IV's reign England was covered with a spider's-web of coach-lines, with the main threads radiating out from the capital and linked laterally by a larger number of cross-threads. Twenty coaches daily took passengers from London to Brighton; nine to Dover; eleven to Exeter; eleven to

Holyhead; nineteen to Birmingham; thirteen to Manchester. Yet these were only a small fraction of the total
number which thronged the main thoroughfares out of
the capital. Cary's *Road Book* for 1828 gives some 600
different coach-lines starting from London for various
destinations throughout the kingdom. Even that impressive figure is eclipsed by the number of cross-country
lines in the country as a whole. From Manchester eighty-
seven coaches, most of them daily, ran to twenty-seven
different towns as far away as Exeter, Carlisle, Newcastle
upon Tyne, and Aberdeen. From Bath thirty-two to some
two dozen separate destinations, including Southampton, Weymouth, Exeter, and Liverpool. In all Cary lists
nearly a thousand provincial coach-lines, collectively af-
fording (as his publication proudly proclaimed) 'the
Traveller a ready Means of Communications with every
considerable Town throughout the Kingdom'.

After the railways had set new standards of travel, it
was not uncommon for people to look back at the old
coaching days and criticize their discomforts and disadvantages. Yet at the time the British were only too
ready to boast that they had the best roads, the finest
horses, and the fastest coaches in Europe. Travelling
down to London on the outside of the Liverpool coach in
May 1824, fortified by occasional sips from a small bottle
of brandy, Miss Weeton despite her earlier apprehensions
found it an exhilarating experience. Nothing, she declared, would have induced her to take an inside seat.
'Riding on a coach is very easy; I never felt tired or
benumbed with it', and she mentally offered up ten
thousand thanks to Mr McAdam 'for the easy ride I had
the whole of the way. I should have been more shook if
I had journeyed from Wigan to Southport; but on these
roads, the traveller has all the pleasure without any of
the fatigue'. Eleven years later Crabb Robinson recorded
travelling further and faster in one day than he had ever
done in his life. 'The great rapidity of the motion had, I
believe, an effect on my spirits, for I felt no ennui, though
the coach was ill-built and did not allow of my taking a
comfortable nap'. Leaving London at half-past five, he

was in his hotel at Manchester by half-past eight. This represented an average speed of about 12½ m.p.h. for the 186-mile route through Derby and Leek. In 1828 the fastest coach from London to Manchester took 22 hours; so unless Robinson, or his editors, made a mistake, there had been a remarkable improvement in the roads during those previous seven years.

Yet there were undeniable drawbacks to coach travel. Common subjects of complaints were the extortions of landlords and waiters, the peremptoriness of drivers and guards, the rudeness of booking clerks, and the carelessness of porters. In the cramped interior of the coach any unpleasant habits on the part of the other occupants—talkativeness, sneezing, snoring, belching, and tippling—became peculiarly irritating on a long journey. To some what was even worse was the close confinement. The carriage windows, often obscured by condensation or frost, shut out both light and air; loud objections were usually raised by fellow-passengers to even the slightest crack for ventilation; and the atmosphere grew steadily worse as the miles passed. It was not always as bad as this. Jane Carlyle, making her first coach journey from London in July 1836, was lucky enough to find only one other inside passenger on the Manchester night-coach—a taciturn gentleman who rolled up his greatcoat to make a cushion for her, presented her with three lemons, and left her in peace to stretch out at full length on her side of the coach. But it was the recollection of the long journeys in crowded interiors that remained in people's minds. 'The smell of the inside of a coach after a long night of closed windows is a thing never to be forgotten', wrote Mozley feelingly long afterwards.

The outside passengers, cloaked, shawled, gloved, and scarfed, suffered in a different way. Huddled on their hard seats, they were liable to be frozen at night, baked by the sun during the day, drenched by rain or cut by sleet and hail in bad weather, enveloped by dust in dry. Dust was the one great defect of McAdam's new system of road-surfacing and remained so until tar was introduced to give 'tarmacadam' its dustless binding. Journeying to Liverpool by 'Sothern's caravan' in 1825, Miss

Weeton found the continuous cloud of dust, filling mouth and throat and ruining clothes, almost intolerable. Not only did the houses on either side of the road suffer but even the adjoining fields were spoiled by the pollution. 'If Mr McAdam could lay the dust as *well* as the roads, he would be a clever fellow.'

As far as the actual motion of the coach was concerned, the main complaint was of a form of travel-sickness induced by the swinging or rolling action of the vehicle when at full speed. This, however, was not peculiar to stage-coaches; it was a characteristic of all fast, well-sprung carriages. Travelling in his own vehicle down to London, which he reached in fourteen hours, General Dyott in 1837 confessed that long after the journey was over he still felt the physical sensation of the swaying movement of the carriage just as sea-passengers still feel the roll of a ship after they have disembarked. On a fast, heavily laden coach with luggage piled high on the roof, the rolling motion at high speed was decidedly unpleasant. To timid passengers, it brought apprehensions of danger as well as discomfort. Nimrod, scientific as always, pointed out that the lateral motion, or 'rocking', of a coach was greatest at the furthest point from the horses; that is to say, on the roof and at the back. A top-heavy loading of luggage and an ill-matched team of horses aggravated the trouble; though he contended that the danger of overturning was relatively slight. The stiff competition among coach-lines, he observed comfortingly, had resulted in better coaches, better horses, better equipment, and better maintenance. The emphasis on speed had thus paradoxically improved safety.

Even Nimrod had to admit, however, that accidents did occasionally happen; though he thought that human error was more to blame than mechanical failure. The worst accidents were those resulting from the snapping of an axle-tree; the commonest overturning when taking a sharp bend too fast. Nimrod adopted a genial and optimistic view of most things he wrote about, but there is no reason to doubt his verdict that in the 1830s 'travelling by public conveyances was never so secure as it is at the present time'.[2] He added that the old-fashioned type of coachman (that which Dickens was shortly after-wards to immortalize in the person of Tony Weller)—corpulent, rubicund, and addicted to strong drink—was giving way to a new breed of driver, more respectable, more conscientious, and more humane. At the time when he wrote the vogue for gentlemen coach-drivers had waned, but their example had perhaps done something to raise general standards of coach-driving and coach-drivers.

It was the discomfort, however, rather than the danger of which people most complained. Even before the railway age had arrived Dickens' playful imagination had suggested that one of the greatest torments which could be inflicted on a human being, worse than any devised by medieval churchmen for heretics, would be to make him travel ceaselessly as an inside passenger in a small coach with the other seats filled by 'stout men with a slight tendency to coughing and spitting'. There are few public modes of transport in any age, however, that do not suffer from constrictions of space and inflictions of fellow travellers. Early Victorians knew that coach journeys were attended by inevitable rigours and they learned to endure them.

Surtees was less good-humoured than Dickens in his comments on coach travel; but he is usually looking back from the higher standards of the railway age. He ob-serves, for example, in *Ask Mamma* (ch. ii) that

posterity will know nothing of the misery their forefathers underwent in the travelling way; and whenever we hear—which we often do—unreasonable grumblings about the ab-sence of trifling luxuries on railways, we are tempted to wish the parties consigned to a good long ride in an old stage coach. Why, the worst third-class that ever was put next the engine is infinitely better than the inside of the best of them used to be, to say nothing of the speed. As to the outsides of the old coaches, with their roastings, their soakings, their freezings, and their smotherings with dust, one cannot but feel that the establishment of railways was a downright prolongation of life.

Elsewhere he dilates not only on the slowness and cramped accommodation of the old coaches but on the

peril to life and limb from the class of horse often consigned to draw them—'all the jibbers, and kickers, and
vicious horses in the country. People talk of the dangers
of railways, but all horse owners know that there was no
little danger attendant on the coaches. If a man had a
vicious animal he always sold it to a coach proprietor.'
No doubt there was much truth, as well as a tinge of
exaggeration in this. It might, however, be urged on the
other side that the slower speeds and smaller number of
passengers that could be carried on a single vehicle meant
that when accidents occurred, they were rarely fatal.

IV

When Mr Cocking, that forgotten pioneer of a distant
aeronautical age, fell to his death in 1837, Britain was
already launched on the greatest technological revolution of the century. In two great bursts of company
promotion, in 1836–8 and again in 1846–8, the public
supplied the capital for an entirely new transport system, offering standards of speed, cheapness, and comfort that the existing large and efficient stage-coach
organization could not hope to match. Up to 1837 only
some 500 miles of railway had been laid. By the end of
the following year the figure had risen to nearly 750.
This total doubled by 1840, doubled again by 1846, and
doubled once more by the end of 1849. After that the
pace of construction slowed. Even so, at the end of
Surtees' life, England and Wales were provided with over
7,500 miles of track. By that date the railway framework
that was to meet the needs of British society for the next
hundred years was substantially in place. In its universal, pervasive effect on public and private life, it was
probably the greatest single agent of change in Victorian
society. Its significance was not lost on contemporaries.
'The most important event of the last quarter of a century in English history', wrote the barrister William
Johnston in 1851, 'is the establishment of Railroads.' He

was speaking, it should be remembered, of a period which had seen the establishment of Free Trade, Catholic Emancipation, the 1832 Reform Act, Chartism, the introduction of the income tax, and the repeal of the Corn Laws.

Originally railways, with trains of wagons drawn by steam-engines propelling their own wheels, had been primarily envisaged as a cheap method of moving heavy freight. The early railway promoters usually underestimated the profits likely to accrue from human passengers just as they invariably underestimated the costs of construction. What created the railway boom between 1837 and 1849 was the popularity of the new form of conveyance among the travelling public. In the first year of the completed London to Birmingham line half a million passengers used it; by 1845 a million people were annually travelling on it. Over the railway system as a whole the number of passenger-journeys reached nearly 34 million in 1842–3; more than 60 million in 1848–9. In 1836 and again in 1846 something like a railway mania gripped the public as investors drew on the accumulated savings of a wealthy society to send a flood of money into the new industry. At peak periods like 1846–8 half the total national investment went into railways, a sum equivalent to two-thirds of all domestic imports. By 1866 the British public had invested in railways an amount that represented about three-quarters of the National Debt.

With immense profits beckoning, there was an orgy of line-projection, company promotion, and railway constructions. Hundreds of contractors, armies of navvies, invaded the English countryside, leaving in their wake a transformed landscape, with iron roads, stations, bridges, level crossings, tunnels, viaducts, and the raw earth of cuttings and embankments scarring the green fields. Surveyors and solicitors were in universal demand; financiers and stock-jobbers waxed fat; parliament was deluged with railway bills; obscure MPs found their hitherto unrecognized talents rewarded with directorships of railway companies and offers of shares at discount prices. There was savage competition, on occasion even physical clashes, between rival companies, until a more genteel era supervened of doctored dividends, takeover bids, and regional amalgamations. Railway empires rose—and fell. George Carr Glynn, the astute midlands banker and railway monopolist, ended up as a millionaire and member of the House of Commons. George Hudson, the flamboyant Railway King of the north-east, crashed spectacularly and departed in disgrace to the Continent. With money pouring in from the public, engineers and architects were able to give full rein to their professional fancies at the expense of any strict standards of cost-effectiveness. Lines of differing gauges were laid down; the most expensive equipment was installed. Rural stations could be found built in the style of half-timbered Tudor manor houses. Archways with classical columns or medieval battlements adorned the entrance to the larger tunnels. In London majestic buildings in the Greek Doric or neo-Gothic manner marked the terminus of the main lines.

As railway bills piled up on the tables of the House of Commons, the government—perhaps wisely, certainly prudently—clung to a policy of minimum interference. Apart from the imposition of elementary safety regulations, the statutory provision of cheap 'parliamentary' trains at the rate of 1d. a mile for the benefit of the poorer classes, and contingent powers (in the event never taken up) for state purchase on expiry of the original charters, the conditions imposed by the legislature on railway development were not onerous. Later critics, wise after the event, lamented that the government had not, unlike the authoritarian states of Prussia and France, intervened directly to carry out in an orderly, planned, and economical process, over a period of perhaps thirty years, what had been so frantically, untidily, and expensively accomplished by Victorian private enterprise in little more than a decade. Charles Dickens talked, with some justice, of 'a muddle of railways in all directions possible and impossible, with no general public scheme, no general public supervision, enormous waste of money, no fixable responsibility, no accountability'.[3] That attack only came in 1865, however, when his mind had been concentrated by a bad railway accident a few months earlier in which he had been involved. The creator of the Circumlocution Office and the tribe of Tite Barnacles was not usually an advocate for giving greater powers to the civil servants of his day. Early Victorians—public, politicians, and prime ministers—had a justified scepticism about the ability of the state to perform administrative tasks more quickly or more efficiently than private enterprise. In the event the great work of building the Victorian railway system was done, rapidly and effectively, by market forces; done also, it must be said, recklessly and extravagantly.

The loss, however, fell on the investors, not on the general public or taxpayer. The promises of great profits were never realized. Up to 1850 no railway company was making as much as 8 per cent on its capital investment. Shareholders were lucky if they received as much as $3\frac{1}{2}$ per cent dividends. Since many of them had bought at well above the issue price, they would have done better to have left their money in government stock. Surtees had some barbed comments to make about this aspect of railway development. When he describes the Great Golconda Station (Golconda was the old name for Hyderabad, synonymous with a source of endless wealth) he observes that the architect, in building this London terminus of the Great Gammon and Spinach Railway, had apparently taken his idea for the edifice from the *Arabian Nights*—'hence, the splendid dividend of two-pence-halfpenny a share, so complacently announced by the Chairman', despite the fact that the directors in their original prospectus had pitched the likely return at 250 per cent. In the original magazine version of *Mr Sponge* (1849–51) he had even more libellous comments on railway finance, including a reference to the accounts of the Eastern Counties Company being 'cooked' at Albert Gate. This topical reference to the George Hudson scandal was omitted, however, in the book, since by the time it came out Hudson had long ceased to be chairman of the company and that was no longer his address.[4]

The Victorian public, however, had what they wanted. Though their new transport system had cost perhaps as much as three times what it need have done, they had got it in probably a third of the time that would have been taken under a centralized bureaucracy. It was a great, almost a grandiose, achievement which reflected the wealth, optimism, energy, and enthusiasm of early-Victorian society. It touched their imagination as well as their pocket. Turner's 1844 painting *Rain, Steam and Speed* is perhaps the best-known aesthetic reflection of the railway age; but there were others. The literary equivalent of Turner's painting, in terms of the reputation of the artist at any rate, is Wordsworth's 1835 sonnet to 'Steamboats, Viaducts and Railways'.

A lesser poet, though more a man of the world, gave expression to similar sentiments of moral approval in a piece entitled 'The Railway', selected by the *Annual Register* for publication in its volume for 1843. This was C. R. Kennedy, a Cambridge classical scholar, practising barrister, and occasional author, brother of the famous headmaster of Shrewsbury School. Against the accusation that the railways represented only too well the reckless, materialistic spirit of the age, he argued that this 'wondrous' machine, this 'fire-winged courser' with its 'thunderpace', was still a creation of the human brain, itself of divine origin, and was to be regarded therefore as an instrument for the progress of humanity.

Then forward! Still upon thy course prosperity attend!
And thou shalt be to high and low, to rich and poor a
  friend;
And thou shalt scatter wide the seed of plenteousness and
  peace,
And man shall move him to and fro, and knowledge true
  increase.

Poet Laureate and poetaster had this in common: a sense of marvel before this latest achievement of mechanical science, and an optimistic faith that it would contribute to the greater good of society. It was a not untypical Victorian blend of piety and materialism.

V

Since Victorians rarely agreed about anything, there were some, especially in the early years, who looked upon the railways with apprehension and dislike. They included the timid, the old-fashioned, and the inevitable alarmists of the medical profession, as well as those whose property or livelihood was threatened by this new method of locomotion. There was a perceived threat to what the following century would term the environment. The *Oracle*, speaking for farmers, landowners, and sportsmen, prophesied in 1840 that fox-hunting would become impossible and facetiously envisaged a new world of technology in which hunters driving steam-powered vehicles would pursue imported exotic animals of vastly superior speed and strength to the outrun and outmoded fox.

The British public refused to be intimidated. Though few could have been entirely without qualms when embarking on their first journey by train, their apprehensions were outweighed by its novelty and practical advantages. For Charlotte Guest, who went on the Manchester–Liverpool line as early as 1833, her introduction to rail travel was 'a memorable event in my little life'. Despite the entreaties of her mother not to go for fear of accident, 'the temptation of saving so much time and fatigue was not to be resisted'. In the event, 'I never had a pleasanter expedition . . . It is much smoother and easier than a carriage, and the sensation cannot alarm, by reason of its steadiness'. The politician J. C. Hobhouse, who travelled over the same route a year later, confessed that he was 'more affected by this display of human power than by any other work of art, the Simplon Road or the Menai Bridge not excepted'. Having prefaced his remarks by saying that it would be vain to try to describe his sensations, he then proceeded to do so in a passage studded with adjectives like 'prodigious', 'wonderful', 'awful', and 'terrific'. Haydon, the professional student of human emotions, was briefer but more exact when recording his train-trip from Warrington to Liverpool in 1839—'the superb rapidity of Steam travelling was exquisite'. The calmer, aristocratic Charles Greville had his first experience in 1837 between Birmingham and Liverpool. Apart from occasional whiffs of stinking air, he found nothing objectionable and much that was agreeable in this new mode of travel. 'The first sensation is a slight degree of nervousness and a feeling of being run away with, but a sense of security soon intervenes, and the velocity is delightful'. It certainly, he concluded practically, made any other method irksome and tedious by comparison. Dr Arnold of Rugby was in full agreement. Having also made his first railway journey that year (on the Manchester–Birmingham line—95 miles in five hours), he declared that 'nothing can be more delightful, as well as more convenient. It was very beautiful too.'

The caution of railway company directors at first restricted the maximum speed of passenger trains to 30 m.p.h., which meant that the average speed between stations was nearer 20 m.p.h. This, however, was soon exceeded. By 1850 the average speed on the trunk lines had risen to nearly 40 m.p.h., which suggests that speeds of 50 m.p.h. over short stretches could not have been uncommon. The sensation of unprecedented velocity was heightened when two fast trains passed in opposite directions at speeds, relative to each other, of some 60 or 80 miles an hour. The startling effect of these momentary encounters was noted by more than one traveller. 'In passing other Engines', wrote Charlotte Guest, 'you can discern nothing of the features and appearance of those they may contain, and this makes you sensible of the extreme speed at which you are travelling.' Crabb Robinson, whose account of his first rail journey, on the same line in the same year, fills two printed pages of his diary, observed that 'the most remarkable moments of the journey are those in which trains pass one another. The rapidity is such that there is no recognising the features of a traveller.' The noise of the oncoming locomotive, he added, was like 'the whizzing of a rocket'. Yet to be conveyed at these wonderful speeds seemed as safe as travelling at a third of that rate in a stage-coach. Of the first 700,000 passengers carried on the

Manchester–Liverpool line only one—the unfortunate Huskisson—was killed; and that entirely because of his own clumsiness.

In the nature of things this immunity could not last. As lines lengthened and traffic thickened, accidents, some fatal, began to multiply. Three people were killed in 1840 when eight carriages overturned on the Eastern Counties railway; four in 1841 when an engine ran off the rails at Cuckfield on the Dover line. In December 1841 came the worst accident that had so far occurred on the railways. Ten people eventually died and eleven were seriously injured when a passenger train ran into a landslip in Sonning Cutting between Twyford and Reading on the Great Western. In the whole of that year twenty-four members of the public were killed on the railways through no fault of their own and a further seventy-two injured; while seventeen more died, officially through their own negligence. This was still a small number compared with the millions of passenger-journeys taking place each year. With the help of the short-lived railway department of the Board of Trade, set up in 1840, the companies learnt by experience such useful safety procedures as clear signalling, use of front and rear lights, and observance of proper intervals between trains, together with tighter discipline over their own servants and occasional prosecutions for gross negligence. In the early years the imposition by coroner's juries of stiff deodands on railway trains involved in fatal accidents (£1,000 in the case of the 1841 accident at Sonning) might have operated as a further sanction against incompetent companies; but deodands were swept away by a reforming legislature in 1846. However, the rate of accidents steadily declined. In 1847–9 the ratio of deaths without contributory negligence was 1 per 4,782,000 rail passengers; by 1856–9 this had dropped to 1 per 8,708,000.

It does not appear that the public thought that there was a disproportionate number of accidents on railways, though they were often more violent and more widely reported. In 1851, for example, in Great Britain and Ireland 10 rail passengers were killed for causes outside

their control; another 22 with contributory negligence;
also 120 employees of the companies or their contractors;
and another 64 casual trespassers on the tracks—a total
of 216. This may be compared with the figure of 250
people who, it was calculated in the 1860s, were killed
every year in London street accidents. Although the
Annual Register in 1852 began to print abstracts of the
official yearly returns of railway accidents, the Victorian
public were accustomed to grim accounts of industrial
accidents in mines and factories, and accepted such ca-
tastrophes as part of life. Charlotte Guest, setting out for
Liverpool in 1837 the day after a bad accident on the
same line, felt that 'if it was the Will of Providence that
any evil should befall us, it was quite certain to happen
by one mode of conveyance as by another'. Belief in a
divine ordering of the universe was useful moral equipment for the age of steam.

As the novelty of the speed wore off, the other features of comfort and economy were increasingly appreciated. There were occasional complaints in the early
years of the uneven surface of the track, caused by the
settlement of the permanent way after heavy rain; but
most travellers were impressed by the steadiness of trains
even at high speed. The comfortableness of the seats
was also praised. In the first-class compartments of the
Birmingham line, for example, seats were upholstered,
with arm-rests and loose cushions. At night special
sleeping compartments were available with convertible
seats. Even the wooden seats of the second-class and the
open trucks of the early third-class represented no particular hardship to a generation accustomed to coach-
travel. Moreover, the design of the carriages steadily
improved. When in 1855 Mrs Carlyle meditated a romantic night-journey to Scotland under the starry heaven,
it occurred to her that it would be prudent to discover
whether the third-class carriages from London to Edinburgh really were still open to the sky. A preliminary
reconnaissance at Euston Station revealed the awful truth.
'Oh, Heavens! the third class was a Black Hole of Calcutta
on wheels! closely roofed-in, windows like pigeon-holes,

and no partition to separate the twelve breaths of one compartment from all the breaths of all the third-class carriage!' She generally travelled second-class; her husband, an apostle of strenuous living, went third. Both of them valued good ventilation above everything else. Not all Victorians shared their preference. Indeed, most probably would have been more sympathetic to Sydney Smith's whimsical observation that when he contemplated the delightful improvements that the railways had made to human life, he was positively ashamed that he had not been more discontented in his youth with the hardships which people in those days endured.

Railway companies encouraged this feeling by providing a number of other amenities for the travelling public. Unlike the coach-lines with their restricted accommodation, there was no need to book rail tickets in advance. Mr Bunting in *Plain or Ringlets* casually assumes that even a horse-box can be produced at a moment's notice when required by a passenger; and, what is more, obtains one after only a brief delay at Golconda Station. In 1854 Miss Martineau was able to travel on the North-Western line in a special invalid carriage. Any amount of luggage could be taken, at first piled on the roof of the carriage in which its owner travelled, after the manner of stage-coaches; later in luggage vans or even special luggage trains. Even dogs could be taken in ordinary passenger compartments by purchasing a cheap dog-ticket. Nervous passengers could cover themselves with an insurance ticket. At many stations there were waiting and refreshment rooms with 'female attendants', as the London and Birmingham Company chastely phrased it in 1839. Even at two o'clock in the morning Charles Dickens was able to get a cup of tea and a bun, albeit 'of enormous antiquity', at Peterborough Station in 1856. (It appears that the refreshment-room bun was already installed as an object of British humour.) At the larger stations the facilities for the hungry traveller were more generous. At Birmingham there was a large restaurant capable of seating several hundred diners, offering a varied menu—chicken, ham, pork, and beef, together with tea or coffee—served within the space of ten minutes at the moderate price of 3s. On the platform W. H. Smith's bookstalls offered a selection of newspapers and popular yellow-back novels with which to while away a long journey. George Bradshaw, a Manchester printer, had made an imperishable name for himself as early as 1839 by publishing his *Railway Time-Tables and Assistant to Railway Travelling*; a tiny book some 3 by $4\frac{1}{2}$ inches in size, containing, in addition to existing railway-times, a series of rail maps, town plans, and a table of hackney-coach fares in Liverpool. For those who wanted more substantial information, Edward Churton produced in 1851 his *Railroad Book of England, Historical, Topographical and Picturesque*, with nearly 600 pages describing the cities, towns, country mansions, and other objects of interest which the traveller might see from his carriage windows.

For those who, either for social status or practical convenience, wished to take with them their own private means of transport, flat wagons were provided on which carriages and their occupants could be conveyed in splendid isolation, leaving grooms and horses to be accommodated elsewhere on the train. On occasion Surtees and his wife in the early 1840s drove the forty miles to Darlington in their 'chariot' and put it on a wagon for the journey south. It was, however, an expensive privilege. The charge for transporting a carriage from Birmingham to Liverpool in 1839, for example, was £3, compared with a guinea for an ordinary first-class fare, not to mention the additional charges payable for the horses and groom. There were other disadvantages. On long journeys the vehicle would become encrusted with dust and grime, and the motion was far from comfortable. The Guests, who took their carriage to Liverpool in 1837 on the mail train from Birmingham, found the swaying of the springs so unpleasant that after a couple of stages they transferred to an ordinary compartment. On a grander scale whole trains could be chartered by private customers. In 1841 Thomas Cook, the enterprising secretary of the South Midland Temperance Association, organized the first publicly advertised train excursion (from Leicester to Loughborough) and so found for himself a new career. Once the railway companies saw the profit to be made from excursion trains, they started running them on their own account for such popular events as prize-fights and public executions.

The remaining attraction of rail travel, its relative cheapness, was slower to assert itself. Pricing in the early years was necessarily experimental. Dr Granville delivered a sharp attack on the fare-fixing policy of the London and Birmingham Company in the two chapters he mainly dedicated to a general eulogy of railway travel. His grievance was that within a few years of the opening of that line fares for first- and second-class passengers had actually gone up; and he put in a plea for standardization of fares on all lines. Given the differences in the initial costs of construction and subsequent incidence of traffic, this seems an unreasonable request. It was true, however, that at first the saving compared with coach fares was not always apparent. The fare from London to Birmingham in 1839 was 32*s*. 6*d*. for a first-, £1 for a second-class fare. In 1838 the Greyhound coach-line was offering inside seats at 25*s*. and outside at 17*s*. for the same journey; though this may have been a calculated attempt to undercut the railway. By the end of the 1840s there were signs that the demand of the public was failing to keep pace with the growth of the railway lines. The figures for first-class passengers in 1848 and 1849 remained almost static, though presumably fares went up since the revenue from these classes was still buoyant. On the other hand, the introduction of the penny-a-mile parliamentary trains had resulted in a great surge of custom even if some of it was at the expense of a slight decline in 1848 and 1849 in the number of second-class passengers. There was also a steady and reassuring growth in the receipts for freight traffic. In any case coach travel had involved all kinds of incidental expenses which were largely absent from trains. When Crabb Robinson went up to the Lake District in 1842 he paid four guineas for his (presumably first-class) fare and did the journey in seventeen hours. By coach only a few years earlier, he reflected, he would have been charged nearly twice as much and would have had to spend two nights on the road. 'This railway travelling', he mused, 'is delightful, and very economical too.' Bishop Phillpotts seems to have been of the same opinion. The opening of the line from Exeter to London, he is reported to have told his son, had been a great boon to him in the performance of his episcopal duties. Apart from the saving of time, he could travel to town in great comfort for £5 whereas in the old days, posting the whole way and breaking his journey at Bath, it had cost him £50 and great bodily fatigue.[5]

There were other ways in which the railway companies tried to attract and retain the support of the public. The London and Birmingham line announced in its published regulations that its servants were not allowed, under any circumstances, to accept gratuities. This rule, if obeyed in practice, would have seemed a palpable improvement to a public inured if not reconciled to the virtually compulsory tipping of coachmen, guards, and waiters in the course of long journeys by coach. Surtees indicates, in fact, that the ban on gratuities to railway staff was generally observed. 'Confound those old iniquities of travelling!' he exclaims in *Ask Mamma* (ch. lviii), 'a man used never to have his hand out of his pocket. Let not the rising generation resuscitate the evil, by contravening the salutary regulation of not paying people on railways.' The Grand Junction Railway from Birmingham to Liverpool went even further. 'All the Company's Servants are strictly enjoined on pain of dismissal, to observe the utmost civility and attention towards all Passengers.' The reputation of the different companies in this respect varied. If Dr Granville, writing in 1841, was right, the busy clerks at Euston Station were not renowned for providing gratuitous information or even civil replies to the questions put to them by inexperienced travellers. Elsewhere, however, at the Great Western at Paddington, at Liverpool, and indeed on other lines generally, he reported that the business of attending to the needs of passengers was usually conducted in a quiet, civil, and reasonable manner.

It was also an advantage, in the matter of relations

with the public, that the railway companies seemed to have had a policy of encouraging a sense of company pride. Their staff, for example, was put into distinctive uniform. On the Manchester–Leeds line, which was largely under Quaker management, Granville commended the excellent appearance of the guards—'smart, active-looking fellows, clad in red, and wearing a glazed, round hat, with the name of the railroad in gold letters upon it'. It was perhaps a remnant of this professional self-respect that made young Thomas Wells go to the gallows in August 1868 (the first execution to be carried out in private under the new law), singing a hymn and clad in his railway porter's uniform of velveteen with the company's initials in red on the collar and a flower in his button-hole. He was an employee of the London, Chatham, and Dover line who had murdered the station-master at Dover after being reprimanded by him for some fault. The case of poor Wells, however, can hardly be considered as characteristic of staff relations on the railways; nor, on the other hand, were the smart, red-uniformed guards that Granville saw necessarily typical of all railway staff. There is not much smartness about the porter sketched by Leech, as an illustration for *Mr Sponge* (ch. xl), in short, loose jacket, waistcoat, baggy trousers, and round, peaked cap. This was at Squandercash Station, in the heart of the country, where standards were not as high as in the metropolis. The credit of the railway staff is restored, however, by Surtees' account of the guard on Miss de Glancey's train in chapter lxii of *Ask Mamma*. This is the smart and popular young Billy Bates, who prides himself on his social tact in putting suitably matched passengers together in the same compartment. He wears white, doeskin gloves, a green and red uniform, and a 'patent leather pouch-belt'.

This, incidentally, especially the last item, tallies so closely with the illustration in *Plain or Ringlets* (ch. lxi), which purports to show Mr Dick Dawdler claiming acquaintance with Mr Bunting, that one cannot help wondering whether there had not been a mistake in the title of the engraving at the time of the publication.

The figure shown speaking to Mr Bunting does not in the least resemble an idle young man-about-town with a mania for seeing trains go off. In his deferential attitude and in his costume—round, peaked hat, high stiff collar, frock-coat, and broad, polished leather shoulder-belt—he matches perfectly the appearance of an early railway guard, even down to the beard which had long been almost an occupational trademark of platform staff. Indeed, railway employees ought perhaps to be credited as much as returning Crimea veterans with popularizing the beard and moustache. John Beames (then a schoolboy at Merchant Taylors), though in retrospect accepting the conventional identification with the Crimean War, observed that 'the fashion began with postmen, railway-guards and porters and though at first laughed at soon spread to the upper classes'. Yet it is clear from a *Punch* cartoon of November 1853, showing a timid lady terrified by the brigand-like appearance of various bearded porters and guards, that the vogue had started before the war, which was not declared until March 1854. If Beames is right, this is an interesting example of a fashion working its way upwards in society; and from two classes, postmen and platform staff, who owed their importance to the railway revolution.

The practice of putting railway employees into uniform seems to have been universal. Supplying them became a large enough industry to support a specialist factory at Crewe and revive the flagging fortunes of Kendal as a clothing town. It was perhaps one of the details which helped the railway companies in their recruitment. Unlike the police, they had little difficulty in attracting good staff. The pay was not unusually high at any of the grades; the hours long and often at night. Yet the prospect of steady employment in a disciplined framework of service to the public seems to have been enough to ensure that the railways could always obtain men of character and responsibility (many from the country rather than from London) and retain them for life.[6]

Perhaps also the innate romanticism of the steam locomotive played a part. It was certainly felt by many of the ordinary public; and the railway companies encouraged it by continuing the early tradition of giving their locomotives distinctive names—though to the classically educated the choice of CHARON for an engine on the Grand Junction Railway in 1841 was not perhaps the happiest that could be made. If Surtees was right (and there is no reason to doubt his accuracy in such a matter), the system of naming extended to carriages. On the train which brought Mr Jorrocks to Handley Cross there were seven first-class coaches, all bearing separate names painted on their smart yellow sides—Prince Albert, Queen Victoria, The Prince of Wales, The Venus, The Mercury, The Comet, and The Star—pulled by a locomotive appropriately named HERCULES. Such poetic touches helped to make the arrival and departure of long-distance trains a spectacle, almost a ritual, for all but the dullest or most blasé of travellers. As in a theatre, the mind of the spectator was first prepared by the magnificence of the terminus building. The great Doric portico at Euston Station was said to be the largest in the world; the grand entrance hall perhaps 'the most magnificent saloon in Europe'. After that came the noise and bustle of the long platforms, the animated crowd of people, the shouting porters, the line of carriages, and in the distance the puffs of steam and smoke from the engine. Describing the departure of the night-train to Liverpool and Manchester, Dr Granville wrote that 'there is hardly a more dramatic or soul-stirring scene enacted by gas-light anywhere in London, than that which may be witnessed any evening under the colonnade of the Euston Square station'. And a couple of pages later, 'if the starting from Euston station be dramatic in effect, the arrival at the Birmingham-station is no less theatrical. The sudden entering under the cover of a vast area, brilliantly lighted up like a fairy region . . . is accompanied by sensations not experienced under any other circumstance.'

Surtees was not given to romantic descriptions but he permitted himself small verbal flourishes when dealing with steam locomotives. In the scene at the Great Golconda Station, which is a kind of Surteesian version of Dr Granville's vignette of the departure of the night-train from Euston, he describes the ringing of the warning bell, the shouts of the porters along the platform for passengers to take their seats, the frantic rush of late-comers, the slamming of doors, the shrill blast of a whistle, and the long train slowly moving off 'hissing and snorting like an exasperated crocodile'. It is not the most elegant or apt of similes, but Surtees was evidently pleased with it since he had used it before in his description of the arrival of the Jorrocks household at Handley Cross. To the waiting party at the station there came first a distant whistle and then suddenly the sight of the long train itself coming round the bend, 'the engine smoking and snorting like an exasperated crocodile'. This reptilian analogy suggests at least a certain sardonic respect for the outlandish phenomenon that had arrived in the English countryside.

Charles Greville in 1834 wryly observed that by the time people came to read his journal (if they ever did), they would smile at his sense of wonder before the power of the new steam locomotive. By 1875, when that passage first appeared in print, no doubt some did. It could not have been easy for later Victorians to recapture the sensations of Greville, Surtees, and their generation who actually witnessed the railway revolution. For such men the age of the stage coach in which they had grown up became a kind of *ancien régime*, personal memory of which was steadily effaced with each decade of Victoria's reign.

13
A RAILWAY SOCIETY

I

The railway revolution happened so quickly and touched Victorian life at so many points that the danger perhaps is of over- rather than underestimating its effects. The railways themselves were the product of a society which saw in the expansion of manufacture and commerce the secret of wealth and power, and in the application of science and mechanical invention the key to that expansion. Wealth and science made railways possible; the economic demands of British society made them, one might almost say, necessary. Much that happened in the nineteenth century would have happened in any case. The increasing influence of the middle classes, the sharper political consciousness of the nation as a whole, the growth of 'public opinion' as a source of power, the loosening of provincial ties, the weakening of class distinctions, the dominance of the large towns, the steady rise in population—all these tendencies were visible before the coming of the railways. There is no reason to think that they would not have continued; only that the pace would have been slower. The railways did not so much create as accelerate change. They acted as agents rather than initiators; but with such unprecedented force as to make them seem even more significant than they really were.

When thoughtful Victorians looked at their society, it was often the rapidity of change rather than the nature of the changes that impressed them most. Sir Henry Holland, pondering in the late 1860s on a life which had started before the French Revolution, considered that one outstanding characteristic of contemporary English society compared with earlier days was 'the increased *fastness* of living, incident to all classes and occupations of men'. He was, of course, using the word in its literal sense and made the curious addition that it applied not only to politics, commerce, literature, science, and the professions generally, but even to the actual physical way in which people walked about the streets.[1] Already in 1851 William Johnston had concluded that men who could breakfast in London and dine at York, be summoned to town by electric telegraph in a few minutes, and present themselves there within a few hours, necessarily acquired 'a habit of pressure and velocity' in everything they did. 'The effect of railroad habits', he continued, 'is to make us more American than we were.' One cannot suppose this was intended as a compliment.

In the century which followed, the tendency was to look back on the Victorian era as one of leisure and self-confidence, or, less flatteringly, of complacency and conventionality. That was not how Victorians generally thought of themselves. To many it seemed that their society had become restless, volatile, utilitarian, and mercenary, obsessed with change and innovation, forgetful of old values, and heedless of the uncertain future. Some welcomed that future as promising more enlightenment, more social equality, more democracy, and more prosperity; and only regretted that progress was so slow. Optimists and pessimists, however, agreed that the railway locomotive was, for good or bad, a symbol of their times.

II

One curious and early result of the age of steam was a disillusioning feeling that speed had destroyed the romance of travel. People, it was complained, were now simply transferred from one place to another. It was no longer an enlightening or adventurous experience, merely a procedure governed by timetable in which there was no place for casual diversions or unexpected encounters. This was to some extent also true of the fast stage-coach; but it was the greater rapidity and isolation of the railway compartment that made these criticisms occur so forcibly to the more sensitive users of the railroads. Once high speed became commonplace, perverse human nature felt a sense of loss. A conservative lawyer like Johnston was not alone in having mixed feelings about rail travel. The mercurial Haydon, who had exclaimed over the 'superb rapidity' of trains in 1839, expressed different emotions in 1842 when he took a trip to Windsor to see the Royal Picture Gallery.

The rapidity of railroad communication destroys the Poetry & mystery of distant places. You went to Windsor as an exploit for two days. Now, down you go in an hour, see it in another & home in a third. It is painfully attainable, & therefore to be despised.

There was thus an aesthetic, even moral, price to be paid for fast travel of which early Victorians were clearly conscious. Haydon and Surtees did not have much in common, but in his more vernacular style Surtees uttered the same thoughts. 'Railways have destroyed the romance of travelling', he wrote in *Mr Romford* (ch. viii). Trains and trucks offered no scope for a novelist. 'One journey is very much like another, save that the diagonal shoots across country are distinguished by a greater number of changes... It's "Away you go!" "Here you are!" ' The directors of railway companies were not in the business of providing material for novelists and concentrated on such mundane matters as safety, comfort, and punctuality; but the effect on an ungrateful public was a degree of boredom.

From this came an unexpected development. When railway travellers got tired of looking out of their carriage windows, they fell back on books and magazines to pass the time. Where their lively Gallic neighbours would have resorted to conversation, the taciturn English preferred to read. The railways, by denying their public (as far as they could) any real-life adventure, drove them to find it between the covers of a novel. 'One of the peculiarities of modern travel', observed Surtees archly in *Plain or Ringlets* (ch. xxxiii), 'is the great demand there is for books, a book to prevent people seeing the country being quite as essential as a bun to prevent their being hungry.' Nobody had foreseen that the steam locomotive would promote English literature; but so it proved. The railways made the fortune of Messrs W. H. Smith and contributed handsomely to the incomes of many forgotten lady-novelists of mid-Victorian England. Railway travel demanded distraction rather than edification. For all his Methodist upbringing, the young W. H. Smith realized that travellers wanted to be amused, not improved; and that if they were to be persuaded to buy light travel literature in large quantities, the price would have to be nearer that of a newspaper than of a conventional novel. Previously cheapness had been the mark of disreputable literature. Smith's achievement was to put before the travelling public attractive but respectable reading matter at a low price. Before long the distinctive yellow covers of his *Railway Novels*, produced in collaboration with Chapman and Hall at 2s. a volume, vied with the white of newspapers on station bookstalls. Worthy but dull and more expensive books were driven from the field and other publishers were obliged to follow the new fashion. By the middle of the century rival series of cheap novels began to appear under various catchy titles—*Parlour Library, Home Library, Seaside Library*— offering the predominantly middle-class public a wide range of inexpensive, readable fiction.[2]

In their unpretentious way they were feeding the appetite of an increasingly literate society, as well as fitting in with the expanding industries of travel and tourism. Surtees was perhaps being gently ironic in his description of the bookstall at Roseberry Rocks railway station but there is some social significance in what he said. Mentioning first the attractions of the refreshment room, he added, 'nor is food for the mind forgotten in providing for that of the body. The books look so new and gay, and, above all, are so cheap—a shilling for what used to cost a guinea a few years since.' In the marketing and supply of this mental nourishment the railways clearly played an important role.

This was not the only connection between the railways and the spread of respectable, if mostly ephemeral, literature. A feature of the intellectual world of the Victorians was the growth not only of the daily and weekly press but of periodicals catering for special interests. By the 1850s there were journals for most religious denominations and all the great professions; journals for sportsmen, farmers, and gardeners; for actors and musicians, engineers, chemists, and economists; journals for women and their families. The low price and national circulation of these magazines were only possible because of the railways. Stage-coaches had offered fast communications and a wide network of routes but they were not adapted for the transport of bulky freight. The canals carried heavy freight but were too slow and geographically too restricted. The cheap postal service introduced in 1840 would have been overwhelmed by its own popularity had it been forced to rely on horsed transport. Only the steam train provided the combination of speed of delivery, low cost, and ability to carry bulk consignments, on which an effective national distribution of periodical literature depended. Without the railway, Surtees wrote, 'cheap postage, cheap papers, cheap literature, extended post-offices, would have been inefficient, for the old coaches would never have carried the quantity of matter modern times has evoked'. That for the first time in British history a market existed for mass literature of both an entertaining and informative kind can be reckoned, just as much as the penny post, among the benefits of the railway.

The flat-rate, pre-paid 1d. post came into force in January 1840. Its effect was remarkable and immediate. The total of chargeable letters passing through the London General Post Office more than doubled by the end of the year; and nearly trebled by the end of 1841. The long-term effects were even more striking. The number of letters delivered in England rose from 79 million in 1839 to 529 million in 1863, representing an average of 25 for each member of the population. Previously most letters were paid for by the recipient at a rate which depended on the distance they had come. Among respectable people it was considered somewhat derogatory to be sent a pre-paid letter—presumably because this implied either an inability or a reluctance to pay on the part of the person to whom it was addressed. For the poor, however, the arrival of an unexpected letter, accompanied by a demand for a shilling or more in postage, was a discomforting and even alarming experience. Even among the middle classes regular family correspondence of purely personal interest could be a financial infliction.

It is not surprising that MPs, who enjoyed the privilege of free postage, were besieged by requests for franks by their acquaintances or that ladies stored up their gossipy letters to friends until they could obtain the precious signatures that would relieve their correspondents from any charge. What with the discouraging cost to the public and the abuse of the parliamentary franks, the whole postal system was socially and administratively a singularly clumsy one. Even the cheap 2d. flat-rate postage operating in London was not used as much as might have been expected. According to Surtees it was chiefly employed for commercial purposes. The rich preferred to send their private letters to friends in town by the hand of their own servants. The duke of Wellington used to send parcels of outgoing letters up to London from Stratfield Saye in order to take advantage of the 2d. rate; but he was not a snob and had a very large correspondence. The new 1d. post, and the new adhesive stamp which quickly followed, broke down these little social niceties. Like trains, the penny post offered a cheap, efficient service which private individuals could not match and would have been foolish to reject. With ten deliveries a day in central London in the 1840s, it was possible to send a letter, receive an answer, and dispatch a reply all in the space of twelve hours. In the country districts it would have been equally hard to compete with the facilities it provided. In *Plain or Ringlets* Surtees noted that even dukes no longer disdained to use the ordinary post for sending round social invitations.

With the anticipated increase in letter-traffic and the shrinking of the coach network, it was inevitable that the Post Office would look to trains for the long-distance transport of mail. Disinclined as government usually was to interfere with the industrial life of the nation, steps were taken as early as 1837 to compel railway companies to enter into contracts with the Postmaster-General. Equally striking is the promptitude with which the larger capacity of the railway carriage was exploited for Post Office purposes. Dr Granville in 1840 was able to give an eyewitness description of a new specialized addition to rolling-stock—the big mail-sorting vans attached to fast long-distance trains. In their capacious interior, furnished with tables and lined with pigeon-holes, bags of mail were sorted during the journey and dropped off at various points along the route by the familiar device of snatch-nets put up beside the line. Such instant technical adaptation created a postal service that was beyond anything the stage-coaches could have provided. There is considerable substance in Surtees' argument that not only was the penny post that rare event—a great and beneficial reform that had taken place without any general agitation—but it had come about as soon as was practicable. 'Without the almost simultaneous establishment of railways it would have been almost impossible to have introduced the system.' Only the railways, he continued, could have carried the 'newspaper traffic and correspondence of the present day. The folded table-cloths of *Times*, the voluminous *Illustrated News*, the *Punch*'s, the huge avalanches of papers that have broken upon the country within the last twenty years.'

There was another form of communication which came into existence with the railways and owed its success to them. This was the electric telegraph, an invention which had reached a crucial stage in its scientific development just at the start of the railway age. Pioneered in England by Cooke and Wheatstone, who patented a working instrument in 1837, it was an obvious complement to the railway-lines. As early as 1838 a telegraph connected Paddington with West Drayton and by 1842 had reached Slough. By the mid-1840s the demand for telegraphic communication was so great that Cooke and Wheatstone set up their own Electric Telegraph Company. By 1852 they had built some 4,000 miles of line; ten years later there were 15,000 miles in the United Kingdom. Telegraph lines accompanied the railway lines all over the country and this early association persisted for many years. Until well into the second half of the century it was usually only possible to send a telegram at a railway station. In the Leech illustration of Mr Jorrocks riding into what is probably King's Cross Station for one of his hunting trips into the shires, there may be seen at the entrance to the station forecourt an 'Electric Telegraph Office'. Surtees made little use of telegraphs and telegrams for dramatic purposes in his novels. He does, however, tell us what the uniform of a telegraph boy looked like and even provides the text of an actual telegram. In *Mr Romford* (ch. xxix) Mr Goodheart Green and his head-man, standing in their London stables, see 'a blue and red telegram boy' come 'dribbling down the yard, fumbling for something in his leather-case'. Though Mr Green assumed (as perhaps most Victorians did) that a telegram meant bad news, it contained in fact no more than a complaint from a client (who had clearly not yet learnt the new art of telegraphese) about that skittish animal 'Placid Joe' and an irate announcement that the animal was being sent back to London by the 9.30 train the following day.

III

Cheap literature, penny post, and telegrams were obvious examples of the improvements, technical and otherwise, which the railways brought in their wake. There were other amenities known to the Victorians which, though not created by the railways, were encouraged by them. One was better accommodation for visitors to London and other large cities. That there was a source of additional profit here was clearly realized by the railway companies when they built large hotels at Euston, King's Cross, and Paddington in the middle of the century. It is probable that these in turn indirectly improved the quantity and quality of other London hotels. There was another form of accommodation of greater interest to Surtees and men like him that also, though less obviously, owed something to the new and easier access to the capital. These were the great London clubs which, in his opinion, offered a better and cheaper service than either the big railway hotels or the old-fashioned coaching inns in the centre of the city with their open galleries and noisy courtyards.

Clubs were multiplying in London even before the arrival of the railways; and their character was changing also. The old eighteenth-century clubs like Brooks's and White's were originally owned by a single proprietor who in effect ran them on behalf of a small exclusive set of men for purposes of dining, drinking, and gambling. The new committee-managed subscription clubs which appeared after the Napoleonic Wars were designed for a large membership with a common interest but no special personal acquaintanceship. The Travellers Club (1814), The United Services (1816), and the Athenaeum (1824) were of this type; and they were joined in the 1830s by the two great political clubs, the Carlton and the Reform. There was clearly a considerable demand among the gentry and aristocracy for such institutions. The *British Almanac* in 1841, under the heading 'Principal Club-Houses', listed no fewer than thirty-seven names and addresses. The *Parliamentary Gazetteer* for 1850 noted that club-houses, most of them built during the previous thirty years, were now so numerous that they gave a specific architectural character to many streets in the West End. Surtees bears this out. Twenty years ago, he wrote in one of his articles in *Bell's Life* during the early 1840s, only half a dozen clubs were in existence in London; now they line the streets of St James's, Pall Mall, Cockspur Street, and other fashionable parts.

It was Surtees' contention that these clubs mainly depended on the membership of the country gentry. There is little doubt that they depended for success on a large membership and a small subscription, unlike the old proprietary clubs which depended on a wealthy, exclusive membership and had correspondingly high charges. Among the new subscription clubs, for example, the Athenaeum, aiming at a membership of a thousand, started in the 1820s with an entrance fee of £10 and £5 annual subscription. In 1850 the entrance fee was twenty guineas and the annual subscription six. By that time the membership had risen to 1,300 which gave the club a yearly revenue of about £9,000. In *Plain or Ringlets* a decade later Surtees quotes, without identifying, the balance sheet of another club which he described as one of the largest in London with an annual revenue of some £15,000. For a modest subscription of some £8 or £10 a year, he wrote appreciatively, the club member had reading rooms, writing rooms, billiard rooms, smoking rooms, library, baths—everything in fact except beds. So superior were the comforts of a large London club compared with anything that hotels could offer, he asserted, that many men, when they came up to London, avoided hotels. Instead they took a bachelor bedroom in one of the many lodging-houses in the neighbourhood, and spent their days in the club. 'Clubs, in fact,' he concluded handsomely, 'are the greatest and cheapest luxuries of modern times.' They were a home from home for the provincial squire; and their mere existence was an inducement to go up to the capital; 'that is what the Clubs do. They invite visits.'

In his enthusiasm he even declared that without clubs the railway system would have been incomplete. It could also be argued that without the railways the clubs would not have been able to maintain the large provincial membership which they needed to make themselves financially secure. It was the cheapness of the train fares that enabled the country member, without undue expense, to run up to town for a few days, and rendered more tolerable the annual shopping trip to London undertaken at the solicitation of his wife and daughters.

Compared with the total cost of a family expedition to
the capital, the club membership subscription was a
positive bargain when set against the benefits it conferred.
Though the railways did not create the clubs, they
undoubtedly helped to maintain them. In so doing
they contributed to the emergence of what by the mid-
Victorian period had become a feature of male society in
the capital.

It was a development that was not without its critics.
One objection to the West End clubs was that their masculine exclusiveness distorted normal social relationships.
In the late 1860s Sir Henry Holland was writing with a
degree of testiness about the 'inordinate multiplication
of the London Clubs—institutions absorbing much of the
time and talents which might else be given to domestic
life, or to life in other forms'. He looked on these 'anti-
domestic' male fortresses as a dubious mixture of good
and bad elements. The journalist Redding disliked them
for other reasons. To him the great subscription clubs
were little more than 'large taverns with the same unso-
cial company' and he regretted the decline of the older,
more intimate, social clubs of the eighteenth century.
There was a temptation perhaps, in reaction to the large,
bland, impersonal nature of the mid-Victorian subscription clubs, to exaggerate in retrospect the wit and
intellect of the old proprietary institutions, and forget
the drunkenness and gambling. If 'taverns', the new-style
clubs with their mass membership were at least well
conducted. There was less heavy drinking and few
temptations to indecorous behaviour within their respectable walls. Some observers praised them as exercising a positively moral influence. Crabb Robinson
thought that they had changed the character of London
society for the better and were instrumental in saving
young men from the evils of rash marriages on the one
hand and dissipation on the other. Goldwin Smith some
years later also inclined to that view. 'Instead of being
denounced as hostile to marriage, the Clubs ought to
be credited with keeping young men fit for it.' Surtees,
on the other hand, appeared to think that there was a
certain danger to young men from mixing too much with

older, successful men. They would be taken in by their conversation, acquire a prematurely mercenary view of life, and devote too much of their time and money to club-life 'instead of their marrying and settling quietly as their fathers did'. This rather captious criticism is slightly inconsistent with Surtees' general praise of clubs; but he was talking about young men only, and his real target was the obsession with money-making. His normal point of view is that of a middle-aged squire up in London for a few days, rather than that of a young bachelor making a career in the metropolis. Comfort and economy are uppermost in his mind, not larger questions of morality and domesticity.

Surtees deals with clubs, in fact, as he does with rail ways and postal services. He notices them as part of the changing social scene but makes little use of them for purposes of plot. This is partly perhaps because his principal male characters hardly qualified as members of a respectable London club. Mr Bunting perhaps, grandson of an admiral, might have passed muster, but not Mr Romford, nor Mr Sponge, and certainly not Mr Jorrocks. It is the same with his railway scenes. They are brief and incidental. There are no dramatic encounters in carriages; no providential train accidents to remove an unwanted character or create a timely widowhood. In that sense Surtees is not a novelist of the railway age as Dickens can be said to be. Yet Surtees is clearly a novelist in the railway age. The accumulation of references, casual and brief as they are individually, is considerable. Though there are no great railway scenes, there is much incidental information about them. They had clearly become an integral part of the world in which all but his early novels are set. When Mr Romford, for instance, wishes to move his entire hunting establishment— hounds, horses, and humans—from Minshull Vernon to Firfield, he transports them by train in the modern fashion. There are incidental Surteesian comments on the psychology of railway passengers: their reluctance to allow other people into their compartment at the start of a long journey and the ingenious devices used to deter them—coats arranged on the seat in such a way as to suggest a live occupant, babies held up at the window (it being a well-established fact, says Surtees gravely, that there is nothing like a baby to keep men out of a carriage). There are the everyday details—the electric telegraph, omnibuses meeting the trains at rural stations, adhesive labels on the luggage, yellow and white striped rail-tickets, the choice of pretty girls to serve in the station refreshment-rooms. We learn of a perceptible increase in the items of luggage which ladies found necessary once they realized that the railways provided almost unlimited space for them; of the over-manning at large stations; of the habitual unpunctuality of cross-country lines; of the new jargon which the rail-timetables intro-duced into the English language—11.30 a.m., for instance, instead of half-past eleven in the morning. It all seems very familiar. Yet how many writers of the time had Surtees' eye for the trivial commonplaces which make his world so like our own?

It is of less importance that Surtees has the unusual distinction for a Victorian novelist of being the author of a popular brochure, *Hints to Railway Travellers*. This was not a guide on the model of *Bradshaw* but an article in the *New Monthly Magazine* giving advice on how to make the most of a trip to London without spending too much money. It was considered sufficiently useful, however, to be reprinted as a bookstall pamphlet in 1852. This piece of occasional journalism was presumably inspired by the events of 1851, the year of the Great Exhibition: which, said the Census Commissioners, 'attracted persons to London from all nations, and produced a greater and more general movement of the population than has ever before been witnessed'. Surtees' more illuminating comments on the railway age, however, are found in his novels rather than in this fugitive piece.

IV

In the general economy of the country one of the most significant achievements of the railways was to replace the canals as the principal method of transporting heavy freight. For the ordinary Victorian household, however, one of the immediate obvious benefits was the rapid conveyance of perishable goods. There was, for example, a noticeable enlargement of the areas from which the big cities drew fresh foodstuffs. In 1857 the journal of the Royal Agricultural Society noted the stimulus given to market gardening in Bedfordshire by the opening of the Great Northern line. It was a two-way traffic; the trains which took fresh vegetables to London brought the capital's manure back to the gardeners. In more modest fashion London households found that they could send fresh fish from Billingsgate down to friends in the country, and sportsmen in the country send boxes of grouse to friends in London, with reasonable assurance that the contents would arrive in eatable condition. The London shops, too, were extending their trade into the provinces. It was no longer necessary for ladies to have their dresses made locally. They could examine fashion-plates in their magazines, send off an order by post, and have the garments sent down by rail with a minimum of expense and delay. Whole outfits could be supplied by the larger London stores like Swan and Edgar, or Marshall and Snelgrove. No longer need their husbands depend on the local hotel or inn for their drinks. Crates of wine could be sent down by train at competitive prices and probably of better quality. Fortnum and Mason were ready to supply the materials for entire dinner-parties. This facility of ordering by post and receiving by rail, Surtees once reflected, meant that 'London is fast absorbing the retail trade of the country'. It was only because the duke of Tergiversation's ball in *Plain or Ringlets* was designed to strengthen his influence in the county that part of the catering was entrusted to local shops.

Others besides the respectable found the speediness of rail transport useful. Poached game from the country-side, including some no doubt taken from ducal estates, could be spirited away overnight and be on sale in London the following morning. In *Tom Hall* Surtees describes how this was done. Mr Crowbar, a 'member of a new fraternity that is now fast springing up over the country', was the indispensable middle-man in this nocturnal activity. In his spring-cart he would travel 'by night through a long tract of agricultural country, to pick up all the poached game, stolen fowls, stolen pigeons, stolen anything that was left at his different houses of call, to be by him conveyed to the railway station'. Crime apart, Surtees notices other curious secondary effects which the coming of the railways had on the English countryside. Formerly, rural dwellers away from canals and seaports habitually used wood for fuel; now cheap coal could be had wherever there was a railway line. As a result fox-coverts were becoming tangled and overgrown, because 'brushwood had ceased to be profitable since the introduction of coal into the country by the Gobblegold Railway'. The greater use of coal is a commonplace item among the various social repercussions of railways; but we are rarely reminded of the effects on woodlands.

Surtees' countryman's attitude is even more noticeable in what he has to say about the more destructive effects of the railways on English rural society. In the standard railway histories there is usually mention of the new towns created out of what were little more than villages, like Swindon and Crewe, or old towns rejuvenated by a new prosperity, like Derby, Doncaster, and Carlisle. Surtees has little interest in these. The only comparable phenomenon of that kind in the novels is Pickering Nook in *Mr Romford* (ch. xlix), and even that is for a sporting reason. This once quiet spot, the haunt of retired families, elderly ladies, and nightingales, had accidentally become a junction-point for five separate railway lines and was now a 'perfect ant-hill of industrious locomotion'. Because of its rail-facilities in all directions, it was selected by Mr Stotfold as the headquarters for his peripatetic pack of staghounds.

Surtees' sympathies are with the rural victims of railway expansion, not its urban beneficiaries: in particular the coaching inns left to a slow and painful decline when the traffic on which they depended disappeared from the roads. So many examples of them appear in his novels as to give the impression that England in the middle of the century was littered with these relics of a once great transport system. In *Handley Cross* there is a little sketch of 'The World Turned Upside Down' (an only too appropriate name)—'one of those quaint way-side inns out of whose sails the march of railroads has taken the wind'. It was once an attractive place: a substantial old stone mansion, standing a little off the road and approached by a drive, its front garden laid out with gravelled walks, topiary, and climbing roses. It had been a posting house and though never a busy establishment it was a favourite with newly married couples and with coach-drivers, who usually made some excuse for pulling up outside its honeysuckled porch. In *Mr Sponge* there is a similar establishment, 'The Old Duke of Cumberland Hotel', kept by a retired butler of the Scattercash family. Formerly enjoying considerable popularity, it had been 'left high and dry' by the railway line that passed through Granddiddle Junction, to which it was 'sufficiently near to be tantalised by the whirr and the whistle of the trains, and yet too far off to be benefited by the parties they brought'.

Two more of these melancholy survivals deserve a mention. The first is 'The Crooked Billet' in *Ask Mamma*, whose prosperity was suddenly overthrown by the Crumpletin Railway. From being a 'first-class wayside house at which eight coaches changed horses twice a-day', it had sunk into 'a very seedy unfrequented place' that only came to life on the rare occasions during the winter when the local hunt met there. What made its decline more painful was that its proprietor knew when he bought it that a railway was soon to be built nearby but had contemptuously ignored the threat. Himself a former coach-driver, the 'velvet-collared, doeskin gloved John of the fast Regulator Coach', he could not bring himself to believe that the gentry and aristocracy would ever condescend to travel by such a new-fangled, ignoble means of conveyance as a train, however handy it might be for conveying goods and heavy merchandise. It was 'utterly and entirely out of the question'. So he used up all his savings in renovating the 'Crooked Billet' at the very moment when the surveyors moved into the county to map out the line of the new railway. A companion in misfortune, though commanding less of Surtees' compassion, was 'The Lord Hill' at Dirlingford. This was a town hotel and posting-house of a type 'now fast disappearing before the march of modern civilisation'. Even in its prime, however, it had been a decidedly unattractive establishment: 'a great, gaunt four-storeyed small-windowed red brick house, standing right in the middle of the High Street'. At one time it kept twelve pairs of post-horses and seven coaches changed their teams there twice a day. Such a constant throng of travellers had bred a certain contempt for ordinary coach-passengers. Those of this class who misguidedly chose to break their journey here were 'treated like cattle at a market, pushed and squeezed and fed anyhow'. All the courtesy and service of which the hotel was capable went to the superior species of human beings who travelled in their own vehicles and dispensed their money liberally on fresh horses and leisurely meals.

The fate awaiting these casualties of the transport revolution was a slow slide into stagnation and poverty. Sometimes they even failed to survive as a public hostelry at all. The great national coach-network had supported so many establishments, large and small, along its routes that when it withered away, some of the inns and hotels which lived off the system could no longer maintain a separate existence. Surtees drops a few clues on what became of them. 'The large comfortable old posting-houses that existed prior to the railways', he observes in *Plain or Ringlets* (ch. lxii), 'have all disappeared or been converted into schools or convents, or such-like purposes.' At the 'Old Duke of Cumberland' the former Scattercash butler had, fortunately for himself, received a warning from a friendly patron not to lease the house beyond the date fixed for the opening of the railway. The actual loss fell, therefore, on the owner, who was obliged to let his tenant keep the place at a derisory rent until he could 'convert it into that last refuge for deserted houses—an academy, or a "young ladies" seminary'. Since both hotels and boarding schools require many bed-rooms, the suggestion is plausible enough. If Surtees was right, the railways made a contribution to Victorian middle-class education that went beyond ferrying pupils backwards and forwards three times a year.

Individuals suffered as well as buildings from the decline of coaching inns. For the stage proprietors and their expert staff the change must have been particularly severe. The knowledgeable, hard-working men who used to preside over the stable-yard—Surtees says he knew one in the old coaching days who looked after twenty-five horses with only one helper—became a vanishing breed. After the middle of the century, he observed, all that one could usually find at an inn were either decrepit veterans too old to find other employment or young hobbledehoys who hardly knew how to put on a bridle. Indoors, men-waiters had been replaced by women. In the main he had a low opinion of the small hostelries which had contrived to survive the railway revolution by making economies and reducing services. 'Third-rate country-inns in England are deplorable places', he wrote in *Plain or Ringlets* (ch. lxii). A man would have to be either a keen sportsman or desperately in love, he thought, to stay at one of them for the purpose of pursuing foxes, or ladies, or even a combination of both. The food would be bad; the wine worse; and the only resemblance to the old days would be the exorbitant bills. He resented particularly the excessive charges for boarding a groom or feeding a horse. 'There is no branch of our rural economy', he concluded severely, 'that requires more revision and amendment than the country inns; in fact there is no economy about them at all.'

Though in the quieter country districts the local employment offered by the railways for porters, clerks, gangers and platelayers probably did not make up for the loss of road-traffic, there were some rural areas to which they brought increased trade. Tourism and the holiday habit were not created by the railways but were certainly greatly stimulated by them. The consequences for the inhabitants of the favoured localities were mixed. Those who catered for the tourists profited; other residents had less reason to rejoice. Lakeland, for instance, suffered greatly from an inrush of tourists and day-trippers. Local celebrities like Wordsworth and Miss Martineau had to put up with constant intrusions during the holiday season. It was not surprising that the lady found it advisable to move elsewhere during the summer or that the poet came to the conclusion that appreciation of romantic scenery required a cultivated mind and that the working classes would do equally well if they limited their excursions to the fields near their own homes. The uncultured classes, however, seemed bent on using the opportunities presented by the railways to visit famous beauty spots, invade the gardens of literary lions, or at least experience the sights and smells of the seaside. The first excursion train from London to Brighton in 1841, attracted nearly two thousand trippers and needed six engines to pull its packed carriages. At the Great Exhibition of 1851 the combination of cheap 1s. 6d. entrance days and cheap excursions trains resulted in the arrival of vast but orderly crowds of working-class people. On one memorable day, 7 October, there were over 109,000 visitors. By the middle of the century the cheap railway excursion had become an established social institution. In 1855, during the Crimean War, the South-Eastern Railway was advertising express excursions from London to Folkestone and Dover every Sunday with return fares of 5s. third, 7s. second, and 10s. first class.

Surtees had no great interest in day-trippers or casual tourists as distinct from the more resident middle-class holiday-makers whose activities he chronicled in *Plain or Ringlets*. He appreciated, nevertheless, that the railways had widened the opportunities of travel and recreation for the whole of the community. 'Thanks to George Stephenson, George Hudson, and the many other Georges, who invested their talents and valuable money in the invaluable undertakings,' he wrote in his milder ironical vein, 'railways have brought wealth and salubrity to everyone's door.' By the end of his life he thought that the old social distinctions between different holiday resorts had largely broken down. People visited first one and then another until they finally decided which was their favourite. They then adopted it as if it were their own peculiar property, sang its praises, and disparaged all its rivals.

What was for Surtees the best and greatest recreation of all had hardly been affected by the coming of railways. Fox-hunting, contrary to the early apprehensions of sporting journalists, continued to flourish despite the occasional deaths of horses that strayed on the line, and no doubt many unreported casualties among foxes and hares. Indeed, Surtees affirmed that more harm to hunting was done by the railways in encouraging people to go up to London to spend their money than by any direct local damage to its activities. Though men paid as much in subscriptions to their clubs as their fathers did in hunt subscriptions, that was a mere trifle compared with what rising social expectations made them spend on travel and holidays. Moreover, there was a counter-benefit of a sort. The same trains that took the country squire and his lady up to London in the summer, in winter brought London sportsmen down to the shires. Those whose occupation only allowed them an occasional day in the field no longer had to confine their outings to the Surrey Hunt or the Middlesex Staghounds. By dint of an early start from Euston or Paddington they could enjoy a run between mid-morning and dusk, and still get back to sleep in their own beds. Lord George Bentinck made a name for himself in the early 1840s by hunting in Wiltshire in the morning and turning up on the benches of the House of Commons in the evening, his hunting clothes only partially concealed under a paletot. The sagacious Mr Jorrocks, we are told, also saw the possibilities opened up by the railroads for both business and sport. He began at an early date to make excursions into the Midlands, taking orders for tea one day, hunting the next, and sometimes doing both together. Euston Station and the terminus of the Great Northern Line at King's Cross, he used to declare, were the two best cover-hacks in the world.

In this respect railways had a double advantage. They

made it possible for London sportsmen to hunt regularly in some of the best counties, and also to make a round of the different hunts as the fancy took them. Unlike the provincials, the metropolitan man could put in an appearance as easily in one county as another. 'Railways', wrote Surtees, 'make sportsmen very ubiquitous. One day they are with the Queen's, another with the Quorn, a third with the Craven, or perhaps the Cheshire.' In the old days even a brief expedition from London demanded time and preparation. Horses and groom had to be sent on in advance. When news came of their arrival, a seat on a coach had to be booked and domestic engagements cancelled. Then there was the constant risk that, on arrival, frost or snow would leave the sporting visitor to kick his heels in some out-of-the-way hostelry until the weather changed.

The use of railways for hunting which Surtees was able to describe in the 1840s increased in popularity as the century went on. In the 1860s the railway companies were offering cheap fares for hunting men and occasionally put on special trains for particular meets. So much was this a part of Victorian sporting life that when the volume on 'Hunting' in the *Badminton Library* was published in 1886 a whole chapter was devoted to 'Hunting from London'.

V

The more cosmopolitan character of the sporting world was a reflection in miniature of a national tendency. People were moving around, more often and further afield than their fathers. In the process provincial outlooks were quietly dissolving. It would be more accurate perhaps to say local rather than provincial since the effect was seen among Londoners as well. According to James Burn, the constant presence in the capital of visitors from other parts of the country, with their families and domestics, was breaking down the old prejudices of the true-born

Cockney against provincials. Douglas Jerrold felt as early as 1840 that London had lost its mystery. The stage-coach had started the decline; the railway had completed it. Distance had once lent, if not enchantment, at least prestige to the capital, but 'there is no distance when there is a railroad'.[3]

It was in the countryside, however, that the weakening of local feeling and local interests were most clearly seen. The habit of travel fostered by the railways, the more frequent contact with people from other parts of the kingdom, the common stock of intellectual topics formed by the national press, the expansion of public boarding schools, annual holidays at the seaside, all these features of Victorian society were insensibly enlarging people's mental horizons. Though Surtees himself belonged to a traditionally conservative class, he believed that these developments constituted progress. He had few regrets for the passing of the old, narrow provincial life. In *Mr Romford* (ch. xvi) he observes genially that since the amalgamation of countries and counties produced by the railways, there had been a general improvement in society—'improvement in wit, improvement in wine, improvement in "wittles", improvement in everything'. Almost the only consequence of rail travel which earned his displeasure was the invasion of even the smallest provincial race-meeting by disreputable strangers from the underworld of the sport. There were now, he complained, fifty 'legs' where a quarter of a century earlier there had been but one.

Like lesser mortals Surtees could display inconsistencies. In the mid-1830s he had shared the common view that the railways would damage hunting; and towards the end of his life he opposed the building of the Derwent Valley branch railway-line that seemed likely to cross his property. The tendency to forget considerations of the public advantage when one's own personal interests are threatened is a perennial trait of human nature. For the wider social and political effects on country society, however, he had nothing but praise, even though it was tinged occasionally with cynicism. By the time he came to write *Plain or Ringlets* in the later 1850s, he had a number of reflections to make on the beneficial consequences of the railways. They had emancipated entire families from the contracted surroundings of provincial life. They had enlarged the matrimonial market for the young of both sexes. Familiarity with a wider world made local issues and personal feuds shrink in importance. Neighbours, he thought, did not go to law with each other so often. 'It may appear strange,' he wrote, 'but we believe our oft-lauded friends, the railways, have had a good deal to do in repressing the old spirit of litigation and making parties keep the peace together.' People found that obnoxious neighbours lost their power to vex when they were at the other end of a railway-line. Distance had a calming influence: it was intimacy that bred acrimony. He attributed the quarrelsomeness of the Scotch to their clannishness; and quoted old Lord Eldon who once satirically asked whether certain litigants in his court were first cousins or merely country neighbours. He accounted for the undeniable decline in party political animosities in the constituencies by similar arguments. Men who had acquired a taste for foreign travel, sportsmen who hunted in a dozen counties, shot grouse in Scotland, or sailed a yacht on the Solent, felt little inclination to represent their county in parliament: a privilege, according to Surtees, which simply meant that they spent their money in entertaining and their time in doing other people's business. 'In truth, the country gentlemen were a land-locked, leg-tied tribe, before the introduction of railways—coaching was uncomfortable, and posting expensive, besides which a journey took such a time.' They therefore travelled rarely and preferred to be somebody in their own county town than a nobody in London. Now they had discovered the advantages of absence. In the old days of enforced social intimacy, the squire's country home was looked upon by friends and neighbours as a kind of 'great, unlicenced inn' where they and their servants could call in at will for refreshment. Now the squire and his wife were finding new and better ways of spending their money and were not sorry to make judicious economies at home that would serve to pay for their new amusements abroad.

In helping to break down provincial society, the railways also helped to weaken some of the more obvious marks of class distinction. In their own fashion they imposed a degree of uniformity in social habits which conflicted with the older conventions. Dukes might travel first class and domestic servants third; but the trains would be hauled by the same locomotive and they would arrive together at the same destination. Once it would have been beneath the dignity of a bishop to travel by public stage-coach. Later it would have been absurd if he had refused to avail himself of the superior speed and comfort of the train. At one stroke, Surtees observed, steam had broken down the social prejudice against public transport. Others took the same view. 'The railroad is the true leveller', wrote another social critic, Cyrus Redding. As a veteran liberal journalist, who had as a child seen John Wesley and as a boy remembered the news of the French Revolution, he joked that William Pitt would have had the railways prosecuted in court for their egalitarian tendencies. Surtees agreed with the argument though he expressed it in a more matter-of-fact way. 'Railways', he observed in *Ask Mamma*, 'have taken the starch out of country magnificence.' People who once would never have dreamed of calling on a great man in anything less than a post-chaise, now thought nothing of driving up to his house in a one-horse fly, or even getting the station omnibus to drop them off at the gates.

The county magnates themselves had left off some of their pomp. Dukes were not what they used to be; at least, not in the estimation of others, especially those who had wealth and social position of their own. They could no longer, Surtees thought, command the respect and political allegiance which formerly they could take for granted. As he put it in *Plain or Ringlets* in his chapter on 'Old and New Squires':

Time was—before the establishment of railways—that the
Squires used to respond to the call of their chiefs with the
greatest alacrity, but the whistle of the engine has somewhat
dispelled the authority of the leaders, and made men think
more for themselves than they did. In truth, there is perhaps
no class of Her Majesty's subjects more benefited by the introduction of railways than the country gentlemen generally.

Where once, he went on, after a university education
and perhaps a Grand Tour on the Continent, they had
been content to return home, sink themselves in provincial life, and breed children from their neighbours'
daughters, now they were as much an emancipated class
as any. It is an unusual, almost paradoxical, observation;
and it needs to be tempered by the reflection that Surtees
had no love for dukes and was hardly displeased to note
any decrease in their influence. The contrast he makes
and the extent of the change he records are a little too
sharp to be entirely convincing. Not all squires had bowed
down respectfully before the higher aristocracy in the
past; and dukes were not without social and political
influence even after the railroads had penetrated their
fiefdoms. Yet a levelling tendency must have been perceptible for Surtees to be able to describe it so emphati-
cally. He exaggerated, no doubt; he could hardly have
been inventing.

It may also be true that Surtees attributed too much to
the railways; but if so, he was not alone. It is noticeable
how many elderly Victorians, looking back over their
lives, mention the coming of the railways as one of the
great formative agencies of their time. Those who welcomed the social changes which took place in the nineteenth century and those who deplored them were
equally likely to point to the railways as one of the causes.
Discussing the significance of the Great Exhibition of
1851 as the first great demonstration of the nation's
progress since the accession of Victoria, the old showman George Sanger wrote:

Times were indeed better. As compared with the days of my
boyhood, it was almost as though a miracle had been wrought
in the land. The giant of steam was responsible for much of

the transformation. Railways were stretching over the country, rendering a transport and interchange of commodities possible with a quickness and at prices that the old folks could never have dreamt of.

James Burn, though shirking the 'tedious task' of recounting all the social changes in his time, found space to mention 'the railways, with their surpassing interest and revolutionising influence'.

These were men who had known hardship and risen from humble beginnings. Sir Henry Holland, an example of the successful Victorian professional man, displayed a more reserved attitude to the popular concept of 'progress' and its various agents. One of the most revealing social changes in his lifetime, he thought, was the degree of fusion that had taken place between the higher and middle classes. With the prudence of a physician he forbore to express either approval or dislike of this development, apart from a severe footnote on the vulgarity of dress 'now so prevalent among English gentlemen'. He did, however, suggest a number of reasons for the greater intermingling of social classes—the spread of wealth and education, the change in the character of the House of Commons, the growth of public meetings and private associations, and the increase in the number of clubs and joint-stock companies. All these different trends, he thought, had contributed to the blending of classes that once kept themselves distinct from each other. Then he added, as though an afterthought, 'even the modern methods of travelling may be concerned in the result; as well as those changes in ordinary apparel which among professional men as well as others have abolished many of the distinctions formerly accepted in the world'.[4]

There is a fine confusion of causes and effects in his explanations. Those who live through a great social transformation are able to grasp the visible manifestations more readily than the underlying causes. In reality, perhaps, the most important feature of British society in the nineteenth century was that its great increase in wealth mainly benefited the middle classes rather than the old landed aristocracy. Though Surtees did not trouble himself with all the consequences of this, he was at least positive about the central fact. 'No-one', he wrote in the late 1840s, 'with any experience of life will deny that there has been a very great extension of wealth among the middle classes of society within the last quarter of a century, and greatly increased expenditure on their part.' There was, in fact, a general perception not only that money was being made faster but that it was being made by classes which in origin had been outside the intellectual and cultural tradition of the old governing caste. It was this that made moralists and theologians, poets like Tennyson, parsons like Kingsley, publicists like Carlyle, aesthetes like Ruskin, denounce obsessive materialism and the relentless pursuit of riches. It was less fashionable to point out, as that man of quiet common sense, the Revd Thomas Mozley did, that the vastly increased wealth of the country had made it possible to carry through in safety many changes that in other circumstances would have been risky experiments. He instanced the more humane treatment of criminals, the more sympathetic attitude to the needs of the poor, the provision of free national education, and the extension of the parliamentary franchise. All these reforms had come about, he believed, because prosperity had enabled the ruling classes to act with unhurried discretion and to give generously from their own abundance.

Many Victorians no doubt regretted the passing of the elegance and formality which, through the golden haze of memory, they thought had characterized higher society in Georgian England. Yet even those who mourned the past would have been loath to give up the comforts and cleanliness of the present. Surtees for one would not have exchanged the practical conveniences of the new Victorian age for the elegancies of the old. He was too much of a countryman to admire money for its own sake. On the frantic pursuit of wealth and all its alleged consequences he could be as stern a moralist as any. 'Certainly money is an essential, but not so absorbing an essential as some people make it', he observed in *Ask*

Mamma (ch. li). Elsewhere he praised the moderation of people who were happy to live on secure if limited incomes—what he called the 3 per cent people as compared with those who devoted themselves to the 'raving rapacity of modern cupidity'. Yet he was not a worshipper of times past. Though he was not greatly in favour of the society that developed during his life, he was not greatly against it either. Progressivism and reactionism are both species of idealism; and Surtees was not an idealist. Independent, matter-of-fact, observant, and detached, he thought some of the changes which had happened in his time were to be regretted, but possibly even more were to be welcomed. He lacked the fervour, the imagination, and the optimism of many early Victorians. On the other hand he lacked their capacity for self-deception, their religiosity, their moralizing, and their seriousness. The only typical Victorian qualities he exhibited perhaps were his sense of personal privacy and his proud self-reliance. For the rest, he was a very un-Victorian man, observing with an ironic eye his own rapidly changing society. There may have been more like him than we are apt to think. It is easy to mistake the surface of a society for its substance.

NOTES

Place of publication is London, unless otherwise stated.

Introduction
1. In *Ask Mamma* (Jorrocks Edition, n.d. but post-1901).

Chapter 1
1. J. A. Thomson, *The Smuggling Coast* (Dumfries, 1989), 83–90.
2. R. D. Altick, *Presence of the Present* (1990), 61.
3. F. von Raumer, *England in 1835*, 3 vols. (1836; repr. Irish UP, 1971), i. 182, 261, ii. 120.
4. *Squire Osbaldeston, His Autobiography*, ed. E. D. Cuming (1927), 19, 214.
5. *Memoir and Letters of Sir Thomas Acland*, ed. A. H. D. Acland (1902), 262.
6. E. Lytton Bulwer, *England and the English*, 2 vols. (1833), i. 95; Captain Gronow, *Reminiscences*, 2 vols. (1889), i. 325.

Chapter 2
1. Grantley F. Berkeley, *My Life and Recollections*, 4 vols. (1865–6), i. 295 ff.
2. *Letters of Thomas Carlyle to His Brother*, ed. E. W. Marrs (1968), 413 (Nov. 1836).
3. Cyrus Redding, *Fifty Years' Recollections*, 3 vols. (1858), iii. 179.
4. *Heads of the People, Portraits of the English*, 2 vols. (1841), i. 221–7.
5. Earl of Lytton, *Life of Edward Bulwer, 1st Lord Lytton*, 2 vols. (1913), i. 117.
6. W. Fletcher, *Reading Past and Present* (Reading, 1839).
7. Revd T. Mozley, *Reminiscences Chiefly of Oriel College and the Oxford Movement*, 2 vols. (1882), ii. 167, 249; and *Reminiscences Chiefly of Towns, Villages and Schools*, 2 vols. (1885), ii. 396.
8. *Letters of Sidney Godolphin Osborne*, ed. Arnold White, 2 vols. (1890), i. 23., ii. 88.
9. A. D. Gilbert, *Religion and Society in Industrial England* (1976), 100.

Chapter 3
1. Thomas Raikes, *Journal*, 4 vols. (1856–8), iv. 310.
2. Alexis de Tocqueville, *Journeys to England and Ireland*, ed. J. P. Mayer (1958), 67.
3. *House of Commons Reports 1857: Lambeth Election Petition*, 14.

4. *Charles Kingsley, Letters and Memories,* ed. by his wife (1892 edn.), 234; Una Pope-Hennessy, *Canon Charles Kingsley* (1948), 153.
5. Rosamund Lawrence, *Charles Napier* (1952), 205–8.
6. Mozley, *Oxford,* ii. 99–100; *History,* xlix. 244 (review by W. L. Burn).
7. *Diary of B. R. Haydon,* ed. W. B. Pope, 5 vols. (1960–3), ii. 209.
8. *Heads of the People,* i. 338.
9. Mozley, *Towns,* ii. 360.
10. Quoted in A. S. Turberville, *The House of Lords in the Age of Reform* (1958), 427.

Chapter 4

1. *Memoir of Lord Abinger,* by his son (1877), 172–5.
2. See generally Carolyn Steadman, *Policing the Victorian Community 1856–80* (1984).
3. *Osbaldeston,* 52.
4. Vera Wheatley, *Life and Work of Harriet Martineau* (1957), 378.
5. *Autobiography and Letters of Mrs Margaret Oliphant,* ed. Mrs Harry Coghill (Leicester, 1974), 309.

Chapter 5

1. *Dyott's Diary 1781–1845,* ed. R. W. Jeffery, 2 vols. (1907), 222–3.
2. *Memoir of John Grey of Dilston,* by Josephine Butler (Edinburgh, 1869), 265; *Dyott's Diary,* ii. 388.
3. *R. S. Surtees by Himself and E. D. Cuming* (1924), 156 ff.
4. See 'Speech of George Game Day at Huntingdon on 17 June 1843' (pamphlet, 1844, which ran into 12 editions) and 'Speech of 27 January 1844' (pamphlet, 1844).
5. Thomas Hughes, *Portrait of a Brother* (1873), 90; *Memoir of J. J. Gurney,* ed. J. B. Braithwaite, 2 vols. (Norwich, 1855), ii. 373.
6. N. McCord, *The Anti-Corn Law League* (1958), 56–64, 175–6, 184–7.
7. Cuming, *Surtees,* 230.
8. *Journal of The Royal Agricultural Society,* 2nd series, iv. (1868), 123 ff. Article by J. Bailey Denton, 'Land Drainage and Improvement by Loans'.

Chapter 6

1. *Memoir of John Grey,* 327–8 n.
2. *Heads of the People,* i. 209 ff., ii. 277.
3. Ibid. ii. 1 ff.
4. *Under Five Reigns,* ed. by her son (1911), 161.
5. Cecil Woodham-Smith, *Florence Nightingale 1820–1910* (1950), 95; Susan Chitty, *The Beast and the Monk: Life of Charles Kingsley* (1974), 74.

Chapter 7

1. *The Whistler at the Plough* (1852), 35.
2. *Memoir of J. J. Gurney,* ii. 303–4.

3. G. Huxley, *Lady Elizabeth and the Grosvenors* (1965), 22, 36.
4. *The Diaries*, ed. Sir Alfred Pease (1907), 128, 144, 193.
5. Algernon West, *Recollections 1832–1886*, 2 vols. (1899), i. 272.
6. *Diary of Henry Crabb Robinson*, ed. T. Sadler, 3 vols. (1869), iii. 233.
7. J. Pope-Hennessy, *Monckton Milnes*, 2 vols. (1949–51), ii. 10.
8. *Journal of The Royal Agricultural Society*, vii. (1846), 15–16.
9. *Reminiscences by Goldwin Smith*, ed. A. Haultain (1910), 12, 30.
10. F. Shepperd, *London 1808–1870: The Infernal Wen* (1971), 371–2.
11. W. H. Dunn, *J. A. Froude*, 2 vols. (1961–3), i. 161–210.

Chapter 8

1. John Wigley, *Rise and Fall of the Victorian Sunday* (Manchester 1980), 182.
2. Carola Oman, *The Gascoyne Heiress* (1968), 289–90; *Diary of Lady Frances Shelley*, ed. R. Edgcumbe, 2 vols. (1912–13), ii. 256, 353.
3. G. J. Holyoake, *Sixty Years of an Agitator's Life* (1906), 126–7.
4. John Beames, *Memoirs of a Bengal Civilian* (1984 edn.), 112.
5. *England As It Is*, 2 vols. (1851), i. 121.
6. *Lady Charlotte Guest, Extracts from her Journal, 1833–1852* (1950), and *Lady Charlotte Schreiber . . . 1853–1891* (1952), ed. Earl of Bessborough.
7. *Monckton Milnes*, ii. 61.
8. *Life of Edward Bulwer*, i. 267.
9. Sir Theodore Cook (Editor of *The Field*), in *Osbaldeston*, p. xxxi.
10. Pierce Egan, *Book of Sports* (1832), 382.

Chapter 9

1. Marrs, (ed.), *Letters of Thomas Carlyle*, 480.
2. *Life of Edward Bulwer*, ii. 388.
3. Nimrod, *The Chace, the Turf and the Road* (1837), 279 ff.
4. *The Oracle* (1842), 29.
5. Mozley, *Oxford*, ii. 151.
6. Quoted in J. J. Tobias, *Nineteenth Century Crime: Prevention and Punishment* (Newton Abbot, 1972), 16–19.
7. Mozley, *Towns*, ii. 252 ff.; *Oxford*, ii. 165–6.
8. Ravensdale in the text, but this must be a misprint.
9. Cuming, *Surtees*, 111.

Chapter 10

1. *New Letters of Jane Welsh Carlyle*, ed. A. Carlyle, 2 vols. (1903), i. 200.
2. Gwen Raverat, *Period Piece* (1954), 84.
3. Author's recollection.
4. *Autobiography*, ed. J. E. Morpurgo (1949), 105–7, 313.
5. *Schooldays with Kipling* (1936), 71.
6. I am indebted to Mr Mark Curthoys of the University of Oxford History project for these details.

7. Earl of Albemarle, *Fifty Years of My Life* (1877), 135, 184.
8. *Period Piece*, 84.
9. J. A. R. Pimlott, *The Englishman's Holiday* (1947), 130.
10. *Journal of a Governess*, ed. E. Hall, 2 vols. (1936–9), ii. 382.
11. Berkeley, *Life and Recollections*, ii. 342–9.

Chapter 11

1. Holyoake, *Sixty Years*, 28, 237.
2. West, *Recollections 1832–1886*, i. 230.
3. *The Jerningham Letters*, ed. Egerton Castle, 2 vols. (1896), ii. 121, 146.
4. Mark Girouard, *The Victorian Country House* (1971), 25–6.
5. Sir John Mowbray, *Seventy Years at Westminster* (1900), 55–6; J. O. Johnston, *Life of H. P. Liddon* (1904), 35.
6. Holyoake, *Sixty Years*, 235.
7. *Sketches by Boz* (1892 edn.), 54–5.
8. *Rogue's Progress*, ed. J. L. Bramley (1965), 192–204.

Chapter 12

1. *Greville Journal*, 28 January 1834.
2. In *The Chace*, 102–19.
3. *Letters*, ed. M. Dickens and G. Hogarth (1893), 591.
4. Altick, *Presence of The Present*, 61.
5. *Memoir of the Rev. John Russell*, by E. W. L. Davies (1878), 68–9.
6. J. Simmons, *The Railway in Town and Country 1830–1914* (1986), 40–1.

Chapter 13

1. *Recollections* (1872), 268.
2. Sir H. Maxwell, *Life of W. H. Smith*, 2 vols. (1893), i. 85–6; Amy Cruse, *The Victorians and their Books* (1935), 222, 234–6.
3. James Burn, *Autobiography of a Beggar Boy*, ed. D. Vincent (1978 edn.), 58; *Heads of the People*, i. 321–3.
4. *Recollections*, 267.

BIBLIOGRAPHICAL NOTE

Besides the novels and *The Analysis of the Hunting Field* I have used the original material printed in two compilations edited by E. D. Cuming, the pioneer of Surteesian studies.

1. *Town and Country Papers* (1929), containing a selection of Surtees' journalistic writings.
2. *Robert Smith Surtees 1805–1864 by Himself and E. D. Cuming* (1924), containing his autobiographical fragments and other unpublished material.

A comprehensive bibliography of Surtees' writings and of books and articles about him is given in the edition of Frederick Watson's standard biography *Robert Smith Surtees* (1933) published by the R. S. Surtees Society in 1991.

INDEX

Italics are used to indicate: (i) printed books and periodicals; (ii) fictional places and characters. References to individual books by Surtees will be found listed in alphabetical order under his name.